Low-Income Consumers as a Source of Innovation

Aline Krämer

Low-Income Consumers as a Source of Innovation

Insights from Idea Competitions in Brazilian Low-Income Communities

Springer Gabler

Aline Krämer
Freising-Weihenstephan, Germany

Dissertation, Technische Universität München, 2014

ISBN 978-3-658-08929-0 ISBN 978-3-658-08930-6 (eBook)
DOI 10.1007/978-3-658-08930-6

Library of Congress Control Number: 2015932769

Springer Gabler

Printed on acid-free paper

Springer Gabler is a brand of Springer Fachmedien Wiesbaden
Springer Fachmedien Wiesbaden is part of Springer Science+Business Media
(www.springer.com)

PREFACE

The PhD thesis by Aline Krämer focuses on low-income consumers as a source of innovation. In the first part „Insights from Theory“ Aline Krämer gives an overview of the relevant literature, including open innovation, and idea competitions as a method of user integration. In the second part she shares „Insights from the Field“, describing and analysing idea competitions conducted in the context of the Base of the Pyramid (BoP) in Brazil as one of the emerging economies. While there are numerous studies on open innovation in the context of developed countries and markets, they are scant in the context of developing countries, particularly the BoP. It is no surprise, since it is quite challenging to gain access to this field. Aline Krämer is one of the first ones to collect data in this area, and conduct high-quality research. Her empirical findings show that idea competitions are feasible instruments to involve BoP consumers in the innovation process, generating creative ideas and concepts. Furthermore, idea competitions help companies identifying trends and lead users in BoP markets. This has strong implications for theory and practice alike. It is research with impact in terms of science and society.

Researchers interested in open innovation, particularly user integration, will find interesting insights and findings for theory and method development. Practitioners, who seek to explore and exploit the opportunities in BoP markets, will find useful information to enhance the innovation process. This holds true for SMEs and large, multinational companies. Thus, the present PhD thesis by Aline Krämer targets a broad readership, and I hope the theoretical insights and empirical findings will be widely disseminated.

Univ.-Prof. Dr. Frank-Martin Belz
Technische Universität München
TUM School of Management
Freising, 26th of November 2014

ACKNOWLEDGEMENTS

Writing this dissertation, I mostly only saw what I had to forgo. I am very grateful to now be able to take a look at what I have gained – and thank the many people who have supported me on this research journey.

First and foremost, I would like to thank my supervisor, Univ.-Prof. Dr. Frank-Martin Belz, for giving me the leeway to pursue my personal research interests. His constructive feedback taught me to focus and structure my research – skills that will be invaluable for my future career. At his Chair of Corporate Sustainability Brewery and Food Industry at the Technische Universität München, Prof. Dr. Belz provided me with the ideal research and work environment. This made my time as a PhD candidate not only an insightful, but also a fun experience.

I would also like to extend my appreciation to Univ.-Prof. Dr. Prof. h.c. Dr. h.c. Ralf Reichwald for inspiring me with his research and for accepting to be my second supervisor. Furthermore, I owe thanks to Univ.-Prof. Dr. Jutta Roosen, PhD, for agreeing to chair my doctoral examination committee.

My colleagues at the Chair of Corporate Sustainability Brewery and Food Industry at the Technische Universität München deserve special thanks: Dr. Roxana Codita, Dr. Sandra Silvertant, Dr. Jasmin Vella, Dr. Birte Schmidt-Riediger, Dr. Sunita Ramakrishnan, and Marc Requardt. Their expert input and encouragement was invaluable when pursuing this research project. They were not only great colleagues, but have become special friends that I would not want to miss. I owe particular thanks to Dr. Roxana Codita. She was an invaluable sounding board for my ideas over the past couple of months, always lending me her expert advice. Also, I would like to thank Jeanette Kralisch and Gisela Rosemeyer for their technical support, their patience as well as for always having a warm word for me.

Furthermore, I am particularly indebted to Prof. Dr. Aguinaldo dos Santos and the whole research team of the Research Center for Design and Sustainability at the Federal University of Paraná, Brazil. Without him and the support of his team, this research project would not have been possible. The list of team members and supporters is long, but each of them deserves to be named in person: Agnese Brasca, Abel Chang, Eduardo Camargo (Aliança Empreendedora), Jairo da Costa, Alessandra M. Enriconi, Fernanda Franzoni Zaguini, Naotake Fukushima, Nivaldo Gomes, Andrea Hernández Nájera, Cláudio Pereira, Gheysa Prado, João Gabriel Pontual

Falcao, Benedikt Schmitz, Prof. Andrea Sell Dyminski, Eduardo Sell Dyminski (Soliforte), Carolina Tapia Torres, João Victor, Tiago Volpato, Sara Worms, and, last but certainly not least, Cláudia Zacar. Furthermore, I would like to express my gratitude to Dr. J.C. Diehl of the TU Delft for his support to kick-off this research project with first interviews.

I further owe special gratitude to the people in the communities of Aguas Claras (Piraquara), Jardim Boa Vista (Campo Magro), and Vila Zumbi (Curitiba). They did not only participate in the idea competitions and lend me their time during the interviews – but also taught me what hospitality means. The people I talked to were poor in the terms' narrow sense, but certainly rich in knowledge and insights. What is more, the conversations with them encouraged me to further pursue my research and work on inclusive business models and the opportunities they offer to create value for all.

Special thanks further go to my dear colleague, co-founder of Endeva and friend Christina Gradl. She is a constant source of inspiration and a wonderful person to work with. The discussions with her as well as her expert input have tremendously supported and improved this research project. I would also like to thank my Endeva colleagues and friends Martin Herrndorf, Claudia Knobloch and Shuan SadreGhazi for their input and feedback.

I am also indebted to Jeremiah Hendren. He did not only edit this dissertation, but also helped me to structure my arguments and put them into clear-cut words and sentences.

I would also like to thank my dear friend Kathi Pamp for helping me on the final stretch, as well as Nadja Fiedler and Nina Kiesgen. Further, I thank all my friends for staying my friends, although I barely had time for them over the past years – and many more people that I have not mentioned by name, but whose support I have enjoyed along the way.

Finally, I would like to acknowledge the Kurt Fordan Stiftung für herausragende Begabungen e.V., the Stiftung der Deutschen Wirtschaft as well as the Emerald/CAPES Brazilian Management Research Fund Award for financially supporting my research project.

My deepest gratitude goes to my most enduring supporter, Stefan Menden. His true love, incredible patience and everyday support gave me the strength to finalize this research project.

Last but not least, I would like to thank my family: my parents Marita and Werner Krämer, as well as my sister Sina Krämer and my brother Markus Krämer. My parents have taught me to pursue my interests and dreams – and their unconditional love has given me the courage to do so.

Aline Krämer

München, August 2013

TABLE OF CONTENTS

LIST OF FIGURES AND TABLES

FIGURES

Please note: The author apologizes that no higher quality images could be provided in figures 27, 28, 35, 36, 44.

TABLES

LIST OF ABBREVIATIONS

ATM	Automated teller machine
BoP	Base of the pyramid
CAT	Consensual assessment technique
COHAPAR	Housing agency of Paraná (Portuguese: Companhia de Habitação do Paraná)
COPEL	Energy company of Paraná (Portuguese: Companhia Paranaense de Energia)
CPF	Tax number (Portuguese: Cadastro de pessoas físicas)
CS	Creativity score
DI	Confederation of Danish Industry
e.g.	For example (Latin: exempli gratia)
ECB	European Central Bank
ECG	Electrocardiogram
et al.	And others (Latin: et alii/alia)
etc.	And so forth (Latin: et cetera)
ff.	And following (Latin: foliis)
FFE	Fuzzy front end
FFM	Five factor model
FINEP	Brazilian funding authority for studies and projects (Portuguese: Financiadora de Estudos e Projetos)
i.e.	In other words (Latin: id est)
IBGE	Brazilian Institute for Geography and Statistics (Portuguese: Instituto Brazileiro de Geografia e Estatística)
Ibid.	In the same place (Latin: ibidem)
ICC	Intra-class correlation coefficient
IEA	International Energy Agency
IFC	International Finance Corporation
ITU	International Telecommunication Union
LED	Light-emitting diode
LU	Lead user
LUS	Lead-user score

n	Sample size
NDS	Research center for design and sustainability (Portuguese: Núcleo de Design e Sustentabilidade)
NGO	Non-governmental organization
NIH	Not invented here
NOS	Nokia Open Studios
NPD	New product development
OECD	Organization for Economic Cooperation and Development
PAC	Governmental program to accelerate economic growth (Portuguese: Programa de Aceleração do Crescimento)
PIN	Personal identification number
PPP	Purchasing power parity
PSI	Population Services International
PVC	Polyvinylchloride
QFD	Quality function deployment
R$	Brazilian Real
R&D	Research & development
RG	Identity card number (Portuguese: Registro Geral)
SECI	Socialization, externalization, combination, and internalization
sig.	Significant
SIM card	Subscriber identity module card
SME	Small and medium-sized enterprises
SPSS	Superior Performing Software System
TOA	Time of adoption
UFPR	Federal University of Paraná
UNDP	United Nations Development Programme
UNFPA	United Nations Population Fund
UoA	Units of analysis
URL	Uniform resource locator
USD	United States Dollar
WHO	World Health Organization
WRI	World Resources Institute

We should not discount completely the merit of providing certain goods and services to the people at the bottom of the economic pyramid, but the fact remains that poor people are not at the bottom of the knowledge, ethical, or innovation pyramids. Unless we build on the resources in which poor people are rich, the development process will not be dignified and a mutually respectful and learning culture will not be reinforced in society. (Gupta 2013, 18)

1 Introduction

Can low-income consumers make a contribution to corporate innovation processes? Since the groundbreaking work of von Hippel, researchers have affirmed that consumers in middle- to high-income markets can indeed contribute to innovation. Von Hippel has identified users[1] who develop new products and services on their own, in particular when current market offers do not meet their needs (see, e.g., von Hippel 1982/1986/1988). Following his research, scholars have empirically shown that integrating consumers can be a key success factor for innovation (see, e.g., Gruner and Homburg 2000). Moreover, studies have investigated how companies can identify and build on user innovations, and how they can leverage the knowledge of users by integrating them into new product development processes (see section 2.1).[2] Yet most of these studies focus on similar sectors and contexts – namely, middle- to high-income market segments of industrialized countries (see table 58, section 2.1).[3] While they do not claim that their findings are restricted to this context, no study has yet shown that these findings are (or are not) context independent.

At the same time, there is anecdotal evidence that user innovations are not a phenomenon that only occurs in high-income markets. Anil Gupta, professor at the Indian Institute of Management, found a variety of examples of what he names "grassroots innovations" – that is, innovative solutions developed by low-income

---

1 The terms consumer, customer, and user will be used as synonyms in the present study, although they have slightly differing meanings: A *user* can be defined as a person who makes use of or operates something. Thus, the term is centered around the act of employing a good or service. User can refer to individuals or "user firms." A *consumer* is a person who purchases goods or services for personal use (not for manufacturing or reselling) and consumes them. Thus the term refers to an actor in a market and is focused on the act of consuming. A *customer* can refer to an individual or an organization that buys goods or services from a store or another business. It thus widens the definition to other organizations and businesses. A customer, in contrast to a consumer, is more focused on the act of buying something.

2 For example, literature has evolved around specific techniques for integrating consumers, such as innovation workshops, idea competitions, and toolkits (see, e.g., Reichwald and Piller 2006; Soll 2006; Piller and Walcher 2006; Walcher 2007; Silvertant 2011; Schrader and Belz 2012).

3 For example, studies that focus on the consumer goods industry most typically examine user innovators in the field of sports-related consumer goods or other leisure activities (see the literature review by Bogers et al. 2010, 863).

consumers (Gupta 2010/2013).[4] Nonetheless, the contributions low-income consumers can make to new product development remain underexplored. In their recently published article in the Journal of Product Innovation Management, the university professors Viswanathan and Sridharan (2012, 51) claim that

> *much of the academic literature on product development is anchored in empirically advanced economies and relatively affluent markets. In contrast, very little is known about product development for base of the pyramid markets (BoP).*

This emphasis of academic research may result from the fact that middle- to high-income markets have, for various decades, remained the main focus of most corporate activities. Recently, however, this trend is undergoing a shift. According to *The Economist* (2010b), "multinationals expect about 70% of the world's growth over the next few years to come from emerging markets." In his book entitled *The Fortune at the Bottom of the Pyramid* (2004), the business strategy professor C.K. Prahalad suggested exploring the market potential of the part of the world where billions of consumers reside – and where the population is only expected to grow.[5] Although most of the consumers residing in developing and emerging economies only have a small income, their aggregated purchasing power is high. Hammond et al. (2007, 13) estimate that the poorest four billion consumers – those who earn less than 8 USD per day measured in terms of local purchasing power (PPP) – spend five trillion USD PPP per year (Hammond et al. 2007, 13). Moreover, low-income consumers often pay higher prices for basic goods and services and receive them at a lower quality – a phenomenon often referred to as the "poverty penalty" (Prahalad and Hammond 2002; Mendoza 2011). *The Economist* (2010b) concludes that "companies need to learn how to appeal to the billions of people who live outside Shanghai and Bangalore, from the rising middle classes in second-tier cities to the farmers in isolated villages."

---

4 They include herbal pesticides – to replace chemical ones – developed by rural farmers in India, or a frying pan from an Indian inventor that conserves energy due to its thermal efficiency (Gupta 2010, 143).

5 The United Nations Population Fund (UNFPA) estimates that in 2050, the world population will have risen by more than two billion people (from 7.2 to 9.6 billion), most of whom will reside in developing and emerging economies (UN 2013).

Figure 1: Global income pyramid

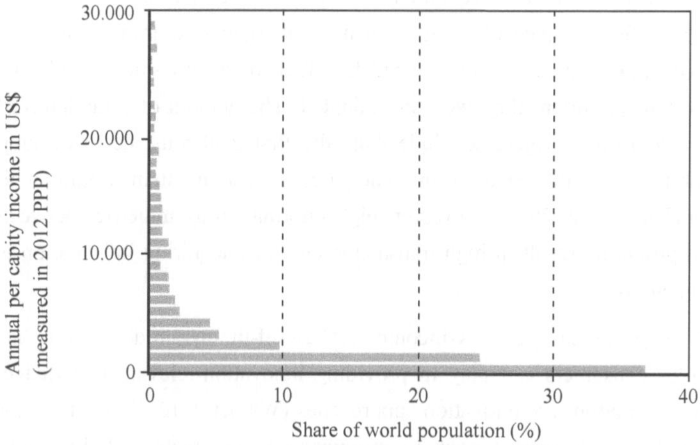

Source: UNDP 2008, 18.

But what is the role of user innovators as companies explore the business opportunities in low-income markets? And why are innovations needed in the first place? A variety of authors point to the fact that new solutions are needed in low-income markets to overcome the endemic challenges that characterize this market environment – be they a lack of infrastructure, constraints in the regulatory environment, or the low literacy of consumers (see, e.g., Christensen et al. 2001; Hart and Christensen 2002; Prahalad 2004; Gradl et al. 2008, 40; Krämer and Belz 2008, 221ff.; UNDP 2008, 17ff.). Some even argue that adapting products, processes, and business models to the characteristics of low-income markets is essential for succeeding in this marketplace (ibid.).[6]

However, companies aiming to enter low-income markets face an innovation gap. Their technological knowledge enables them to develop and produce almost any kind of solution; however, the life circumstances of consumers in low-income markets are "completely alien" to product developers of large global firms (Viswanathan and

6 For example, solar products overcome a lack of grid connections; mobile payment systems address issues of banking infrastructure; financial mechanisms such as group lending resolve financial constraints; and voice-driven ATMs or color-coded medicines overcome barriers of illiteracy. Some authors even argue that the challenges prevalent in low-income environments trigger innovation (SadreGhazi 2008, 64; Hart and Christensen 2002).

Sridharan 2012, 51; see also Weidner 2010). In fact, numerous innovation projects targeted at low-income markets have failed for this particular reason (Webb et al. 2009, 8). One example is projects offering inexpensive alternatives to traditional three-stone cookstoves. Although these stoves need less fuel, omit less smoke, and thus minimize indoor air pollution, they were not adopted. The authors of a randomized evaluation of a cookstove project conclude that "the first goal must be to develop cookstoves that people would actually want to acquire, use, and maintain" (Duflo et al. 2012; see also Hanna et al. 2012). However, high information asymmetries between consumers and producers result in high transaction costs, as acquiring information is time and cost intensive.

To address this gap, literature on low-income or "base-of-the-pyramid" markets has stressed the roles consumers can play in providing innovation-relevant knowledge. They advocate for "bottom-up innovation" approaches (Waibel 2012, 73ff.) that hear and incorporate the voices of low-income consumers and "co-create" solutions with them (see, e.g., Hart and Sharma 2004; Hart 2005; London 2007/2008; Simanis et al. 2008; Simanis and Hart 2008/2011; Sridharan and Viswanathan 2008, 461; Waibel 2012). However, for the most part, these studies remain on a conceptual level – or else very practitioner-oriented. Only a few exceptions exist that follow a qualitative empirical approach.[7] For the most part, these studies call for "a new approach to innovation" (Simanis and Hart 2011, 11). Viswanathan and Sridharan (2012, 51) have even questioned

> *the extent to which insights generated by traditional product development research anchored in formal, advanced market contexts will be applicable to the task of developing innovative products for BoP contexts.*

However, considering the vast body of research on innovation – which has provided a variety of theories, concepts, and empirical insights – one may question why research in the context of low-income markets should start from scratch. Thus it stands to reason to first consult mainstream innovation literature for relevant concepts and theories. This is the point of departure of the present study.

The next section (1.1) outlines the concrete research questions of the study as well as the theoretical and practical contributions it aims to make. Section 1.2 then provides an overview of the study.

---

[7] See the studies by Simanis et al. (2008), Viswanathan and Sridharan (2012), and Waibel (2012).

1.1 Research questions and contributions of the study

As outlined above, this study aims to explore how low-income consumers can be integrated into innovation – more specifically, to what extent they *are* a source of innovation. This approach is expected to enhance the capacity of companies to develop new solutions for these markets by leveraging the knowledge of their target group. In doings so, the study builds on previous findings from mainstream innovation research.

Innovation literature suggests a variety of methods that actively integrate consumers into innovation processes.[8] These methods are viewed in contrast to traditional market research techniques, which see the target group only as objects of research ("speaking when spoken to"), and not as active contributors. The present study hones in on investigating one particular technique called **idea competitions**. The method was found to be an ideal technique for integrating consumers into the "fuzzy front end" of innovation processes – that is, the period between the generation of an idea and its approval for development (Reichwald and Piller 2006; Soll 2006; Piller and Walcher 2006; Walcher 2007; Silvertant 2011). This stage is said to be the most chaotic and uncertain stage (Lynn and Akgun 1998; Kim and Wilemon 2002, 270; Bucherer and Eisert 2012, 185); but it is also a stage that determines the success of an innovation project if conducted properly (Cooper 1988, 243; Cooper and Kleinschmidt 1994).[9] Idea competitions provide access to information and knowledge that are relevant for this stage of the innovation process but usually difficult to tap (ibid.).

Moreover, the technique seems particularly suitable for integrating low-income consumers. For example, ideas can be handed in as drawings, texts, or verbal descriptions, helping to overcome challenges of low literacy (Jung and Chipchase 2008; Gau et al. 2012). The method can be conducted online and offline – with the latter being more appropriate for the realities in low-income markets where most consumers have no access to the internet, although this is slowly changing (ITU 2013[10]) While the method has been attempted in low-income markets (Jung and

8 The empirical studies of, e.g., Pobisch (2009) and Ramakrishnan (2011) investigate innovation workshops, while those of Walcher (2007) and Silvertant (2010) examine idea competitions.

9 Later stages encompass development and commercialization, which include prototype development and testing, production, market introduction, and diffusion. For further elaboration, see section 2.1.1.

10 ITU (2013) reports that in developing countries, 31% of the population is online (compared with 77% in the developed world).

Chipchase 2008), no empirical studies have made use of idea competitions to inform new product development processes targeted at low-income markets.

Thus the main question of the present study is the following: **What can we learn from applying idea competitions in low-income markets?** More specifically, the study aims to test if the contributions attributed to the technique hold true in low-income markets. Previous research has found that idea competitions serve to (1) generate creative ideas, (2) identify creative and innovative consumers, and (3) provide access to information and knowledge relevant for the subsequent stages of the innovation process.

(1) Identification of creative ideas

Creative ideas offer valuable input for the early stages of innovation processes, as they reveal relevant information about unaddressed needs, aspirations, or trends (Belz et al. 2009, 16). Idea competitions encourage consumers to generate creative ideas related to the topic of the competition (Walcher 2007; Belz et al. 2009; Silvertant 2011). While anecdotal evidence exists that low-income consumers are able to generate creative ideas, this has not been empirically investigated. Consequently, the following research question is asked:

Research question 1: To what extent can offline idea competitions generate creative ideas from low-income consumers?

(2) Identification of lead users and creative consumers

Second, due to their competitive character and measurable outcome, idea competitions are discussed as a method to identify particularly creative and/or innovative consumers (Walcher 2007, 185ff.; Belz et al. 2009, 17ff.; Silvertant 2011, 69ff.). This is relevant, as not all consumers possess innovation-relevant knowledge. More specifically, scholars view the method as a means of identifying lead users – a special type of consumer who significantly enhances the outcome of innovation processes (see, e.g., von Hippel 1986/1988). Anecdotal evidence indicates that certain consumers in low-income markets may be classified as lead users. For example, Gupta (2010, 137–138) argues that the "lack of material resources spurs knowledge-intensive innovations by common people in the informal sector," which offer "new problem-solving techniques that can [even] be applied in different contexts." Viswanathan and Sridharan (2012, 66–67) have identified consumers who "created innovative and affordable solutions to their 'vexing and perennial' needs, primarily because of the absence of market solutions." However, the question of how these innovators or lead users can be identified remains unanswered. Moreover, it is unclear whether idea competitions serve as a viable method to identify them. Consequently, the following research question must be addressed:

Research question 2a: To what extent can offline idea competitions identify low-income consumers with lead-user characteristics?

A variety of studies show that some individuals who are not classified as lead users (so-called "non-lead users") may still be able to provide creative input relevant for innovation (Silvertant 2011, 256ff.; Ramakrishnan 2012, 169 ff.; Schrader and Belz 2012, 345ff.). While this type of "creative mainstream consumer" (Silvertant 2011) has been identified through idea competitions (Silvertant 2011, 259) and innovation workshops (Belz et al. 2011; Ramakrishnan 2012; Schrader and Belz 2012), no studies have attempted to further characterize them. However, knowing what characteristics set them apart may be of particular value, as not all innovation endeavors targeted at low-income markets may require input from lead users – particularly if the aim is product adaptation rather than breakthrough innovation. In addition, being able to identify creative mainstream consumers may significantly help enhance the efficiency and effectiveness of integrating consumers into innovation, since participants who do not show their characteristics could be screened out earlier in the process. Thus, the present study addresses the following question:

Research question 2b: What are the common characteristics of low-income consumers who produce creative ideas in offline idea competitions?

(3) Identification and transfer of innovation-relevant knowledge[11]

As a technique that enables "open innovation," idea competitions are expected to provide access to innovation-relevant knowledge that is usually hard to tap, as it "sticks" to consumers (von Hippel 1994; 2005, 67). Innovation research distinguishes between need-related and solution-related information, which can be transferred in its tacit or explicit form (Nonaka and Takeuchi 1995; Nonaka et al. 1996; Reichwald and

[11] The terms information and knowledge will be used as synonyms in the present study, although they have differing meanings. For a justification of this approach as well as for further explanation, please see section 2.3.4.

Piller 2006, 108; Reichwald et al. 2007, 24; Walcher 2007, 20). However, research has neglected to examine what types of information and knowledge idea competitions actually provide. Innovation research also suggests that some types are more useful for innovation processes than others. For example, Senker (1993) and Mascitelli (2000) stress the acquisition of tacit knowledge to be of particular relevance for innovation. However, studies on idea competitions have not yet examined what types of innovation-relevant knowledge the technique yields. Thus the following research questions deserve attention:

Research question 3a: What types of information and knowledge can be obtained through idea competitions conducted in low-income contexts?

Research question 3b: What types of information and knowledge are most useful for innovation processes geared towards developing solutions for low-income consumers?

To gain access to relevant information and knowledge, previous research has merely focused on the **outcome** of idea competitions – namely, the identification of creative ideas and innovative participants. While this has provided valuable results (Piller and Walcher 2006; Walcher 2007; Silvertant 2011), it can be assumed that relevant information and knowledge is also transferred throughout the whole **process** of idea competitions, which typically provides some level of interaction between the organizers (i.e., product developers or designers) and target consumers. According to knowledge management theories, this interaction can help transfer innovation-relevant knowledge (Nonaka and Takeuchi 1995). Nonetheless, studies in the context of open innovation and user integration have mostly neglected to examine whether there are specific factors that enable a successful transfer of innovation-relevant knowledge from the consumer to the company. Consequently, the following research question can be asked:

Research question 3c: What factors enable the transfer of innovation-relevant knowledge from participants to designers/developers during offline idea competitions in low-income contexts?

Theoretical relevance

Why apply and study idea competitions in low-income markets? And what can we learn from doing so? The research questions outlined above already indicate a two-fold theoretical contribution of the present study:

(1) By transferring insights from innovation research to a new context, the study aims to find out whether the objectives of idea competitions, outlined by previous research (see above), can be met by applying the method in low-income contexts. The contribution lies in **testing existing propositions in a new context**, as the empirical studies of idea competitions identified through an extensive literature review[12] were only conducted in industrialized countries with high- and middle-income consumers (see, e.g., Soll 2006; Piller and Walcher 2006; Walcher 2007; Silvertant 2011).

(2) However, the focus of this study does not lie in testing theory. **By extending previous research on open innovation and consumer integration to a new context, the study aims to complement and expand existing findings** – and ultimately contribute to building middle-range theory (Merton 1968).[13] Scott (1995, 151) argues that too often we study propositions in "systems close to us in time and place." This, however, prevents us from gaining radically new insights, as familiar systems "are most difficult to see with fresh eyes. […] [They] co-opt and corrupt our vision because we are likely to share many of our [research] subjects' beliefs and assumptions. We need the frame-breaking experiences that only come from examining and comprehending organizations operating in other places and other times." Gradl

---

[12] The literature review was conducted using Business Source Premier (EBSCOhost), a research database service. It features the full text of more than 2,200 journals, about 1,100 of which are peer reviewed. Also, a limited number of books are offered (see http://www.ebscohost.com/academic/business-source-premier). Furthermore, standard books on innovation were consulted and a thorough search with Google Scholar was conducted. However, it should be mentioned that most books and papers screened were published in English and German. Due to practical limitations of this research project, academic work published in other languages was not considered.

[13] Middle-range theories are intermediate steps toward general or "grand" theories. They study concrete phenomena – as opposed to "grand theory," which attempts to explain the entire social world. To develop middle-range theories, empirical findings are generated. They are the basis for producing testable hypotheses about the phenomena encountered. Robert K. Merton (1968, 39), who coined the term middle-range theory, explains that they are "theories that lie between the minor but necessary working hypotheses that evolve in abundance during the day-by-day research, and the all-inclusive systematic efforts to develop a unified theory that will explain all the observed uniformities of social behavior, social organization and social change." For further explanation, please see Merton (1968), Boudon (1991) or Weick (1995).

(forthcoming) also suggests that although studying phenomena in the “bare context” of low-income markets may not be generalizable, these findings may certainly help us observe what we take for granted with “fresh eyes” and derive insights on an abstract level.

Mainstream research on idea competitions still leaves a variety of questions open. For example, it remains unclear what type of innovation-relevant knowledge idea competitions generate. Furthermore, little to no research has been done on how this information and knowledge can be transferred from consumers to companies (i.e., product developers or designers). Conducting idea competitions offline may reveal further insights regarding these unaddressed questions. Consequently, the contribution of this study will lie in developing preliminary hypotheses for the context of low-income markets, which can be tested in future studies. Ideally, these hypotheses may also provide new impetus for innovation research in other markets.

Practical relevance

In addition to its theoretical relevance, the topic of the present research endeavor stems from a practical challenge. Businesses seek to enter the untapped and rather unknown low-income market with suitable products and services. However, they frequently lack precise market information as well as a good understanding of their target group’s needs and of the context in which the products or services will be used. Thus a variety of products that were introduced into low-income markets have never been accepted by the consumer.

Consequently, this study aims to develop practical recommendations for corporate practitioners to gain access to information about consumers’ needs, wants, traditions, and aspirations, as well as about their view of potential solutions that address these needs and suit their context. Few methods have been tested which actively integrate consumers into innovation in low-income markets. Thus, this study strives to provide practitioners with a practical and tested tool to tap the potential of their target group to develop solutions for their very own needs. Nonetheless, it should be stressed that idea competitions cannot replace the research and development activities of a company. Furthermore, the results obtained from this method still need to be complemented and triangulated with the results of other market research methods.

Table 1: Research questions

Objective of the idea competition	Research question	Unit of analysis	Expected contribution	
			Test theory	Build theory
(1) Generation of creative ideas	(1) To what extent can offline idea competitions generate **creative ideas** from low-income consumers?	Ideas	✓	X
(2) Identification of lead users and creative participants	(2) To what extent can offline idea competitions identify low-income consumers with **lead-user** characteristics?	Participants	✓	X
	(2b) What are the common **characteristics** of low-income consumers who produce creative ideas in offline idea competitions?	Participants	X	✓
(3) Identification and transfer of innovation-relevant information and knowledge	(3a) What **types** of information and knowledge can be obtained through idea competitions conducted in low-income contexts?	Ideas, Process	X	✓
	(3b) What types of information and knowledge are most **useful** for innovation processes geared towards developing solutions for low-income consumers?	Ideas, Process	X	✓
	(3c) What factors **enable** the transfer of innovation-relevant knowledge from participants to designers/developers during offline idea competitions in low-income contexts?	Process	X	✓

Source: created by author.

1.1 Outline of the study

The study is divided into six chapters.

The present chapter introduced the topic of the study. It outlined the justification for the main research questions and explained the theoretical as well as practical contributions of this study.

The second chapter presents relevant insights from innovation research regarding the main research questions. It serves to develop a theoretical lens, which provides orientation during the research process. It is divided into three parts: The first section of the chapter (2.1) discusses the state of the art in literature on open innovation and customer integration into innovation processes. The second section (2.2) then takes a closer look at consumers as a source of innovation. The third section (2.3) starts off by describing the design and implementation of a specific method to integrate consumers – namely, idea competitions. It presents the state of the art in research on the technique as well as its objectives. Each of the three sections also offers conceptual considerations on the relevance of the insights from innovation research for research on low-income markets. For this purpose, the stream of literature on the "base-of-the-pyramid" (BoP) approach is consulted. Furthermore, the identified research gaps are presented in an intermediate conclusion to each section.

The third chapter outlines the research design chosen for this study. The first part (3.1) starts with conceptual considerations on the status of theory building in low-income contexts. It also clarifies the underlying research paradigm of the study. The next part of section 3.1 explains the research strategy chosen. It clarifies why the qualitative approach is appropriate given the nature of the research questions and the topic under study. Furthermore, details are provided on the case-study approach and on how case studies were selected and applied. The second part of the chapter (3.2) gives detailed information on the research methods. It starts with outlining the design and implementation of the idea competitions. Following, the methods for data collection and analysis are described along the three units of analysis (UoA): ideas, participants, and process.

The fourth chapter presents the results of the three case studies. Each of these case studies represents an idea competition conducted in Brazilian low-income communities. Each case study report follows the same structure, presenting the setting and then examining the three units of analysis: First, the creativity of the ideas generated is evaluated. Second, the characteristics of participants are analyzed. Third, the types of information and knowledge obtained from the process are analyzed – considering both what types were most useful for the innovation process and which factors enabled their transfer.

The fifth chapter compares and discusses the results of the three case studies and derives conclusions. While chapter four examines each case study independently, this chapter aggregates findings in a cross-case analysis (Yin 2003, 133). This analysis is done separately for each research question. The results are triangulated with findings from other studies wherever possible and relevant. Ultimately, the chapter aims to provide answers to the research questions, and hypotheses are drawn from the findings where suitable.

The last chapter summarizes the theoretical and practical contributions of the study. It also points towards the limitations of the study. Last, recommendations for further research are developed.

Figure 2: Overview of study

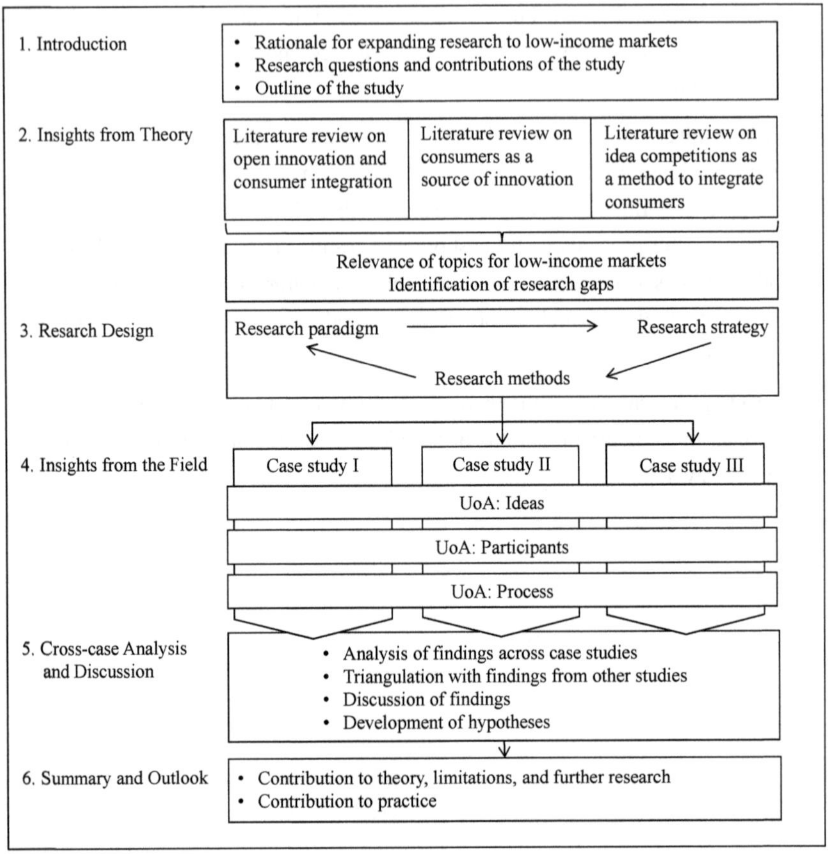

Source: created by author.

2 Insights from theory

The present study builds on insights from two streams of research: innovation research – in particular open innovation and customer integration – and research on low-income or "base of the pyramid" (BoP) markets. Of these two areas, innovation research provides the main theoretical background of this study.

BoP markets are a rather new research area. However, BOP literature offers a valuable contribution by drawing research interest towards low-income contexts and markets (see, for example, Prahalad and Hammond 2002; Prahalad 2004; Hart and London 2005; Brugmann and Prahalad 2007). Recently, more and more academic studies are being published based on empirical data and in connection with existing literature streams and methodologies (see, e.g., London and Hart 2004; Sánchez et al. 2007 Seelos and Mair 2007; London et al. 2009; Badry 2009; Webb et al. 2009; Halme et al. 2012; Herrndorf 2013). However, the majority of BoP articles are still conceptual in nature and lack empirical analysis and theoretical grounding (see also section 3.1.1).

This study argues that research on low-income markets (or "BoP" research) could more explicitly build on innovation research, particularly in the area of open innovation and consumer integration. In turn, applying theoretical insights from innovation research to low-income markets can create new insights.

Consequently, this chapter is structured as follows:

- The first section of each of the following three main sections (2.1, 2.2 and 2.3) introduces key concepts from innovation literature (2.1.1, 2.2.1, and 2.3.1–2.3.4).
- The subsequent sections discuss the relevance of these insights for low-income or BoP markets by reviewing BoP literature (2.1.2, 2.2.2, and 2.3.5).
- The chapter then identifies and characterizes research gaps. They are discussed at the end of each section as part of an intermediate conclusion (2.1.3, 2.2.3, and 2.3.6).

2.1 Underlying concepts of open innovation and consumer integration

The first part of this section provides an overview of the state of the art in open innovation and consumer integration. It explains why companies increasingly open up their innovation processes and why consumers may have particularly relevant input for these processes. After clarifying the "why" questions, the "how" dimensions are discussed, providing an overview of the methods to integrate consumers. Finally, the approach is critically evaluated.

The second part discusses the relevance of the insights from innovation research for low-income markets. For that purpose, the relevance of innovating for these markets is explained. Furthermore, this section elaborates on how innovating for low-income markets can be approached and what role consumers can play in this endeavor. The section concludes with a brief summary of the similarities between both research streams as well as a discussion of shortcomings and research gaps.

2.1.1 State of the art in open innovation and consumer integration

The Latin origin of the word "innovation" (*innovare*) denotes the renewal or change of existing solutions (Tidd et al. 2005, 10). These new solutions not only build on novel ideas for products, processes, or any other aspect of a firm's activity, but also imply improvement in efficiency or usefulness. Josef Schumpeter, one of the earliest researchers to draw attention to the importance of innovation, was also the first to point out that in contrast to invention, innovation involves a commercial transaction (Schumpeter 1912; see Freeman and Soete 1997, 6). To find market success, innovations must be met by a market demand.

Innovations create benefits on an individual and societal level: They help manage resource constraints or increase productivity, thus creating value. Innumerable types of innovations are distinguished in the literature. For the purpose of this study, these types can be organized along two questions: (1) What is new? and (2) How new is it?[14]

14 Hauschildt and Salomo (2007, 3) further distinguish the subjective dimensions of innovations – that is, the question, "For whom is it new?" Here, they refer to the fact that innovations can be new to a geographical area (a region or the world), a sector, a market, a market segment, an organization, or an individual.

Answering the question "What is new?" clarifies the object of innovation. Generally, three types of innovations are distinguished:[15]

- **Process innovations** change the way in which products and services are produced and delivered (e.g., a change in the manufacturing methods and equipment to process food). This includes significant changes in techniques, equipment, and/or software (Tidd et al. 2005, 10; OECD 2005; Reichwald and Piller 2006, 99; Hauschildt and Salomo 2007, 9).
- **Product and service innovations** refer to changes in products and services offered by an organization. These include significant improvements in components and materials, technical specifications, incorporated software, user friendliness, or other functional characteristics. (e.g., functional food enriched with selected vitamins and minerals) (OECD 2005; Tidd et al. 2005, 10; Reichwald and Piller 2006, 99; Hauschildt and Salomo 2007, 9).
- **Business model innovations** can be defined as changes in the way a "business creates value in its products and services and captures that value in the form of revenue from its customers" (Chesbrough 2007, 16).

The question "How new is it?" refers to the degree of novelty. Three types can be classified:

- **Incremental** innovations mean small-scale improvements of an existing product or service through value-adding attributes. So called "me-too" products or extensions of product lines count as incremental innovations – they only imitate or slightly improve existing products (Verworn and Herstatt 2007, 115). Incremental innovations generally are associated with lower risk and better short-term profitability (Magnusson and Kristensson 2010, 150).
- **Radical** innovations differ significantly from former solutions and mostly imply revolutionary changes. "These innovations incorporate technology that is substantially different from existing products and fulfills customer needs either significantly better than existing products or addresses different types of needs [...]" (Bucherer and Eisert 2012, 186). They are generally regarded as more risky, but they also promise high profitability when they succeed in the marketplace (Verworn and Herstatt 2007, 115).

---

15 Other researchers distinguish further types of innovations, for example, marketing innovations. As they are not relevant for the focus of this study, they were not defined or explored further. For additional insights, please see: Tidd et al. 2005 or the OECD Guidelines for Collecting and Interpreting Innovation (2005).

- **Disruptive innovations** are products or services that take root in simple applications (Hart and Christensen 2002, 52). They usually perform worse than an established, mainstream product. However, they have new characteristics such as portability, simplicity, ease of use or a lower price (Ahlstrom 2010, 18). Disruptive innovations thus enable market entry for completely new users who were previously unable to use the established product due to its complexity or price (Christensen et al. 2001; Ahlstrom 2010, 18). These innovations thus often compete against non-consumption (Hart and Christensen 2002, 52). Moreover, disruptive innovations have the potential to move up in the market, eventually displacing established competitors.

The **innovation process** can be divided in three major stages: the fuzzy front end, development, and commercialization. In practice, these stages encompass a variety of steps, as seen in figure 3 (see, e.g., Herstatt 1999; Cooper et al. 2004; Kotler and Armstrong 2004).[16] These steps, however, cannot be seen as a linear, step-by-step process. Rather, several feedback loops between technological alternatives and customer needs are necessary (Bucherer and Eisert 2012, 185).

Figure 3: Stages of the innovation process

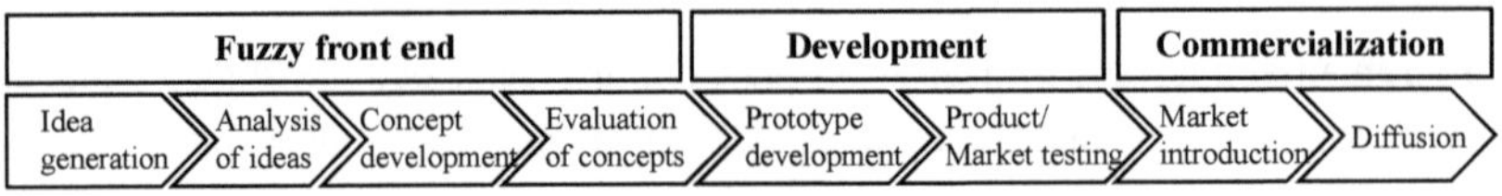

Source: created by author.

This study focuses on the first stage – the "fuzzy front end." It is defined as the period between the generation of an idea and its approval for development (Kim and Wilemon 2002, 269; Verworn et al. 2008, 1). As the name indicates, the fuzzy front end has been found to be the most chaotic stage, as it is where most "setbacks and surprises" happen (Bucherer and Eisert 2012, 185). Researchers describe the fuzzy front end as "intrinsically non-routine, dynamic and uncertain" (Kim and Wilemon 2002, 270). Uncertainty may come from either market forces or technological conditions (Lynn and Akgun 1998). Thus, during the fuzzy front end, information

16 There are two reasons to include the diffusion of new products in the innovation process: Many inventions might seem great in a research lab but fail to see the light of the day. Thus, successful diffusion is vital to the economic success of inventions (Rogers 1995). Second, consumer information and feedback during the diffusion process eventually leads to new incremental or radical innovations.

needs to be gathered to reduce uncertainty. Indeed, it can be empirically shown that the quality of execution of pre-development activities directly relates to the success of innovation projects (Cooper and Kleinschmidt 1994). Companies with excellent records of successfully introducing new products conduct more analyses during the fuzzy front end (Cooper 1988, 243) or pre-development phase. They also invest in their idea and in concept generation and conduct more rigorous screening and evaluation of the ideas generated (Booz et al. 1982, 26). Nonetheless, this phase often receives less attention than the later stages and is thus considered the greatest weakness in product innovation (Khurana and Rosenthal 1997). In particular, little attention has been devoted to understanding and managing the phase of idea creation (Magnusson 2009, 581; see also Dahl and Moreau, 2002).

As low-income markets remain rather unexplored, high market uncertainty can be expected, the degree of which is determined through "knowledge about customers' needs and wants" amongst other factors (Verworn et al. 2006, 4). To gain access to this knowledge in the early phases of the innovation process, scholars have advocated for opening up innovation processes (von Hippel 1988/2005; Chesbrough 2003/2006; Reichwald and Piller 2006). The following sections provide a brief introduction of the benefits of opening up these processes, the methods for doing so, and the risks.

Open versus closed innovation

The idea that new products and services should be exclusively developed within a firm's boundaries has long dominated the thinking of both practitioners and researchers. Following this approach – often referred to as "**closed innovation**" – companies mainly rely on internal resources to develop new products and services (Chesbrough 2003, 21ff.). Consequently, they create their own research and development units, which are important drivers for large-scale industries such as the chemical industry. To ensure state-of-the-art research, a highly qualified workforce is often bound to the company through incentives. Where closed innovation prevails, the scientific landscape often consists of isolated "knowledge islands" (Chesbrough 2007, 21–24). Technologies that are developed outside of the firm's boundaries are often rejected (Chesbrough 2007, 30) – a phenomenon referred to as the "not invented here (NIH) syndrome," first documented by Katz and Allen (1982).[17]

---

17 Katz and Allen (1982, 7) define it as "the tendency of a project group of stable composition to believe that it possesses a monopoly of knowledge in its field, which leads it to reject new ideas

In opposition to this rather traditional view, researchers and practitioners today reason that resources outside a company can be vital for new product development – or, as Henry Chesbrough puts it: "Not all the smart people work for you" (2006, 34). As useful knowledge can be widely distributed, companies should tap the knowledge and creative potential of external sources. These may be suppliers, customers, business partners, competitors, start-ups, universities, other research institutions, or even governments (von Hippel 1988). Chesbrough names this model "**open innovation**" as opposed to "closed innovation" (Chesbrough 2003 21ff.; see figure 4)[18]. He defines open innovation as "the use of purposive inflows and outflows of knowledge to accelerate internal innovation, and expand the markets for external use of innovation, respectively" (Chesbrough et al. 2008, 1).

Chesbrough recognizes that the idea of opening up innovation processes is not new: "Many models have [already] been developed to explain how firms can exploit external knowledge" (Chesbrough et al. 2008, 7). For example, they can imitate a competitor, consult with their customers, tap the knowledge of start-ups, consult public sources, fund university research or form strategic alliances with other companies.

While there is a wealth of antecedents in academic literature on the use of external knowledge, the open innovation paradigm elevates external knowledge from playing a supplementary to a primary role:

> *In open innovation, external knowledge plays an equal role to that afforded to internal knowledge in earlier conception. [...] In the proprietary model of innovation, useful knowledge is scarce, hard to find, hazardous to rely upon (a root cause of the NIH syndrome). In open innovation, useful knowledge is generally believed to be widely distributed, and of general high quality. Even the most sophisticated R&D organizations need to be well connected to these external sources of knowledge.*[19] (Chesbrough et al. 2008, 8–9)

---

from outsiders to the detriment of its performance." Katz and Allen investigate the NIH syndrome between company units (i.e., opposition to input from marketing departments). However, it can be assumed that the rejection of external knowledge is even bigger (Reichwald and Piller 2006, 89).

18 Chesbrough argues that companies "should organize their innovation process to become more open to external knowledge and ideas" – a process he terms as the "outside-in" process. In addition, he suggests that companies take "unused internal ideas to the outside" – referred to as the "inside-out" process (Chesbrough 2006, 21).

19 While the open innovation model developed by Chesbrough encompasses cooperation with start-ups or independent research institutions, the present study focuses on innovation processes that the company engages in with its users or consumers.

The model reflects the increased mobility of people and knowledge in the twentieth century (Chesbrough 2007, 34–41). "Knowledge islands" have dissolved more and more.

Figure 4: Open vs. closed innovation

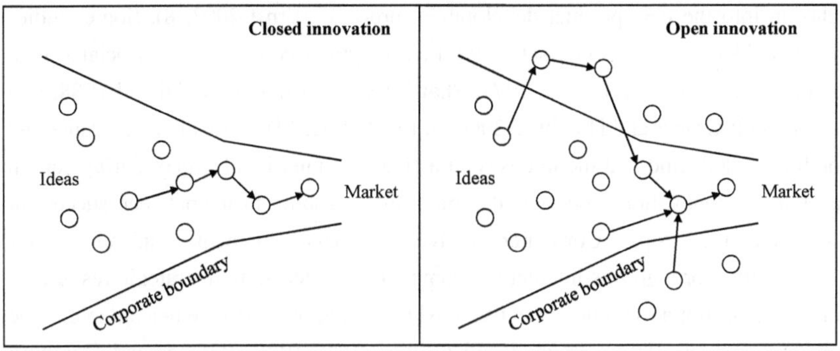

Source: Chesbrough 2003, xxii.

However, Chesbrough himself reckons that external validity of the open innovation approach has yet to be proven, as the evidence for this model mostly looks at high-tech industries (such as IT or pharmaceuticals) and the research has been largely focused on US-based companies. Thus, it remains an open question whether the concept applies to low-tech industries as well as to industries outside the US or the industrialized world (Chesbrough 2003, 5).

Active versus passive consumers

Companies have an incentive to rethink their innovation approach: Empirical studies show that – depending on the sector – up to 90% of inventions do not succeed in the marketplace (Reichwald and Piller 2006, 106; see also Crawford 1987; Cooper 1999). Studies in innovation management have long tried to explain why some inventions fail and others succeed (Ernst 2002, 1). Broadly speaking, external and internal success factors are distinguished (Reichwald and Piller 2006, 106–107). External factors that influence innovation success may lie in the regulatory environment – for example, the protection of intellectual property rights – or in the company's infrastructure or location – for example, its closeness to scientific hotspots (Reichwald and Piller 2006, 106; see also: Cooper and Kleinschmidt 1987; Cooper 1988; Cooper 1999; Ernst 2002). Internal factors could be an innovation-friendly corporate culture, corporate strategy, organizational factors, the commitment of senior management, the design and proficiency of activities carried out in the individual phases of the innovation process – particularly the early phases – and the use of market information throughout ("market orientation") (ibid.).

Market orientation involves "consultations with the customer, leading to her/his inclusion into the new product development process" (Ernst 2002, 8). Some studies provide evidence that this interaction with customers or consumers is associated with product success (Rothwell et al. 1974; Shaw 1985; Urban and von Hippel 1988; von Hippel 1988; Gruner and Homburg 2000, 3; Ernst 2002, 14). For example, Gruner and Homburg (2000) find that the intensity of active consumer involvement during certain stages of the innovation process is the main distinguishing factor between successful innovations and "flops." Consumer involvement creates competitive advantages for the company. Through this interaction, companies get access to a strategic resource – namely, the information inherent in users, which would otherwise be unavailable to the firm (von Hippel 1988; Campbell and Cooper 1999, 508ff.; Gruner and Homburg 2000, 2). This information enables companies to better anticipate market changes (Sawhney and Prandelli 2000, 258) and increase the market acceptance of new products or services by making them "fit to market" (Reichwald and Piller 2006, 152), thus minimizing risks (Soll 2006, 18).

However, other studies show contrary results. For example, Cooper (1986) finds that intense concentration on a few customers ("customness") has a negative influence on innovation success (see also Ernst 2002, 8). Campbell and Cooper (1999, 507) find that partnerships with customers during the innovation process were no more successful than in-house projects. This difference in findings is largely due to the two following aspects.

(1) **The "who":** First, success depends on the **type of consumers** involved. Campbell and Cooper (1999, 517) themselves point out that "empirical evidence [...] exists that partner selection is critical to achieving benefits from closer customer interaction." Indeed, a variety of studies show that selecting the right consumers for innovation makes a significant difference, since some consumers are simply more capable of making relevant contributions to innovation processes. In particular, "lead users" are said to enhance the outcome of innovation processes significantly.[20] They are a special

[20] Lilien et al. (2002, 1043) find that annual sales of lead-user product ideas generated at 3M are conservatively projected to be 146 million USD after five years – more than eight times higher than

type of consumer who senses needs earlier than others, and thus benefits greatly from the advent of new products or services that address these needs (von Hippel 1986/2005). Furthermore, they have the ability to transform their need-related information into solutions – that is, to engage in innovative activities (Reichwald and Piller 2006, 108). They either modify existing products or develop entirely new ones (Lüthje and Herstatt 2004, 554). Herstatt and von Hippel (1992, 213–214) argue that due to the high expected benefit, lead users "can provide the richest need and solution data to inquiring market researchers."

(2) **The "how":** Second, **the role of the consumer** during the innovation process is crucial. The consumer's passive involvement only gives access to explicit information, while their active cooperation reveals implicit, solution-related information vital for innovation (see section 2.3.4).

Traditional market research mostly views consumers in this passive role, as "demanders" (Ernst 2002, 9) who "speak only when spoken to" (von Hippel 1978, 243). The manufacturer's role, in this view, is to hear and incorporate "the voice of the customer" (Griffin and Hauser 1993) – that is, to capture the needs and preferences of consumers and develop appropriate solutions. For this approach, von Hippel coins the term "**manufacture-active paradigm**" (von Hippel 1978, 40ff.). However, from such a passive role, few insights for innovation can be expected. Moreover, studies show that the customers themselves are slowly "stepping out of their traditional roles" to become "active players" and "co-creators of value" (Prahalad and Ramaswamy 2000, 80). According to Sawhney and Prandelli (2000, 258), a shift from a perspective of exploiting customer knowledge by the firm to a perspective of knowledge co-creation with customers can be observed. Von Hippel finds that users develop or modify products for their own use in 10 to 40% of cases (von Hippel 2005, 19–20).[21,22] In his

forecast sales for the average contemporaneously conducted traditional project. They also found that each lead-user project is projected to create a new major product line for a 3M division.

21 Through numerous studies, von Hippel investigates innovative users (see, e.g., von Hippel 1976/1978/1986/1988/2005) and finds evidence that dates back to the 18th century. For example, Adam Smith reports that "a great part of the machines made use of in [...] manufactures [...] were originally the invention of common workmen, who [...] naturally turned their thoughts towards finding out easier and readier methods of performing it" (Smith 1776; see von Hippel 2005, 21). In this example, the workmen can be regarded as users of the product. Acquiring a wealth of implicit information or use information when handling the machines, they were well suited to coming up with a better solution.

22 However, von Hippel rightly notes that all studies were probably affected by a response bias, as users might be more inclined to say "yes" when asked if they innovate or not.

pioneering work on user innovation beginning in the '80s and '90s, von Hippel has coined the term "**customer-active paradigm**" (von Hippel 1978, 40ff.) for this phenomenon. It credits consumers with the capacity to solve problems on their own and even to initiate problem-solving processes.

Reichwald and Piller (2006, 131) go a step further. They coin the term "**interactive value creation**,"[23] which sees the customer as a crucial partner for creating value. Building on the work of Chesbrough and von Hippel, they stress that users and manufacturers can engage in cooperative problem-solving processes, which can be activated either by the customer or the company (Reichwald and Piller 2006, 134). Accordingly, Reichwald et al. (2007) distinguish two ways of creating value with customers: (1) Companies can either screen the market for user innovations (2) or they can actively integrate consumers into the innovation process.[24]

The first way is referred to as "**reactive customer integration**," as the customer takes the initiative to innovate (Reichwald et al. 2007, 64–65; Walcher 2007, 28ff.). In that case, the customer has the required "solution information" to adapt or create a product that serves his needs better than the existing offers. User innovations make implicit or sticky information explicit. Kristensson et al. (2004, 6) conclude that "ideas generated by a user in the user's own environment seem more likely to contain those unique features that companies seek but which are difficult to detect. Needs and requirements are likely to be [...] automatically built into the ideas generated" (Kristensson et al. 2004, 6; see also Thomke and von Hippel 2002).

In Reichwald and Piller's classification, the second way of tapping inherent user information and capabilities is to pursue "**active customer integration**" (Reichwald et al. 2007, 65; Walcher 2007, 28ff.). Here, the company takes the initiative to innovate and invites the consumer or customer to contribute. This interaction between the customer and the manufacturer results in a reciprocal learning process: The company learns how consumers use products or what their unfulfilled needs are. The consumer, in turn, learns about new technologies and the opportunities and limitations they provide. In Magnusson's words, "Taken together, such reciprocal learning has the

---

23 This term was translated by the author from the German "Interaktive Wertschöpfung."

24 The different terminology of von Hippel and Reichwald and Piller is due to the fact that the latter look at customer integration from the perspective of the company, who remains "reactive" when users innovate – while von Hippel's "manufacturer-active" versus "consumer active paradigm" looks at who initiates the activity.

potential to bring up ideas for new products" (2009, 582). Along the same lines, Kristensson et al. (2004, 7) observe that a "deepened interaction between a user and a company may increase the likelihood of making new combinations of previously disconnected and unrelated informational elements."

Figure 5: Manufacturer-active and customer-active paradigms

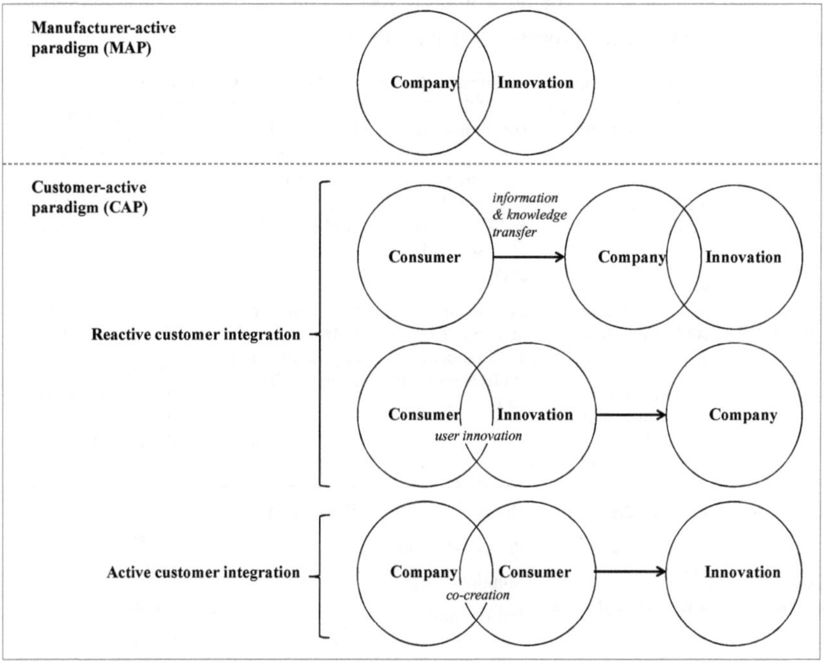

Source: created by author based on Reichwald et al. 2007, 65; Walcher 2007, 28ff.; and Silvertant 2011, 25.

Consumers can make contributions to all phases of the innovation process. Their need-related information is most valuable in the early stages of the process, while their solution-related information can contribute to the development phases. In later phases, they can help enhance products – for example, by testing prototypes – or assist with innovating distribution or marketing channels. However, research finds that particularly their **integration in the early stages has a positive effect on new product success** (Rothwell et al. 1974; Gruner and Homburg 2000; Lüthje 2000, 11–15; Cooper et al. 2004; Kristensson et al. 2004; Magnusson 2009).

Researchers have found different names for the **active roles** consumers can take during the innovation process: They can be thought of as co-innovators, co-creators, prosumers, co-designers, co-producers, and finally consumers and users of new products and services (Prahalad and Ramaswamy 2000; Thomke and von Hippel 2002; Nambisan 2002; Füller and Hienerth 2004; Kristensson et al. 2004, 5; Reichwald and Piller 2006) (see table 2). The present study focuses on the role of consumers in the early phases of innovation processes – that is, the fuzzy front end.

Table 2: Roles and contributions of consumers throughout the innovation process

Phase	Fuzzy front end	Development	Production	Commerciali-zation
Role of Consumer	Consumer as resource (e.g., Nambisan 2002) Consumers as a source of ideas (e.g., Magnusson 2009; Silvertant 2011) Co-innovator (e.g., Füller and Hienerth 2004; Schrage 2006)	Co-designer (e.g., Reichwald and Piller 2006, 163; Seybold 2006) Co-creator (e.g., Sawhney and Prandelli 2000; Nambisan 2002)	Prosumer (e.g., Toffler 1980; Gibbert et al. 2002; Ritz and Jurgenson 2010) Consumers as testers (e.g., Füller and Hienerth 2004)	User and consumer (e.g., Nambisan 2002) Consumers as buyers (e.g., Füller and Hienerth 2004) Consumers as product promoters (e.g., Schreier and Prügl 2008)
Contri-bution	Product ideas Information on needs Evaluation of ideas	Design Prototype testing Solution Information	Production	Evaluation of market potential Diffusion Purchase Providing use information

Source: created by author based on Nambisan 2002, 395; Ernst 2004, 195; Bartl 2006, 28; Soll 2006, 33; Silvertant 2011, 28.

The "fuzzy front end" aims to create and increase the pool of ideas (diverge) and then screen the best ideas (converge). Kristensson et al. find that "creative ideas may offer a successful start to innovation, which is important since research indicates that most projects do not fail at the end, but at the beginning" (2004, 4). The fuzzy front end thus has the highest potential for consumer involvement, as little is pre-defined and the solution space is wide open for input (Reichwald and Piller 2006, 102ff.). Some studies even find that users are able to develop more original ideas than company executives at this stage (Kristensson et al. 2002, 59; Magnusson 2009; Poetz and Schreier 2009, 12).

Despite evidence that companies could significantly improve their new product development process, the question remains why many shy away from integrating consumers during the early stages of innovation. For example, a study by Gruner and Homburg (2000, 11) finds that the intensity of consumer involvement is highest in the market launch stage (4.14 on a 7-point Likert scale, with 1 representing no interaction and 7 maximum interaction). Interaction in the idea generation stage is lowest (2.42 on a 7-point Likert scale). No evidence supports this tendency; however, it may be due to a lack of knowledge on the side of the company about how to integrate consumers into innovation.

Methods of consumer integration

The general shift in innovation management from closed to open innovation (Chesbrough 2003/2006), from the manufacturer-active paradigm to the consumer-active paradigm (von Hippel 1978 40ff.; von Hippel 2005) also influences the way the consumer's role is perceived – and consequently also the methods with which market information is gained. In general, the consumer transforms from being viewed by companies as a passive object of investigation to having an active role. **Conventional market research methods** belong to the manufacturer-active paradigm, as they are mostly targeted towards obtaining representative information *about* consumers. They can generally be distinguished into quantitative and qualitative methods. Quantitative methods such as surveys can be a first step to get an overview of the market and the target group (i.e., market size, age structure, or income data) or assess the market potential of a product (demand) (Meffert et al. 2005, 154–158). They are also used to capture the reactions of consumers to new products and services, for example through consumer panels[25]. These methods mostly follow testing purposes, strive to be representative, and select their samples accordingly. Qualitative methods – such as qualitative interviews, observations, focus groups, or ethnographic methods – are more exploratory in nature. They aim to describe unknown phenomena (Lüthje 2000, 21). In early stages of the innovation process, they are applied when a company is still trying to find out which need to address. In later stages, qualitative research methods can, for example, be applied to test and enhance prototypes. However, Jeppesen (2005, 349) reckons that

[25] A consumer panel is group of consumers who are asked to give their opinions about (new) product or service solutions. The technique is often employed for new product development initiatives.

> *the utility of such methods depends on the analyst's ability to accurately and completely condense from the interview data the product attributes consumers feel are important. A problem may arise if the information gatherers filter the voice of the consumer through their own biases. Additional problems may arise from the fact that consumers constantly form new preferences and thus may change their opinion by the time the actual product is released [...]. The methods suffer from the sticky information problem in that the expenditure required to transfer information in a useable form is high.*

Qualitative methods do not strive to be representative, but rather choose participants according to criteria that are driven by content ("theoretical sampling" – see Miles and Hubermann 2005, 27–29). In their aim to address future needs, however, the optimal selection criteria of the sample often remain unclear, as the target group of the future is unknown. Both qualitative and quantitative methods bear the risk of assessing only present needs of today's consumers (Lüthje 2000, 21), because the information on new product needs is collected from a random or typical set of consumers (Lilien et al. 2002, 1042). The outcome can thus be constrained by consumers' real-world experience – a phenomenon also referred to as "functional fixedness"[26] (Duncker 1945; Adamson 1952; Lüthje 2000, 22). Usage patterns hinder them from thinking "outside the box" and discovering original ways of using objects. Furthermore, grounding innovation development on present samples can lead to reactive, rather incremental innovation. Kristensson et al. (2004, 5) state that "traditional market research techniques only manage to skim the surface of user needs and desires" (see also Tidd et al. 2005).[27] Lüthje and Herstatt (2004, 554) thus conclude that

> *most traditional market research techniques do not offer appropriate ways to discover new product attributes and ideas outside the well-known solution space; mainly, customer reactions and answers to stimuli or questions are recorded; consumers are not induced to formulate emerging needs for new solutions [...].*

---

[26] Duncker defines functional fixedness as a mental block against using an object in a new way that is required to solve a problem (Duncker 1945). Usage patterns and the familiarity with an existing product or solution hinder conventional customers from moving past the original intention of the object and consider alternative applications (Duncker 1945; Adamson 1952, 288; von Hippel 1986, 792; Lüthje and Herstatt 2004, 554).

[27] In addition to these general techniques, which can also be applied for purposes beyond innovation, there is a whole range of techniques specifically developed to integrate the voice of the customer into the innovation process – for example, Quality Function Deployment (QFD). The objective is to gear the whole innovation process towards the needs of the customers; it is applicable when a company has a concrete idea – and potential customers can articulate their needs and requirements (Reichwald and Piller 2006, 111).

New market research methods aim at integrating consumers actively and deeply into one or, ideally, all stages of the innovation process ("customer-active paradigm"). With higher levels of integration and interaction (see figure 6), they are more likely to tap consumers' latent needs. They unveil tacit or "sticky" information as well as solution-related information (von Hippel 1994, 430; Neale and Corkindale 1998; Slater and Narver 1998; Narver et al. 2004; Reichwald and Piller 2006, 55; Krämer and Belz 2008). Consequently, these methods do not merely generate information *about* the market or the consumer – they gain access to the information and knowledge *of* consumers (Pobisch 2010, 55ff.; Silvertant 2011, 31) or create it *with* them (Sawhney and Prandelli 2000, 258; Silvertant 2011, 31). In doing so, the innovation process is no longer dominated by the company.

The following table provides an overview of market research methods that give consumers an active role (see table 3):

Table 3: Examples of new market research methods

	Innovation workshops	Toolkits
Description and objective	• Structured workshops are facilitated by a moderator. • Creativity techniques can be applied to stimulate participants. • Participants usually consist of a group of consumers or a mixed group of consumers, experts, and company professionals. • The aim is to create new ideas and concepts that may result in innovation.	• Integrated toolsets enable users to create and test designs for custom products or services, which can then be produced by manufacturers. • Users can experiment within the frames of this toolbox, changing, e.g., colors, forms, designs, materials, or the taste of a product • The aim is for users to find the optimal solution to a problem through "trial and error."
Stage of innovation process	• All stages, but most commonly applied for "ideation" or concept development	• Later stages, mostly concept development
Benefits	• In-depth interaction with the target group • Applicable in all stages of the innovation process • Solution space is open	• Enables the integration of a broad group of people • Reduces transaction costs, as the "trial-and-error process" is entirely transferred to the customer • Can be conducted online or offline

Shortcomings	• Time-intensive selection and recruiting of participants, as well as preparation of the workshop • Only conducted offline, with small groups of selected participants	• Only applicable at later stages • Limited solution space
Sources	Hansen and Raabe 1991, 185; Lüthje 2000; Reichwald and Piller 2006, 162; Pobisch 2010, 72ff.	von Hippel 2001; von Hippel and Katz 2002; Thomke and von Hippel 2002; Franke and Piller 2004; Eichwald and Piller 2006, 163; Prügl and Schreier 2006
	Virtual communities	**Idea competitions**
Description and objective	• Innovation communities created by companies encourage consumers to share and exchange information on a specific topic ("community-based innovation"). • Alternatively, companies can tap communities that are initiated by users. • The aim is to tap innovation-relevant information and ideas.	• Idea competitions ask consumers to submit new ideas to a given task within a given time frame. • Ideas are assessed along predefined criteria by a group of experts; the best ideas are usually awarded with a prize. • The aim is to increase the pool of possible solutions and identify creative participants.
Stage of innovation process	• Mostly early stages	• Mostly early stages
Benefits	• Enables the integration of a broad group of people • Supports identification of "user innovations" • Solution space is open	• Enables the integration of a broad group of people • Supports identification of "user innovations" • Solution space is open • Competitive character stimulates creativity • Can be conducted online or offline
Shortcomings	• Limited direct interaction with consumers • Only conducted online	• Limited direct interaction with consumers if applied online
Sources	Kozinets 2002; Bartl et al. 2004; Füller et al. 2004; Bartl 2006; Reichwald and Piller 2006, 184.	Ernst 2004; Reichwald and Piller 2006, 172; Walcher 2007, 38ff.; Silvertant 2011, 58ff.

Source: created by author.

Pobisch et al. (2007) arranged the methods mentioned above according to their level of consumer-company interaction (high/low), and the level of consumer integration into the innovation process (one stage/various stages).[28] Figure 6 visualizes the difference between conventional and new market research methods.

Figure 6: Level of interaction and integration

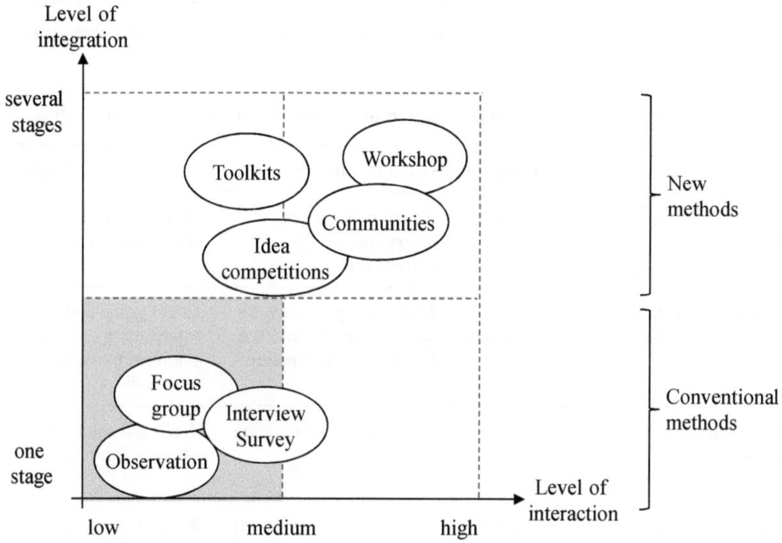

Source: based on Pobisch et al. 2007, 11.

The challenge lies in finding the right method for the right purpose. Conventional and new methods of market research do not substitute each other. Rather, they can be seen as complementary, as they gather qualitatively different information and grant consumers different roles. Generally, it can be said that a lower degree of interaction and integration is more apt to generate insights about needs and wants, while a higher degree can help evoke suggestions for concrete solutions. It is clear that different degrees of participation are justified in their own ways, as they provide different types

[28] "Interaction" denotes how deeply the two actors (the company and the consumer) interact with each other during the innovation process (e.g., through conjointly developing ideas/solutions) and in how far the method is able to generate lessons on both sides. "Integration" means how far the consumer is included as an active part in the innovation process (e.g. in how many stages of the innovation process).

of information. And it is not always the case that a high level of participation generates the best outcome.

However, Lüthje concludes that when engaging in innovation endeavors, a "proactive approach seems to be more promising than conventional market research with a representative sample of existing customers that often show a conservative attitude towards new technology." Furthermore, "methods enabling a direct manufacturer-customer-interaction can particularly reduce the danger of wrong interpretation of market information" (Lüthje 2004, 684).

Table 4: Types of information obtained from different degrees of interaction and integration

Low	**Degree of interaction and integration**		**High**
Role of consumers	**Object of observation**	**Active provider of information and knowledge**	**Co-creator, source of innovation**
Description	Target group remains passive, is merely observed	Target group is asked for information or consulted for specific information	Target group and organization engage in joint activities and "co-create"
Main type of information obtained	Need-related information	Need-related information	Need- and solution-related information
Method	Participant observation	Interviews, surveys, focus groups	Workshops, toolkits, communities, idea competitions

Source: created by author.

A critical look at open innovation and consumer integration

While many authors point out the benefits of open innovation in general – and customer integration in particular – possible risks and challenges of the approach cannot be ignored.

Indeed, the costs associated with open innovation are not well studied; both sides may incur transaction costs. Integrating open innovation into an organization might affect corporate culture and strategy as well as internal innovation processes. Managers who want to push open innovation internally might invest time and resources to achieve the needed buy-in from their colleagues or boss. Their opponents within the company might fear a loss of ownership or control over the innovation process through, for example, premature dissemination of ideas and findings (Campbell and Cooper 1999,

509). Also, consumers and the company may disagree over the allocation of property rights (Bogers et al. 2010, 870).

In addition, the integration itself can be costly for both sides. To enable consumer integration, companies need to invest in certain infrastructure – for example, tools and human resources (Reichwald and Piller 2006, 154). Also, there might be uncertainties arising from the selection of the right consumers, the time and intensity of involvement, and the ability and willingness of the consumer to provide the right kind of knowledge. Furthermore, the costs of evaluating and finally integrating the knowledge generated with consumers needs to be considered, especially in light of possible internal resistance – for example, the "not-invented-here" syndrome (Katz and Allen 1982).

Consumers, on the other hand, bring their time as well as knowledge and creativity into the interaction, which they could also invest in other endeavors (opportunity costs). They also might face psychological costs such as stress and the fear of underperforming (Reichwald and Piller 2006, 148).

All in all, it must be stressed that open innovation can only be a complementary approach to other R&D activities and does not always fit the circumstances. There are many cases where closed innovation processes have their justification. The benefits and risks need to be evaluated in advance. Consequently, some authors support a "balanced innovation approach" (Enkel et al. 2009, 312; Neyer et al. 2009, 417) that combines the strength of both closed and open innovation.

2.1.2 Relevance of concepts for low-income markets

Low-income markets are often seen as "new markets for [...] old products" (Prahalad and Lieberthal 1998, 69–70). Prahalad and Lieberthal thus conclude that "as a result of this imperialist mind-set, multinationals have achieved only limited success in those markets" (1998, 69–70). They state that instead of marketing inexpensive versions of top-of-the-pyramid products, companies should tailor new products, services, and business models to the needs and capacities of low-income consumers, as well as to the specific context in which they live. Some authors even argue that **innovation is a *conditio sine qua non*** to overcome the market constraints prevalent in low-income contexts (Prahalad 2004; Gradl et al. 2008, 40; Krämer and Belz 2008, 221ff.; UNDP 2008, 17f.). The major **challenges** businesses face include a lack of physical infrastructure, which leads to high transaction costs when, for example, sourcing raw material or delivering products and services, and little access to credits and insurance, which may hinder consumers as well as producers from participating in a market system as their irregular incomes may not suffice to finance larger purchases. A lack of knowledge and education among consumers may also pose a challenge when marketing and selling products that are not self-explanatory, such as medicines or irrigation systems (UNDP 2008, 5–6).

Product and service innovations can especially help address a lack of knowledge and education. For example, the Bolivian microfinance organization PRODEM FFP serves its illiterate consumers with voice-driven smart ATMs in local languages with color-coded touch screens and fingerprint recognition (Hernández and Mugica 2003). Product innovations can also overcome a lack of infrastructure: Mobile phone–based payment services, such as M-Pesa in Kenya, provide consumers with virtual bank accounts, which address a lack of access to financial services by partly replacing a banking infrastructure.[29] Pharmaceutical companies have developed fixed-dose combinations to reduce the pill burden for low-income consumers when treating malaria or HIV/AIDS, as with every pill, the patient needs to have clean water and food available (Haupt and Krämer 2012, 19).

Process innovations often address issues surrounding *affordability* and *availability*. To sell yoghurts fortified with nutrients in Bangladesh, Danone sought ways to enable local production (Webb et al. 2009, 2). One major constraint in the production process was frequent energy shortages. Thus, the company added a biodigester to the plant, which enables environmentally friendly low-tech and low-cost production. The biodigester powers the factory's lighting and heating systems by transforming waste into electricity (Matlak 2008). Amul Dairy, a large Indian milk producer, found ways to innovate the collection of milk by organizing farmers as well as creating an efficient handling system that maintains the cold chain. The automated and computerized collection system speeds up the weighing, quality testing, and payment processing (UNDP 2010, 17).

A **business model innovation** combines different types of innovations to create and capture value. The company Grameen Shakti combines a product innovation – namely solar home systems – with an innovative distribution and financing model which

---

[29] For further information, see company website: http://www.safaricom.co.ke/ – accessed May 1, 2013.

addresses a lack of infrastructure and financial resources in low-income markets. To pay back the credit, consumers pay the same amount they would have paid for kerosene, candles, or other energy sources. The solar home systems are assembled and distributed by trained villagers who benefit from this income opportunity.[30]

The examples above are not mere "stripped-down versions" of pre-existing innovations from high-income market segments that are made available to low-income consumers (Tiwari and Herstatt 2012a, 4). Rather, they are diverse products, services, and business models specifically tailored to the needs of the poor. These innovations are often regarded as "**disruptive**," as they have fewer features and are therefore less expensive, while maintaining adequate quality which makes them attractive for underserved consumers (Christensen et al. 2001; Hart and Christensen 2002).[31] Making such products and services available to low-income consumers often contributes significantly to improving their living standards and productivity (Ahlstrom 2010, 19; see also Hart 2010). For example, Nokia life tools, a mobile application, provides agricultural information to farmers – such as crop prices and weather forecasts – and thus saves them time and resources (Nokia 2008).

Some innovations developed for low-income markets also have the potential to "trickle up" and **disrupt** markets in the developed world. For example, the mobile phone Nokia 1100 was particularly created for developing countries, with features such as a built-in flashlight and dust resistance (Whitney 2010, 173). According to Whitney, the phone has "steadfastly maintained its ranking as the best-selling consumer electronics product of all time, with more than 200 million units sold." The reason for this success is that the embedded flashlight also appeals to many people in the developed world (Whitney 2010, 174). Similarly, General Electric created an ultrasound device for the Chinese market that is inexpensive and uses raw materials sparingly, thus meeting demand in high-income markets as well, where solutions are badly needed that reduce healthcare costs without reducing the quality of care (*Economist* 2010).

Innovations are of vital importance in low-income markets, because they overcome market constraints and thus help companies to enter and eventually succeed in the market place. Innovations can also support the sustainability of a company's venture,

---

30 For further information, see company website: http://www.gshakti.org/ – accessed May 1, 2013.

31 Other authors refer to "Ghandian innovations" (Prahalad and Mashelkar 2010), "grassroots innovations" (Gupta 2010) or "frugal innovations" (Tiwari and Herstatt 2012a/2012b/2012c).

as they often "**leapfrog**" conventional practices, meaning that they help move directly to more efficient ways of consumption and production by immediately making use of, for example, renewable energy or biodegradable packaging.

Relevance of open innovation for low-income markets

Despite the many examples of successful innovation in low-income markets, many other ventures have not found success. Webb et al. (2009) cite the case of PuR, a water purifier developed by P&G. About 1.1 billion people use water from unimproved sources (WHO 2000). Although from an outside perspective there are clear benefits from consuming higher quality water, the project failed. Webb et al. (2009, 17) explain that the company did not address the lack of knowledge amongst the target group. As water-borne bacteria are not visible, the target customers did not see the need to pay for the filter. Thus, the obvious need was not met by demand, and in the end the company abandoned the commercial version of the product, mainly due to the high costs of educating consumers (Weidner et al. 2010, 568).

What distinguishes successful ventures from failures? Some authors argue that success depends on the **companies' ability to acquire information as well as an understanding of the low-income market** – that is, of people's needs and how to address them (Paton and Halme 2007; Simanis et al. 2008; Mohr et al. 2010; Chikweche and Fletcher 2012). In low-income markets, knowledge about potential consumers and the market environment is not readily available (London and Hart 2004, 13; see also Grosh and Glewwe 1995). Companies typically refer to national statistics – particularly household data – to get an overview of a potential market and its size.[32] However, most poor people live in urban slums or rural areas which are hardly covered by national statistics as it is difficult to capture data about people without a legal residence. Anderson and Billou (2007, 33) argue that the poor might even be reluctant to participate in, for example, a census questionnaire, as this might cause problems with local authorities. Also, data on income and household spending is often inaccurate, because the poor mostly operate in the informal economy or – in some countries – their income is in the form of remittances (de Soto 2000). In addition, businesses lack a support infrastructure of service providers that are

---

32 The WRI and the IFC thus funded a research project that sheds light on the size of the market of the poor (Hammond et al. 2007). Although this aggregated data gives a good overview of various sectors, it is currently one of the few sources of information.

specialized on gathering data (UNDP 2013, 33). Weiser et al. (2006, 19ff.) conclude that

> *underserved markets are not described accurately by many of the market information and analysis systems that are commonly used by businesses. [...] Businesses [thus] end up gathering wrong information, or gathering it in ways that provide a skewed image of potential sales and profits in underserved communities.*

Besides quantitative data, also **qualitative data** on the needs and preferences of low-income consumers and their behavior is hardly available. Companies particularly lack tacit information about habits, norms, values, traditions, beliefs, aspirations, and needs of consumers (Ricart et al. 2004; Webb et al. 2009, 7). According to Schmidt and Sofka (2005, 4),

> *social, cultural, cognitive, administrative, institutional and organisational differences are especially pronounced when foreign firms search for valuable sources for innovation abroad [...]: The targeted knowledge is largely tacit in nature and hence difficult to assess. It is challenging to identify and collect promising sources of knowledge, put them into an adequate context and act accordingly, if linguistic, cultural and social barriers cause misinterpretations, mistakes and delays.*

London (2008, 3) argues that not only foreign companies but also local companies face this information gap when trying to enter low-income markets: "Being native to a country does not necessarily make one native to the BoP; host-country nationals should not automatically assume they are familiar with the BoP." Since acquiring information is time and cost intensive, high information asymmetries between consumers and producers result in high transaction costs when innovating for the market of the poor.

One way to gain access to the information and knowledge necessary for innovation is through **engaging in partnerships with external actors from low-income markets** – be they individuals, groups of individuals, or organizations (Hart and Sharma 2004; Sánchez et al. 2007; Gradl et al. 2008; UNDP 2008). Indeed, Sánchez et al. (2007, 28) find in their qualitative, case-based study that "firms that have created a more innovative business model are those that developed embedded ties with local community members, NGOs and local governments in the business model design process, favoring a bottom-up development process."[33] They call this approach "becoming socially embedded."

In addition to Sánchez et al. (2007) and researchers in the area of innovation management (see section 2.1.1), various authors who research low-income or BoP markets agree that "the knowledge needed to generate unique and disruptive ideas often lies outside the organization" (Hart and Sharma 2004, 8). Although few of the respective articles on the BoP refer to the concept of "**open innovation**," most of them describe the same idea. They explain that the closed innovation approach of protecting "resources and knowledge from unintended leakage outside the firm boundaries" and relying on a limited number of established partners is doomed to failure, as the experience of corporate executives is also only centered on dealing with the urban elite (London and Hart 2004, 3–5). Rather, it is found that "the critical knowledge for success lies beyond the firm's [established] boundaries" (Hart and London 2005). Through opening up their boundaries for **new external partners**, companies not only gain access to but also co-create the information and knowledge they lack (Hart and Sharma 2004; London and Hart 2004; Chesbrough 2006; Brugmann and Prahalad 2007; Rivera-Santos and Ruffin 2010).

In contrast to the open innovation literature, these authors describe the key external partners for businesses in low-income markets as "**non-traditional partners**" and often as "**non-market actors**" (London and Hart 2004; Chesbrough 2006; Rivera-Santos and Ruffin 2010; Gradl et al. 2010). The partners common to businesses in developed markets – such as established suppliers, universities, research institutions, or other businesses – often do not operate or even exist in low-income markets (UNDP 2013, 22, 33). Likewise, the informal sector plays a more substantial role in these environments (de Soto 2000; London and Hart 2004, 3). Non-traditional partners can help companies gain market access and understand how to operate in this new context, as they are more likely to be embedded in the informal environment, are linked to local powers and can support companies to overcome formal institutional voids (see also de Soto 2000; Webb et al. 2009, 14; Rivera-Santos and Ruffin 2010, 3, 9). In one of the

---

33 In the above-cited case of PuR, for example, P&G engaged in partnerships with a number of NGOs, such as Population Services International (PSI) and Cooperative for Assistance and Relief Everywhere (CARE), and restructured its business model. The partners support P&G to promote PuR and also train local health workers to aid in the distribution of the sachets. While the commercial version of the product was abandoned, PuR is now sold to development organizations at cost, with funding from donors and individuals.

very first articles on the topic – "Serving the World's Poor, Profitably," – Prahalad and Hammond (2002, 54) argue that

> *partnerships maximize the existing infrastructure – both physical and social. MNCs seeking partners should look beyond businesses to NGOs and community groups. They are key sources of knowledge about customers' behavior, and they often experiment the most with new services and new delivery models.*

Hart and Sharma (2004, 10–11) particularly stress the inclusion of so-called "**fringe-stakeholders**," arguing that this "unseen periphery of the firm's stakeholder network" can enable "a panoramic view of a firm's changing external environment" and enhance the capacity of the company to think creatively. In their analysis of partnership networks in low-income markets, Rivera-Santos and Ruffin (2010) also find that cross-sector partnerships are relevant for innovation. They find that these partnerships are "laboratories of product and business model innovation," allowing companies to "develop appropriate products" (Rivera-Santos and Ruffin 2010, 136).

In the articles cited above, a whole variety of "non-traditional" or "fringe" partners are mentioned. They include other businesses, local entrepreneurs, cooperatives, non-profit organizations, communities, village-level governments, or individual consumers (Chesbrough et al. 2006; Brugmann and Prahalad 2007; Seelos and Mair 2007; Webb et al. 2009). While these different types of partners deserve equal attention, this study focuses on low-income consumers as a source of information and innovation.

Relevance of customer integration for low-income markets

Innovation research discusses different roles consumers can play in innovation (see section 2.1.1):

(a) Companies can gather information *about* the consumer, capturing explicit needs and preferences ("manufacturer-active paradigm"). Thus, consumers – or potentially other external partners – are regarded as a **source of information and knowledge**.

(b) When given a more active role, consumers are further regarded as a **source of innovation**. Innovation can happen in different ways: Consumers might take the initiative to innovate, transforming their needs into a solution ("user innovation"), which can be identified and further developed by companies (so-called "reactive consumer integration" – see Reichwald and Piller 2006, 131). Alternatively, the development process can also be initiated by the company, who aims to engage consumers in a reciprocal learning and co-creation process (so-called "active consumer integration" – see Reichwald and Piller 2006, 131).

These potential consumer roles can both be found in the current BoP literature:

(a) Source of information and knowledge: A variety of authors suggest that companies should not assume that they know the needs of the poor. Rather, they should learn "from the bottom up" by hearing and incorporating the voices of low-income consumers (Hart 2005; London 2007; Simanis et al. 2008; Simanis and Hart 2008; Sridharan and Viswanathan 2008, 461; Waibel 2012). This direct cooperation with individual consumers – or groups of consumers – is regarded as an effective way to access information (Prahalad and Hammond 2002, 56; Hart and London 2005; London 2008; SadreGhazi 2008, 63): It is assumed that personally interacting with the target group provides access to tacit information on needs and preferences. The "unfiltered" and implicit information obtained in this way is put in context and can contribute to a better understanding of local norms, beliefs, habits, and traditions – and ultimately to designing solutions that consider and respect them (Hart and Sharma 2004).

A variety of examples can be found which show that closely observing users and tapping their need-related information can result in new products and services. For example, Nokia observed low-income consumers sharing phones. However, phone sharing did not allow them to leave numbers or personal messages on the phone, which was a need expressed by the consumer. The company thus developed software that allows one to save several address books on one phone that can be accessed by entering a PIN (Chipchase 2006).

(b) Source of innovation: Low-income consumers are not only a source of information, but also a source of innovation. In order to survive, they creatively deal with their living situation. In fact, creative activities can result from necessity (Walcher 2007, 46ff.). Fukushima (2009) finds that low-income consumers often modify products with material they encounter, or create new products out of recycled materials – so called "vernacular solutions." Consequently, a variety of authors – such as Gupta (2010), Viswanathan and Sridharan (2012, 53, 60), and Fukushima (2009) – argue that low-income contexts are a pool for user innovations. These solutions are a good starting point for creating new products, as they provide solution-related information.

Figure 7: Consumers as a source of information and innovation

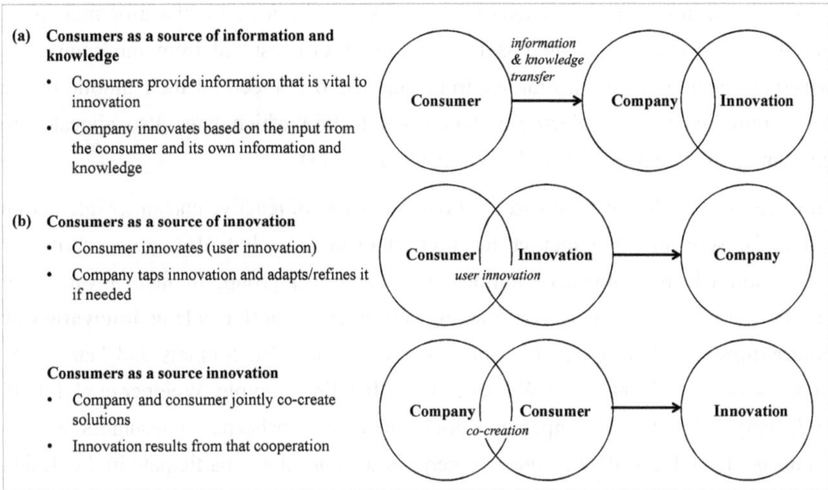

Source: created by author based on Reichwald et al. 2007, 65; Walcher 2007, 28ff.; and Silvertant 2010, 25.

Indeed, many companies have already successfully built on user innovations when adapting products or business models to the low-income context. For example, a water-efficient irrigation system brought to market by IDE India was based on an invention by a farmer.[34] The appliance manufacturer Haier also benefitted from identifying a user adaptation: The company observed that Potato growers in the Sichuan region used washing machines to rinse off the mud from the vegetables. A.T. Kearney (2007, 54) reports that "instead of blaming customers for misuse, Haier developed a machine with wider pipes that could wash potatoes and other vegetables in addition to clothes without being clogged. […] The result was a strong increase in use of Haier's products among low-income consumers – and market leadership in China." Body Shop executives observed African women using slices of pineapple to cleanse their skin. Subsequent research showed that active ingredients in pineapple clear dead skin cells better than chemical formulations (Prahalad and Hart 2002, 13). As Whitney (2010, 176) concludes, "Using user insights to create a more abstract view of the problem frequently leads to innovations […]."

[34] Source: Interview with Niraj Subrat (BoP Conference at the TU Delft, November 2009).

Finally, learning from low-income markets even offers opportunities to incubate **disruptive innovations** (Christensen et al. 2001): The idea for the aforementioned mobile phone with a built-in flashlight (Nokia 1100) resulted from the company's observing people in low-income environments use the screen on their mobile phone for lighting when their electricity failed – a feature which later also appealed to consumers in the developed world (Whitney 2010, 173).

However, current literature stresses not only the value of reactive consumer integration – that is, screening the market for user innovations – but also active consumer integration which co-creates solutions with the target group. In fact, a variety of articles put a strong emphasis on granting consumers an **active role as innovators or co-creators** (London 2008, 3ff.; Simanis et al. 2008, 77ff; Simanis and Hart 2008; Simanis and Hart 2009, 15ff.; Waibel 2012, 63ff.). For example, Weidner et al. (2010, 567) emphasize that "companies should involve subsistence consumers as co-producers […]. Innovative solutions emerge when consumers participate in the design of products […]." Simanis et al. (2008, 64) call for an "embedded innovation strategy" which is based on "close, personal engagement of the community in the design and evolution of a business." They argue that "such a co-venturing approach would marry the capabilities and knowledge of corporations with those of the communities and embed the business within the existing socio-cultural institutions." Similarly, Viswanathan et al. (2011, 567) conclude the following:

> *Another important aspect of product development in subsistence marketplaces is in engaging subsistence communities at every stage in the design and development process, and not treating them solely as end consumers […]. It is essential to treat customers and communities as partners […].*

While there seems to be almost unanimous agreement amongst a variety of researchers that consumers are a valuable source of information and innovation, BoP literature provides surprisingly little information on two aspects: First, it remains unexplored whether specific groups of consumers are more suitable partners for innovation than others. Second, little information is provided on specific methods for tapping consumer knowledge.

Relevance of methods of consumer integration for low-income markets

Current BoP research relates best practice examples and anecdotal evidence but generally fails to provide guidance regarding concrete methods for including the target group into innovation. However, there seems to be agreement on two key insights: First, it is argued that conventional approaches to innovation and new product development face limitations when conducted in low-income contexts. Second, authors agree that new methods are required that are more adapted to the specific constraints in low-income markets. Pitta et al. (2008, 397) summarize that "a change of focus to the BoP will require new techniques and freedom from accepted knowledge."

(a) Limitations of conventional market research methods

In an exploratory study of business ventures that target the low-income market, London and Hart (2004, 9) find that "relying on existing product development knowledge restricted the design process." Weidner et al. (2010, 562) stress that

> *researchers are typically trained in methodologies that have been finely honed with Western consumers, such as focus groups, surveys, and experiments. [...] [T]hese techniques have limited effectiveness in subsistence marketplaces [...]. [L]acking personal connections with poverty and low literacy, managers and researchers need to bridge the resource and literacy gap in conducting effective market research.*

Challenges of applying conventional market research methods mentioned in the current body of literature can be clustered as follows:

First, the methods are often difficult to conduct in **infrastructure-weak environments**. Low-income consumers mostly reside in rural areas or shantytowns and are thus hard or even dangerous to reach. The support infrastructure for conventional market research is also often lacking (Gradl et al. 2008; UNDP 2008, 31; UNDP 2010, 26).

Second, results gathered may be **misleading** (Weiser et al. 2006) or hard to grasp. Quantitative data lack accuracy because the poor are undercounted by official censuses and income data are often not reported, as transactions are carried out informally (Weiser et al. 2006; Weiser 2007). Also gathering qualitative data might represent challenges, as language barriers can make it difficult to build rapport with an interviewee. Moreover, low-income consumers are firmly embedded in their regional culture, which is marked by values, habits, and specific behavior or consumption patterns. Thus, they might not recognize that this contextual information can be valuable to others and are rather unlikely to express it in, for example, surveys or focus groups (Krämer and Belz 2008, 217ff.). At the same time, market researchers unfamiliar with this context may find it difficult to interpret certain tacit information by just observing or surveying consumers (and not interacting with them).

Third, due to a **lack of education**, many consumers in low-income markets are not aware of certain needs (e.g., hand-washing or taking vitamins) or are not used to thinking creatively about a product feature they might desire. It is thus difficult to verbally communicate this information (Gradl et al. 2008, 35; Krämer and Belz 2008, 217ff.). Often, they might not even understand a certain question due to their lack of experience in abstract thinking (Krämer and Belz 2008, 217ff.).

In addition, low-income consumers might face difficulties in transferring information to others when personal contact and **trust** are lacking (Polanyi 1958; Senker 1993). Barki and Parente (2010, 18), who have conducted research in low-income settings in Brazil, note that "low-income consumers highly value face-to-face contact. […] Trust between people is much stronger than trust towards institutions, or in contracts."[35] However, trust needs to be established. Whitney (2010, 182) relates that "many of our subjects had never met anyone from outside of their local culture, so they tended to be shy or suspicious when interacting with our interviewers."

Another shortcoming of conventional research approaches is that they primarily gather **information about current, explicit needs**, which might not be sufficient to address a completely new target market in a sustainable way (Slater and Narver 1998, 1002ff.; Krämer and Belz 2008, 217ff.).

(b) The need for adapted or new methods

Some more practitioner-oriented publications have started to consider these challenges and adapt existing market research methods accordingly. For example, the Confederation of Danish Industry (DI) developed a whole toolbox that provides hands-on guidance on market research methods that work in low-income contexts (DI 2011). Essentially, they explain how participant observation, interviews, or focus groups need to be designed to address the challenges mentioned above – the lack of infrastructure,

[35] Note that this insight was collected in the context of consumer purchasing behavior. However, it might also apply to market research.

trust, or education.[36] Doing so, they draw on existing experiences as well as knowledge from the area of design thinking and development work.

Academic literature, in turn, repeatedly refers to "**immersion**" as an alternative approach for gaining insights on low-income consumers. Company representatives (e.g., market researchers or product developers) immerse themselves in low-income communities – into what Hart and Sharma describe as a "radically different physical and mental context" (2004, 14). While still applying conventional market research methods such as participant observation and interviews, immersion can be specifically tailored to the needs of innovating companies. A major difference to conventional methods is that stays may last up to several days or weeks, increasing trust as well as the frequency and level of interaction with the target group (Viswanathan et al. 2011; Viswanathan and Sridharan 2012). Thus, it is expected that immersion contributes to developing a deeper understanding of consumer needs, as tacit knowledge is transferred through direct interaction. Ultimately, this interaction shall "spark the imagination", and contribute to exploring "the feasibility of new approaches for meeting consumer need in a radically different, innovative and sustainable manner" (Hart and Sharma 2004, 14-15). To illustrate, Hart and Sharma (2004, 10) cite the following example of Hindustan Lever Limited, the Indian subsidiary of Unilever:

> *[The company] requires its managers to spend six weeks in rural areas to generate knowledge about the hygiene needs and practices of the rural poor. This knowledge resulted in new product ideas (combined soap and shampoo bar) and promotional programs (such as street theatre) for rural markets.*

Weiser (2007, 34) cites another example of CEMEX, a large cement manufacturer:

> *Instead of using its standard approaches to gathering and analyzing data for product development, the company sent managers to live in the communities for a year to observe how individuals planned and financed their 'do-it-yourself' projects. This firsthand knowledge led to the development of an entirely new approach to selling cement to low-income households.*

---

[36] For example, the target group often lacks education or practice in abstract thinking. Thus, stating "to what extent" they would use a certain product or prefer it over others may not be a productive question. The toolbox provides concrete information for these situations, suggesting the use of visual material and games. For example, it suggests using a tool called "ranking values" in focus group situations – an activity that asks participants to rank a number of alternative products or services. Drawing an "activity map" with consumers – for example, concerning when they use different energy sources – may yield insights into use patterns.

However, Hart and Sharma (2004, 14) advise that "to be able to absorb knowledge [...], managers need to empathize with differences in perspectives." They thus recommend that "product development managers should begin intense interactions with fringe stakeholders only after suitable cultural and ecosystem sensitivity trainings." Prahalad and Hammond (2002, 54) also stress that "the traditional workforce is so rigidly conditioned to operate in higher-margin markets that, without formal training, it is unlikely to see the vast potential of the BoP market." In addition, it is recommended that corporate representatives stay longer periods of time in the environment to gain trust and be able to have more frequent interactions with the community. Immersion may thus be a suitable method to tap information on implicit needs. The repeated and more direct exchange – called "reactive consumer integration" – may further enable them to identify local solutions or even detect user innovations.

However, while both immersion and the adapted versions of conventional market research methods mentioned above grant the target group an active role in generating valuable market *information*, they do not foresee an active role in developing appropriate *solutions* ("active consumer integration"). The "BoP Protocol" is the only method that could be identified in the current body of BoP literature that specifically aims for co-creation.

The BoP Protocol, developed by Professor Stuart Hart and Eric Simanis of the Johnson School at Cornell University, is an approach that builds on the long-standing experience of ethnographic research and development practice when innovating for low-income markets (Simanis et al. 2008; Simanis and Hart 2008). These disciplines call for a shift in mindset, from viewing beneficiaries of development projects as mere recipients – which causes dependency and alienation – to seeing them as development "experts" who know what they need and what works in their living context (Waibel 2012, 73ff.). The approach thus aims to avoid a paternalistic attitude and values the cultures and traditions of the poor (Simanis et al. 2008, 62). In its essence, it builds on similar insights as the open innovation approach by giving consumers a voice and an active role which empower them and lead to solutions that are more acceptable and of value to the target group, and thus sustainable in the long run.

Turning these insights into a concrete, step-by-step approach, the BoP Protocol suggests that company representatives immerse themselves into the low-income context to engage in a "deep dialogue" with their target group and a process of mutual learning and co-creation (Simanis et al. 2008). The envisioned outcome is a fully co-created business model that marries "the capabilities and knowledge of corporations with those of the communities and embed[s] the business within the existing socio-cultural institutions" (Simanis et al. 2008, 62).

However, a major downside of the BoP Protocol is that the process of co-creation – according to the authors – should last a full year and requires considerable financial and personal commitment. Thus, like extended immersion, the BoP Protocol may not be compatible with business practice, which requires faster, more result-oriented approaches. In fact, Simanis and Milstein acknowledge in one of their latest papers that the approach of the BoP Protocol needs to be more aligned with "business fundamentals" (Simanis and Milstein 2012, 84–85).

Table 5: Objectives and methods to integrate consumers

Role of consumer	**Source of information and knowledge**	**Source of innovation**	
Objective / Method	Tap information and knowledge	Tap user innovations	Co-create
Observation	●	◐	○
Interviews, Surveys	●	◐	○
Immersion	●	●	○
BoP Protocol	●	●	●

Key
○ Method does not meet objective
◐ Method partly meets objective
● Method fully meets objective

Source: created by author.

Moreover, the approaches of immersion and the BoP Protocol face similar constraints as other market research tools. First, they address a random sample of consumers and provide no guidance on how to find and interact with those who have the most valuable insights for a particular innovative endeavor. Second, they are generally more geared towards assessing consumers' current and explicit needs and preferences rather than focusing on future needs. It thus comes as no surprise that, after the first pilot projects that followed the "BoP Protocol", Simanis and Milstein (2012, 85) reached the following conclusion:

> *Together with a team of women from low-income villages and slum communities, we began co-creating business concepts. Unfortunately, the community's ideas were plain and simplistic […]. In the name of co-creation, two months were spent trying to move the community team toward more compelling concepts while ensuring they retained a sense of ownership.*

In contrast, methods discussed in mainstream innovation research, as outlined in section 2.1.1, focus on tapping future needs by identifying the types of consumers who may have the most valuable insights for a particular innovation project. This discussion is almost entirely lacking in current BoP literature.

A critical look at low-income consumer involvement in innovation

Criticism of the BoP proposition as such was first expressed by Prof. Dr. Aneel Karnani in his papers "Misfortune at the BoP", "The mirage of marketing to the BoP" and "Romanticizing the poor" (Karnani 2007a/2007b/2009; see also Jaiswal 2007 and Landrum 2007). He criticizes the estimates of the BoP market size put forth by, for example, Prahalad as too optimistic. His main argument is, however, that the BoP should not be targeted as consumers but rather as producers, emphasizing the approach of buying from them to raise their income. He stresses making markets more efficient, so that the poor can capture more value, and investing in their education and skills to increase productivity (Karnani 2007a, 109). While these points were certainly already captured in the BoP proposition – particularly in articles and papers that refer to opportunities at the BoP as "inclusive business" (see, e.g., UNDP 2008) – his criticism balances and complements the debate.

As discussed above, low-income consumers are already engaged in activities that result in user innovation. While academics and practitioners stress the value of engaging them in co-creation efforts, few critical viewpoints have been expressed thus far. Articles that put forth the idea of integrating low-income consumers into innovation mostly neglect questions around ownership and intellectual property. Open questions are, for example, whether and how low-income consumers are informed from the beginning of the commercial objectives of the projects as well as of the rights they have to their ideas. Furthermore, researchers and practitioners rarely clarify how consumers might benefit from potential commercial success – either through compensation or royalties.

To balance the discussion above, it should be noted that integrating low-income consumers into innovation processes does not guarantee success and is certainly not a "cure-all" approach (Simanis and Milstein 2012, 84). Rather, it can only be seen as one component of new product or business model development.

2.1.3 Intermediate conclusion and research gaps

Looking at both innovation research and BoP literature, certain similarities stick out. Both research streams agree that innovation is vital to succeed in the marketplace. External partners – particularly consumers – are regarded as a source of information and innovation. Giving them an active role by integrating them into the innovation processes is considered a successful approach to address the prevalent lack of market information and understanding. However, two research gaps remain:

(a) Lack of suitable methods for consumer integration

In both streams of literature, evidence can be found that conventional research methods – such as surveys – can only yield limited insights for innovation. To fill this gap, innovation research suggests applying methods like innovation workshops or idea competitions that focus on gaining specific, innovation-relevant insights. These methods have received considerable attention by researchers. The empirical studies of, for example, Pobisch (2010) and Ramakrishnan (2012) investigate innovation workshops, while those of Walcher (2007) and Silvertant (2011) examine idea competitions. Nonetheless, they would benefit from further empirical exploration (see, e.g., Reichwald and Piller 2006, 173; Soll 2006, 3; Haller et al. 2009, 2; Silvertant 2011, 69ff.). Furthermore, to the author's best knowledge, these methods have only been documented and empirically studied in developed markets.

In turn, BoP literature highly emphasizes "co-creation" and "bottom-up innovation" (see, for example, SadreGhazi 2008; Simanis et al. 2008; Simanis and Hart 2008). However, articles on the topic are mostly conceptual in nature – or very practitioner-oriented. Hardly any empirical studies exist that examine open innovation approaches in low-income contexts. Exceptions are approaches like "immersion" or the "BoP Protocol" (Hart and Sharma 2004; Simanis et al. 2008; Viswanathan et al. 2011; Viswanathan and Sridharan 2012; Waibel 2012, 63ff.). However, apart from these studies, there is little empirical evidence and analysis about which methods work in low-income environments and the concrete outcomes of their application.

Whitney (2010, 187) thus suggests that established methods tested in developed markets could – with adaptations – also be applied to low-income markets. His reasoning is that "the daily life of the BoP is as complex and as difficult to understand as the daily life in developed economies." To close this gap, the extent to which existing methods in innovation research can be applied or how they need to be adapted needs to be further explored.

(b) Lack of insights on suitable types of consumers

Whitney (2010, 187) argues that in both high- and low-income markets, designers and product developers have to "go beyond what users say they want." Researchers warn that companies should not uncritically cater to the demands of current consumers, as usage patterns and familiarity with existing products or solutions may hinder them from thinking "outside the box" – a phenomenon often referred to as "functional fixedness" (Duncker 1945; Adamson 1952; von Hippel 1988; Lüthje 2000, 22). However, innovation research suggests that there is a specific type of consumer able to develop innovative solutions for future markets. In fact, a whole research stream has evolved around how to identify these types of consumers (see, e.g., von Hippel 1986/1988; Kristensson et al. 2002/2004; Lüthje 2000/2004; von Hippel 2005; Soll 2006; Walcher 2007; Silvertant 2011; Ramakrishnan 2012).

This discussion is almost entirely lacking in current BoP literature. While the importance of innovating or co-creating with low-income consumers is stressed, little insight is given on how to identify consumers who may have the most valuable input. The methods discussed in BoP literature rather address a random sample of people and do not focus on individuals (or organizations) with particular characteristics or capabilities.

The following two sections will thus take a closer look at the two gaps identified above. Section 2.2 will summarize insights from innovation research on how to identify "lead users" who can indeed be considered a "source of innovation." What is more, it will discuss the relevance of these findings for low-income markets. Section 2.3 provides an introduction to idea competitions – a method that has shown promising results when actively engaging consumers in creating solutions. It is also discussed as a method to identify creative and innovative consumers. Finally, the section discusses the extent to which the method could be of relevance for low-income markets.

2.2 Consumers as a source of innovation

While literature on open innovation stresses the potential of consumers as a source of innovation, it is debatable whether all consumers have valuable input in this area. Von Hippel writes in this regard that "users steeped in the present are […] unlikely to generate novel product concepts which conflict with the familiar" (von Hippel 1986, 791). These type of users, who are often chosen in market research, "are poorly situated with regard to the difficult problem-solving tasks associated with assessing unfamiliar product and process needs" (von Hippel 1986, 792). He thus devotes most of his research to identifying those users with the most valuable input (see, e.g., von Hippel 1976/1978/1982/1986/ 1988/2005).

The question is, how can this user be identified? This following section (2.2.1) summarizes the characteristics of lead users and how they are operationalized. The characteristics identified here serve as a basis for the empirical part of this study. Moreover, building on the insight that "lead userness" is not a dichotomy, but rather a continuum (Magnusson 2009), the section provides an overview of further types of lead users and non-lead users (Silvertant 2011, 256ff.; Ramakrishnan 2012, 169 ff.; Schrader and Belz 2012, 344ff.).

Consumers that innovate, however, are not a phenomenon that is limited to certain markets or contexts. In fact, there is evidence that consumers in low-income markets are particularly creative when it comes to developing solutions for their pressing needs. Chapter 2.2.2 provides a brief overview of the so far rather preliminary research in that area. Last, chapter 2.2.3 clearly lays out the research gaps which deserve further investigation.

2.2.1 Characteristics of lead users

Various studies have already embarked upon identifying and testing characteristics of lead users in industrial as well as consumer goods contexts (see, e.g., Lüthje 2000/2004; Soll 2006; Walcher 2007). Nonetheless, besides some definitional characteristics, there is still only a limited understanding of who consumers with high "lead userness" are (Schreier and Prügl 2008, 332). Clarifying these users' distinguishing characteristics will enable companies to identify them reliably and efficiently – and ultimately to leverage their potential.

Future needs and high expected benefits – lead users according to von Hippel

The term lead user was coined by von Hippel (1986, 796). He points out two characteristics that he found to be inherent in these innovative consumers:

(1) **Future needs**: Lead users face general needs in a marketplace, but months or years before the bulk of that marketplace encounters them.

(2) **High expected benefit**: Lead users are positioned to benefit significantly from a solution to those needs.

The first criterion can be understood in analogy to theories of diffusion of innovations (Rogers and Shoemaker 1971; Rogers 1995), which show that diffusion curves for new products and services are bell-shaped (normal/Gaussian distribution). Consequently, a small group of consumers **face needs earlier** than others and adopt new products before the bulk of the market. According to von Hippel, lead users are even ahead of the innovator and the early adopter, as they face needs before respective products even exist (see figure 8). This is due to the fact that lead users operate in use contexts (in the present) that will be relevant for the majority of consumers only in the future. They experience "tomorrow's needs today" (Herstatt and von Hippel 1992, 213). As Lüthje and Herstatt (2004, 557) describe it, unlike ordinary customers "users at the leading-edge do not have to imagine themselves in a yet non-existing situation. The 'new' is already familiar to them." Lead users are thus characterized as being "**ahead of the market**" (von Hippel 1986; Lüthje and Herstatt 2004, 557). Some studies also characterize them as **trend leaders** or trendsetters[37] (Herstatt and von Hippel 1992, 213–214; Sawhney and Prandelli 2000, 262; Walcher 2007, 194ff.). Hirschmann (1980, 285-288) states that "the desire to seek out the new and different (i.e., inherent novelty seeking) is conceptually indistinguishable from the willingness to adopt new products (i.e., innate innovativeness)." Thus, being "ahead of the market" or being a "trend leader" is often measured by the "time of adoption" (TOA) – the time between market introduction and the purchase of a new product (Lüthje 2000, 64–65; Soll 2006, 105; Walcher 2007, 194ff.).[38]

---

[37] Midgley and Dowling (1978, 236) use the term trendsetter in the sense of an early adopter or innovator.

[38] The reasoning behind this approach is that "innovating users and the market initiators might be the same people (…), [as] both use initiation as well as the development of genuine new products involve creative tasks and require that the user conceives solutions that are in conflict with the familiar" (Lüthje 2004, 685).

Figure 8: Time of adoption

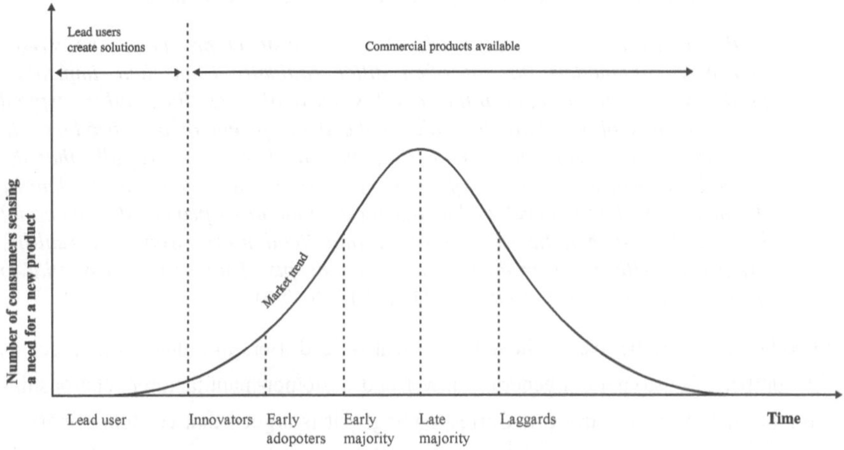

Source: adapted from Walcher 2007, 194ff.; see also: Rogers 1995, 72 and Hippel et al. 1999, 12.

The new needs that lead users sense do not correspond to an existing market offer; they are thus said to be highly **dissatisfied** (Lüthje 2004, 686). Dissatisfaction while using existing products and services can be a trigger to become aware of new needs and to see which products can be improved. This explains the second criterion von Hippel mentions: The greater the **benefit** a consumer expects from a new solution, the greater his willingness to devote resources to obtain it (von Hippel 1986, 797; see also Morrison et al. 2004, 351).[39]

Lead users in industrial and consumer markets

Although von Hippel mentions examples of lead users from both industrial and consumer goods markets in his earlier articles (see, e.g., von Hippel 1986, 799, 802), his later research rather focuses on **industrial markets** (see, e.g., Herstatt and von Hippel 1992; von Hippel et al. 1999; von Hippel 2005), with a focus on high

---

Another reason for early adoption can also be seen in a high risk affinity; innovators and early adopters are alleged to feel a lower risk when purchasing new developments (Robertson et al. 1984, 12; Walcher 2007, 194ff.).

39 "The bell-shaped diffusion curves for new products and services reveal that not all individuals within a user population expect a high benefit from innovations at the same time" (Lüthje 2004, 685).

technology. He argues that innovations in the consumer goods industries are mostly incremental, meaning that even ordinary users could have valuable input:

> *In the relatively slow-moving world of many consumer products, new cereals and new car models do not often differ radically from their immediate predecessors. Therefore, even the "new" is reasonably familiar, and the typical user can thus play a valuable role in the development of new products. In contrast, in high technology industries, the world moves so rapidly that the related real-world experience of ordinary users is often rendered obsolete by the time a product is developed or during the time of its projected commercial lifetime. For such industries I propose that 'lead users' who have real-life experience with novel product or process concepts of interest are essential to accurate marketing research.* (von Hippel 1986, 796)

In addition, it may be less challenging to identify lead users in industrial markets, as the number of customers is generally lower and customer-manufacturer relationships are more direct and/or stronger. Correspondingly, it is argued that consumer markets are too vast, heterogeneous, and fragmented to be screened for lead users and that end-users are not motivated or qualified enough to actively contribute to innovation processes (Hansen/Raabe 1991, 172; Lüthje 2000, 2). However, Lüthje (2000, 2) states that this has not been empirically proven.

Consequently, researchers have embarked on investigating whether the lead-user concept also applies to **consumer markets** (Lüthje 2000; Shah 2000; Franke and Shah 2003; Soll 2006; Walcher 2007). First, anecdotal evidence for innovations in consumer markets that were initiated or developed by motivated and qualified consumers could be identified (Utterback et al. 1976, 4; von Hippel 1982, 118; 1986, 803; Urban and von Hippel 1988, 581; Lüthje 2000, 3). For instance, Lüthje and Herstatt (2004, 555) cite the examples of "TipEx," which was developed by a secretary in the 1950s[40], or early versions of protein shampoos and ready-mix cakes, which stem back to housewife recipes.[41]

---

40 Being an artist in her free-time, the secretary recalled that artists paint over their mistakes on canvas, and thus she came up with the idea that typing errors could be corrected the same way. She began to use bottled tempera water-based paint in the office and quickly started to receive requests from her colleagues. From mixing the tempera at home, she moved to open up a company in 1956 that grew into a million dollar business (Reichwald and Piller 2006, 125).

41 A more recent example is the string cleaner, a device to clean guitar strings, which was entirely developed and commercialized by a user who is a professional musician. For more information, see company website: http://www.thestringcleaner.com, accessed May 1, 2013.

Second, empirical studies in consumer markets were conducted. For example, Utterback et al. (1976, 4) as well as Lawton and Parasuraman (1980, 31) compare product innovations from industrial and consumer markets and find that in both segments, almost the same percentage of products was initiated through customer input.[42] Other authors found that high-involvement consumer industries, such as sports equipment, account for a high incidence of user innovations (Lüthje 2000/2004; Shah 2000; Franke and Shah 2003; Bogers et al. 2010, 859ff.). Shah's findings reveal that it was always an end-user who invented the first versions of the basic equipment in each of the investigated fields (snowboarding, windsurfing, and skateboarding).[43] Lüthje shows that a third of the respondents of a survey (n=153) had generated ideas for improved or new products; 9% had built prototypes or marketable products for the outdoor industry (Lüthje 2004, 693).

Following these results, Lüthje (2000) is the first author to theoretically deduce and empirically test characteristics of lead users in consumer markets, for whom he coins the term "progressive customer"[44] (Lüthje 2000, 45).[45] The characteristics are based on the criteria from von Hippel (1986, 796): that innovative consumers face needs earlier and are thus dissatisfied by a certain market offer. However, Lüthje (2004, 685) points out that the leading-edge status of a consumer can only be relevant for a certain industry or type of product.

Empirically testing which characteristics discriminate between innovating and non-innovating users, Lüthje introduces the characteristics **product-related knowledge** and **use experience** for lead users in consumer markets (2000, 24–40; 2004, 686).[46] He argues that new needs and dissatisfaction are often revealed through intensive use of certain products (see also Price and Ridgway 1983, 680). Through intensive use, the

---

42 In their comparative exploration of several consumer markets, Lawton and Parasuraman (1980) also find that 12.7% of the innovation processes were stimulated by users. Utterback et al. (1976) find high levels of consumer activities for electronics innovations – 32.1% of innovations were initiated by detailed user requests (see also Lüthje 2000, 46 and Lüthje 2004, 684).

43 Shaw's research is an explorative field study that investigates the sources of an existing innovation (ex-post).

44 This term was translated by the author from the German "fortschrittlicher Kunde."

45 Lüthje implements these characteristics to identify adequate customers. He uses a questionnaire that tests the characteristics that have to be simultaneously fulfilled (compensation is not possible – see Lüthje 2000, 150). In doing so, Lüthje proves the existence of lead users in consumer markets in two industries: outdoor equipment and parlor games. In a next step, he even shows that the identified customers deliver promising product ideas and concepts when integrated in creativity workshops (Lüthje 2000, 194–199).

46 For insights on use experience as a lead-user criterion, see also Hienert et al. 2007.

consumer realizes how a product has to be modified to satisfy his needs. Usage seems to enhance the ability of the consumer to transform his dissatisfaction into new product features or entirely new products. Studies indeed show that "lead userness" increases in proportion with a user's depth of experience with a certain product (Lüthje 2000, 34ff., 65ff.; Lüthje 2004, 693). **Product-related knowledge** which is defined as knowledge concerning the product architecture (e.g., material as well as technical know-how) allows the consumer to specify technical details. It can, for example, be acquired through a (technical) profession or hobby (Lüthje 2004, 690; Hienerth et al. 2007, 22; Silvertant 2011, 208, 242). Knowledge that the consumer already possesses can be enhanced or expanded at low cost, which is why users tend to innovate in an area in which they are already proficient (Bilgram et al. 2008, 439). However, Lüthje also shows that innovative users need only a good technical understanding and not necessarily highly specified technical knowledge (Lüthje 2000, 68). Magnusson and Kristensson (2010) even find that a very high level of technical knowledge hinders innovation.

The idea that consumers with use experience and product-related knowledge are better suited to innovate is in line with research around "**absorptive capacity**." This concept stresses the role of prior knowledge for learning. Pre-existing knowledge increases the ability to absorb, evaluate, and utilize new knowledge (Cohen and Levinthal 1990; Sawhney and Prandelli 2000, 263; Lüthje and Herstatt 2004, 558; Bilgram et al. 2008, 434). Due to their expertise in a certain field, lead users are thus more likely to productively make use of information relevant for developing new solutions that address their "new" needs.

Product-related knowledge is also the consequence of high involvement, which stems from a certain importance the product plays in the life of the consumer (Greenwald and Leavitt 1984, 591; Mittal 1995, 664; Soll 2006, 118). **Involvement** means a strong disposition to use a certain product (Trommsdorff 1995, 1067). Highly involved people actively pursue and process information. The frequent occurrence of user innovations in high-involvement industries underpins this assumption.

Studies also mention **opinion leadership** as a characteristic of lead users. This concept is related to but not identical with innovativeness (Robertson 1971, 184; Soll 2006, 109). Opinion leaders have expert knowledge in a certain field (Trommsdorff 1993, 217) and are said to influence the opinion of people in their social network (Lazarsfeld et al. 1944[47]; King and Summers 1970, 43; Granovetter 1985; Childers 1986, 184; Soll 2006, 109; Walcher 2007, 194ff.). People tend to seek information from their peers when they are overwhelmed with information that they are not able to process or when they receive information that is inconsistent with their current knowledge or opinion – which is also referred to as "cognitive dissonance" (Festinger 1957, 12). As "followers," people often consult the "opinion leaders" in their social network (Walcher 2007, 194ff.). The adoption of new products by certain opinion leaders might be perceived as an indicator of quality and thus reduce uncertainty (or "cognitive dissonance") as well as the need to pursue further information. Opinion leaders themselves, however, make their decisions based on their expertise and independently of their social environment (Midgley and Dowling 1978; Hirschmann 1980; Price and Ridgway 1983; Manning et al. 1995; Soll 2006, 109; Walcher 2007, 194ff.). This is in line with the previously stated characteristics of lead users – that is, product-related knowledge and use experience. Thus, Bilgram et al. (2008, 443) argue that opinion leadership is already contained in the original lead-user criteria.[48]

Opinion leadership as a characteristic of lead users has been pointed out to have beneficial side effects – namely their contribution to the diffusion of innovations (Urban and von Hippel 1988; Schreier and Prügl 2008). However, in contrast to "lead userness," opinion leadership is a rather widespread characteristic (King and Summers 1970, 48; Soll 2006, 110).

In conclusion, it can be said that studies differ in their findings on the characteristics of lead users. Seven characteristics of lead users in consumer goods industries have been operationalized and tested in previous studies (see table 6 below and annex II). However, these characteristics have only been tested in high-income markets in developed countries.

47 Lazarsfeld et al. (1944) coined the term opinion leader. They showed that the opinions of certain people in a social network had an influence on the US presidential election in 1940.

48 Indeed, studies confirm that lead userness and/or lead users' innovative activities are positively correlated to opinion leadership. Morrison et al. (2000) empirically show that the majority of lead-user companies in their sample are also regarded as opinion leaders in their industry. However, it should be noted that the study had organizations, not individuals, as a unit of analysis. Walcher (2007, 239ff.), who focuses on individuals, shows that participants who obtained a high creativity score in his study are also opinion leaders.

Table 6: Summary of lead-user characteristics

Characteristic	Description	Examples for operationalization[49]
High expected benefit / Dissatisfaction	Through a latent dissatisfaction with existing market offers, new needs emerge. Dissatisfaction can motivate a consumer to search for new solutions.	Dissatisfaction is applied to measure high expected benefit (Urban and von Hippel 1988).
Ahead of the market / Trend leadership	Lead users are said to face new needs earlier than others. They thus lead trends. Their desire to seek out the new also results in a willingness to adopt new products "ahead of the market."	Time of adoption is the time between market introduction and the purchase of a new product (Lüthje 2000, 64–65, 254; Soll 2006, 105; Walcher 2007, 194ff.; Silvertant 2011, 285ff.).
High expected benefit / Innovative activity	Lead users face needs that they cannot satisfy, as related products or service offerings are not available. However, they have a high expected benefit from these solutions. To alleviate the "tension" between expectations towards a product and the product's performance, lead users spend time and resources to create the solutions themselves ("user innovations").	Innovative activity is applied as a measure for high expected benefit, whether the person has already experimented with product improvements or created new solutions (Franke and Shah 2003, 163; Lüthje 2004, 686; Silvertant 2011, 285ff.).
Product-related knowledge	Lead users possess (technical) knowledge about a product, such as how to assemble or construct the product, knowledge about components, materials, or appropriate technologies.	Overview of the market of the product (Soll 2006, 149; Silvertant 2011, 285ff.) Knowledge of the functions or materials of the product (Soll 2006, 149) Occupation or hobbies indicate product-related knowledge (Lüthje 2000, 68; Herstatt 2003; Lüthje 2004; Hienerth et al. 2007; see also Bilgram et al. 2008; 427).
Use experience	Lead users need to have an understanding of how the product functions to be able to develop a new product or improve an existing one. This is mostly acquired through frequent use of the product or similar products. Using the product, they are able to determine possible reasons for their dissatisfaction with existing solutions.	Frequency of use (e.g., days per year) and the total period of use (e.g., since *x* years) (Lüthje 2000, 254; Franke and Shah 2003; Schreier and Prügl 2008, 340).

49 For an overview of the questions/items used in questionnaires of other studies, please see table 58 in chapter 5.

Involvement	Lead users are said to have a special interest in a product they care about or they use very often. They show their involvement through knowing existing market offers and frequently researching new solutions that better serve their needs – or even develop them on their own.	Level of interest in the product or frequency of use of product-related information sources (Lüthje 2000/2004; Franke and Shah 2003; Bilgram et al. 2008, 427; Schreier and Prügl 2008).
Opinion leadership	Lead users tend to have greater knowledge about products and are able to sense as well as influence the opinions of people in their environment.	Frequency of conversations with others about the product/topic and whether or not they share their experiences (Soll 2006, 148; Silvertant 2011, 285ff.).

Source: created by author.

Towards a lead-user typology

Empirical research on lead users usually segments user samples into lead users versus non-lead users (e.g., Urban and von Hippel 1988), implicitly suggesting that there is a dichotomy. However, in their paper on "the nature of lead users," Morrison et al. (2004, 358) argue that "the assumption and use of a dichotomous distribution of lead users in the population as suggested in the literature has not been empirically tested." They find that lead userness is not a binary but rather a bell-shaped construct. This leads them to recommend that "a lead user dichotomy should not be used, as it is not a good representation of the population mix and its use throws away useful information" (Morrison et al. 2004, 358).

Based on qualitative empirical findings from two lead-user workshops, Schrader and Belz (2012, 344ff.) develop a model that still builds on the dichotomy between lead users and non-lead users, but includes further types. These more gradual categories may help translate the idea of lead userness as a continuous construct into an actual **typology**. As the first attempt at such a typology, Schrader and Belz's model distinguishes between two types of lead users and three types of non-lead users. Type I are lead users who actively innovate and have done so already, while type II are those who have the potential and capabilities to innovate but have not yet implemented their own ideas. Both types are regarded as interested in contributing to corporate innovation processes. Type III are users with the capabilities to produce creative ideas and motivation to be integrated into innovation processes, but who do not show lead-user characteristics. Silvertant (2011, 256ff.) names them "creative mainstream consumers." Schrader and Belz (2012, 345) stress that they "are of particular interest as recruits for user integration." Magnusson (2009, 590) specifies that these rather "ordinary users" have relevant input precisely because they lack technological knowledge, which prevents them from restricting their creative thinking. However, most ordinary users are not creative but simply interested – these belong to type IV and are referred to as "interested mainstream consumers" (ibid.). The remaining participants, type V, are neither creative nor interested in contributing to innovation processes (see figure 9).

Figure 9: Types of lead users and non-lead users

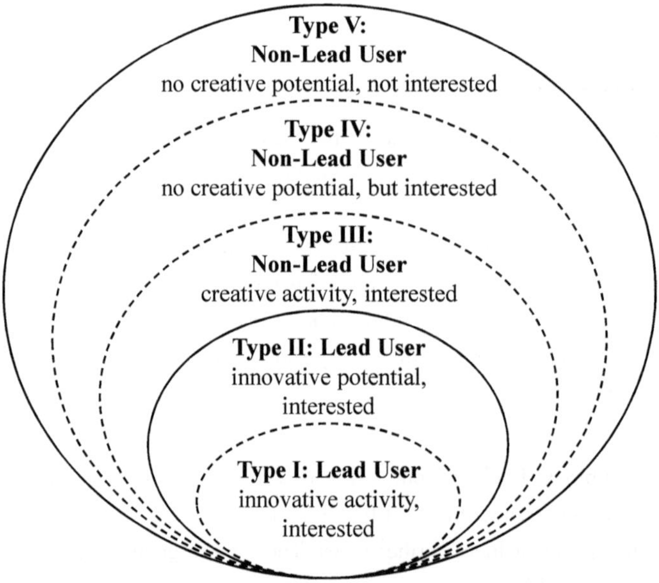

Source: based on Schrader and Belz 2012, 345; see also: Silvertant 2011, 256ff.

While there are numerous studies on lead users, "non-lead users" are under-researched. Only a few studies look closely at this user group – without, however, distinguishing different types of "non-lead users" or identifying their characteristics (Kristensson et al. 2002; Kristensson et al. 2004; Magnusson 2009; Magnusson and

Kristensson 2010).[50] Consequently, Schrader and Belz (2012, 346) argue that "a future challenge will be to develop recruitment instruments that are capable of excluding type IV individuals at the recruitment stage of the innovation process." One way would be to identify the characteristics of the non-lead users of type III (or "creative mainstream consumers") to be able to more clearly distinguish them from type IV users. However, little is known about type III consumers' particular characteristics. Hence, further research is needed.

2.2.2 Relevance of lead-user identification for low-income markets

While BoP literature stresses the importance of external partners for innovation, little insight is given on how to find and select these partners, particularly when it comes to integrating low-income consumers into innovation. The methods discussed in literature – for example, immersion or the BoP Protocol – rather address a random sample. Nonetheless, anecdotal evidence in BoP literature points towards the fact that some low-income consumers may be better suited to provide input than others. Beshouri (2006, 66), for example, points out potential opinion leaders in communities as partners:

> *Communities are frequently in a better position than companies are to resolve issues that make it uneconomic to serve low-income groups. [...] People in local communities – not only the mayors and barangay (village) captains but also school principals, teachers, religious leaders, and residents themselves – are in the best position to help companies deal with the challenges of doing business in low-income areas.*

A variety of publications refer to the creative and innovative capabilities of low-income consumers, albeit without further examining their characteristics. Gupta (2010, 138) argues that a lack of material resources spurs "knowledge-intensive innovation by common people in the informal sector." Along the same lines, SadreGhazi (2008, 64) reasons that market constraints can trigger innovation. Fukushima (2009) identifies "vernacular solutions" developed by Brazilian low-income consumers, referring to improvised solutions which use materials their creators have at hand and creatively combine in new ways. Furthermore, Viswanathan and Sridharan (2012, 60) point out that low-income consumers are often "prosumers," as they frequently have to "trade

---

50 For example, Kristensson et al. (2002) and Kristensson et al. (2004) contrast the innovative abilities of ordinary users and company professionals. Magnusson (2009) contrasts ordinary users with company professionals and lead users.

off the choice between buying and self-producing as a result of low and uncertain incomes." Nair et al. (2012) identify a variety of user innovations developed by residents in Indian slums. They cite the case of a potter who invented a machine that makes non-sticky clay pans with characteristics similar to Teflon and which last longer than common clay pans, which need to be replaced every 15 days. The same potter also invented a clay water filter and clay chiller, which exploit the material's porosity and thermal properties, respectively.

Viswanathan and Sridharan (2012, 66–67) analyze the results of a course they held that aimed at developing new products for low-income markets through virtual and actual immersion in the field. In their conclusions, they directly refer to the lead-user concept:

> *In all the [13] case studies, the product teams encountered consumers who were willing to share insights on their current, homemade solutions to significant needs. These "lead users" were found to create innovative and affordable solutions to their "vexing and perennial" needs, primarily because of the absence of market solutions.*

However, they do not systematically show that the users identified can truly be considered lead users in the term's original sense (see section 2.2.1), nor do they elaborate on how to identify them. In fact, no study could be found that examines whether innovative consumers in low-income markets show the "lead-user characteristics" researched in only high-income markets thus far. Nonetheless, Viswanathan and Sridharan conclude that there is "a potential BoP parallel to the existing 'lead user' concept in the NPD [new product development] literature and [an] opportunity to examine the different nuances the BoP context imparts to this concept" (Viswanathan and Sridharan 2012, 66).

2.2.3 Intermediate conclusion and research gaps

The lead-user concept has been conceptually and empirically explored by a variety of researchers (see section 2.2.1). However, two research gaps can be observed:

(1) Lack of lead-user research in the context of low-income markets

Since von Hippel's pioneering work, most studies that could be identified through an extensive literature review[51] were conducted in the United States of America as well as

---

[51] The literature review was conducted using Business Source Premier (EBSCOhost), a research database service with the full text for more than 2200 journals, 1100 of which are peer reviewed.

Europe.[52] Most of these studies focused on industrial goods. Lüthje (2000) was the first researcher to extend the lead-user concept to the consumer goods industry, and his study was followed by a variety of studies (see table 7). However, they were also mainly conducted in Europe with a focus on the sports industry or hobby-related high-involvement industries (see, e.g., Bogers et al. 2010, 859ff.).[53] The target populations addressed by the studies range from members of kitesurfing communities to university students. Based on their profession and their interests in, for example, outdoor sports, it can be assumed that most potential lead users addressed were middle- to high-income consumers.

Not a single study could be identified that was conducted outside of Europe or the USA. None of the studies identified was conducted in emerging or developing countries, nor did any specifically address low-income consumers. In fact, when it comes to innovating for low-income markets, there seems to be a general lack of insight into the types of consumers most suitable for contributing to innovation as well as the characteristics that set them apart. Thus Viswanathan and Sridharan (2012, 66–67) suggest exploring a potential "BoP parallel to the existing 'lead user' concept." However, they do not define nor investigate the concept in that context. In fact, the question of whether lead-user characteristics serve to identify innovative consumers in low-income markets remains unaddressed and requires further research.

Also, a limited number of books are offered (see http://www.ebscohost.com/academic/business-source-premier). Furthermore, standard books on innovation were consulted and a thorough search with Google Scholar was conducted. However, it should be mentioned that most books and papers screened were published in English and German. Due to practical limitations of this research project, academic works in other languages were not considered.

52 The products studied range from the semiconductor industry to medical equipment and library systems (von Hippel 1976; von Hippel 1977; Shaw 1985; von Hippel 1986; Urban and von Hippel 1988; Herstatt and von Hippel 1992; Gruner and Homburg 2000; Morrison et al. 2000; Olson and Bakke 2001; Lilien et al. 2002; Lüthje 2000/2004; Morrison et al. 2004; Bartl 2006; Soll 2006; Jokisch 2007; Hienerth et al. 2007; Silvertant 2011; Schrader and Belz 2011; Ramakrishnan 2011; also see annex II).

53 Single studies looked at, e.g., the mobile industry, household appliances, and the food and beverage industry.

Table 7: Selected lead-user studies in the consumer goods industry

Source	Product/sector	Country	Sample
Lüthje (2000)	Outdoor sports, parlor games, public transport	Germany	Pilot: users of outdoor products who are in databases of German outdoor sports companies; case study for parlor games: active elderly people
Kristensson et al. (2002)	ICT	Sweden	University students, service developers
Franke and Shah (2003)	Outdoor sports	Germany	Members of sports communities (sailplaning, canyoning, boardercross, handicapped cycling)
Kristensson et al. (2004)	ICT	Sweden	University students, service developers (employees of firm)
Lüthje (2004)	Consumer outdoor products	Germany	Customers of two outdoor product manufacturers
Franke et al. (2006)	Kitesurfing	Europe	Members of European kitesurfing communities
Soll (2006)	Household appliances	Germany	Visitors of the German website of BSH
Walcher (2007)	Sports shoes	Germany	Adidas customers
Schreier and Prügl (2008)	Sailing, technical diving, kitesurfing	Austria, Germany, international	Visitors of website www.streckenflug.at; members of the international diving community Global Underwater Explorers (GUE); European kitesurfing communities
Magnusson (2009)	Mobile phone service	Sweden	Professional service developers from Telia Mobile; students from Karlstad University
Silvertant (2011)	Food and beverages (packaging)	Germany	University students, customers, visitors of website

Source: created by author.

(2) Lack of research on types of innovative or creative consumers

Also, the extent to which other, non-lead users can support companies in gaining innovation-relevant insights remains an open question. As discussed in section 2.2.1, Silvertant (2011, 256ff.) and Belz and Schrader (2011) have begun to develop a typology of lead users and non-lead users. It also considers consumers who may not be as innovative as lead users but could still share relevant insights for specific innovation endeavors. However, further exploration of the characteristics of "non-lead users," or "creative consumers," may be a fruitful area of study for two reasons.

First, identifying genuine lead users is a cumbersome and time-intensive process, particularly because they are rare. Second, for many (rather incremental) innovation projects, lead users' future-oriented, cutting-edge knowledge may not be as relevant. In fact, it may often suffice to identify consumers who show creative capabilities. This may potentially apply to innovation endeavors targeted at low-income markets where companies often possess relevant technological knowledge but lack insight into the context and characteristics of the market.

The next section introduces idea competitions as an underexplored method to close the gaps in research and innovation in low-income markets.

2.3 Idea competitions as a method to integrate consumers into innovation

Idea competitions have recently started to gain popularity in corporate practice. [54] Research in the field of innovation management has also begun to view the method as a tool to initiate dialogue with consumers (Hansen and Raabe 1991) and integrate them into the fuzzy front end of innovation processes (Bartl 2006; Piller and Walcher 2006; Soll 2006; Walcher 2007; Belz et al. 2009; Ebner et al. 2009; Silvertant 2011). However, only a few studies take a systematic look at idea competitions in the context of innovation (Ernst et al. 2004, 129; Piller and Walcher 2006, 308; Soll 2006, 2, 59; Walcher 2007, 5; Silvertant 2011, 5). Haller et al. (2009, 2) constitute: "A deep understanding of the instrument is still lacking."

[54] Companies set up idea competitions for a variety of reasons – e.g., for marketing purposes (Haller et al. 2009, 17) or social causes (McKinsey 2009). However, most competitions are applied to initiate a dialogue with consumers (Hansen and Raabe 1991) and integrate them into the fuzzy front end of innovation processes (Reichwald and Piller 2006; Walcher 2007; Belz et al. 2009; Silvertant 2011). For an exemplary overview of practical examples, see Haller et al. (2009, 29).

To lay the ground for a better understanding, the first part of this section (2.3.1) provides an overview of the current state of the art of idea competitions. The subsequent sections focus on the objectives of idea competitions, which are said to support innovation projects in three ways:

(1) First, they **generate creative ideas** that serve as input at the early stages of innovation processes (section 2.3.2).
(2) Second, they help **identify creative consumers or even lead users**, who may have relevant input for innovation (section 2.3.3).
(3) Third, they can serve to **identify and transfer innovation-relevant information and knowledge** (section 2.3.4).

Section 2.3.4 also discusses the different types of innovation-relevant information and knowledge, and provides an excursus on the crucial distinction between information and knowledge – terms which are often confused or used imprecisely. The section then describes how information and knowledge is transferred between individuals.

Finally, the relevance and feasibility of the method for low-income markets is discussed in section 2.3.5. An intermediate conclusion reflects all previous discussions – and points towards research gaps.

2.3.1 Design and implementation of idea competitions

In idea competitions, a private or public organization invites a specific or general target group to hand in submissions related to a specific topic within a given time frame. These submissions are then evaluated by an expert jury according to pre-defined criteria and awarded a prize according to their performance (Walcher 2007, 40).[55] Following this definition, the **process** of idea competitions can roughly be described in four phases: (1) set-up (2) realization, (3) evaluation and awarding (4) follow-up.

Although researchers have defined these phases (Walcher 2007, 39; Haller et al. 2009, 3; Silvertant 2011, 58ff.; see also table 8), they generally offer little guidance on how the phases should be designed to achieved a specific, target-oriented outcome (Soll 2006, 59; Piller and Walcher 2006, 308; Wenger and Haller 2010; Füller et al. 2011, 269). A few exceptions exist that focus on particular aspects of idea competitions. For

[55] Walcher's definition provided the basis for subsequent studies (e.g., Ebner et al. 2009; Haller et al. 2009; Silvertant 2011).

example, Füller et al. (2011) investigate the benefits of combining idea competitions with online communities to enhance the outcome. Other studies zoom in on the evaluation phase, investigating the potential of "open evaluation" – that is, having ideas evaluated by peer users (Möslein et al. 2010). Others investigate how to design prizes (Wenger and Haller 2010).

The subsequent summary thus provides a detailed overview of the current state of the art in designing and implementing idea competitions. The empirical part of this study (chapter 3) builds on the findings of this overview when adapting the method to the context of low-income markets.

Table 8: Design elements of idea competitions

Phases	Design element	Variations	Literature
Set-up	Objective	Generation of ideas ("ideation"); identification of lead users; generation of innovation-relevant information and knowledge	Soll 2006 Piller and Walcher 2006 Walcher 2007 Silvertant 2011, 58ff.
	Object	Product, service, process, business model	Ebner et al. 2009 Silvertant 2011, 58ff.
	Topic/Task	High / low specificity of the task	Piller and Walcher 2006 Ebner et al. 2009 Silvertant 2011, 61
	Target group	Specified target group (e.g., age, country, interest, income) or unspecified	Piller and Walcher 2006 Ebner et al. 2009, 346
	Time frame	Short / long / very long term	Walcher 2007 Silvertant 2011, 62
Realization	Channel	Online, offline or mixed	von Hippel and Katz 2002 Ebner et al. 2009, 346 Silvertant 2011, 58ff.
	Promotion	Through specific/thematic channels or broad; through online channels (communities, websites); offline (posters, flyers)	Belz et al. 2009, 53 Silvertant 2011, 66ff.
	Collection of ideas	Online submissions, via toolkits, per mail, physically handing in ideas	Soll 2006, 30 Silvertant 2011, 66ff.

Evaluation and awarding	Evaluation	Self-assessment, evaluation by an expert jury (internal and/or external experts), user evaluation (peer review)	Nambisan 2002 Piller and Walcher 2006 Reichwald and Piller 2006 Silvertant 2011, 64ff. Möslein et al. 2010
	Assessment of ideas (criteria)	Specified, unspecified	Amabile 1996 Silvertant 2011, 64ff.
	(Prize) Incentives	Monetary prize / non-monetary prize, mixed	Ernst et al. 2004 Ebner et al. 2009, 346 Wenger and Haller 2010 Silvertant 2011, 63
Follow-up		Interviews, innovation workshops	Belz et al. 2009, 70–78

Source: adapted from Walcher 2007, 38ff.; Ebner et al. 2009, 345ff.; Haller et al. 2009; Silvertant 2011, 58ff.

(1) Set-up

Idea competitions can be initiated by private or public organizations (Reichwald and Piller 2006, 174; Walcher 2007, 40; Haller et al. 2009; Silvertant 2011, 59ff.). Most commonly, idea competitions are initiated by companies.

The set-up phase of an idea competition must define its objective as well as the object to be innovated, the task that is "handed over" to the consumer, the target group, and the time frame. In the context of innovation, idea competitions are mostly conducted to pursue one or all of the following three **objectives**: (1) to generate creative ideas with customers or other external partners ("ideation") (Soll 2006, 3; Silvertant 2011, 69ff.), (2) to identify lead users (Walcher 2007, 38ff.; Silvertant 2011, 69ff.)[56] or particularly creative consumers, and/or (3) to generate innovation-relevant information and knowledge, such as information on unsatisfied needs of consumers (Belz et al. 2009, 16) (see sections 2.1.5–7).

Participants are asked to submit ideas for a certain **object**, be it a new product, service, process, or a business model within a given time frame (Ernst 2004; Piller et al. 2006; Haller et al. 2009; Silvertant 2011, 58ff.). Depending on the design of the competition, ideas can be submitted online or offline and in the form of a visual and/or textual

[56] Furthermore, Ebner (2008) as well as Ebner et al. (2009) investigate idea competitions as a means to develop online communities. As this objective is of minor importance for the purpose of this study, it is not elaborated on.

description. Participants can hand in ideas, concepts, sketches, or prototypes (Haller et al. 2009).

The **topic** of the competition can be highly specified or broad (Walcher 2007, 42; Belz et al. 2009, 41–42; Silvertant 2011, 58ff.). Broad topics that leave the solution space open are found to enhance creativity (Soll 2006, 102). However, topics that are too broad may confuse participants and yield submissions that are too diverse.

The **target group** of a competition can remain unspecified or be limited to people with certain characteristics and capabilities, such as age, gender, interests, or income level (Reichwald and Piller 2006, 174; Haller et al. 2009; Silvertant 2011, 60ff.). The participation of people with particular characteristics can be encouraged by promoting the competition through certain communication channels (e.g., offline only in certain regions or online only in certain communities) (Silvertant 2011, 66ff.). Researchers stress promoting idea competitions not only in the target market but also in analogous markets (von Hippel 1986, 800; Lilien et al. 2002, 1047, 1056; Silvertant 2011, 58ff.).[57]

The **time frame** of idea competitions can be short or long, lasting from minutes to months, depending mostly on the complexity of the task (Reichwald and Piller 2006, 175; Walcher 2007, 41; Silvertant 2011, 60ff.), the objective of the competition, and the context and media chosen.

(2) Realization

During the realization phase, the idea competition is promoted for a certain period of time, after which ideas are collected:

The promotion of idea competitions highly depends on the "channel" chosen – whether the idea competition is realized online or offline. **Offline** idea competitions are promoted through local news channels (e.g., newspaper, radio, or television), word to mouth, direct mailing, or other promotional material such as posters, flyers, or the packaging of a product (Belz et al. 2009, 53; Silvertant 2011, 60ff.). The ideas can be submitted in person or via mail. Offline idea competitions are favorable if the target group does not have access to or is not competent in using the internet (Belz et al. 2009, 28). This applies to specific target groups, like children or elderly people, and

57 Hienerth et al. (2007, 20–21) find that users from analogous markets contribute solutions that are significantly more novel.

often to low-income settings. However, most studies focus on online idea competitions. A lack of research on offline competitions and their specific characteristics can be observed.[58]

Online idea competitions are carried out on an online platform, which can vary in technical complexity. These platforms either allow participants to upload their ideas or they provide toolkits for idea generation (Silvertant 2011, 60ff.). Platforms can also include community functions, enabling an exchange between participants as well as "peer review" of ideas (Belz et al. 2009; Haller et al. 2009). Online idea competitions enable a broader reach as they can be promoted worldwide through communities, blogs, online forums, and electronic newsletters at considerably low costs (Soll 2006, 30; Silvertant 2011, 60ff.). Thus, a higher number of ideas can be generated. Furthermore, online idea competitions facilitate the management of ideas, as well as the discussion, evaluation, and further development of these ideas with the target group (Belz et al. 2009, 28; Walcher 2007, 62).

(3) Evaluation and awarding

After the realization phase, the ideas must be evaluated. To identify the best ideas, submissions are often assessed by a **jury of experts**. However, self-assessment or assessment by other participants ("peer review" or "open evaluation") are also viable options (Walcher 2007, 111 ff.; Belz et al. 2009, 49; Haller et al. 2009, 5; Wegener and Haller 2010; Möslein et al. 2010). The jury might comprise company representatives, external experts, or both (Haller et al. 2009, 19; Silvertant 2011, 64). The topic of the competition should ideally be closely related to the domain of their expertise (Amabile 1996, 33; Walcher 2007, 111ff.; Silvertant 2011, 64). Haller et al. (2009, 5) report that including external experts "can help to overcome the not-invented-here syndrome by acting as gatekeepers."

Evaluation of results is "far from [being] standardized. Sometimes, gut feeling or criteria from idea management are used," report Haller et al. (2009, 5). There are no uniformly accepted criteria for idea evaluation (Magnusson 2009, 585). Idea

---

58 Some studies, however, have offline components. For example, Bartl (2006) compares the characteristics of participants recruited online for the "Virtual Lab" organized by Audi with participants who are recruited through the Audi customer center, i.e., offline (Bartl 2006, 272). The idea competition conducted by Silvertant (2011) was partly marketed offline and also allowed offline submission of ideas via mail. Most ideas, however, were handed in online (Silvertant 2011, 132).

competitions mostly apply innovation-specific **criteria**, for example, criteria from creativity research[59] that can reliably evaluate the ideas' creative performance (Kristensson et al. 2004, 10; Reichwald and Piller 2006, 174; Walcher 2007, 43ff.; Haller et al. 2009, 5; Silvertant 2011, 73ff., 89ff.). For example, both Walcher (2007, 43ff.) and Silvertant (2011, 73ff., 89ff.) find the Consensual Assessment Technique (CAT) developed by Amabile (1996) to be an appropriate technique for the evaluation of ideas (see chapter 3). The CAT construct of creativity was proved reliable and valid in previous studies.[60] Besides criteria for measuring creativity, the CAT further provides concrete advice regarding the size of the jury and its qualifications as well as the assessment of criteria (see chapter 3).

Participation is often awarded with a non-cash and/or cash **prize** – most commonly for the three best submissions (Reichwald and Piller 2006, 175; Walcher 2007, 39; Silvertant 2011, 63). Sometimes, the winners do not get a prize, but are simply publicly announced as winners. These gains in reputation can also be perceived as incentives (Reichwald and Piller 2006, 175; Belz et al. 2009, 44; Silvertant 2011, 63). Additional possible incentives include appreciation, detailed feedback, or the chance to design an idea that will be realized by a company (Belz et al. 2009, 44). Regardless of the extrinsic motives, participants are also found to be intrinsically motivated to participate in idea contests because they are fun and the completion of a task provides satisfaction and a feeling of competence (Füller 2006; Haller et al. 2009, 6). Another intrinsic incentive is the opportunity to take part in creating a new product (Sawhney and Prandelli 2000, 263).

Idea competitions often yield a high number of ideas, which shows the high motivation of participants (Soll 2006, 210). However, empirical research has not yet been able to provide clear-cut insights on how the most creative people can be incentivized to take part (Silvertant 2011, 63): Frey (1997) stresses the danger of high extrinsic incentives, which might "crowd out" participants who are primarily intrinsically motivated (the so-called "crowding-out effect"). In contrast, Sawhney and Prandelli (2000, 263) as well as Belz et al. (2009, 44) regard a reward for participation as necessary for idea competitions in a business setting. Generally, extrinsic incentives can have a positive influence on creativity, but should be well balanced (Amabile 1996, 150; Soll 2006, 102).

---

[59] For an overview of techniques to measure creativity, see Walcher (2007, 43ff.).

[60] For a list of studies that applied the CAT with reliable results, see Walcher (2007, 59ff.).

(3) Follow-up

The follow-up phase serves to stay in touch with the most creative or innovative consumers and to continue to involve them in innovation. For example, in-depth interviews can be conducted or innovation workshops can be organized with them (Belz et al. 2009, 70–78; Pobisch 2010; Ramakrishnan 2012). These workshops may serve to further explore or refine the ideas suggested by the participants (concept development), or even to develop and test prototypes.

2.3.2 Idea competitions to generate creative ideas with consumers

In the context of innovation, idea competitions are mostly conducted for "ideation" purposes – that is, to generate ideas with (potential) consumers (see, e.g., Reichwald and Piller 2006, 173–176; Piller and Walcher 2006; Walcher 2007, 38ff., 106ff.; Ebner et al. 2009, 345; Belz et al. 2009, 15; Silvertant 2011, 69ff.). The focus lies not only in the quantity of ideas generated, but also in their quality (Soll 2006, 102; Silvertant 2011, 221ff.). Submissions can encompass ideas to improve existing products (incremental innovations) or the development of completely new ideas. In Walcher's study, for example, 10% of the 82 ideas submitted were assessed to be radically new – the remaining ideas were considered as valuable suggestions for product improvement (Walcher 2007, 256ff.; see also Piller and Walcher 2006, 304). In the study of Silvertant on competitions for beer and honey packaging, one third of the 59 and 70 submitted ideas, respectively, were evaluated as creative (Silvertant 2011, 221ff.). A very small number was ranked as highly original; the remaining ideas served to tap trends and innovation-relevant knowledge (Silvertant 2011, 224).

The creative ideas of users can work as "an inspiration for the innovation process [...] [and] can actually cause a company to become more innovative by breaking the current dominant logic" (Magnusson 2009, 591). This is partly because company professionals are often bound by existing technology and thus face difficulties in thinking "outside the box." Being exposed to creative solutions from outside of the company may help them to overcome their "**functional fixedness**" (Duncker 1945; Adamson 1952; Lüthje 2000, 22).

However, Füller et al. (2009, 95) reckon that "consumers engaging in virtual co-creation projects will rarely be able to determine the final design of a product." Indeed, idea competitions rarely lead to ready-to-implement concepts or prototypes (Belz et al. 2009, 16; Magnusson 2009, 591; Silvertant 2011, 223). At the same time, product designers hardly look out for *the one* creative idea at the early stages of innovation processes. In fact, they are well aware that an "idea may go through many iterations and changes as it is examined, studied, discussed, and developed" (Koen et al. 2001, 51). Consequently, the objective of the fuzzy front end is first and foremost to "diverge" – that is, to create a wealth of quality inputs to inspire the project team (Kim and Wilemon 2002, 273ff.; Soll 2006, 55; Silvertant 2011, 222). At the fuzzy front end, it may thus be beneficial to gain input from various sources rather than focus on one idea from only one source. Kim and Wilemon (2002, 275–277) state that

> *building and sustaining the sources of ideas is as important as managing the fuzzy front end phase […] Through frequent and intimate communication with customers, project members can gain new and diverse viewpoints beyond those of a team. Customer involvement in the fuzzy front end helps the project team get a clearer understanding of both customer needs as well as future needs (e.g., Chandy and Tellis, 1998), probable markets sizes and growth. Moreover customers can play roles not only as buyers, and users, but also as important information sources.*

The competitive character of idea competitions can trigger creativity, increase the quality of submissions (Ernst et al. 2004; Haller et al. 2009, 5), and, most importantly, identify lead users (see e.g., von Hippel 1986/1988/2005). The following section explains why idea competitions are a suitable method for identifying lead users.

Figure 10: The fuzzy front end of innovation processes

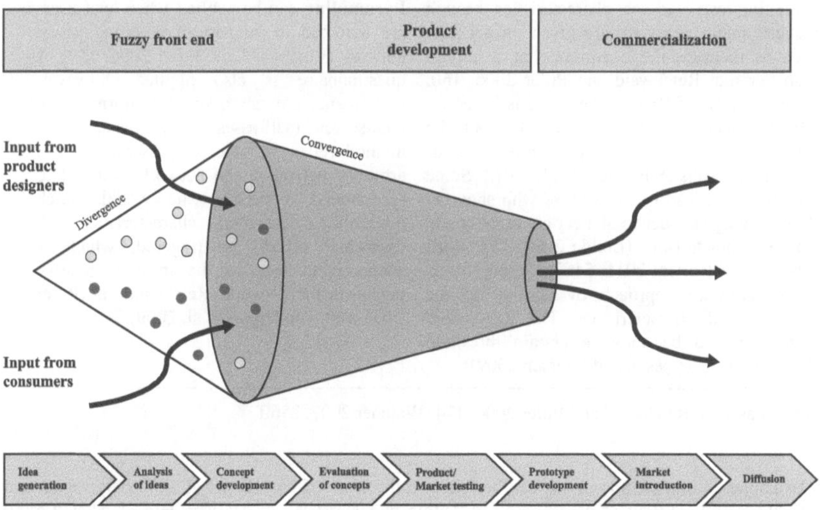

Source: created by author.

2.3.3 Idea competitions to identify lead users and creative consumers

Based on the research findings of von Hippel (see, e.g., von Hippel 1986/1988/2005) on "lead users," researchers have tried to identify those consumers who can provide the most valuable input to innovation processes – particularly in its early stages (Soll 2006, 19). However, as described in section 2.2, identifying lead users is difficult and cumbersome. To address this challenge, innovation researchers have tried to find methods that support lead-user identification, the most prominent of which are called screening and pyramiding (Ernst et al. 2004; Reichwald and Piller 2006; Walcher 2007; von Hippel et al. 2009; see table 9).

Table 9: Methods of lead-user identification (selection)

Screening	**Pyramiding**
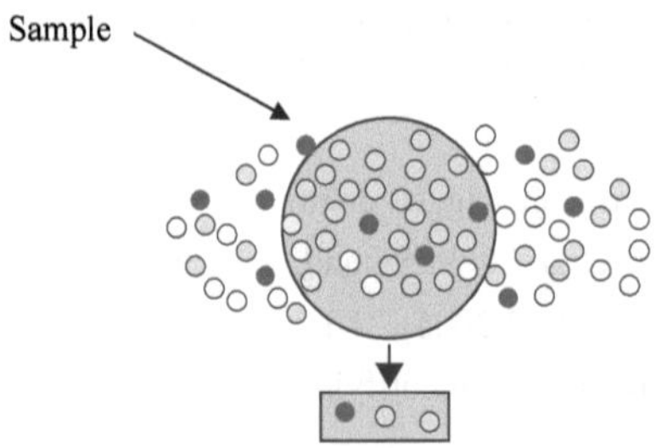	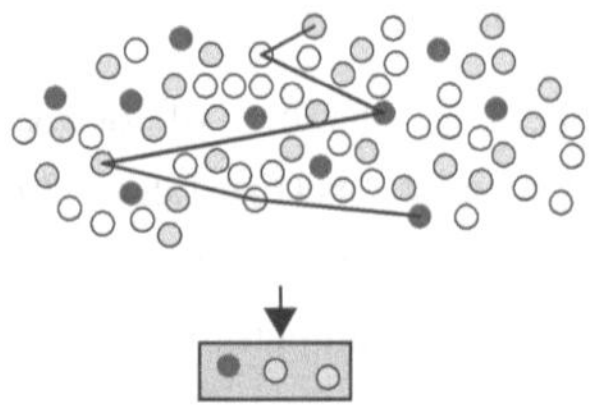
Screening tests lead-user characteristics through a questionnaire; answers are given on a Likert scale to measure the occurrence of a certain characteristic (Reichwald and Piller 2006, 160; Silvertant 2011, 54ff.). The method is based on self-assessment. After consumers fill out the questionnaire there is no coherent procedure for evaluating results (Silvertant 2011, 54ff.). Some authors define lead users as those who show an above-average incidence of a certain number and type of characteristics (Lüthje 2000, 151; Bartl 2006, 188; Silvertant 2011, 54ff.). Others follow a compensatory approach by adding up the scores of all characteristics. The aggregated score needs to be above a certain threshold (Jokisch 2007; Jeppesen and Laursen 2009).	**Pyramiding** can be applied when lead users are assumed to be part of a strong social network (Reichwald and Piller 2006, 159). A questionnaire is also applied; however, participants are not asked to inform about themselves (self-assessment). Instead, the method relies on objective assessment: An arbitrary person in the network is asked to recommend a person who would match predefined lead-user characteristics. A "snowball effect" is triggered, which is supposed to lead to the most innovative person in the network (Reichwald and Piller 2006, 160; von Hippel et al. 2009).[61]

Source: based on Reichwald and Piller 2006, 174; Walcher 2007, 256ff.

[61] Examples of this method in use can be found in the work of von Hippel et al. (1999); Olson and Bakke (2001); Lilien et al. (2002) and Lüthje and Herstatt (2004). Von Hippel et al. (2009) compare the techniques of screening and pyramiding (see also Silvertant 2011, 54ff.).

However, both methods require one-to-one interaction with customers and the use of a questionnaire. Thus, they are more suitable for the business-to-business ("B2B") sector, which has fewer customers.

For both consumer and industrial goods, some researchers have found **idea competitions** to be a viable method for lead-user identification (Reichwald and Piller 2006, 176; Walcher 2007, 256ff.; Belz et al. 2009, 17; Silvertant 2011, 210ff.). The method facilitates the participation of a high number of consumers who enjoy engaging in creative activities and communicating their ideas (Ernst et al. 2004, 122; Bartl 2006, 76; Reichwald and Piller 2006, 176; Hienert et al. 2007, 9; Walcher 2007, 267ff.; Silvertant 2011, 57). The submitted idea then indicates the creative capabilities of the idea owner (Walcher 2007, 186ff., 239ff.; Silvertant 2011, 210ff.). Indeed, studies have identified a **high incidence of lead-user characteristics amongst winners of idea competitions**. For example, Soll (2006, 204) and Walcher (2007, 253ff.) show that the most creative ideas were submitted from participants with new, unsatisfied needs. Walcher (2007, 253ff.) and Silvertant (2011, 210ff.) show that they are often trend and opinion leaders. A person's participation in an idea competition is further testimony to his or her high involvement in the topic of the competition. Researchers argue that this high incidence of lead-user characteristics amongst winners is due to a triple selection process, as the method combines pre-selection by the company with self-selection and selection by others, often experts (Walcher 2007, 127ff.; Belz et al. 2009, 18; Silvertant 2011, 70, 228ff.; see also figure 11):

- **Pre-selection** means that companies address a certain group through targeted promotion. The target group might be likely to be familiar with the topic and to contribute creative ideas. They might be, for example, design students or certain experts in the field (Belz et al. 2009, 18). Alternatively, targeted promotion can exclusively address the target group of the end product. For example, in developing a service for retirees, the competition could address elderly people and their caregivers.
- **Self-selection** means that participants who chose to take part "select themselves," as they regard themselves to be able to make a contribution to and/or win the competition (Bartl 2006, 273; Walcher 2007, 258; Silvertant 2011, 228ff.; Füller et al. 2011, 269). Füller et al. (2011, 269) comment that "while self-selection has often been seen as a bias in scientific research, it can be clearly seen as an advantage for idea competitions […] [as] self-selection not only helps to overcome the local

search bias (Lüthje et al. 2005), but also ensures a participant's intrinsic interest in the activity and topic." Furthermore, previous research shows that "creative people are more likely to participate in co-creation platforms than their less creative counterparts (Füller 2010), indicating that the principle of self-selection may lead to better solutions as more qualified participants are willing to engage." (Füller et al. 2011, 269; see also Bartl 2006, 273).

- **Selection by others** (e.g., experts) is conducted along pre-defined evaluation criteria. Usually, winners are defined by assessing the output of their creative ideas (Walcher 2007, 258; Silvertant 2011, 228ff.). To ensure that these winners can be considered lead users, studies often combine the evaluation of the outcome with a screening questionnaire which tests if the winners comply with certain characteristics (Walcher 2007; Silvertant 2011).

Figure 11: Triple selection process of lead users through idea competitions

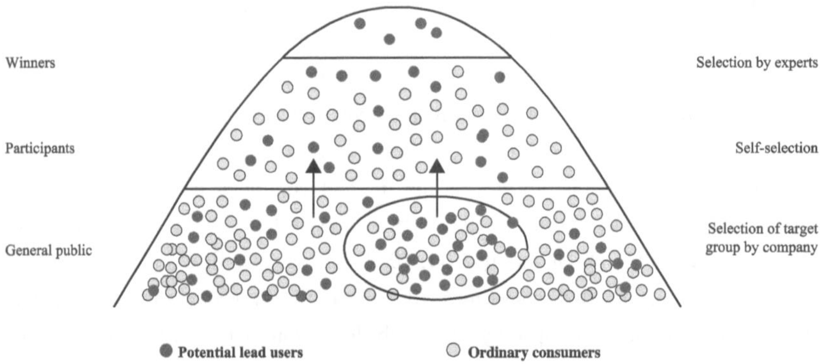

Source: based on Belz et al. 2009, 18 and Silvertant 2011, 229.

The lead users identified in this way are said to provide the most valuable input to innovation processes, as they do not only possess information about their needs, but are also able to transform them into concrete solutions ("solution-related information"). The next section explains the different types of information and knowledge needed for innovation purposes and discusses why idea competitions serve to tap them.

2.3.4 Idea competitions to tap innovation-relevant knowledge

As presented in the previous sections, idea competitions are expected to yield **two outcomes**: to generate creative ideas and to identify particularly innovative and creative consumers – namely, lead users. Both of these outcomes, in turn, are a source of information and knowledge that is relevant for innovation purposes.

The lead users identified are seen as "carriers" of information and knowledge (von Hippel 1988; Mascitelli 2000, 189; see section 2.2 and 2.3.3). They are set apart by their ability to sense future needs earlier than others and to transform their needs into concrete solutions. The information inherent in lead users can be tapped by interacting with them or via the solutions they create, their ideas.[62]

The ideas generated through competitions need to be analyzed to extract information and knowledge. Conducting an analysis of the pool of ideas from two online competitions, Silvertant is able to identify certain patterns: The ideas reflect problems consumers are facing and provide suggestions for how they could be solved (Silvertant 2010, 224ff.). Furthermore, the ideas provide implicit or sticky information, which the organizing company would not have been able to identify through conventional market research methods (Silvertant 2010, 224ff.). Besides these valuable conclusions, however, Silvertant's analysis does not systematically show which types of information and knowledge could be derived from the pool of ideas generated. The same applies to other studies on idea competitions: While they theoretically distinguish different types of information and knowledge (Piller and Walcher 2006, 307; Walcher 2007, 20ff.; Silvertant 2010, 29), they do not investigate which types were specifically produced by idea competitions. To lay the ground for the empirical part of this study, which will investigate this question, the different types of information and knowledge discussed in innovation management and specifically open innovation literature are explained in the following subsection.

Second, the following subsection points towards another shortcoming of empirical research on idea competitions: Studies mainly focus on the *outcomes* of the method – the ideas generated and participants identified – and few studies look at the *process* itself. Exceptions are, for example, the studies of Silvertant (2011) and Bartl (2006). Silvertant analyses how the process of idea creation and evaluation influences the

[62] The information can further be tapped by involving them after the competition – e.g., through innovation workshops – into the further development of ideas.

quality of the ideas (Silvertant 2011, 237). Bartl (2006, 274) examines factors that influence the capability of participants to transfer innovation-relevant insights when taking part in virtual idea generation methods. However, no studies could be identified that analyze the innovation-relevant knowledge that can be obtained from the *process* of idea competitions. Likewise, none analyzes how insights are transferred from the "knowledge owner" to the "knowledge seeker." Nonetheless, theories of knowledge management have investigated these aspects in the general context of corporate innovation (Nonaka and Takeuchi 1995; Cohen and Levinthal 1990). The insights from this field that are relevant for this study are briefly summarized below.

Types of information and knowledge

Information and knowledge that are relevant for (open) innovation purposes are generally categorized as need-related and solution-related information as well as tacit and explicit knowledge.

Need-related information encompasses desires, preferences and user requirements regarding functionality, performance, quality, and design of the product. **Solution-related information** helps transform needs into a good or service (Reichwald et al. 2007, 24; Walcher 2007, 20ff.). The latter is traditionally attributed to companies (Reichwald et al. 2007, 24). However, research on the role of consumers in innovation processes also grants them the ability to provide solution-related information (see section 2.1.6).

Following Polanyi, researchers further distinguish between two forms in which knowledge is conveyed: explicitly and implicitly (or tacitly) (Polanyi 1958, 14; Nonaka 1991/1994; von Hippel 1994; Reichwald and Piller 2006, 69). **Explicit knowledge** can be codified "in words and numbers and shared in the form of data, scientific formulae, specifications, manuals and the like" (Nonaka and Konno 1998, 42). However, knowledge often cannot be managed like other resources as some aspects of it are difficult to grasp – they are tacit.

Tacit knowledge is said to be particularly relevant for innovation (Senker 1993; Hernández-Serrano et al. 2002; von Hippel 2005, 67; Goffin and Koners 2011). It is regarded as highly personal and is often possessed unconsciously. As Polanyi (1966, 4) puts it, "We know more than we can tell." Although the term "tacit knowledge" is widely used in innovation literature (see, for example, Takeuchi and Nonaka 1986; Mascitelli 2000; Hernández-Serrano et al. 2002; Goffin et al. 2010), it is also criticized as being a "black box" or "residual category" that encompasses all types of knowledge that cannot be easily codified (see, e.g., Styhre 2004, 178). However, Styhre acknowledges that "the concept of tacit knowledge can be very useful in practice without being satisfyingly defined within a theoretical discourse" (Styhre 2004, 179). Two different understandings dominate the current body of literature: When Polanyi refers to "tacit knowledge," he describes things that go unsaid due to a lack of understanding of the subject. For example, we cannot fully understand through logic alone how one orchestra conductor is better than another. In contrast, Nonaka and Takeuchi (1995) as well as von Hippel (2005, 67)[63] – who uses the term "sticky knowledge" – talk about subjects that people may understand, but which are costly to articulate and tap (Boisot 1998, 57; see also, Styhre 2004, 180). The present study follows this second concept of tacit knowledge. It has both a cognitive dimension, consisting of "beliefs, ideals, values, schemata, and mental models, which are deeply ingrained in us and which we often take for granted" (Nonaka and Konno 1998, 42), and also a technical dimension including concrete know-how and skills (Nonaka 1991, 98; Nonaka and Konno 1998, 42; see also Senker 1993, 210).[64] Through socialization, tacit knowledge is often tied to a certain context or environment. Thus, it can be assumed that it is only of use in such a context (Nonaka and Takeuchi 1995; Grant 1996 and 1997; Büschken and Blümm 2000).

The types of information described above (need-related and solution-related), as well as the forms in which they are conveyed (explicitly or tacitly), are frequently referred to in innovation literature, albeit not systematically. Figure 12 presents the different possible combinations of types of information and forms of knowledge transfer identified in literature. The figure shows how both need- and solution-related information can theoretically be transferred either tacitly or explicitly. However, the extent to which these correlations hold in practice has yet to be examined.

---

63 Von Hippel (2005, 67) writes: "The stickiness of a unit of information is defined as the incremental expenditure required to transfer that unit of information to a specified location in a form usable by specified information seeker. When expenditure is low, information stickiness is low, when it is high, stickiness is high."

64 Senker (1993, 212) writes: "Accumulated technical knowledge may be stored in the form of a patent or as documented know-how. More often, relevant information [to solve problems which crop up in the course of innovation] exists randomly in society as tacit knowledge and relates to the context of a specific problem."

Figure 12: Relationship between different types of innovation-relevant knowledge

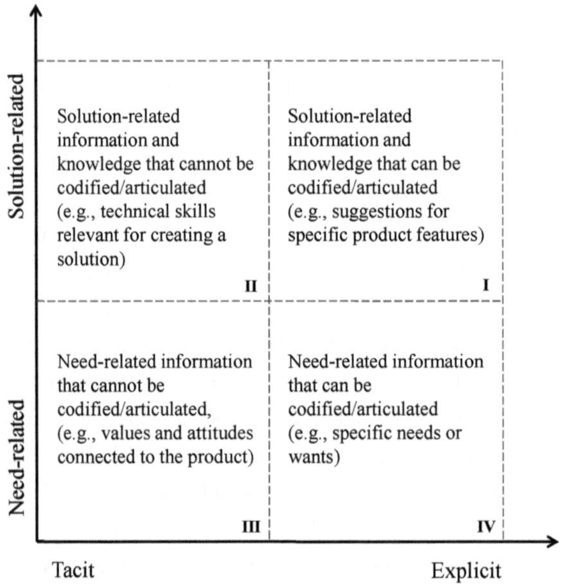

Source: created by author.

Distinguishing between information and knowledge

The precise definition of the terms information and knowledge has been a profound philosophical debate dating back to Plato (see, e.g., Styhre 2004). Studies in information science suggest that we understand data, information, and knowledge as a hierarchy (see figure 13). Data (or raw facts) that are related to each other become information, and knowledge, in turn, is information that is combined, put in context, and/or applied. Davenport and Prusak (1998) writes that "most people have an intuitive sense that knowledge is broader, deeper, and richer than data or information." In English, the word *knowledge* can encompass skills, know-how, expertise, capabilities, and experiences.[65]

[65] The most frequently cited working definition of knowledge is that of Davenport and Prusak (1998, 5): "Knowledge is a fluid mix of framed experience, values, contextual information, expert insight and grounded intuition that provides an environment and framework for evaluating and incorporating new experiences and information. It originates and is applied in the minds of knowers."

Figure 13: Data, information, and knowledge

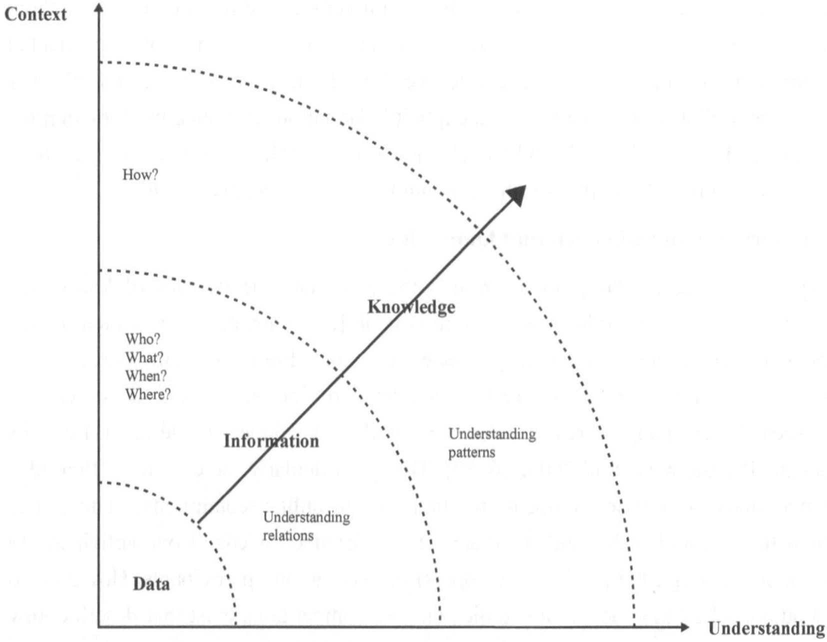

Source: adapted from Bellinger et al. 2004.

Studies in knowledge management and innovation literature, however, often do not follow such clear-cut definitions. In fact, they often fail to properly define "information" and "knowledge." Likewise, those studies that do define the terms use highly differing definitions, while other researchers even use the terms synonymously.

For example, the term "explicit knowledge" is widely used in innovation literature (von Hippel 1994; Nonaka and Konno 1998, 42; Reichwald and Piller 2006, 69; Walcher 2007, 20ff.; Silvertant 2011, 29ff.). Zeleny (2005), however, argues that "all knowledge is tacit," and only once it is captured, or made explicit, it becomes information. At the same time, von Hippel (2005, 67) uses the term "sticky information" to describe information that is costly to transfer but nonetheless vital for new product development. In essence, he refers to what others would name "tacit knowledge." Similarly, one could argue that what innovation literature calls "solution-related information" could already be considered knowledge, as creating solutions involves a certain level of expertise and experience.

Concluding, it can be said that the boundaries between information and knowledge are blurry. This study, therefore, sticks to the terminology in the research of key authors that lay the groundwork for this study. It refers to need- and solution-oriented information, as coined by, for example, Reichwald and Piller (2006), and Walcher (2007), as well as to tacit/implicit and explicit information, as coined by, for example, Nonaka and Takeuchi (1995) and Nonaka and Konno (1998). When referring to these four types at once, the study uses the term *innovation-relevant knowledge.*

Transferring innovation-relevant knowledge

Bogers et al. (2010, 867) point towards the fact that "the transfer of knowledge between a user and a producer is a central issue in […] innovation." As a method that opens up corporate innovation processes to input from external sources, idea competitions are expected to create some level of interaction and direct contact between the company representatives (i.e., product developers or designers) and its (potential) customers (Soll 2006, 56–57). This is particularly the case for offline idea competitions or online competitions tied to an online community. Thus, idea competitions could enable and moderate the transfer of knowledge from participants to the organizer (e.g., the product developers) or even among participants. However, to the author's best knowledge, no studies on idea competitions exist that describe **how innovation-relevant knowledge is transferred** from the consumer to the company professionals or **what factors enable this transfer**.

The only related studies found examine the transfer of knowledge among participants. For that purpose, some researchers combine idea competitions with online communities to foster interaction or "co-opetition" among participants, which is found to yield a higher quantity and quality of ideas (Füller et al. 2011, 270; Hutter et al. 2011). They examine, for example, the benefits participants obtain by revealing their knowledge as well as how and why they support each other (Hutter et al. 2011).

On the other hand, research in the area of knowledge management has thoroughly studied how knowledge is generated and transferred (Cohen and Levinthal 1990; Nonaka and Takeuchi 1995). For example, Nonaka and Takeuchi published several books and articles on precisely this topic (Nonaka 1991/1994; Nonaka and Takeuchi 1995).[66] In their well-known book *The Knowledge-Creating Company* (1995), the

[66] Due to a lack of shared definitions (see the above-described difference between definitions by Polanyi 1958 and Nonaka and Takeuchi 1995) scholars also disagree when it comes to the question

researchers examine the codification of tacit knowledge. They describe that "knowledge is created through [a] conversion between tacit and explicit knowledge" which happens along four steps (Nonaka 1994, 18–19): (1) From tacit to tacit, (2) from tacit to explicit, (3) from explicit to explicit, and (4) from explicit to tacit. This is also referred to as the SECI-model, which stands for socialization, externalization, combination, and internalization (Nonaka 1994), with each term describing the stage (or mode) of knowledge conversion (see figure 14).[67] Socialization happens through "observation, imitation, and practice" (Nonaka 1991, 99). However, systematic insights are missing as knowledge is transferred in its tacit form (Nonaka 1991, 99). Transferring tacit into explicit knowledge is difficult and can be costly. But it is possible through "externalization," which "requires expression of tacit knowledge and its translation into comprehensible forms that can be understood by others." This process "involves techniques that help to express one's ideas or images as words, concepts, figurative language (such as metaphors, analogies, or narratives), and visuals" (Nonaka and Konno 1998, 43). As soon as knowledge is externalized, it can be combined with other types of explicit knowledge. Internalizing knowledge means incorporating the explicit knowledge into one's very own tacit knowledge base (Nonaka and Konno 1998, 45). However, the conversion between the different types of knowledge is not linear, but rather it moves back and forth along this continuum.[68]

A very similar process is described by Cohen and Levinthal (1990) in their concept of "**absorptive capacity**." They define it as "a firm's ability to recognize the value of new information, assimilate it, and apply it to commercial ends" (1990, 128). Like in Nonaka and Takeuchi's phases of knowledge transfer, four phases can be identified from this definition: (1) knowledge identification and acquisition, (2) its assimilation

---

of whether tacit knowledge can be converted into explicit knowledge. In his work from 1958, which coined the term, Polanyi negates this, explaining that tacit knowledge can only be transferred in its tacit form (i.e., through socialization): "An art cannot be specified in detail, cannot be transmitted by prescription, since no prescription for it exists. It can be passed on only by example from master to apprentice" (Polanyi 1958, 52). Nonaka and Takeuchi's work, in turn, is based on the assumption that the transfer is possible (Nonaka and Takeuchi 1995).

67 The conversion from tacit to explicit and back is referred to as the epistemological dimension of the SECI model. Nonaka also distinguishes an ontological dimension, which looks at those who carry knowledge: individuals, groups, or organizations. Through a spiral process of knowledge creation, knowledge can move from tacit to explicit (and back), as well as from individuals to groups and finally to organizations.

68 In fact, a variety of authors argue that knowledge is rarely exclusively explicit or tacit, but can also appear in a mixed form and thus have different grades of "codifiability" (see, e.g., Li and Gao 2003; Reichwald and Piller 2006, 70).

and (3) transformation, and its (4) application or exploitation. The first phase refers to the identification and acquisition of valuable external knowledge; it corresponding to socialization and externalization in Nonaka and Takeuchi's model. Assimilation refers to what Nonaka and Takeuchi call combination with one's own knowledge set. Transformation and application/exploitation refer, respectively, to the internalization of knowledge and ultimately its use.[69]

Furthermore, knowledge management literature names a variety of factors that enable the transfer of knowledge – for example, personal interaction (Senker 1993, 212), prior knowledge, and trust (Sawhney and Prandelli 2000, 261–262; Soll 2006, 58). However, no studies could be identified that examine what factors enable the transfer of knowledge from the consumer to the company professionals throughout the process of idea competitions.

Figure 14: SECI Model: "Modes of the knowledge creation"

From / *To*	Tacit knowledge	Explicit knowledge
Tacit knowledge	**Socialization**	**Externalization**
Explicit knowledge	**Internalization**	**Combination**

Source: Nonaka 1994, 19.

[69] While both Cohen and Levinthal (1990) as well as Nonaka and Takeuchi (1995) develop their concepts with the firm as a unit of analysis, these concepts have been applied to individuals, groups, or even nations (see Nonaka and Takeuchi's ontological dimension). The present study focuses on the level of individuals.

Concluding, there is a good understanding of the types of information and knowledge that idea competitions can yield. However, they have not been empirically investigated. Furthermore, there seems to be a good understanding of how knowledge is transferred from one person to the other, be it in the context of innovation or in other contexts. However, no study thus far has examined how knowledge is transferred throughout the process of idea competitions or what factors enable this transfer.

2.3.5 Relevance of idea competitions for low-income markets

Idea competitions have gained increasing popularity – also in the context of low-income markets. There are a number of practical examples that apply competitions to identify or generate ideas for products, services and business models which work in low-income contexts in emerging and developing countries. However, the examples found are almost exclusively conducted online and rarely engage the actual target group – that is, the consumers of the product and service ideas generated. Rather, the idea competitions identified mostly address employees, scientists, researchers, engineers, and designers from all over the world (see table 10, which shows an exemplary selection). Business plan competitions, such as Ashoka Changemakers or the SEED Award, are closest to the actual target group, as they address entrepreneurs in developing countries. Yet, these competitions are usually not conducted to generate ideas. Rather, they aim to identify promising business models which are already in place. None of the examples found has been documented or empirically analyzed. The examples can only be found on the respective websites.

The Nokia Open Studios (NOS) idea competition was the only one identified that was conducted with low-income consumers (Jung and Chipchase 2008). This competition targets residents of shantytowns in Brazil, China, Ghana, and India. The respective communities were chosen based on the researchers' aim "to learn from [them] what we are unlikely to find elsewhere either because of their unique context, or because within that context trends are much easier to spot" (Jung and Chipchase 2008, 3). While the results of this study have not been published in an academic journal or the like, they are documented as a whitepaper accessible online. The researchers report the following **strengths of the method** when applied for idea generation (or "ideation") purposes, which seem to particularly address the challenges of conducting idea competitions in low-income markets (as outlined in section 2.1.2).

First, the method generates an “obvious output” – namely, a documented idea – that “can become a vehicle by which to engage and stimulate discussion amongst [...] stakeholders” (Jung and Chipchase 2008, 23). In fact, they were able to collect 222 ideas from three communities (ibid., 8), which underpins the assumption that idea competitions do serve to generate ideas with low-income consumers.[70]

Second, the method grants participants “ample incubation time [...] to internalize the theme and their ideas” and lets them “work at their own pace, a process that encourages reflection and adds depth to the entries.” This advantage is particularly obvious when comparing the idea competitions with other methods. For example, Jung and Chipchase (2008, 21) report that the ideas which resulted from a one-day workshop were “directly influenced by the discussion or the stimulus material made available to the participants.” A street survey was also used with low-income consumers; however, it revealed only spontaneous reactions and did not serve to yield deeper innovation-relevant knowledge.

Due to the minimal guidance for participants, idea competitions support “discovering topics that can easily be overlooked by other inherently more guided methods” (Jung and Chipchase 2008, 22). Furthermore, seeking people’s opinions is appreciated by the target group and can contribute to building trust. Repeated visits in the community to promote the competition build relationships with key informants. In addition, using visual material such as drawings can help overcome challenges associated with low-literacy of participants (Viswanathan et al. 2011) and contribute to acquiring implicit information.

In Jung and Chipchase’s analysis of the ideas generated, they first clustered them along themes that emerged from the submissions.[71] Then, they discussed the clusters in search of conclusions. The results provided valuable insights into the needs,

---

[70] The motivation of people to participate encompassed extrinsic as well as intrinsic motives. Most participants sought to take advantage of the “rare opportunity to express their ideas on an intellectual level to outsiders.” Others wanted to “elevate their standing within the community through contact with representatives of a respected corporation,” “show off creative skills,” “reflect on their own life,” or simply conduct “a fun family activity” (Jung and Chipchase 2008, 19).

[71] The themes identified were: Device symbolism (mobile phones in the shape of a mango or a heart), functional enhancement for special needs (loud speakers for announcements, emergency alarms, environmental conditions, pen drive), mobile convergence and magical function (such as a “peace button” as part of the phone).

aspirations, lifestyles, and living conditions of the participants.[72] Being able to talk to the creators about their ideas further contributed to gaining a better understanding for the specific use context and living conditions of the entrants. For example, one entrant designed a phone that shows the level of pollution, hoping that this would raise people's awareness for environmental matters. Another designed a phone that allows carrying multiple SIM cards as a way to lower telephone costs (Jung and Chipchase 2008, 13–17).

Table 10: Selected idea competitions in the context of low-income markets

Organizer	Target group	Topic (examples)	Description
Ashoka Change-makers	Entrepreneurs in developing countries	Competition topics range from clean water to sustainable urban housing.	Changemakers hosts collaborative online competitions to identify and connect the best social innovators and implementers. Participants compete to surface the most promising solutions, and then collaborate to refine, enrich, and implement them.[73]
Empowering people award (Siemens)	Inventors and developers all over the world	The award seeks low-tech solutions or products for basic supply problems in developing and emerging countries across a variety of sectors.	The aim of the "empowering people. Award" is to identify low-tech solutions or products making them accessible to everyone. The innovations are aimed at enabling sustainable improvement in the supply of basic needs in developing countries.[74]
Google Project 10^{100}	Individuals from all over the world	Categories include community, opportunity, energy, environment, health, education, and shelter.	Online call for ideas to change the world by helping as many people as possible.[75]

[72] Winners were identified via a close review of the entries, which were debated by the research team. Besides the criterion "relevance of the idea for the community", no other criteria are reported.

[73] Ashoka Changemakers website, accessed May 1, 2013, http://www.changemakers.com

[74] "empowering people. Award," Siemen's website, accessed May 1, 2013, http://www.empowering-people-award.siemens-stiftung.org

[75] "Project 10 to the Hundred," accessed May 1, 2013, http://www.project10tothe100.com

Inno Centive Rockefeller Foundation	Scientists and researchers with technical knowledge	Exemplary topics might be solar water treatment systems, small-scale river turbines, or low-cost rainwater harvesting storage tanks.	The series of challenges are organized to tap the knowledge of the platform's network to create solutions for pressing development challenges.[76]
Nokia Open Studios (NOS)	Low-income consumers in shanty towns in Brazil, China, Ghana, and India	The topic was "Design your dream phone."	Offline design competition with the objective of generating information about the role of future technologies in participant's lives by giving residents the opportunity to articulate their needs and aspirations (Jung and Chipchase 2008).
Open IDEO	Designers and tinkerers worldwide	Topics encompass ideas for business models ("How might we use social business to improve health in low-income communities?") as well as product and service solutions ("How might we improve maternal health with mobile technologies for low-income countries?").	OpenIDEO is an online platform for creative thinkers. The objective is to design for social good.[77]
SEED Awards	Entrepreneurs in developing countries	Award seeks to find entrepreneurial and innovative ideas that are locally driven and have potential to contribute to sustainable development in emerging or developing countries.	The SEED Award is an annual awards scheme conducted online. It is designed to find the most promising, innovative and locally led start-up social and environmental entrepreneurs in countries with developing and emerging economies.[78]

Source: created by author.

[76] "The GlobalGiveback Initiative Challenge," InnoCentive website, accessed May 1, 2013, https://www.innocentive.com/ar/landing/global-giveback.gsp
[77] "OpenIDEO," accessed May 1, 2013, http://www.openideo.com
[78] "SEED Initiative," accessed May 1, 2013, http://www.seedinit.org

In conclusion, the study from Jung and Chipchase does provide preliminary evidence that (a) idea competitions serve to generate creative ideas with low-income consumers and (b) that analyzing the ideas can yield innovation-relevant knowledge. Nonetheless, the study does not distinguish and examine specific types of information and knowledge, nor does it shed light on how they are transferred from the idea creator to the company. Furthermore, their study does not thoroughly assess the characteristics of the entrants – apart from assessing their socio-economic characteristics (Jung and Chipchase 2008, 8ff.). All in all, it can be concluded that idea competitions are a promising method to integrate low-income consumers into innovation and an area that warrants further research.

2.3.6 Intermediate conclusion and research gaps

In corporate practice, idea competitions have gained increasing popularity.[79] Surely, the method cannot substitute the research and development (R&D) activities of a company (Soll 2006, 55; Silvertant 2011, 226). Nonetheless, its results can complement the work of the R&D department. Through including customers in the fuzzy front end, companies can increase their idea pool and gain access to relevant knowledge. Consequently, idea competitions can increase the efficiency of the innovation process through reducing innovation time and related costs and through increasing the acceptability of new products and services. Researchers have thus shown increasing interest in the method. Nonetheless, empirical research still shows two major gaps.

(a) Lack of empirical research on idea competitions that inform innovation for low-income markets

While there are several studies on idea competitions as a method to integrate consumers into the early stages of innovation processes (e.g., Soll 2006; Walcher 2007; Silvertant 2011), the method remains relatively underexplored (Soll 2006, 3; Haller et al. 2009, 2; Silvertant 2011, 69ff.). Furthermore, all empirical studies on idea competitions focus on competitions in the developed world (Soll 2006; Piller and Walcher 2006; Walcher 2007; Silvertant 2011). To the author's best knowledge, no academic studies are known that empirically analyze idea competitions conducted to inform product development processes for low-income markets. Only one practical example could be identified: The Nokia Open Studios (Jung and Chipchase 2008). The

[79] For an exemplary overview of practical examples, see Haller et al. (2009, 29).

results presented in the whitepaper point towards the applicability of this method in low-income contexts. The organizing company managed to generate a considerable number of ideas with consumers, and analyzing these ideas supported the identification of trends. The reported success factors are in line with recent innovation research.

Furthermore, a number of studies that identified user innovations from low-income contexts could be found (Fukushima 2009; Gupta 2010; Nair et al. 2012; Viswanathan and Sridharan 2012). There is additional anecdotal evidence of the creative capabilities of low-income consumers (see section 2.2.2). This leads to the assumption that "creative mainstream consumers," or even lead users, can also be found in low-income contexts. However, there are currently no empirical studies that investigate whether idea competitions serve to identify creative or innovative users in low-income contexts. Adapting and applying idea competitions to the context of low-income markets could help close this research gap.

(b) Lack of empirical research on the types and transfer of information and knowledge generated throughout idea competitions

Studies on idea competitions have thus far mostly focused on the information and knowledge that can be obtained from the outcomes of idea competitions – namely, (a) creative ideas and (b) lead users (e.g., Soll 2006; Walcher 2007; Belz et al. 2009, 14–18; Silvertant 2011). Nonetheless, the specific types of innovation-relevant knowledge they yield have received little attention. Furthermore, few studies have taken a process perspective when analyzing the results of idea competitions.

A gap in the research lies in determining how innovation-relevant knowledge is transferred throughout idea competitions and what factors enable this transfer. Knowing what types of insights can be expected could enable the method be used more strategically with more targeted results. Similarly, understanding how insights are transferred from consumers to companies could influence the way idea competitions are designed, which in turn could influence the quality of the results. Thus, investigating these research gaps would not only benefit product development for low-income contexts, but also make a contribution to innovation research in general.

3 Research design

The present chapter describes the research design of the study. As illustrated in figure 15, a research design is composed of three key elements (Creswell 2009, 5): (1) the underlying **research paradigms** on what constitutes knowledge, (2) the **research strategy** chosen to test or build knowledge, and (3) the **methods** for data collection and analysis.

Section 3.1 first frames the context for this research endeavor by providing a brief overview of the different views on testing and building theory about phenomena in low-income or BoP markets. Second, it elaborates on the underlying research paradigm as well as the research strategy chosen. It then discusses case studies as a research strategy, and explains how case studies were selected and applied.

Section 3.2 starts with describing the design and implementation of the idea competition. This is done to provide transparency and contribute to further research in this area, which might build on and refine the approach. Moreover, the methods for data collection and analysis are described along the three units of analysis: ideas, participants, and process.

Figure 15: Key elements of a research design

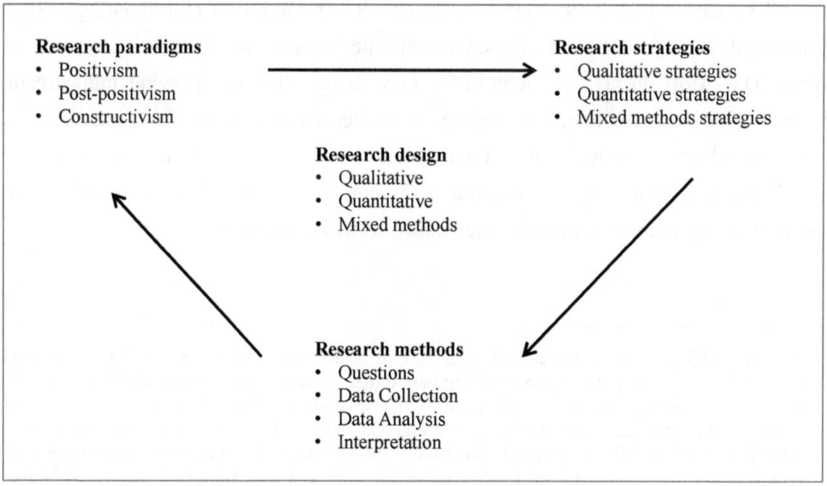

Source: adapted from Creswell 2009, 5.

3.1 Research paradigm and strategy

3.1.1 Theory building in BoP contexts

The role of business in contributing to development objectives, such as poverty alleviation, is a fairly new topic – both in business literature and in practice. Even newer is the concept that development can be fostered through core business activities, and not only through philanthropy. The first book on this topic was published in 2004 by C.K. Prahalad, and the first papers came out slightly before (Prahalad and Lieberthal 1998; Prahalad and Hammond 2002; Prahalad and Hart 2002). Articles on the relevance of innovation in that context soon followed (e.g., Hart and Christensen 2002; Anderson and Billou 2007; Mendoza and Thelen 2008; SadreGhazi 2008; Simanis et al. 2008; Gupta 2010; Waibel 2012). As discussed in chapter 2, most of these studies are descriptive or conceptual in nature.[80] This reflects the early stage of research and knowledge in this field, which still requires "exploring and understanding" (Creswell 2009, 3) as well as theory building (see also London and Hart 2004, 2).

Herrndorf (forthcoming, 39) points out the different views on building theory in BoP contexts. As outlined in table 11, some researchers argue that no new theory is necessary ("BoP as business as usual"), while others stress that a specific "BoP theory" is needed ("BoP as a special phenomenon"). Herrndorf (forthcoming, 43ff.) further elaborates that, between these two extreme poles, more moderate views can be found. The "BoP through the lens of" – view argues that by applying mainstream theory to low-income contexts, one can gain a better understanding of original theories and extend them by exploring their boundaries. Similarly, the "BoP as a polar case" – view recognizes that insights from the BoP context may even help alter, refine, or further develop mainstream theory (Herrndorf, forthcoming, 43).[81]

80 The same findings apply to research on other aspects of the "base of the pyramid" (BoP) concept, which is largely descriptive or conceptual in nature (e.g., Prahalad and Hammond 2002; Hart and London 2005; Brugmann and Prahalad 2007). Those studies that build on empirical evidence mostly follow a qualitative approach (e.g., London and Hart 2004; Sánchez et al. 2006; Seelos and Mair 2007; London 2009; Waibel 2012; Herrndorf, forthcoming). However, it can be observed that more recently, the number of quantitative empirical studies is increasing (e.g., Badry 2009 and Klein 2008).

81 Herrndorf (forthcoming, 44) cites the example of stakeholder theory to illustrate this point: "While businesses might traditionally seek to interact with stakeholders of strategic importance, besides their stockholders and customers, BoP research suggests to talk to 'fringe stakeholders,' that are

Table 11: Views on building "BoP theory"

Approach	Concept of BoP markets	View on existing theory	Focus of theory testing and building	Examples
"BoP as business as usual"	BoP markets do not differ in quality or nature from more established markets.	Existing theory can explain phenomena in BoP markets.	Existing theory can be used to explain BoP phenomena.	Akula (2008)
"BoP through the lens of"	BoP markets are different from upscale markets and those in "developed" countries.	BoP markets can be understood through more established theory.	Insights from BoP markets can help determine the boundaries of established theory (and the conditions in which they apply).	Hart and Christensen (2002); Webb et al. (2009a); Rivera-Santos and Rufín (2010)
"BoP as a polar case"	BoP markets are different from "normal" markets, but mainly in size rather than in quality ("less formal").	BoP markets can be partly understood by existing theory, but it has gaps that could be filled by theorizing from BoP data.	BoP data can be used as "polar cases" to extend or improve existing theory, not for building specific BoP theory per se.	Hart and Sharma (2004); Seelos and Mair (2007)
"BoP as a special phenomenon"	BoP markets are fundamentally different from upscale markets and those in "developed" countries.	Applying standard theory is misleading and prevents a proper understanding of BoP markets.	Building new models that target and explain the specifics of BoP markets.	London and Hart (2004); Prahalad (2004); Simanis and Hart (2011)

Source: Herrndorf, forthcoming, 41ff. (with slight adaptations).

The latter two views are in line with the objectives and approach of the present study, which argues that the body of knowledge already existing in innovation management cannot be ignored. In fact, the present study has two objectives: (1) to transfer insights from mainstream innovation research to the context of low-income markets, testing its

'remote, weak, poor, disinterested, isolated, non-legitimate, or nonhuman' (Hart and Sharma 2004, 10), challenging traditional insights into selecting and prioritizing stakeholders."

boundaries; (2) to generate new insights by applying what is known in a new context. This may eventually help to enhance existing concepts and theory – or even contribute to building middle range theory (Merton 1968).

3.1.2 Research paradigm

Guba and Lincoln (1994, 105) advise making a study's underlying research paradigm explicit.[82] They define paradigm as a "basic belief system or worldview that guides the investigator, not only in choices of method but in ontologically and epistemologically fundamental ways" (ibid.). Table 12 provides an overview of three different research paradigms: positivism, post-positivism, and constructivism.[83] The post-positivist paradigm[84] assumes that reality is imperfectly comprehensible "because of basically flawed human intellectual mechanisms and the fundamentally intractable nature of phenomena" (Guba and Lincoln 1994, 109). It is a more critical view as opposed to the positivist standpoint, which argues that there is only one objective reality which can be captured and understood. Constructivist paradigms, on the other hand, claim that reality is subjective; it is constructed by the human intellect and hence value-, time- and context-bound (Lincoln and Guba 1985, 37).

As elaborated above (chapter 1 and section 3.1.1), the present study builds on existing theory and concepts which it aims to test and eventually alter. However, its primary ambition is to expand theory by adapting the lead user concept to low-income markets, by proposing characteristics of creative consumers and by developing a model for transferring innovation-relevant knowledge through idea competitions. In doing so, the study mostly builds on the post-positivist viewpoint that knowledge develops as theory is continuously generated, tested, and refined through replicated findings that are "probably true," albeit always "subject to falsification" (Guba and Lincoln 1994, 109).

---

82 They further point out that the use of qualitative and quantitative methods do not indicate a certain research paradigm, as they can both be used for studies with a positivist, post-positivist, constructivist or any other paradigm (Guba and Lincoln 1994, 105).

83 Please note that this is a simplification, as some authors distinguish additional paradigms – e.g., critical theory and other related ideological positions (see Guba and Lincoln 1994, 110), advocacy/participatory and pragmatism (see Creswell 2009, 6ff.). Also note that these views have a history and are products of sophisticated discussions and debate. It is, however, beyond the scope of this study to elaborate on these questions. For more insights, see, for example, Morgan and Smircich (1980), Guba and Lincoln (1994), Gephart (2004), Creswell (2009).

84 Post-positivism originated from the work of Karl Popper (1963) and Thomas Kuhn (1970).

Table 12: Basic beliefs of alternative paradigms

	Positivism	Post-positivism	Constructivism
Ontology *What is the nature of reality?*	There is only one "real" reality (naïve realism).	Reality is only "imperfectly apprehendable" (critical realism).	There are different (and sometimes conflicting) realities that are "constructed" (i.e., the product of the human intellect). They are local and specific.
Epistemology *How can knowledge be acquired?*	Objectivist: Findings are "true"; the investigator determines "how things really are."	Objectivist: Findings are "probably true"; one can approximate but never fully grasp reality.	Subjectivist: Findings are "created" in interaction among investigators and respondents.
Methodology	Hypothesis are verified; chiefly quantitative methods	Falsification of hypothesis; may include qualitative methods	Hermeneutical/ dialectical

Source: created by author based on Guba and Lincoln 1994, 109ff.

3.1.3 Embedded research design

Creswell explains that many research designs lie on a continuum between qualitative and quantitative, only being able to say that they *tend* to one side of the continuum or the other (Creswell 2009, 3). These research designs are called mixed methods designs. According to Creswell (2006, 67), this study can be classified as an embedded design, which "is a mixed methods design in which one data set provides a supportive, secondary role in a study based primarily on the other data type." While this study is **primarily qualitative**, quantitative data sets provide a supportive, supplementary role. This is in line with Miles and Huberman (1994, 41), who believe that the "quantitative-qualitative argument is essentially unproductive." They "see no reason to tie the distinction to epistemological preferences" and show that both methods (and thus data) are complementary, compensating for the weaknesses and blind spots of each other (see also Eisenhardt 1989, 533; Dul and Hak 2008, 23).[85]

[85] This view, however, is not shared by all researchers. In fact, some researchers argue that qualitative and quantitative research (and thus data) would be incompatible. These different views are essentially based on wholly different philosophical convictions (Yin 2003, 15). Consequently, there is no "right" or "wrong."

Aiming to further investigate propositions derived from innovation theory (see chapter 2), the study has a small deductive element. The respective research questions ask to what extent insights about idea competitions and lead users hold true in low-income contexts (see table 1, chapter 1, research questions 1 and 2a) and whether they have to be modified for this particular context. In other words, they identify "the scope conditions" of the theory (George and Bennet 2005, 75). These deductive parts, however, only serve as the basis for discussing the potential modifications and further development of existing concepts (see chapter 5), building the basis for the inductive parts of the study.

Although employing quantitative methods, this research is still primarily inductive as it focuses on understanding low-income consumers as a source of innovation in the early phases of new product development – a rather new research topic. This is in line with Creswell, who points out that a qualitative approach is appropriate "if a concept or phenomenon needs to be understood because little research has been done on it" (Creswell 2009, 18). This is also apparent in the nature of research questions 2b–4c, which are open questions, asking "what" (Yin 2003, 1–2; Creswell 2009, 18) (see table 1 in chapter 1).

What is more, the qualitative approach is well suited to studying phenomena in low-income markets as it is characterized by its flexibility, which makes it particularly suitable for studying complex, real-life situations in their particular context. It also aims for an in-depth and holistic understanding and tries to get closer to what is being studied, with sensitivity to the context (Punch 2005, 234–256). Consequently, "the possibility for understanding latent, underlying or non-obvious issues is strong" (ibid.). Samples are small and guided by theoretical rather than probabilistic considerations. Also, its methods offer a greater flexibility and are more diverse (Punch 2005, 234–256).[86]

---

[86] This is also relevant for more pragmatic reasons: Getting access to low-income communities requires establishing relationships and trust (Seelos and Mair 2007, 53; Badry 2009, 4; Viswanathan and Sridharan 2012, 563), which takes time. Also, qualitatively investigating small samples more in depth seems to be more feasible in low-income markets than implementing quantitative methods such as surveys (see section 2.1.2).

3.1.4 Case studies as a research strategy

The present study builds on case studies as a research strategy (Eisenhardt 1989; Yin 2003; Punch 2005, 144).[87] Case studies can be used to test and generate theory (Eisenhardt 1989, 535; see also Bonoma 1985; Miles and Huberman 1994; Yin 2003; Myers 2009). Creswell (2009, 13) defines case studies as "a strategy of inquiry in which the researcher explores in depth a program, event, activity, process, or one or more individuals. Cases are bounded by time and activity, and researchers collect detailed information using a variety of data collection procedures over a sustained period of time."

Case studies are recommended for "new topic areas" (Eisenhardt 1989, 532), when existing theory on the topic of interest is limited and when the topic is broad or complex (e.g., when there are more variables of interest) (Dul and Hak 2008, 24). As outlined above, this is the case for the present study. Furthermore, case study research has successfully been employed – for both theory testing and building purposes – in the context of innovation research (e.g., Leonard-Barton 1988) as well as for research on low-income markets (e.g., Sánchez et al. 2006; Seelos and Mair 2007; London 2009; Halme et al. 2012).

Embedded multiple case study design

The specific research questions of this study are explored applying an embedded multiple case study design (Scholz and Tietje 2002; Yin 2003, 40) (see figure 16). Designs are "embedded" when the same case study investigates more than one unit of analysis (Yin 2003, 40). Here, there are three units of analysis within a single case: the ideas, the characteristics of participants, and the process of the idea competition. As multiple-case designs are likely to be stronger than single-case designs, the case study is replicated three times (Yin 2003, 52). The replication is a parallel, not serial – that is, the case studies do not build on each other's outcomes, but rather explore the same questions in parallel (Dul and Hak 2008, 44).

---

87 According to Yin (1981/1984), Eisenhardt (1989, 534), Punch (2005, 144) and Creswell (2009, 13), a case study is more a strategy than a method.

Figure 16: Basic types of case study designs

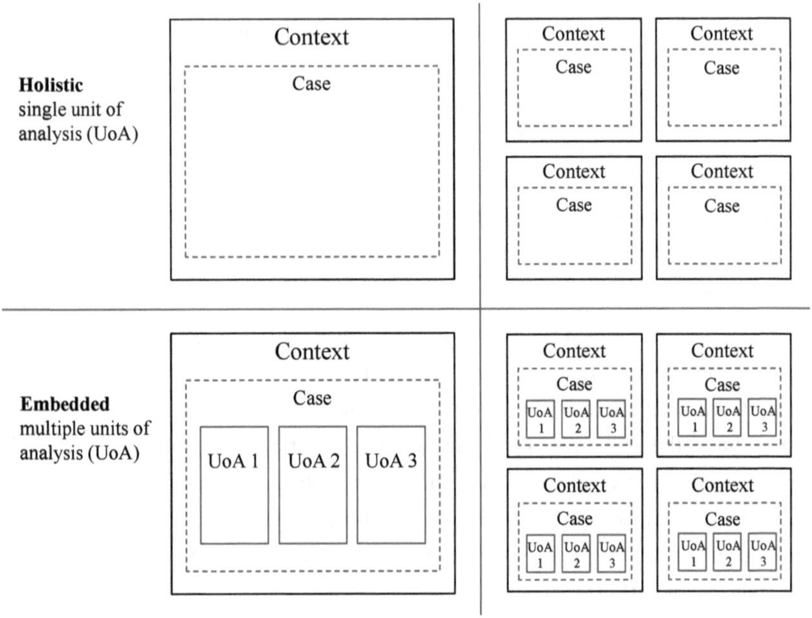

Source: Yin 2003, 40.

Data collection and analysis in case study research

The unique strength of the case study method is its richness in data. It can apply various data collection methods and process multiple sources of evidence (Eisenhardt 1989, 534; Yin 2003, 8; Punch 2005, 145), with "data needing to converge in a triangulated fashion" (Yin 2003, 12). Furthermore, Bonoma (1985, 203) points out that case studies – like other qualitative methods – "rely heavily on verbal reports (personal interviews) and un-obtrusive observation as primary data sources. However, the case method is distinguished from other qualitative methods in that it involves numerous other data sources, some of which are quantitative" (see also Eisenhardt 1989, 534–538; Punch 2005, 145; Gibbert et al. 2008).[88]

[88] Miles and Huberman (1994, 42–43) distinguish three levels of enriching qualitative studies with quantitative data. The first level is called "quantitizing," where qualitative information is counted directly or converted into ranks or scales. The second is that of "linkage between distinct data types" – e.g., qualitative information is compared to numerical data. The third way is an overall design strategy, in which both methods determine the study design ("multi-method approach"). The

To explore the different units of analysis (or research questions), a **data collection protocol** was developed (see section 3.2.1). The data collection and analysis were conducted in an iterative process. The data was then organized and analyzed for patterns based on the units of analysis (ideas, participants, and process). As recommended by Eisenhardt, this was done separately for each case study (**"within-case analysis"**). Eisenhardt (1989, 540) comments that "within-case analysis typically involves detailed case study write-ups for each site. These write-ups are often simply pure descriptions, but they are central to the generation of insight […] [T]he overall idea is to become intimately familiar with each case as a stand-alone entity," allowing for "unique patterns of each case to emerge." After compiling the individual case study reports, they are analyzed to find cross-case patterns (**"cross-case analysis"** [Eisenhardt 1989, 540–541]). Tabular displays are used to summarize evidence (Eisenhardt 1989, 542). Through the within- and cross-case analyses, patterns and relationships between variables become evident (Eisenhardt 1989, 541). Based on these relationships, existing hypotheses can be confirmed or tentative hypotheses can be formulated – which are supported with existing literature where possible (see figure 17).[89]

Figure 17: Case study approach

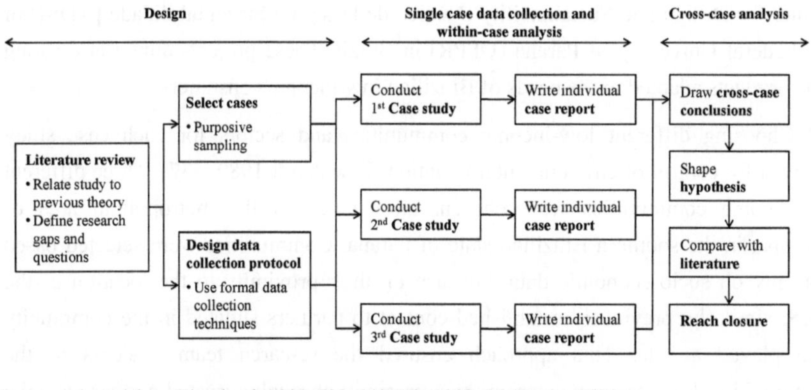

Source: adapted from Eisenhardt 1989, 533, 540; Yin 1989, 56; Dooley 2012.

present study mostly applies "quantitizing," but also links qualitative and quantitative data to provide richer detail as well as for triangulation purposes (Miles and Hubermann 1994, 41).

89 Note that the steps described above are not straightforward and consecutive, but rather involve "constant iteration backward and forward between steps" (Eisenhardt 1989, 564).

Case study selection

The present case studies were selected based on concrete research questions. This targeted, theoretical approach is also referred to as "purposive (or theoretical) sampling" – as opposed to "statistical (or probability) sampling" (Eisenhardt 1989, 537; Patton 1990, 169 ff.; Miles and Hubermann 2005, 27–29).[90] In this method, sample units are selected for having "particular features or characteristics which will enable detailed exploration and understanding of the central themes" (Ritchie and Lewis 2003, 78).

The following criteria were relevant when choosing the cases: (1) The case studies needed to offer potential for real-time study of the fuzzy front end of the innovation process (i.e., the idea-generation phase). (2) Due to the study's particular focus on low-income markets, the cases had to be implemented in low-income communities situated in a developing or emerging country. (3) The products to be innovated needed to come from a sector that is relevant for low-income markets.

The case studies chosen fulfilled these criteria in an ideal way:

(1) The idea competitions were part of the market research and idea generation phase of larger product development projects conducted by a research team of the Research Center for Design and Sustainability (Núcleo de Design e Sustentabilidade [NDS]) of the Federal University of Paraná (UFPR) in Brazil. These projects aimed at creating new products adapted to the needs of Brazilian low-income consumers.

(2) Choosing different low-income communities and sectors for each case study allowed for control of environmental variation (Eisenhardt 1989, 537). Three different low-income communities were chosen, all situated in the metropolitan area of Curitiba, in the southern Brazilian state of Paraná. Communities were selected based not only on socio-economic data, but also on their proximity to the location of the NDS; similarly, previously established contact to partners situated in the community also played a role. This approach ensured the research team's access to the communities. Furthermore, entering the community through a trusted partner gave the

---

90 Theoretical sampling, which was first described by Glaser and Strauss 1967, "is a particular kind of purposive sampling, in which the researcher samples incidents, people or units on the basis of their potential contribution to development and testing of theoretical constructs" (Ritchie and Lewis 2003, 80).

project legitimacy. Consequently, potential risks when working in low-income communities – for example, being assaulted – were reduced

(3) Three different sectors were chosen: housing and furniture solutions, water management, and energy and lighting solutions. These sectors are highly relevant when addressing the needs of the poor (see Hammond et al. 2007). They also address key consumption areas which are crucial for furthering sustainable consumption and production (see Tukker et al. 2008).

Methodological rigor in case study research

Criticism against case study research points towards a lack of both rigor and a basis for scientific generalization (Yin 2003, 10). According to Yin, the grounds of this criticism do not lie in case studies as a research strategy, but rather in the "sloppiness" of the researcher. Sound case study research has to follow a systematic procedure. Often, criticism of case study research is also due to misunderstandings about what this particular research strategy can achieve. The goal is to expand and generalize theories (analytic generalization) and not to enumerate frequencies (statistical generalization). Consequently, case studies are "generalizable to theoretical propositions and not to populations or universes" (Yin 2003,10).

Four conditions are related to the **quality of a case study design** (Yin 2003, 34; Punch 2005, 254–255; Gibbert et al. 2008): construct validity, internal validity, external validity, and reliability. Construct validity ensures that the phenomena encountered in the field match the theoretical constructs chosen. To achieve construct validity, this study establishes a "chain of events" and makes use of multiple sources of evidence, which are triangulated (Yin 2003, 34). Furthermore, construct validity is enhanced due to the fact that the study explains how access to data has been achieved and how it was analyzed (see chapter 3.2) (Gibbert et al. 2008). In addition, peers from the research team were given the opportunity to review the case study and provide feedback (Yin 2003, 34-35; Gibbert et al. 2008). Internal validity is achieved as the research framework is explicitly derived from literature, building on logically consistent arguments (Gibbert et al. 2008). In the analysis stage, it is also achieved through the triangulation of results with literature (Eisenhardt 1989, 545; Yin 2003, 34–36; Gibbert et al. 2008). To enhance internal validity, rival explanations are addressed where possible and appropriate (see chapter 5) (Yin 2003, 34, 133ff.; Punch 2005, 254–255). External validity asks if findings are generalizable to theoretical propositions (analytic generalization) (Yin 2003, 34; Punch 2005, 254–255). This can be addressed through applying a multiple case study design that allows replication (see "literal replication" in Yin 2003, 52) and cross-case synthesis (Yin 2003, 133). The present study was carefully and systematically set up, intending to meet all the conditions outlined above for ensuring construct, internal, and external validity (see chapters 3 and 5). Careful documentation ensures that other researchers doing the same case would come to the same conclusions ("inter-rater reliability"). To achieve reliability, the present study carefully documented the evidence used (Yin 2003, 34, 37–39). Furthermore, the data was gathered and coded by more than one researcher wherever possible (see section 3.2).[91]

Role of the researcher

The post-positivist paradigm requires a researcher to be objective and detached from the research subject. Other research paradigms, however, acknowledge that researchers are influenced by the values and beliefs predominant in society, which guide their investigation (Guba and Lincoln 1994, 114). Qualitative research methods in particular result in higher involvement of the researcher, as they often require personal contact with the research subject.

The present author was actively involved in the set-up and implementation of the idea competitions. This role can be described as an "insider participant observer" (Labaree 2000). This process took several weeks and allowed deep insights to be gained (see section 3.2). Active participation and interaction with the research subjects supported building trust, which some scholars view as a precondition to gain access to and conduct research in low-income communities (Seelos and Mair 2007, 53; Badry 2009, 4; Viswanathan and Sridharan 2012, 563). This involvement may have had effects on the researcher's views of the research subject. However, as related above and below, the author focused on reducing bias and staying neutral by designing a research approach based on various, triangulated sources of evidence, and by involving other researchers in the data analysis, always ensuring inter-rater reliability. Also, replicating the competitions three times (case studies) strengthened the patterns that emerged from the data, thus reducing biases that may have resulted from proximity with the research subject.

---

[91] Eisenhardt (1989, 538) recommends employing "multiple investigators [...] to make visits to case study sites in teams," assigning them different roles. The objective is to allow "the case to be viewed from the different perspectives of multiple observers." This was employed whenever feasible.

3.2 Research methods

For the purpose of this study, three idea competitions were conducted in low-income communities in southern Brazil. Each competition conducted represents a case study, providing the "frame" for the data collection and analysis. Idea competitions have **four phases:** set-up, realization, evaluation & awarding, and follow-up (see section 2.3.1). The design and implementation of each phase is outlined in the next section (3.2.1).

Data collection and analysis is organized based on three units of analysis (UoA): (1) ideas, (2) characteristics of participants, and (3) the process of the idea competition. Sections 3.2.2–3.2.4 describe the methods applied for data collection and analysis. Figure 18 provides an overview of these sections.

Figure 18: Data collection and analysis for each case study

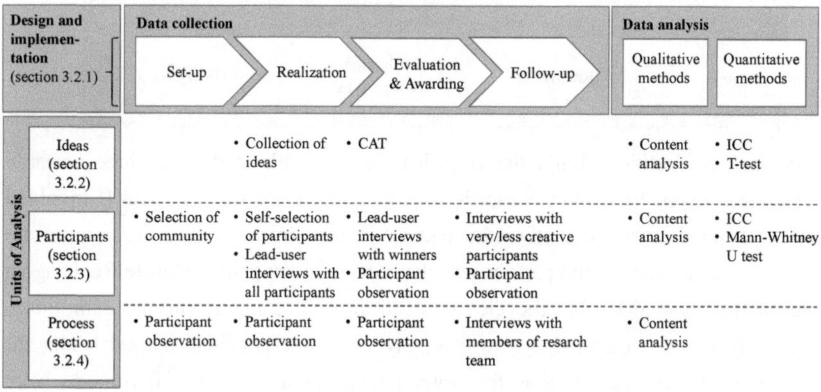

Source: created by author.

3.2.1 Design and implementation of idea competitions

There is little research about how idea competitions should be designed to ensure quality results (Soll 2006, 2ff., 59; Haller et al. 2009, 2; Wenger and Haller 2010; Füller et al. 2011, 269). The studies of Walcher (2007) and Silvertant (2011) have started to fill this gap by describing the phases of the idea competitions they conducted in their studies. The booklet for practitioners by Belz et al. (2009) as well as the paper by Haller et al. (2009) provide further information on design options of idea competitions. However, these studies mostly provide guidance on conducting online idea competitions and draw their findings from those conducted in high-income environments. The only documented offline idea competition that could be identified was a study by Nokia in Brazil, Ghana, and India called the "Nokia Open Studios (NOS)" (Jung and Chipchase 2008; see section 2.3.5).

For the purpose of this study, the design and implementation of offline idea competitions builds on the best practices drawn from the aforementioned studies. Due to a lack of guidance and standardization in the design and implementation of offline idea competitions, the chosen approach is described in detail. One the one hand, this is done to provide transparency in the decisions taken at each step. On the other hand, this description aims to contribute to further research in this area, which could build on and refine the approach (see chapter 6 on further research options).

Context

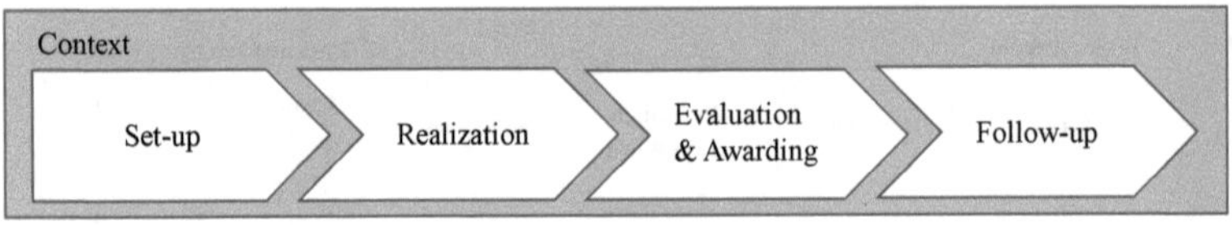

Three idea competitions build the empirical basis of this study. All three research projects were supported by a consortium of partners. Case studies I and II involved partners from the private sector who had an interest in translating the results into practice. In case study I, the partner was the recycling company Soliforte Reciclagem Ltda., a Brazilian SME that recycles waste from civil construction and demolition. Case study II was supported by the company Tigre, the Brazilian market leader for PVC pipes and fitting solutions for water management systems. All projects were funded by the Funding Authority for Studies and Projects (Financiadora de Estudos e Projetos [FINEP]) of the Brazilian Innovation Agency. To gain access to low-income communities, it was crucial to find additional partners who already had strong roots in the target communities (Seelos and Mair 2007, 53; Badry 2009, 4; Viswanathan and Sridharan 2012, 563). To conduct the first idea competition, the project team cooperated with the residents' association (associação dos moradores). For the second and third competitions, the Brazilian housing agency Companhia de Habitação do Paraná (COHAPAR) participated as a partner. Having conducted projects in low-income communities in the metropolitan area of Curitiba for around 20 years, COHAPAR proved to be a suitable partner to gain access to the target group. As COHAPAR also builds a considerable amount of houses in low-income communities as part of the housing program "Minha Casa – Minha Vida" ("My house – my life"), which was launched by the Brazilian government in 2009, it is also a potential client for the end-products of the three projects.[92]

Table 13: Context of case studies: names, sectors and partners

	Case study I	Case study II	Case study III
Name of research project at NDS	"Eco-Agregado"	"Projeto Amana"	"Projeto LED"
Sector	Housing/furniture solutions	Water	Energy/lighting solutions
Project partners	Research Center for Design and Sustainability (NDS) Company: Soliforte Partner to access community: residents' association Funding: FINEP	Research Center for Design and Sustainability (NDS) Company: Tigre Partner to access community: COHAPAR Funding: FINEP	Research Center for Design and Sustainability (NDS) Partner to access community: COHAPAR Funding: FINEP

Source: created by author.

Set-up

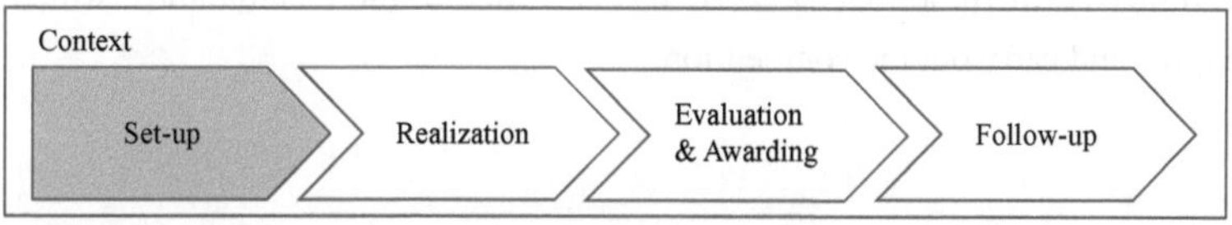

As a first step, the whole research team was trained by the main researcher – the author of this study – on the technique and the different steps of the idea competition in a half-day workshop. The workshop also defined the **objective** of conducting idea competitions: to inform the idea generation stage of subsequent the product development processes. As previously mentioned, the **topic** of the competition aimed to address a relevant need of low-income consumers (see table 14). In case study I, relevance was ensured by building on previous field research on the needs of low-income consumers, conducted by the NDS.[93] In cases II and III, the topic was defined

92 The housing program forms part of the national growth plan, the "Programa de Aceleração do Crescimento" (PAC). The plan foresees considerable subsidies for the construction of houses for the low-income population.

93 An ethnographic pre-study was conducted between March and April, 2009, by the NDS in the community Aguas Claras: The research team conducted a series of interviews, house visits,

in cooperation with the project partner COHAPAR, bringing in their experience in assessing needs of low-income communities. In addition to being relevant, the topic needed to be understandable to low-income consumers (Belz et al. 2009, 42). Thus, pre-tests were conducted in April 2009 and 2010 with selected inhabitants from the target communities (case studies I and III) and with the cleaning personnel of the university, who are all from a low-income background (case study II).[94] In addition, the topics needed to be broad enough to ensure a creative outcome (Soll 2006, 102). The topic also defined the **object** to be created: case study I looked for solutions, case studies II and III aimed to generate products (see table 14).

As mentioned above, the **target groups** of the idea competitions were low-income communities situated in the metropolitan area of Curitiba. The community of the first idea competition (case study I) – the community "Aguas Claras" in Piraquara – was identified through previous contacts of the NDS, which had conducted field studies in that community and thus had an established contact to the residents' association, the partner organization. The identification of communities for case studies II and III – the communities "Jardim Boa Vista" and "Vila Zumbi" – was supported by COHAPAR. As a project partner, it offered to conduct the idea competition in an area where it was already working. Furthermore, COHAPAR has an office in the communities, which helped promote and carry out the competition.[95]

---

participant observation, a focus group as well as the paparazzi research method. Interviews were recorded and transcribed. Field notes, pictures, and videos were taken and impressions were written down in a research diary. These methods were conducted to understand the needs of low-income consumers in the field of housing and furniture solutions. It was found that low-income consumers of the respective community have a great desire to amplify the perceived space in their house. This can be achieved through solutions that organize their belongings efficiently.

94 A small competition was announced during their lunch break, during which about 20 people were asked to submit their ideas. Two ideas were submitted, which is a return rate of 10%. Conversations with participants and their respective questions regarding the competition also confirmed that the topics were easy to understand.

95 For further information on the characteristics of these communities, see chapter 4.

Table 14: Set-up

Design element	Case study I	Case study II	Case study III
Objective	Generation of creative ideas Identification of lead users and creative participants Identification and transfer of innovation-relevant knowledge		
Topic/Task	Create solutions to organize your house!	Create a product to collect rainwater!	Create a product that lightens up your house and saves energy!
Object	Solution	Product	Product
Target group	Community "Aguas Claras," Piraquara	Community "Jardim Boa Vista," Campo Magro	Community "Vila Zumbi," Curitiba

Source: created by author.

Realization

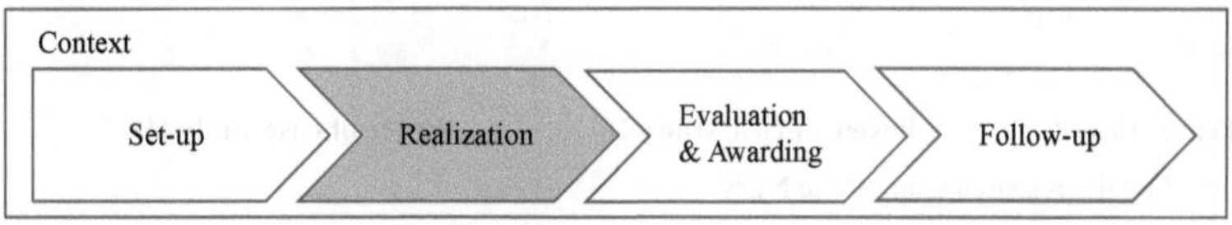

In all three cases, the idea competitions were conducted offline. The competitions were intensely **promoted** over two weeks, using offline and online marketing channels.[96] A team of about ten junior researchers spent three afternoons in the community to distribute flyers door-to-door and put up posters in key spots such as the local schools, bars, small grocery stores, and churches (see figure 19). Walking through the community and door-to-door, they explained to people the topic as well as the participation procedure and handed out participation forms. Also, the local project partners helped promote the project. In addition, key persons, or "multipliers," of the community – such as school teachers, bar or shop owners, social workers, and the president of the residents' association – helped further promote the competition. Furthermore, a car with loudspeakers (the so-called "carro de som") drove through the community announcing the competition – a common and very popular marketing

[96] While online competitions are often promoted over longer periods (e.g., 8–10 weeks, see Belz et al. 2009, 31), this was not considered necessary for offline competitions that are conducted in somewhat small communities. Rather, the intense promotion ensured the necessary outreach and created "momentum" within the target communities. The project partners advised that this momentum would have gotten lost if the period of the competition had been extended.

technique in Brazilian low-income communities, which is usually used for sweets or consumer products like cleaning tools. For each competition, an online blog was created to report on the status of the project. The URL of the blog was communicated through the flyers.

Figure 19: Promotional posters

Poster of case study I **Poster of case study II** **Poster of case study III**

Source: created by the research team of the NDS.

After promoting the competitions for two weeks in each community, the ideas were **collected** on a fixed date and during a set period. For the first competition (case study I), ideas were collected at the building of the residents' association, whereas in the second and third competition (case studies II and III), the buildings of the COHAPAR in the respective communities were used. All three buildings were ideal as they are situated in the center of the community and are known and frequented by the community members. The research team was present for a whole day to collect the ideas. To hand in an idea, people were asked to register by filling out a form that had been distributed during the promotion phase (see figure 20). On the form, participants had to fill out their full name, address, phone number, and tax or identity number (CPF/RG). They were also asked to sign the terms of the idea competition on the form, which ensured that the information provided by the participant could be further used by the research team ("rights of use"). The research team assisted participants with low literacy in filling out the form. Furthermore, the terms were verbally explained to all participants.

The front of the form contained two spaces: one for the title of the idea and one for a verbal description. The backside of the form provided space to draw the idea. However, drawings were not required – ideas were also accepted as a textual or oral description (which was videotaped).

Figure 20: Front page of the participation form

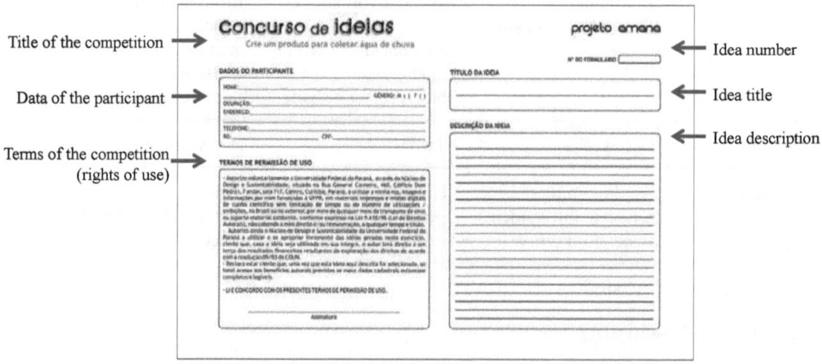

Source: created by the author, in cooperation with the research team of the NDS.

Most participants brought a filled-out form on the idea collection day, which already contained the drawings or textual description of their ideas. In a few cases, they filled out the form on the spot. Participants with difficulties in either writing or designing/drawing their idea were assisted by a facilitator. When handing in their ideas, participants were briefly interviewed to gather demographic data (age, income, profession, etc.) as well as their motivation to participate. Participants were also videotaped giving a short verbal description of their idea. This was done to clarify questions of the research team and to ensure that drawings and descriptions would not be misunderstood. Also, semi-structured interviews were conducted during the idea collection day (see section 3.2.3).

Table 15: Realization

Design element	Case study I	Case study II	Case study III
Media	Offline	Offline	Offline
Promotion	Poster; flyer; mouth-to-mouth; involving key informants; blog/project website	Poster; flyer; mouth-to-mouth; house visits; involving key informants; announcement with loudspeakers; blog/project website	Poster; flyer; mouth-to-mouth; involving key informants; presentation at local school; announcement with loudspeakers; blog/project website
Timeframe	Two weeks	Two weeks	Two weeks
Collection of ideas	Handing in ideas in person at the residents' association office	Handing in ideas in person at COHAPAR office	Handing in ideas in person at COHAPAR office

Source: created by the author.

Evaluation and awarding

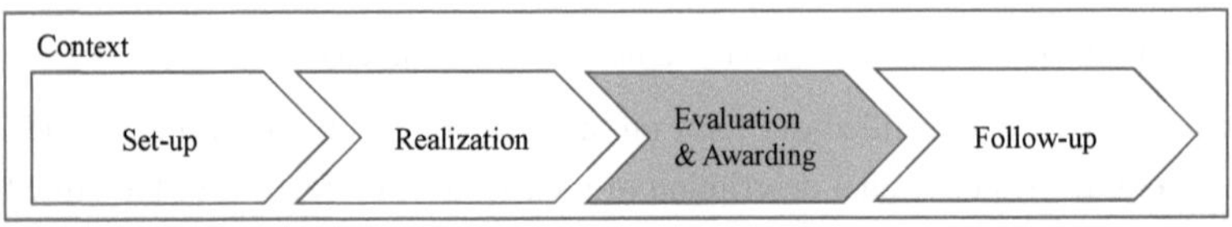

To **evaluate** the creativity of the ideas, the Consensual Assessment Technique (CAT) was applied (see section 3.2.2 for further detail). The **evaluation panel** was selected and conducted according to the requirements of Amabile (1986). It consisted of at least one academic expert, at least one expert from the private sector – in most cases from the partner company – and at least one expert from a non-profit organization. All jury members had knowledge about or experience in developing products for low-income consumers as well as the topic of the competition.

Having identified the three best ideas of the idea competition through the CAT, the winners were informed and personally given their prizes. To announce the winners to all participants, a car with loudspeakers drove through the community. Such reputation gains are often perceived as additional incentives for participants (Reichwald and Piller 2006, 175; Belz et al. 2009; Silvertant 2011, 63). In all three cases, **material prizes** were offered (see table 16), which are regarded as fair for idea competitions in a business setting (Belz et al. 2009, 44).[97] However, a good balance was sought between incentivizing participants and not "crowding out" participants who are primarily intrinsically motivated (Frey 1997). Intrinsic incentives could be, for example, the opportunity to take part in creating a new product (Sawhney and Prandelli 2000, 263) or simply a feeling of enjoyment or competence (Füller 2006; Haller et al. 2009, 6).

In the case of the first idea competition, an award ceremony was held at a social gathering of the residents' association. The winners of the second competition were awarded prizes at the building of the COHAPAR, while winners of the third were awarded in their own homes.

Table 16: Evaluation and awarding

Design element	Case study I	Case study II	Case study III
Evaluation	1 academic expert 1 company expert 1 NGO expert	1 academic expert 21 company experts 2 NGO experts	3 academic experts 1 company expert 1 NGO expert
Assessment of ideas (criteria)		CAT criteria	
Prizes	Shelf (room divider); warm blanket	DVD Player; CD player with radio; small couch	High-quality LED lamp; LED torch with radio and phone charger; small portable LED lamp
Awarding	Award ceremony at community center	Awarding at COHAPAR; announcement with loudspeakers	Awarding at recipients' homes; announcement with loudspeakers

Source: created by author.

Follow-up

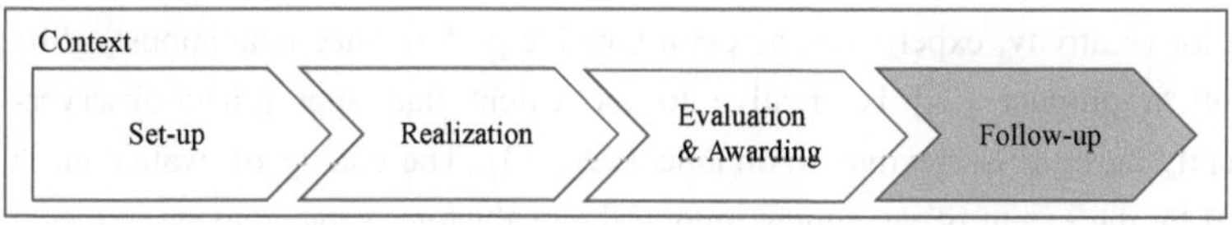

[97] In case study III, the first prize was related to the topic of the competition. In case study I, this was only possible for the first prize, as there was no budget for offering three pieces of furniture. In case study II, offering a prize related to the topic would not have been possible as no rainwater collector exists for low-income houses. Thus, the research team opted for prizes that were known to be attractive incentives.

After each idea competition, a follow-up phase took place which involved several field visits. Interviews were conducted with the winners of the competitions as well as other participants (for sampling decisions, see section 3.2.2).

3.2.2 Ideas: Creativity analysis

The first research question asks whether idea competitions serve to generate creative ideas with low-income consumers. But when can an idea actually be regarded as creative? Previous research found the Consensual Assessment Technique (CAT) developed by Amabile (1996) to be an appropriate technique to quantitatively assess the creativity of ideas (Walcher 2007, 43ff.; Silvertant 2011, 282).[98] It is a generic measure of creativity which has mostly been applied by creativity researchers but recently also gained popularity in innovation research (see table 17). In addition, the technique has been used in the context of idea competitions (Piller and Walcher 2006; Soll 2006; Walcher 2007; Ebner 2008; Silvertant 2010). Furthermore, the CAT construct of creativity was proven to be reliable and valid in previous studies (Amabile et al. 1997).

Research question 1: To what extent can offline idea competitions generate creative ideas from low-income consumers?

Unit of analysis: ideas

The CAT focuses on the assessment of the result of a creative activity rather than on the person (Amabile 1996, 65; see also Walcher 2007, 43ff.). It is not based on a specific theory or definition of creativity, but rather on the conviction that the creativity of ideas (or any other artifacts) can be reliably assessed by experts in the respective field. In fact, Amabile (1996) shows that while there is no undisputed definition for creativity, experts can assess a creative performance unanimously. She writes that "a product [...] is creative to the extent that appropriate observers independently agree it is creative" (Amabile 1996, 33). The quality of evaluation is determined by the extent of agreement among the evaluators' subjective assessments (Amabile 1996, 33; see also Silvertant 2011, 74).

Furthermore, creativity is understood as a continuum – ideas can have differing degrees of creativity (Amabile 1996, 34). As recommended by Amabile (1996, 43ff.),

98 For a comprehensive overview of techniques to measure creativity, see Walcher (2007, 43ff.).

studies that apply the CAT have most commonly used four criteria to measure creativity, which were assessed along a Likert scale: *originality*, *usefulness*, *degree of elaboration*, and *feasibility*:

Originality is commonly referred to as the most obvious attribute of creativity in products (Kristensson et al. 2002, 55; Kristensson et al. 2004, 6; Magnusson 2009, 585; Silvertant 2011, 73). Although being the "most respected trait in creativity," products also need to solve a problem that is vital for the person – that is, they should be **useful** (Amabile 1996, 21; Kristensson et al. 2004, 6; Magnusson 2009, 585; Silvertant 2011, 74). The degree of **elaboration** indicates the creative capability of transforming an idea into an elaborated solution (Piller and Walcher 2006, 314; Walcher 2007, 116; Silvertant 2011, 74). As creativity does not automatically evolve into innovation, Kristensson et al. (2004, 6) suggest considering "the probability and ease of developing an idea into a final product." Consequently, the **feasibility** dimension is included (Walcher 2007; Magnusson 2009, 585). The criterion ensures that ideas can actually be transformed into a viable solution, which is vital for innovation (Amabile 1996; Kristensson et al. 2004, 6).

Table 17: Studies that apply the CAT method for assessing ideas from consumers

Study	Criteria applied
Lüthje (2000, 192)	Newness Originality Feasibility Elaboration
Kristensson et al. (2004, 5–6)	Originality Value Realization Number of ideas
Piller and Walcher (2006, 314)	Originality Customer benefit[99] Number of beneficiaries Degree of elaboration
Hienert et al. (2007)	Novelty Value Realizability

[99] Piller and Walcher (2006) as well as Walcher (2007) differentiate usefulness on two scales: expected customer benefit and number of expected beneficiaries.

Walcher (2007)	Originality Customer benefit Number of beneficiaries Degree of elaboration
Magnusson (2009)	Originality User value Producibility
Silvertant (2011, 73ff.)	Originality Usefulness Degree of elaboration Feasibility

Source: based on Silvertant 2011, 72.

The four dimensions used in this study – originality, usefulness, degree of elaboration, and feasibility – are meant to be applied by a jury of experts. Amabile (1996, 41ff.) defines several **requirements** for the composition of the jury as well as the design and implementation of the evaluation workshop, which are summarized in table 18.

Table 18: Requirements to implement CAT

Category	Requirement
Requirements for task	01. Clearly interpretable result
	02. No specific capabilities needed to accomplish task
	03. Free idea development (i.e., open solution space)
Requirements for experts/jury	04. Experts that are familiar with the topic
	05. Number of experts between 3 and 10
Requirements for implementation	06. Random order of assessments
	07. Dimensions: originality, utility, elaboration, and feasibility
	08. Subjective assessment
	09. No consultation between experts
	10. No influential instructions through workshop leader
Requirements for assessment	11. Minimum level of ICC > 0.7

Source: Walcher 2007, 63, 109; Silvertant 2011, 90 [based on Amabile 1996, 40ff.].

The present study complies with the requirements presented above. First, the tasks for the participants were kept relatively open: "Create a solution to organize your house!"; "Create a product to collect rainwater!"; or "Create a product that lightens up your house and saves energy!" Participants did not need any specific capabilities to accomplish the task. Collecting various sources of information (i.e., the drawings, a textual description of the ideas, and a videotaped verbal description) ensured that results were clearly interpretable.

The members of the jury need to be experts regarding the topic (Amabile 1996, 42). However, their level of expertise does not need to be identical (Amabile 1996, 41). For the purpose of this study, an interdisciplinary jury was set up with between four and five members, who all showed expertise related to the competition topic (see section 3.2.1).

Also, the requirements for the implementation were fulfilled: The set-up of the CAT workshop was a half-day session, which started with a short presentation of the research project, the idea competition and the steps of the CAT. The introduction was kept strictly neutral, focusing merely on a description of the technique and the process, in order not to influence the experts (Amabile 1996, 75; Walcher 2007, 116; Silvertant 2011, 94ff.). Each expert was seated separately to ensure independent evaluation. They each received the submitted ideas in a different, random order. The ideas were complemented with the transcripts of the verbal descriptions; the names of the creators were hidden and ideas were merely numbered to avoid bias. The jury was instructed to carefully consider each idea and, in a second step, group them along the following scale: very creative, creative, not very creative. Ratings were supposed to be in relation to each other (and not in relation to other ideas outside the competition). Then, they were given rating sheets (see figure 21) to assess each idea according to the four creativity dimensions (originality, usefulness, elaboration, and feasibility), measured on a 5-point Likert scale (1 = very low, 5 = very high) (see Walcher 2007, 53; Silvertant 2011, 96). Then, the scores for each dimension were added together to calculate the score per idea per rater ("partial creativity score").

Figure 21: CAT assessment sheet

	Very low	Low	Medium	High	Very High
Originality	☐ 1	☐ 2	☐ 3	☐ 4	☐ 5
Utility	☐ 1	☐ 2	☐ 3	☐ 4	☐ 5
Elaboration	☐ 1	☐ 2	☐ 3	☐ 4	☐ 5
Feasibility	☐ 1	☐ 2	☐ 3	☐ 4	☐ 5
			∑ sum (creativity score)		☐

Source: based on Silvertant 2011, 93.

Based on this evaluation, a **creativity score** of a single idea was calculated by adding the creativity scores from each expert (i.e., the sum of the rating of each dimension).[100]

$$CS_{ip} = \sum_{e=1}^{n} \sum_{d=1}^{m} R_{e_{ip}d_{ip}}$$

The creativity score is thus "additive-compensatory," meaning that there is no minimum threshold for each dimension and that the creativity dimensions can compensate each other.

Due to the varying number of experts, the creativity score of each idea could range from 16 to 80 points in case study I (four experts), and from 20 to 100 points in case studies II and III (five experts). To make the creativity scores comparable across case studies, the scores were standardized: they were divided by the number of dimensions (d) and the number of experts (e), so that final scores ranged from 1 to 5.

---

[100] The creativity score CS of an idea i of a participant p is composed of the ratings R of all creativity dimensions d across experts e; m indicates the number of creativity dimensions and n the number of experts.

To be able to compare more creative with less creative ideas – and to relate the scores to characteristics of their participants – two groups were formed. This follows the approach developed by Walcher (2007, 114ff.) and Silvertant (2011, 104). Ideas below the center scale belong to group CS_{low}; ideas equal to or above the center scale belong to the group CS_{high}. This means that a creative idea has to have a score of at least $CS_{high} \geq 3$, a less creative idea a score of $CS_{low} < 3$. The advantage of choosing the center scale – as opposed to the arithmetic mean – is that it is independent of the values of the scores achieved by the ideas (Silvertant 2011, 104).

The **analysis** of the data obtained through the CAT was done with the support of Excel and SPSS (Version 21.0). The outcome of the CAT is only a good indicator for creativity if agreement among the jury is high (Amabile 1996, 33). Agreement across jury members shows that the dimensions have the same meaning to each of them, although no definition of creativity or the dimensions was provided. There are a number of statistics which can be used to determine inter-rater-reliability (Amabile 1996, 68; see also Wirtz and Casper 2002, 16; Gwet 2010). One is the **intra-class correlation coefficient** (ICC) for interval-scaled scores (Shrout and Fleiss 1979; Amabile 1996, 47–71; Wirtz and Casper 2002, 163ff.). The basic principle of the ICC corresponds to that of the analysis of variance. The ICC can range from 0 to 1. The closer the ICC is to 1, the lower the variation between raters. If the ICC is 0, there is no consensus between the ratings; if the ICC is 1, the raters have given the same score. An ICC of at least 0.7 is regarded as an indicator for good reliability (Amabile 1996, 68–76; Wirtz and Casper 2002, 157ff.). However, the specific threshold can be defined on a case-by-case basis. In any case, it should be above a value of 0.3, which indicates fair agreement (Wirtz and Casper 2002, 25).

There are different ways of calculating the ICC, which can give different results when applied to the same data (Shrout and Fleiss 1979, 420). Below, a justification is provided for the approach chosen for this study.[101]

- Two-way model: The two-way model was chosen, as all ideas were rated by the same group of experts (within one idea competition). The one-way analysis of variance would have to be applied if the ideas had been assessed by different experts (Walcher 2007, 57ff.; Silvertant 2011, 100; Ramakrishnan 2012, 85). The

[101] For a more comprehensive explanation of the ICC, please refer to Wirtz and Casper (2002) or to Gwet (2010).

two-way model has the advantage that differences in the means of the raters affect all ratings of the ideas in the same way.

- Random raters: The raters can be random or fixed. In the case of this study, they were random, as the replacement of a rater is not assumed to affect the results of the ICC (Shrout and Fleiss 1979, 420ff.; Wirtz and Casper 2002, 172).
- Unadjusted measures: As opposed to adjusted measures, unadjusted measures do consider mean differences between the raters – and are thus considered the stricter procedure (Shrout and Fleiss 1979, 421ff.; Wirtz and Casper 2002, 169, 181).[102]

An alternative way to determine the degree of rater agreement is through **Cronbach's Alpha coefficient** (Amabile 1996, 68ff.).[103] It is used to measure internal consistency of items to gauge their reliability – that is, it measures the extent to which different items measure the same concept or construct. It can have a value from 0 to 1, with higher values representing higher internal consistency (George and Mallery 2003, 223).[104]

A variety of tests require normal distribution of variables. Thus, the **Kolmogorov-Smirnov goodness-of-fit test (K-S test)** was applied (Neal 1996; Bortz and Döring 2006, 218). It is a nonparametric test which examines if two data sets differ significantly. It can be modified to serve as a goodness-of-fit test for testing normality. In this case, the sample is standardized and compared with a standard normal distribution. A non-significant result indicates normality ($p > 0.05$). If the result is significant, this implies that the subsequent analysis needs to apply non-parametrical tests (Bühl 2008, 338).

To compare less creative ideas with those that have above-average creativity, the means of each group are compared. The mean is the average of a set of numerical values – that is, the sum of all values divided by the number of values (George and Mallery 2003, 98). The **independent sample t-test** assesses whether the means of two groups/samples are statistically different from each other (George and Mallery 2003, 134). The independent t-test requires that the variables be interval-scaled and normally distributed. It is assumed that the two groups have approximately equal variance

102 In SPSS: two-way, random, absolute agreement (see, e.g., Silvertant 2011, 101).

103 Cronbach's Alpha corresponds to the ICC two-way model, fixed, adjusted (in SPSS: two-way mixed consistency; see, e.g., Silvertant 2011, 101).

104 Values of 0.9 and higher are considered excellent. Those above 0.7 are considered acceptable and below 0.7 questionable. Values below 0.3 are unacceptable.

(Leven's Test) – meaning that the degree of distribution is approximately equal. Furthermore, the test assumes that the groups are independent of each other as they contain different sets of individuals (George and Mallery 2003, 134). The null hypothesis assumes that the means of two normally distributed groups of variables are not significantly different; p indicates the error probability. A $p \leq 0.05$ indicates that the means of the two samples are significantly different from each other, which means that the null hypothesis can be rejected (Bühl 2008, 121).

Table 19: Meaning of the error probability p

Probability of error	Meaning	Symbol
$p > 0.05$	Not significant	n.s.
$p \leq 0.05$	Significant	*
$p \leq 0.01$	Very significant	**
$p \leq 0.001$	Highly significant	***

Source: Bühl 2008, 121.

The t-test can be used even if the sample sizes are very small (e.g., as small as ten). However, researchers recommend that effect sizes be measured as well. They quantify the size of the difference between two groups independent of the sample size. In contrast, statistical significance conflates effect size and sample size.[105] This study applied Cohen's *d* for measuring the relative effect size between the means of CS_{high} and CS_{low} (Cohen 1971, 1988).[106] It is reported as a positive number even when the formula produces a negative value (Gravetter and Wallnau 2012, 230). Cohen outlined criteria for gauging small, medium and large effect sizes when comparing independent means (see table 20). The formula for calculating effect sizes is as follows:

$$\frac{x_1 - x_2}{\sqrt{(s_1^2 + s_2^2)/2}}$$

[105] Furthermore, significance tests do not report the size of the effect, but rather the p-value – i.e., the probability of error.

[106] More concretely, the effect sizes between the means of CS_{high} and CS_{low} are calculated for each creativity dimension as well as for the aggregated creativity score (CS).

Table 20: Criteria for evaluating effect size using Cohen's *d*

Magnitude of *d*	Evaluation of effect size
$d = 0.20$	Small effect
$d = 0.50$	Medium effect
$d = 0.80$	Large effect

Source: Cohen 1971, 22ff.; Cohen 1988, 40; Gravetter and Wallnau 2012, 232.

3.2.3 Participants: Characteristics of lead users and creative participants

The next research questions examine the participants – the originators of the ideas submitted. The objective is to determine the extent to which the technique "idea competition" serves to identify low-income consumers with lead-user characteristics. Furthermore, previous studies identified that there are participants who do not show lead-user characteristics, but who nonetheless have valuable ideas and inputs. To investigate these two questions further, a series of interviews were conducted and analyzed through "content analysis" (Mayring 2003).

Research question 2a: To what extent can offline idea competitions identify low-income consumers with lead-user characteristics?

Research question 2b: What are the common characteristics of low-income consumers who produce creative ideas in offline idea competitions?

Unit of analysis: participants

Interviews to determine lead userness of participants

No coherent way to identify lead users can be found in the literature. Primarily, studies disagree on the characteristics through which lead users can be identified. For the purpose of this study, seven characteristics were identified (see section 2.2.1), which have been operationalized and tested in previous studies (Lüthje 2000; Franke and Shah 2003; Bartl 2006; Franke et al. 2006; Soll 2006; Walcher 2007; Schreier and Prügl 2008; Silvertant 2011): *dissatisfaction*, *innovative activity*, *trend leadership*, *product-related knowledge*, *use experience*, *involvement*, and *opinion leadership* (see table 21).

To assess these characteristics, each participant of the idea competition was invited to personally participate in a **semi-structured interview**. The interviews took place immediately after the collection of ideas at the site of the idea competition (i.e., in the community) between April and May, 2009, for case study I and April and May, 2010, for case studies II and III. Participation was voluntary and interviewees were made aware that the results would not influence their participation in the competition. A draft version of the interview questionnaire was pre-tested for its understandability and length with a group of low-income consumers. These lead-user characteristics provided the structure for the questionnaire. They interview questions were developed building on best practices of previous studies (Lüthje 2000; Franke and Shah 2003; Bartl 2006; Franke et al. 2006; Soll 2006; Walcher 2007; Schreier and Prügl 2008; Silvertant 2011; see table 21). To limit the response burden and ensure feasibility, only a limited number of questions per characteristic were asked.[107] However, support questions were asked whenever the interviewer perceived that a question or term was not clear. In addition to answering questions regarding the lead-user characteristics, the participants were asked questions regarding their age, profession, and education.

Since the interviews were conducted in person, the answering behavior of the person was also observed and noted. Short answers were investigated further, asking supporting questions. This process was designed to suit the needs of the target group, which has little experience participating in interviews or surveys and often a lower level of education and literacy. It was also assumed that interviewees may face difficulties with abstract thinking (Viswanathan and Rosa 2007). Also, this specific approach was designed to avoid social desirability of answers, resulting from "the desire of respondents to avoid embarrassment and project a favorable image to others" (Fisher 1993, 303), which is difficult to maintain when support questions are asked and interviewees are observed when answering.[108] This process is more accurate than allowing self-assessment – an approach chosen by most lead-user studies – which makes people inclined to over-assess themselves.[109;110]

---

107 Feasibility was crucial, as the interviews were conducted after the collection of ideas. This means that all interviews had to be conducted on the same day.

108 For further methods of coping with social desirability bias, see Nederhof 1985.

109 The lead-user method, for example, applies a screening approach (Herstatt and von Hippel 1992; Lüthje and Herstatt 2004, 563). Potential lead users are identified and interviewed in person, via email, or by phone, asking structured questions on lead-user characteristics. Other studies apply online questionnaires, asking respondents to provide the incidence of each criterion on a 5- or 7-point Likert scale (e.g., Silvertant 2011, 107ff.). The disadvantage of the latter approach is that there is no way to ensure that respondents fill out the form thoroughly and conscientiously (Silvertant 2011, 217). Furthermore, it is difficult to know whether the respondent understands the question that is being asked.

Table 21: Operationalization of lead-user characteristics

Characteristic	Questions asked in the lead-user interviews of this study	Questions/items applied in other studies	Factor loading of items
Dissatisfaction	Are you unsatisfied with the products/solutions currently available on the market related to ___? If yes, to what degree and why? Do you have needs related to ___ which are not covered by the products currently on the market?	I am dissatisfied with some pieces of commercially available equipment. (Franke et al. 2006, 315)	*0.78*
		I am dissatisfied with the current offer of dishwashers. (Soll 2006, 149)	*0.782*
		I am dissatisfied with the current offers of honey. (Silvertant 2011, 285ff.)	*n.a.*
Trend leadership	If there is a new solution related to ___, available on the market, are you one of the first people to know about the novelty and/or buy it? If yes, why?	I buy the newest articles as soon as they are available on the market. (Lüthje 2000, 254)	*n.a.*
		In my circle of friends, I am generally one of the first to buy novelties in the field of sports shoes. (Walcher 2007, 204ff.)	*0.912*
		I buy new foot products as soon as they are available on the market. (Silvertant 2011, 285ff.)	*n.a.*
Innovative activity	Had you had ideas before the competition related to ___? If yes, what were they? Please describe the idea and whether/how you developed it.	I have improved and developed new techniques in boardercross. (Franke and Shah 2003, 163)	*n.a.*
		I have already helped improve the packaging or packing design of a product. (Silvertant 2011, 285ff.)	*n.a.*

110 The approach chosen could explain the low level of lead-user scores in this study, compared to other studies.

Product-related knowledge	Do you know existing products or solutions related to ____? If yes, what are they? Please describe (e.g., functions, materials).	I have a good overview of the dishwashers available on the market. (Soll 2006, 149)	*0.561*
		I have a very good overview of the sorts of honey available on the market. (Silvertant 2011, 285ff.)	*n.a.*
		I know the functions of dishwashers very well. (Soll 2006, 149)	0.79
Use experience	Which products/solutions related to ___ do you use? How often do you use them and in what situations?	For how many years have you been sailplaning? How many days [per year] do you spend sailplaning? (Schreier and Prügl 2008, 340)	*n.a.*
		I use honey __ times per week. (Silvertant 2011, 285ff.)	*n.a.*
Involvement	How interested are you in products/solutions related to ___ ? Why? With what frequency do you look for information on the subject?	My adidas sports shoes are interesting to me. (Walcher 2007, 213)	*0.933*
		My interest in household products is high. (Soll 2006, 156)	*0.85*
		How interested are you in infotainment for your car? (Bartl 2006, 176)	*n.a.*
		I am very interested in food products. (Silvertant 2011, 285ff.)	*n.a.*
Opinion leadership	Do you share your experiences with others regarding products/solutions related to ____? Do others ask you for recommendations about new products/solutions related to ___?	I speak about household appliances with my friends very often. (Soll 2006, 148)	*0.76*
		I speak with others about packaging/packaging designs very often and share my experiences with them. (Silvertant 2011, 285ff.)	*n.a.*

Source: created by author based on Silvertant 2011, 285ff.

Interviews were also recorded and transcribed, and the transcripts were coded deductively (Mayring 2003, 74). To facilitate coding, anchor examples and coding rules were developed along a 5-point Likert scale, with 1 showing a low incidence of the characteristic and 5 showing a high incidence (Schilling 2006, 33; for anchor examples and coding rules see interview questionnaires in annex I). The answers received by each participant were then coded applying these examples and rules. The coding was conducted by two researchers independently. To ensure inter-rater reliability, the ICC was applied (see section 3.2.2). Differing results were discussed and jointly revised. Where raters still disagreed, the mean of the rating was used.

To determine the lead userness of participants, a lead-user score (LUS) was created. Previous studies differ in the way the score is compiled.[111] For example, some studies define threshold values for each lead-user characteristic (simultaneous approach). Participants are only defined as lead users if they reach a value of, for example, more than 3 points on a 5-point Likert scale for each characteristic (see, e.g., Lüthje 2000, 151ff.; Bartl 2006, 181ff.). Other studies allow the different characteristics to compensate each other (see, e.g., Silvertant 2011, 110ff., 210ff.; Ramakrishnan 2012, 87). Following this approach, a "compensatory model" was chosen – meaning that the scores for each characteristic were added (without defining a threshold for each characteristic or weighting the criteria). This approach seems more appropriate, as this study assumes a continuous distribution of the lead-user score (see Morrison et al. 2004, 358) as opposed to a bi-polar distribution, which assumes that there are only lead users or non-lead users.

Consequently, the lead-user score (LUS) was calculated by summing the scores for each characteristic.[112] The LUS was adjusted, dividing it again by the number of characteristics (seven). Accordingly, the lowest possible adjusted LUS is 1 ($LUS_{low,adjusted} = 1$) and the highest is 5 ($LUS_{high,adjusted} = 5$). The center scale of 3 defines if a LUS can be considered high ($LUS_{high} \geq 3$) or low ($LUS_{low} < 3$). The resulting LUS – which determines the degree of lead userness – can then be analyzed and related to the creativity score which each participant obtained with his or her idea (see chapters 4 and 5).

111 Also, lead-user and non-lead-user groups are formed differently – i.e., along quartiles, means, or the median (Bartl 2006, 188ff.; Tietz et al. 2006, 462; Silvertant 2011, 210).

112 The lowest unadjusted LUS (LUS_{low}) to be obtained is seven points ($LUS_{low} = 7$), the highest thirty-five ($LUS_{high} = 35$). The center scale is at twenty-one (21) points.

To analyze the LUS collected, three statistical methods were applied: Again, the **Kolmogorov-Smirnov goodness-of-fit test** determined if variables were normally distributed. The fact that not every characteristic was normally distributed (see section 3.3.2 and chapter 4) affected the choice of tests that could be applied to analyze the LUS. To determine whether the lead-user characteristics significantly distinguished participants with a high creativity score (CS_{high}) from those with a low one (CS_{low}), the **Mann-Whitney U test** was applied (Doane and Seward 2013, 698).[113] Analogous to the t-test for independent sample means (see previous section), this non-parametric test assumes that the distributions of the two populations are the same, aside from their different locations (ibid.). It requires independent samples from populations with equal variances, but as opposed to the t-test, variables do not need to be normally distributed (ibid.). Furthermore, **Cohen's *d*** was applied for measuring the relative effect size between the lead-user scores achieved by CS_{low} and CS_{high} (Cohen 1971, 1988; see section 3.2.2 for further details).

Interviews and analysis: participants with LUS_{high}

Once the lead-user scores for all participants were identified, the interviewees with the highest lead-user scores were interviewed in depth. They started with an open part, in which the participant was engaged in a conversation. The second part of the interviews was semi-structured along the lead-user characteristics. The interviews lasted 60–120 minutes and were recorded and transcribed.

To schedule the interviews, the potential participants were called after the idea competition to ask for their availability. For three reasons, the interviews were conducted in the participants' homes: First, it was assumed that participants would feel more comfortable in their own environment. Second, reaching places outside of their community (e.g., the city center) would have been difficult and costly in terms of time and transportation – factors which were assumed to influence participation. Thirdly, this approach provided additional information as the home environment could be observed (participant observation). Furthermore, additional family members could be interviewed.

113 For the LU characteristics that were normally distributed, the t-test could also have been applied (see previous chapter). To ensure consistency, and as the Mann-Whitney U test can be considered as the stricter measure, it was applied to both normally distributed and not-normally distributed characteristics.

To analyze the interviews as well as the field notes from participant observation, **content analysis** was applied (Mayring 2003). It is a suitable method to analyze different types of recorded communication – for example, texts, transcripts of interviews, protocols of observations, pictures, and videos (Mayring 2000a, 2). There are various systematic approaches to content analysis. One of the most common approaches is that developed by Mayring (2003), in which three analytical procedures are applied successively or independently: summary, explication, and content-based structuring (Mayring 2003, 58ff.). The first step aims to reduce the material, preserving the main content. The second involves explaining the material through an "explicatory paraphrase," taking the context of the material into consideration. The third step aims to structure the material along categories deducted from theory, or inductively identified from the material itself. The latter two approaches were chosen for this study: First, unclear passages of the interview transcripts were "explained" through taking the context into consideration. Here, information gathered through participant observation was extremely valuable. The material was then coded deductively by categories in line with lead-user characteristics. For the coding, the software MAXQDA was used.

Interviews and analysis: very creative and less creative participants

To identify personality traits of creative consumers, in-depth interviews were conducted, applying semi-structured interviews as well as participant observation. Interviewees were identified based on their creativity score. First, participants whose ideas received high creativity scores (CS_{high}) were selected. Those whose ideas reached the lowest creativity scores (CS_{low}) served as a control group. This decision is a "within-case sampling decision" (Miles and Hubermann 1994, 29): Participants are selected for being extreme examples ("polar types") (Yin 2003; Eisenhardt and Graebner 2007, 27; Mills et al. 2010, 685ff.).

To schedule the interviews, the potential participants of the interview study were called after the idea competition to ask for their availability. The interviews were conducted at the participants' homes between April and May, 2009, (case study I) and April and May, 2010 (case studies II and III). The interviews generally lasted between 30 and 100 minutes. In the first part of the interview, interviewees were engaged in an informal conversation, aiming to provide the interviewee enough room to elaborate on issues he or she wanted to communicate or regarded as relevant. The second part of the interview followed a list of semi-structured questions that were asked in an order which suited the course of the conversation (see figure 22). When additional family members were present, the interactions between them as well as the judgments made about each other were taken into consideration in the field notes. After the interviews, the research team was often invited to stay for a coffee or shown around the house or neighborhood, allowing for additional participant observation.

Directly after the interviews, field notes were written down by the researchers (usually 1–3 people). They encompassed notes taken during the interview, a transcription of the result of the observation conducted in and around the house, and insights on the interaction between family members. The field notes of the different researchers were merged and discrepancies discussed. In addition, the interviews were recorded and transcribed.

Figure 22: Questionnaire for semi-structured interviews with creative participants

Idea competition: What did you think about the idea competition? Why did you participate?
Origin of idea: How did you come up with the idea developed for the competition?
Creative activity: Have you created ideas before? If yes, what type of ideas? Why did you create them? What was important to you when creating them?
Professional background: What is your profession? Please let us know more about it.
Free time: How do you like to spend your free time?
Family background: How many people are in your family? What do they do? What is your relation to them like? How did they react to your participation in the competition?

The field notes as well as the transcribed interviews served as a basis for the **content analysis** of the interviews.[114] In a first step, the transcripts and field notes were grouped by person. Then, participants from CS_{high} and CS_{low} were separated. First, the interviews of CS_{high} were studied closely and categories were built inductively (i.e., from the material). Although the interview transcripts offered a wealth of information, the category system was intended to focus on characteristics of the interviewees. However, other strong patterns relating to the context or abilities of the interviewees were also noted. After having coded 50% of the material using the software MAXQDA, a "formative check of reliability" was conducted, meaning that the categories were revised – new categories were built and others subsumed (Mayring 2003, 74–76). The ultimate objective was to come up with a category system that was

[114] Content analysis was conducted according to Mayring (2003).

exhaustive and mutually exclusive. This consolidation of categories revealed a series of characteristics that were evident for participants from CS_{high}. Then a "summative check of reliability" was conducted, meaning that the codes were applied to the material to test once more if all relevant characteristics would be covered (Mayring 2000a, 3, Mayring 2003, 76). Furthermore, these characteristics were checked to determine whether they sufficiently described all participants from CS_{high}. In a next step, these categories were applied to the interview transcripts from CS_{low} (control group) to ensure that the characteristics could not be found amongst any of the interviewees of CS_{low}. If so, they were deleted or revised.

3.2.4 Process: Identification and transfer of innovation-relevant knowledge

The third aspect of the study aims to find out the types of knowledge that idea competitions yield – and what types are most useful for product development specifically. Furthermore, it aims to examine how knowledge is transferred from participants to the researchers. For that purpose, the ideas collected were analyzed together with the whole research team, and members of the research team were interviewed. Ideas and interviews are analyzed through "content analysis" (Mayring 2003).

Research question 3a: What **types** of information and knowledge can be obtained through idea competitions conducted in low-income contexts?
Research question 3b: What types of information and knowledge are most **useful** for innovation processes geared towards developing solutions for low-income consumers?
Research question 3c: What factors **enable** the transfer of innovation-relevant knowledge from participants to product designers/developers during offline idea competitions in low-income contexts?

Units of analysis: ideas, process

Collection of ideas and analysis

As part of the realization phase, visualizations of the ideas submitted were collected as drawings. To support the explication of the material, textual and verbal descriptions were also requested, and the latter were transcribed. Furthermore, the field notes taken during the competition were compiled in research protocols. Researchers who took part in the collection of the ideas were invited to join the analysis of the ideas, to ensure that any information collected in the field, which was not captured on paper, could be included in the analysis. The analysis was conducted as a half-day workshop.

To analyze the material, **qualitative content analysis** according to Mayring (2003) was conducted. The technique seems suitable for this research endeavor as it takes the context of the material into consideration and puts emphasis on latent or implicit content inherent in the description or the drawings (Mayring 2000b, 468–469; Kohlbacher 2006, 8). The objective of applying this type of analysis is to gain a better understanding of the content of the ideas developed by the participants, extracting insights which could inform the product development process.

To **inductively build categories** (or "codes") that appeared across ideas, all drawings and texts related to one particular idea were grouped and closely read or, in the case of the visualizations, viewed. In a first step, unclear elements of the ideas were clarified by the research team (explication), mostly taking the descriptions by the participants and the field notes as additional sources of information, as well as considering the contexts in which the ideas were created.

Second, the material was organized with the aim of building categories. Topics or characteristics which appeared in more than one idea were written down. To not only capture technical or functional characteristics of the ideas, a special focus was also given to identifying symbolic or semantic aspects of the ideas to understand, for example, what the product means for the consumer, what relevance or status the product has, and what values the consumer associates with the product. This was done to see if this rather implicit information can be derived from the submitted ideas. This is in line with Mayring (2000a, 2), who suggests that content analysis does not only manifest primary content, but also "latent content."

In a third step, these categories were clustered. Then, a "summative check of reliability" was conducted by checking if all ideas could be sufficiently described with these categories, or if topics were missing (Mayring 2000a, 3, Mayring 2003, 76).[115] A single idea could also be described by various categories. At the end of the workshop, the results were discussed among the whole research team. As a result, categories were revised and reduced, subsuming categories or building new ones.

After the categories were made, all ideas were **coded** by two to three researchers using an Excel sheet. To ensure inter-coder reliability (i.e., "the extent to which coders agree in the coding of the same text" [Kohlbacher 2005, 15]), the classification was done by

[115] A "formative check of reliability" after having worked through 10–50% of the material – as suggested by Mayring (2003, 74–76) – was omitted due to the small number of ideas.

at least two researchers independently of each other. Differing results were discussed and jointly revised, and results were summarized in a table. Also, the frequency of each code identified was counted – an approach Miles and Huberman (1994, 42–43) call "quantitizing." However, this quantification of results was handled carefully, as the analysis focused on unveiling latent contents rather than counting frequencies. From these results, patterns and conclusions were derived separately for each case study ("within-case analysis").

Interviews with researchers

The research team, which mainly consisted of product designers, was responsible for designing a product based on the information gathered through desk research and during the idea competitions. They were interviewed with a semi-structured questionnaire. The interviews took place in early 2012, after all idea competitions were over and the product development processes had been completed. Most interviews were conducted via skype.[116]

The interviews were semi-structured along four sets of questions on (1) the benefits and shortcomings of the technique, (2) the insights obtained, (3) the value of the information, and (4) the perspectives of the researchers (see figure 23). Interviews were recorded and transcribed. The results of the transcripts were complemented by field notes taken by the main researcher during the whole process of the idea competitions, who observed the process as a participant.

To analyze the transcripts and notes, qualitative content analysis was applied, conducting first a formative and then a summative check of reliability (see section 3.2.3 for further elaborations). The coding was done inductively (Mayring 2003, 74–76).

---

[116] Researchers who could not participate in an oral interview replied to the questions extensively via email.

Figure 23: Questionnaire for semi-structured interviews with researchers/product designers

Benefits and shortcomings: What benefits and shortcomings does the "idea competition" technique have in comparison to other market research methods?
Insights: What did you, as a co-organizer of the idea competition and product designer, learn from conducting the idea competitions?
Value of information: What information and knowledge obtained during the idea competition was most useful for the subsequent product development/innovation process?
Perspectives: What was your perspective of low-income consumers both before and after the idea competition? What do you think the participants got out of the idea competition?

4 Insights from the field: Case studies

This chapter presents the data gathered through the three case studies. As recommended by Eisenhardt (1989, 539ff.), the case studies are presented and analyzed separately from each other (see "within-case analysis," section 3.2.2). However, the presentation of each case study follows the same structure:

The first section of each case study presents the **setting**, introducing the topic of the competition, the target community, and the partners involved. The second section takes a close look at the level of creativity of the **ideas** gathered in each idea competition. The third section examines the **participants** who submitted the ideas – considering, first, their socioeconomic profile and, second, the extent to which they show lead-user characteristics. Furthermore, the third section aims to explore the characteristics of those participants with high creativity scores.

The last section of each case study takes the **process** of the idea competition as a unit of analysis. Through interviews with the team of product designers who set up and implemented the idea competitions, it aims to explore the types of innovation-relevant knowledge they obtained through the method – as well as the factors that enabled this knowledge transfer.

4.1 Case Study I: Project "Eco-Agregado"[117]

4.1.1 Setting: Topic, target community, and partners

Brazilian low-income families often cannot meet their housing needs. Their domiciles are frequently improvised, with walls made from discarded materials or dirt floors; they lack access to water or sewage systems; or they simply live with too many people under the same roof (Caixa Economica Federal 2011, 13ff.; IDB 2012). Many of these houses are illegal settlements. However, only legal houses can receive social benefits (i.e., subsidies for electricity or water). The governmental program "Minha Casa Minha Vida" – launched in 2009 – aims to address this housing deficit by building and/or reforming three million houses for Brazilian low-income families by the end of

[117] The name of the project, "Eco-Agregado," was created by the research team. It refers to ecological material ("eco") that is aggregated to perform a new function related to housing – i.e., as a piece of furniture or an extension of a house.

2014.[118][119] Due to the governmental support, the households that qualify for the program are willing to invest more in their houses.[120] Consequently, there is a high need for quality goods and services that fit their surroundings. This does not only refer to building materials, but also goods for the interior, like furniture or sanitary installations. However, quality products of this category are rarely available – most products are either too expensive, of low quality, or inadequate for a housing situation that has to accommodate many people.[121]

Topic: The need for appropriate storage solutions

Low-income houses provide shelter to many family members,[122] and space is thus limited. The topic of the "Eco-Agregado" idea competition was to "*Create a solution to organize your house!*" The competition sought solutions that created space – for example, by improving the storage of belongings and thus making the existing space more habitable. The phrasing of the task was intentionally kept open to avoid narrowing down the solution space too early (Soll 2006, 102).

The community: Aguas Claras, Piraquara

The community Aguas Claras in Piraquara was chosen as the first target community due to the established relationship between the initiator of the idea competition, the Research Center for Design and Sustainability (Núcleo de Design e Sustentabilidade

---

118 For further information, see the website of the government program: http://www.minhacasaminhavida.com.br/

119 Housing deficit refers to families that are homeless or live in poor quality houses. According to the Fundação Joao Pinheiro, 85.4% of the families that have up to three minimum wages at their disposal do not have access to appropriate housing (COHAPAR 2010).

120 Households with a household income of less than ten minimum monthly salaries qualify for the program. The minimum monthly salary during the time of the competition (in 2010) was R$510, which was around €230 (exchange rate from September 14, 2010). For further information, see the website of the program "Minha Casa Minha Vida": http://www.portalbrasil.net/salariominimo.htm#sileiro, accessed May 1, 2013. According to Hammond et al. (2007, 117), low-income consumers in Brazil currently spend around 5% of their household budget on housing.

121 Some retailers such as Casas Bahia or Magazine Luiza address low-income segments with innovative business models that give them access to credits and rate payments that are accessible even without a bank account or collateral; however, they often charge high interest rates and sell goods that are of low quality and not tailored to the needs of the consumers (i.e., products don't fit into their rooms with low ceilings, etc.).

122 In the 2010 census, the Instituto Brasileiro de Geografia e Estatística (IBGE) estimated the average number of people per household to be 3.3 (IBGE 2010). During the field visits, however, the absolute number of people per household visited was up to 8.

[NDS]) and the community residents' association.[123] The community is located in the metropolitan area of Curitiba, the capital of the Brazilian state Paraná. It is rather small, with an estimated 100 households. Although many houses are masonry constructions, wooden houses or wooden extensions of houses can be still be found. Most houses are connected to the grid; however, many still lack sanitary constructions. As the community is quite small, no socioeconomic statistics on the community are available.

The project partners: NDS, Soliforte, and FINEP

The idea competition was conducted as part of the field research phase of the research project "Eco-Agregado." The project was supported by the recycling company Soliforte Reciclagem Ltda., a Brazilian SME that recycles waste from civil construction and demolition into aggregates, which are 70% cheaper than raw materials and are sold to consumers as well as to other businesses. Since 2007, the company has been located in the metropolitan area of Curitiba, being the first company of its kind in this area. Soliforte currently only recycles concrete and ceramics, but it aims to amplify its capacities to be able to recycle other materials such as plastic and wood. To enhance value creation, the company also plans to offer specific products related to social housing instead of just recycled material. This was triggered by the fact that the company is surrounded by one of the major low-income communities in the metropolitan area of Curitiba, the "Vila Zumbi." In order to develop new products and services for low-income consumers, the company partnered with the NDS. Jointly, they acquired funding from the Funding Authority for Studies and Projects (Financiadora de Estudos e Projetos [FINEP]) of the Brazilian Innovation Agency and the Fundação Araucária. Out of this initiative, the project "Eco-Agregado" emerged.

The field research phase of "Eco-Agregado" aimed to unveil low-income consumers' needs, wants, and aspirations, and to create initial ideas for focus products and services that the company could develop. The results were intended to inspire product designers during a subsequent idea-generation and product-development workshop.

---

[123] A residents' association ("associação dos moradores") is often created in low-income environments to organize the community and give it a voice in addressing public bodies – e.g., to request public services like electricity or waste collection.

4.1.2 Ideas: Creativity of ideas

To determine the creativity of the ideas submitted, the Consensual Assessment Technique (CAT) was applied (see section 3.2.2). The jury that assessed the ideas consisted of two academics, the director of the company Soliforte and an NGO representative. The requirements of the CAT were fulfilled (see section 3.2.2). Furthermore, the minimum intra-class correlation coefficient (ICC) level (ICC > 0.7) was reached for all dimensions except for *feasibility* (see table 22). Due to the small sample size, the value for *utility* – which is slightly below the minimum ICC level – is acceptable (Wirtz and Casper 2002, 25). The ICC for feasibility is too low. However, the dimension was left in to ensure the comparability of results with the other two case studies, which each show acceptable results for this dimension.[124]

Table 22: Inter-rater reliability in case study I

Dimensions	ICC	Cronbach's Alpha
Originality	0.815	0.846
Utility	0.664	0.619
Degree of elaboration	0.710	0.629
Feasibility	0.221	0.121

Source: created by author.

To determine the creativity, a creativity score (CS) was calculated, ranging from 1 to 5 (5-point Likert scale).[125] The scores of each creativity dimension as well as the score of the CS fulfills the requirements $p > 0.05$ of the Kolmogorov-Smirnov goodness-of-fit test (K-S test), which means that the variables are normally distributed (table 23). The creativity scores for all ideas ($n = 34$) are on a continuum between very low and very high.

[124] Walcher (2007, 61ff.) comes to a similar result. He finds that the values of the feasibility dimension are perceived differently by jury members, or that they state to have no knowledge about it. Citing Amabile, he concludes that the dimension should be rated, but that the result should be considered with care.

[125] See section 3.2.3 for further details. Every idea was assessed by four experts, applying the four CAT dimensions on a 5-point Likert Scale and summing the score of each dimension. Thus, every idea could reach a minimum creativity score (CS_{min}) of 16 points and a maximum creativity score (CS_{max}) of 80 points. To make the scores comparable to other case studies, they were adjusted by dividing them by the number of judges (four) and by the four creativity dimensions.

The arithmetic mean refers to the average degree of *originality*, *elaboration*, *utility*, and *feasibility* of the pool of ideas. The CAT dimension with the highest mean was utility, followed by feasibility. Both dimensions reached a mean above center scale. This means that experts regarded most ideas as useful for consumers and viable. Originality was ranked third and elaboration ranked last – both with values below center scale. This means that ideas were not as new (to the jury of experts) and that specifications of the submitted ideas (e.g., technical specifications, indication of materials to be used) were regarded as rather limited. The mean of the creativity score lay slightly above center scale ($CS_{mean,\ adjusted} = 3.01$).[126] The highest absolute creativity score reached was 4.12, the lowest 1.56 points.

Table 23: Assessment of normality distribution of the CAT dimensions in case study I

Case study I	Originality	Utility	Elabora-tion	Feasibility	CS
Mean	2.77	3.40	2.63	3.22	3.01
Std. deviation	1.10	0.70	0.66	0.43	0.57
Kolmogorov-Smirnov Z	0.491	1.223	0.782	1.279	0.655
Asymp. sig. (2-tailed)	0.969	0.100	0.574	0.076	0.784

Source: created by author.

The ideas can be divided into creative ideas (CS_{high}) and less creative ideas (CS_{low}). The latter are ideas that reach a CS below center scale ($CS_{low} < 3$). They account for 44.1% (n = 15) of the ideas. The creative ideas are those with a CS equal to or above center scale ($CS_{high} \geq 3$). They account for more than half of the ideas (55.9% | n = 19).

A comparison of the creativity dimensions of the two groups shows that the mean of CS_{high} is significantly higher for each dimension. Creative ideas were ranked above center scale, and less creative ones below or only slightly above center scale. The dimension that distinguishes both groups most is originality (delta = 1.72), followed by degree of elaboration (delta = 0.85) (see figure 24). This means that creative ideas were more original and elaborated. An independent sample t-test[127] shows that the differences are significant (see figure 24).

---

[126] The mean of the creativity score (CS_{mean}) has 48.09 points. The adjusted mean is divided by the number of experts and the number of dimensions (see previous footnote).

[127] The independent sample t-test is used when the scores of two different groups of people (creative and less creative) are being compared. It assesses whether the means of two groups are statistically

Figure 24: Comparison of creativity groups in case study I

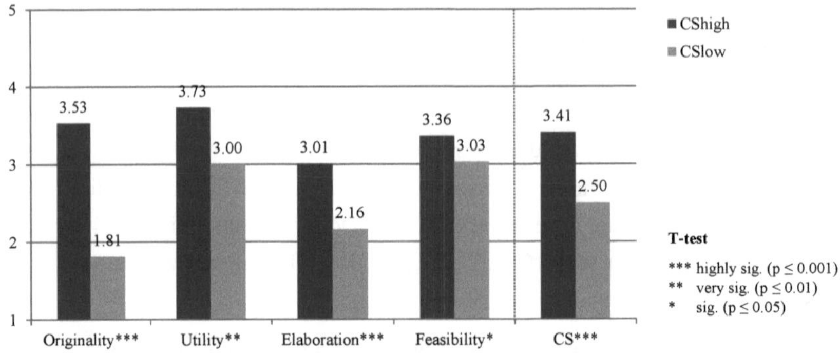

Source: created by author.

Furthermore, Cohen's *d* was calculated (Cohen 1971, 22ff.). For each creativity dimension, it shows a value above 0.8, which indicates a large effect (see table 24).

Table 24: Comparison of means and effect sizes of creativity dimensions – case study I

Case study I	CS_{high}	Std. deviation	CS_{low}	Std. deviation	Cohen's *d*
Originality	3.53	0.70	1.81	0.67	2.50
Utility	3.73	0.50	2.98	0.70	1.23
Elaboration	3.01	0.43	2.16	0.61	1.60
Feasibility	3.36	0.33	3.03	0.48	0.81
CS	3.41	0.32	2.50	0.37	2.63

Source: created by author.

4.1.3 Participants: Analysis of characteristics

The idea competition caught the interest of 26 people, who handed in 34 ideas.[128] As the community of Aguas Claras only comprises around 350 inhabitants, the submission of 34 ideas can be regarded as fairly high: estimating that all households could be reached through the promotion of the competition, the return rate is 9.7%.

different from each other. The t-test requires that the CS and its dimensions be normally distributed, which is given.

128 Most people (23) handed in one idea. Only four people (three of them women) handed in several ideas: One woman handed in four ideas, two handed in three ideas, and two handed in two ideas.

Socioeconomic characteristics of participants

Almost 58% of the participants were women, whereas 42% were men. The average age of the participants was 33.5 years. The highest age was 77, the lowest 10. The median age was 30. The Kolmogorov-Smirnov statistic showed that age was normally distributed ($p_{age} = 0.781$). Breaking participants down into different age groups showed that they are balanced. Only the age groups 51–60 and 61–70 were underrepresented (see figure 25).

Figure 25: Age groups in case study I

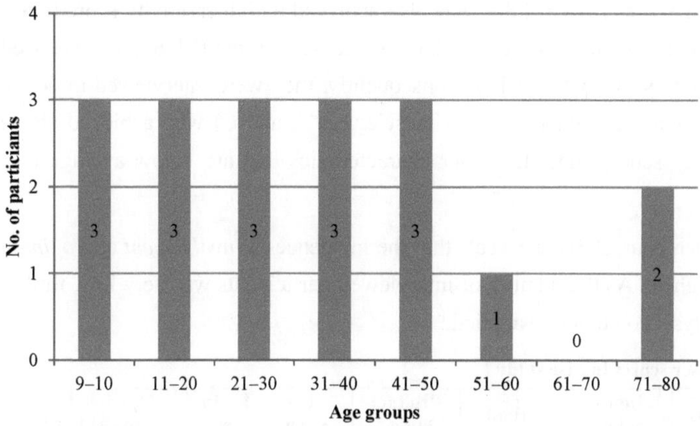

Source: created by author.

Most of the participants were students (36%, n = 22), followed by homemakers (27%). Only one participant was employed as a construction worker. Other participants were either housewives, retired, or self-employed.

The average family income of the participants was R$1,130 per month (around €390).[129] The highest income was R$2,400 (around €830), the lowest R$250 (around €86).[130] All participants thus belonged to the lowest income classes D and E, according

[129] R$ denotes Brazilian Reais.

[130] The exchange rate is from May 2009 – i.e., the time when the interviews took place (1 Brazilian Real = 0.35 Euros).

to the Brazilian Institute for Geography and Statistics (Instituto Brazileiro de Geografia e Estatística [IBGE]).[131]

Quantitative analysis of lead-user characteristics

To be able to compare the results of the qualitative interviews with potential lead users, the answers to the semi-structured questions, which query lead-user characteristics, were quantified. To code the answers, a 5-point Likert scale was applied.

The results of the coding showed that the winner of third place (idea 10) achieved the highest lead-user score (LUS = 4.86). She also achieved a high creativity score (CS = 3.69). The first place winner also received a high lead-user score (LUS = 4.29) as well as a high creativity score (CS = 4.13). Consequently, they were interviewed in depth. In contrast, the remaining interviewees (interviewees A and C) who achieved above average creativity scores show lead-user characteristics that are below average (see figure 26).

The mean of each characteristic reveals that the incidence of *involvement* and *opinion leadership* is highest. As the number of interviewed participants was very low, further methods of analysis could not be applied.[132]

Table 25: Lead-user scores in case study I

Case study I	Dissatis-faction	Inno-vative activity	Trend leadership	Product know-ledge	Use experi-ence	In-volve-ment	Opinion leadership	LUS
Mean	3.20	3.00	3.60	3.40	3.20	4.40	3.80	3.51
Std. devia-tion	1.64	1.58	1.34	1.14	1.10	0.55	0.84	1.00

Source: created by author.

131 The IBGE divides the Brazilian population into five income classes, ranging from A to E, with A being the highest income class and E the lowest. For more information, please see the website of the IBGE: http://www.ibge.gov.br/english/ - accessed May 1, 2013.

132 The small sample size was mainly due to the difficulty of conducting research in low-income environments. For example, the communities were difficult to access, as they are situated in the outskirts of the metropolitan area of Curitiba. Thus, private transport had to be arranged. Security was also an issue when visiting people in their homes rather than at a safer location like the community center. Furthermore, participants with jobs could only be interviewed at night, when it was especially dangerous to access the communities. Lastly, it was difficult to localize the interviewees, as some of them did not have a proper address or phone number

Figure 26: Creativity and lead-user characteristics of CS_{high} in case study I

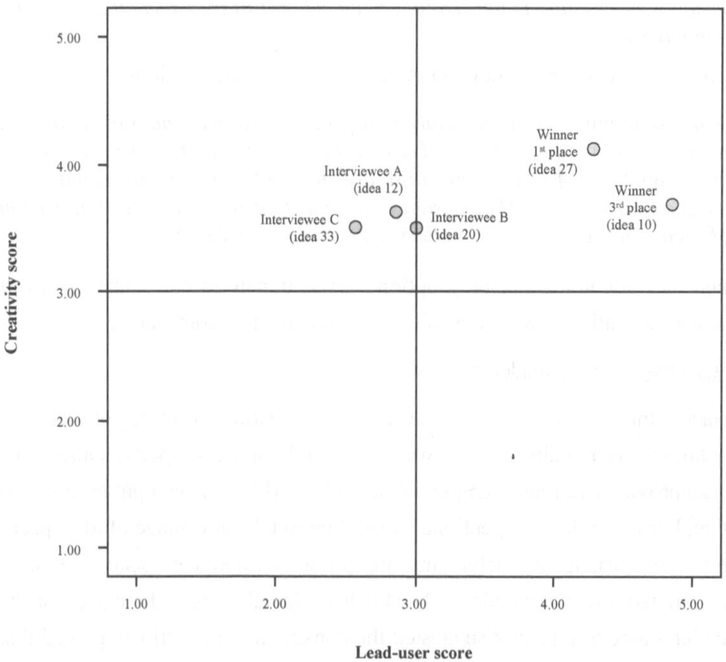

Source: created by author.

Qualitative analysis of lead-user characteristics

Two of the winners of the idea competition (first and third place) were the only interviewees to show above average lead-user scores. To find out if they can be regarded as lead users, in-depth interviews on their lead-user characteristics were conducted and analyzed.

Dissatisfaction

The first and third place winners vividly expressed their *dissatisfaction* with current furniture solutions. The first place winner mentioned the lack of products that were adapted to his particular needs and housing situation:

> *Every piece of furniture is big. They do not work in small houses. And the things that are available for small houses are things you do not want. They are simpler. No, I am definitely not satisfied.*

The winner of the third place came to a similar conclusion:

> *In the shops, everything is big. These products don't fit into a small house. And I like to have space!*

She continued to vividly express her dissatisfaction with current solutions:

> *There are so many pieces of furniture they produce that have nothing to do with the person who uses them. I don't know if the people who design them are not smart enough? [...] A piece of furniture like this shelf costs one thousand reais, and is good for nothing. They design it so that it easily breaks. The maximum life of such a product is a year – afterwards, it starts to distort.*

She explained that oftentimes her only option was to transform and adapt pieces of furniture she was not satisfied with herself – or to have them custom-made.

Innovative activity and trend leadership

The third place winner seemed to be a true expert in creating furniture solutions for low-income houses. Her main concern was to use idle space properly. During the interviews, she provided various examples of new ideas which she had put or aimed to put in practice. For example, she mentioned a solution to take advantage of idle spaces in houses by putting triangular shelves in unused corners, and she spoke of another solution that entailed a foldable table for her kitchen. She also created a closet for the idle space under stairs. She further suggested the construction of a "floating" bed that – by being folded up during the day – could be transformed into a wardrobe or shoe cabinet. She proposed various solutions for pieces of furniture that hang above the floor and thus occupy less space.

Her husband commented that "she always has her own crazy ideas." However, she mentioned that she had more ideas than she could put into practice due to her financial situation. She claimed that whenever she had money, she had her ideas custom-made by a carpenter.

> *I like things that do not exist! [...] I am designing my own dinner table with chairs, as I want it to be different – I don't want the normal things they sell in the shops. That is why I design my furniture and have the pieces made by the carpenter.*
>
> *When I have ideas, I want to see them realized – the other people say "tomorrow I'll do this." But when it is time to carrying things out, I can be insistent.*

She commented that the carpenter always made two versions of the products she designed – one for her and one which he used in a showroom as "they always sell." She stressed that a variety of the solutions she created were copied by other people from the community, which indicates her *trend leadership*.

When asked about his motivation to participate in the competition, the winner of the first place stated that it was "to create something new and original." He submitted two ideas to the competition – the second together with a friend. Both ideas achieved high creativity scores. The competition motivated him to elaborate the ideas and to try to put them in practice. He stated that he frequently had ideas and liked to create new things. In addition, he mentioned that he had had ideas that, at that time, did not exist but that he later saw in the market – a fact that might indicate his trend leadership. He claimed to use the internet frequently to look for new solutions.

<u>Product-related knowledge and use experience</u>

The third place winner clearly stated that her hobby was designing furniture. Besides running a small grocery shop, she was a housewife who spent a lot of the time at home using, cleaning, and often rearranging the furniture to optimize space. Her husband commented that she frequently rearranged things in the house to find better organization solutions. Doing that, she acquired *product-related knowledge* and *use experience* that helped her design her ideas. She has created various pieces of furniture, which she had custom-made by a carpenter:

> *When you have things custom-made, they are oftentimes cheaper. I spend much less having things made, and I can select good materials – for example, high-quality timber. That way the furniture can be used by my great-grandchildren!*
>
> *I always like high-quality material. […] My preferred material is robust wood.*

The winner of the first place was also knowledgeable about materials that could be used for furniture, which he described in detail. For example, when asked if he was able to put his submitted idea into practice, he outlined the materials he would use. He acquired knowledge of materials when working as a construction worker. However, he acknowledged that he had less use experience, as he did not spend much time at home. Nonetheless, he commented that he had put together and dismantled various pieces of furniture, which indicates use experience.

Involvement

Both interviewees uniformly stated that they were very involved and informed when it came to making investments in durable goods. Despite the high information costs, they merely could not "afford" to invest in a product that did not fit in their house/environment or a product which would not last due to, for example, low-quality material. Thus, they oftentimes sought the best possible option within their budget and were willing to spend a lot of time searching for information. The third place winner explained the following:

> *I look in catalogues, I go to shops, I talk to other people, I always go to shops to take home flyers and catalogues. [...] When I want to buy something new, I wait up to a year as I research until I find an affordable solution. I have been wanting to change my dinner table for two years, but I want good furniture. Thus, I think about having it custom-made or buying it.*

The creator of Idea 27 even used the internet for his research: "It is great to do research using the internet – I always take a look."

Opinion leadership

Again, the third place contestant had the strongest tendency of opinion leadership. Due to her excitement, she would even communicate her ideas to people who did not ask her. She stated,

> *I share my experiences with other people – but they are not always interested. But I am! A lot of people saw the solution I implemented to use the space in the corners of the house, a triangle shelf – some people copied this idea.*

Along with actively sharing her experiences and ideas with others, she was frequently sought after by others for her ideas:

> *People asked me about the shelf for the corners. And I have the contact to the carpenter who puts it into practice. I told people to further develop this idea if they had money – for example, to put glass in front to make it look nicer. [...] Also, the carpenter often asked me for my advice. Once, he had a client who wanted to get stairs custom-made. I developed an idea which allows creating storage room under the stairs.*

The winner of the idea competition admitted that he was not very communicative and was rather shy when talking to others: "I have plenty of ideas, but I only sometimes pass them on to others." However, he stated that his friends asked him for advice and help. For example, in the case of the competition, his friend asked him to submit an idea together, as he is known for having good ideas.

Characteristics of creative participants

This section aims to find out if the participants who submitted a creative idea (CS_{high}) distinguish themselves from the creators of less creative ideas (CS_{low}). Thus, interviews were held with four CS_{high} individuals – two of whom were winners of the competition – and with two from CS_{low} as a control group.

Table 26: Overview of interview participants in case study I

CS_{high}			CS_{low}		
Interview no.	**Idea no.**	**CS**	**Interview no.**	**Idea no.**	**CS**
1	10	3.69	**5**	1	2.88
2	12	3.63	**6**	14	2.25
3	20	3.50			
4	27	4.13			

Source: created by author.

The following clusters of characteristics could be identified amongst the group CS_{high}. There was no evidence of these characteristics amongst the control group CS_{low}.[133]

High problem-solving ability

The creator of idea 10 showed a high capacity to solve problems creatively. In addition to her many ideas about how to create or improve pieces of furniture, she applied her creative abilities to create things she lacked, such as toys, carpets, or clothes.

> *I developed the idea for the competition, but I always have ideas. However, nobody from outside [of the community] ever came and asked. I like to present my ideas – it is an opportunity for us to share. [...] In fact, I would have been able to develop 30 ideas for the competition; however, I needed to travel on the day of the competition, which is why I had limited time that day.*

[133] Consequently, comparatively little direct evidence and few quotes from the interviews are reported for group CS_{low}. As laid out in chapter 3, the characteristics for CS_{high} participants were identified through inductively coding their interviews. As the characteristics are supposed to characterize CS_{high} in contrast to CS_{low} (control group), it was ensured that the characteristics identified could not be found amongst any of the interviewees of CS_{low} as otherwise, they had to be deleted or revised. Thus, it was difficult to find a direct quote that would illustrate how CS_{low} did *not* give evidence of the characteristics identified. Rather, the fact that they do not correspond to these characteristics was often shown through participant observation. For example, the lack of ambition and self-confidence of CS_{low} – in contrast to the very ambitious and self-confident group CS_{high} – was observed, as many of them were very reserved and shy, did not speak about any passions or objectives during the interviews, and gave a general impression of resignation.

She explained that she frequently recycled materials and created new things out of them:

> *I always look around. The neighbors throw a lot of things away that can be re-used or re-combined. [...] For example, when people throw away clothes, I always take out the buttons, zippers, pieces of the cloth – and I create new clothes.*

The creator of idea 12 admitted that the idea created for the competition was the first piece of furniture he had invented. However, he explained that he enjoyed solving problems at his workplace. For example, as he was unsatisfied with the way car wheels were repaired, he invented a technique to repair cracked car wheels with cord and glue. He claimed this technique to be more resistant than other techniques. He even opened a little business selling the repaired wheels.

Curiosity and positive attitude towards change

The CS_{high} participants' curiosity was most prominent in the way they approached the research team – they eagerly asked questions about the competition, wanted get information and learn more about its objectives and the project. The creator of idea 20 stated, "I always pay attention to new things!" This was in direct contrast to many other people in the community, who remained skeptical or simply did not show any interest.

In the interviews, all participants of CS_{high} showed a positive attitude towards change. For example, the creator of idea 10 stated that "we have to change – if not, we get sick of the same things." Also, through her elaborations on how she wanted to change her house or her shop, she showed that she enjoyed seeing change and that she approached it proactively. The creator of idea 12 had only recently been elected president of the residents' association. That position entailed strongly advocating for change in his community before local political bodies; and he took action to put his ideas for change into practice. He rented a building in the community where the inhabitants could meet and organize themselves, and acquired donations for the community to organize community dinners and events.

Ambition, dedication, and self-confidence

"Sometimes, when I have ideas, I do cool things," stated the creator of idea 10 self-confidently. She constantly mentioned her willingness to grow:

> *There are people who do not want to get ahead – but I want to grow a lot! [...] I did not have the chance to study – thus, I need to work hard today. When you study, you can be somebody. I tell you, if I had gone to school, I would already be rich!*

She related that she would like to build a furniture factory. She elaborated that she would make two spaces in the factory – one for young people and one for older people – to give both groups opportunities. Furthermore, she dreamed about building a house that would serve as a showroom for the products she created – "a house full of details, a house for visitors and tourists. It will be a unique project. Like this, people will see that an illiterate woman like me can have good ideas."

The creator of idea 12 also showed himself to be a highly ambitious person. He was very dedicated to his position as president of the residents' association, which he carried out in his free time. In the interviews, he vividly laid out the plans he had for the community, and explained how he aimed to put them in practice.

<u>Ability to think and act independently</u>

The creator of idea 10 had a very assertive appearance and seemed to be the one who set the tone at home: "In my house, there is no 'machismo'!" From the way she acted and talked with her husband and children, it became clear that she led the family. She explained that she enjoyed being financially independent, running her own little grocery shop. Previously, she had produced and sold a variety of homemade goods. For example, she made handicrafts, weaving carpets and sewing tablecloths. She also prepared chocolate or food which she sold. "I did everything to make ends meet – except stealing!"

The entrepreneurial ambitions of the creators of ideas 12 and 27 also indicated their drive for independence. Based on his idea to repair car wheels, the creator of idea 12 had opened a little business, which he ran on his own. His position as the president of the residents' association also required a certain degree of independence of thought and action. The creator of idea 27 laid out his plans to produce and commercialize an idea he had developed with a friend – namely, a solution that provides and stores hot water at home without using additional energy.

<u>Environmental consciousness</u>

The creator of idea 10 spoke vividly about her passion for recycling material and creating new things out of old ones: "I bring things home which I find – and sometimes turn them into something new." She complained about people – particularly adolescents – who do not value recyclable materials. "Throwing things away is extravagance! [...] People prefer to buy new things – I, in contrast, value every material and recycle it." She collected buttons and zippers from old clothes as well as nails and pieces of wood from old furniture to re-use them. She also made a variety of things out of PET bottles, such as handbags or toys for kids. She concluded by saying, "[o]ur country is poor because people don't know how to make use of things; if they knew, our country would be rich." Also the creator of idea 12 related that the idea of his business was triggered by his environmental consciousness. Aiming to recycle car wheels, he had come up with a new technique. He also handed in a second idea to the competition that was not related to the topic but a solution to save energy nonetheless – indicating his care for the environment.

Family unity and support

All CS_{high} participants seemed to come from functioning families who supported them. For example, the wife of the creator of idea 27 submitted her husband's idea on the day of the competition, as he had to go to work. Also, he stated that it was his wife who had motivated him to participate, as she believed in his creative abilities. During the interview, the whole family was present. Also, the creator of idea 10 received support from her husband. He was present during the interview, confirmed her statements, and showed himself to be proud of his wife's creativity. Clearly, his wife was the main bread winner of the family, and her husband supported her by dividing up tasks in the household. Also, the creator of idea 12 explained how his wife supported him when he set up his business. His whole family was present during the day of the idea competition, spending time with the research team and supporting the collection of ideas.

In contrast to these CS_{high} responses, no related quotes could be found amongst the participants from CS_{low} that would indicate a match with these characteristics. In fact, many interviews proved the contrary. For example, two interviewees stated that the idea created for the competition was the first idea they had ever created on their own, indicating that finding solutions was not an activity they usually engaged in. Furthermore, they did not show high ambition or self-confidence. Rather, most interviewees seemed to show complacency with their situation, believing that there was little they could change. In addition, they did not show any drive to be independent, nor did they make any comments that would indicate high environmental consciousness. Low family unity and support was particularly striking amongst participants from CS_{low}. For example, when the team made a house visit to conduct the interview with the creator of idea 14, his wife did not allow the team inside, stating, "this is the house of poor people, there is nothing to be seen." The creator of idea 1 was a divorced, single mother who had to care for her children on her own, not receiving any support from other family members.

Table 27: Overview of characteristics of creative participants in case study I

Characteristics of creative participants	Idea no.			
	10	**12**	**20**	**27**
High problem-solving ability	✓	✓	✓	✓
Curiosity, positive attitude towards change	✓	✓	✓	✓
Ambition, dedication, and self-confidence	✓	✓	✓	✓
Ability to think and act independently	✓	✓	X	X
Environmental consciousness	✓	✓	X	X
Family unity and support	✓	✓	X	✓
% of characteristics encountered per person	100%	100%	50%	60%

Source: created by author.

Note: a check mark [✓] was used to code when the characteristic was present, and an X when it was absent.

4.1.4 Process: Identification and transfer of innovation-relevant knowledge

To explore what types of information and knowledge can be obtained from the *process* of idea competitions, two sets of data were analyzed. First, the content of the submitted *ideas* was analyzed (see section 3.2.2). The purpose was to identify patterns and trends that give insights into consumer requirements and preferences regarding a suitable solution for organizing the interior of their house. Winning ideas are portrayed in detail. Second, the researchers/product designers were interviewed on the insights obtained from the whole *process*, after the idea competition was completed. Interview transcripts were analyzed to find out what types of knowledge they obtained, and what types were most useful for the subsequent product development process. The interviews further revealed how the transfer of innovation-relevant knowledge was enabled.

Innovation-relevant knowledge obtained from the ideas

Through the content analysis of the ideas, patterns of similar features and designs can be observed. Concretely, four main topic clusters could be identified, which are listed and explained below in the order of their frequency (for further detail, see table 28). The clusters imply conclusions on consumer requirements.

- **Better utilization of existing space in the house**: In line with the topic of the idea competition, the majority of the solutions suggested using unoccupied spaces in the house. Some proposed the full use of the horizontal dimensions of the room – for example, pieces of furniture that are built into the corner of the room. Other ideas proposed utilizing the vertical dimensions of the room – for example, by designing pieces of furniture that extend from the bottom of the room to the ceiling, leaving no gaps in between. A third group in this cluster suggested the use of idle spaces, such as the space under the ceiling, where no piece of furniture is usually placed (see ideas 16 and 19, figure 27; ideas 10 and 27, figure 28).
- **Multifunctionality**: A variety of ideas present pieces of furniture with multiple functions – for example, a piece of furniture that is both a bed and a seat, and at the same time offers possibilities to store and organize different goods (see Ideas 6 and 26, figure 27; ideas 29 and 10, figure 28).
- **Customized organization and storage**: A third cluster focuses on the requirement for customized organization and storage – the need to store and organize different belongings with the same piece of furniture but separately (e.g., clothes, electronic equipment, and tools). Thus, the designers of these kinds of ideas created different storage solutions within the same piece of furniture – for example, drawers, shelves, and storage racks. The different spaces had different dimensions (small, medium, large), which were designated for different items and sometimes even had different forms (triangular, rectangular, square). Also modular solutions were suggested (i.e., solutions that can be arranged according to user needs) (see ideas 16 and 19, figure 27; idea 10, figure 28).
- **Reduction and recycling of resources**: Some ideas focused on reducing the use of materials or energy consumption as well as on using recycled materials (see idea 10, figure 28). However, this was mostly driven by a desire to reduce costs, and not necessarily by environmental consciousness.

Table 28: Frequency of content clusters identified – case study I

Cluster	Frequency *(absolute)*	Frequency *(in percent)*
Multifunctionality	16	38.1
Better utilization of existing spaces in the house	15	35.7
Customized organization and storage	8	19.0
Reduction and recycling of resources	3	7.1

Source: created by author.

Figure 27: Exemplary ideas from case study I[134]

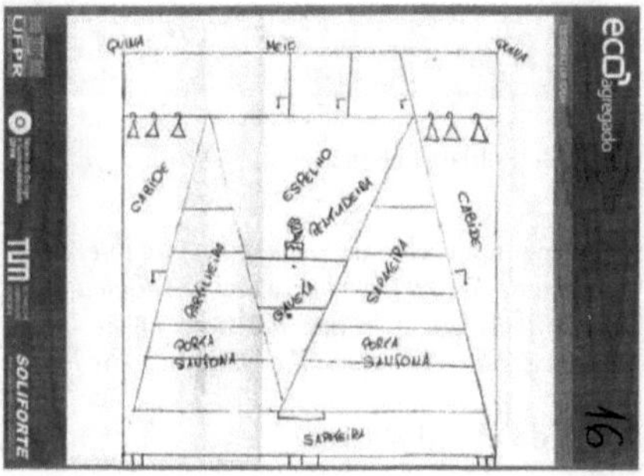

Idea 16 – Multifunctional storage shelf

Description by creator: *The storage solution would go under the ceiling to make good use of space. Its shelves have different sizes, so that different things can be stored. Also, there is an integrated bar to hang things up.*

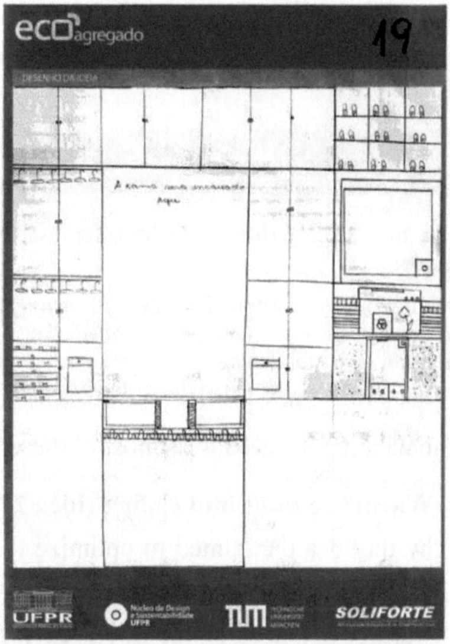

Idea 19 – Storage solution with integrated bed ("guarda-cama")

Description by creator: *The bed – when not in use – can be put back into the wardrobe. Thus, the underside of the bed needs to be pretty – as it will be shown. The bedside tables are also integrated into the wardrobe – and would only be pulled out if needed.*

[134] Ideas were numbered according to the order in which the research team received them. The numbers do not connote any sort of ranking.

Idea 26 – Bed and shelf with wheels for disabled people

Description by creator: *This bed is made for disabled people – it has an integrated shelf so that they can store things they need throughout the day. It has wheels to facilitate cleaning.*

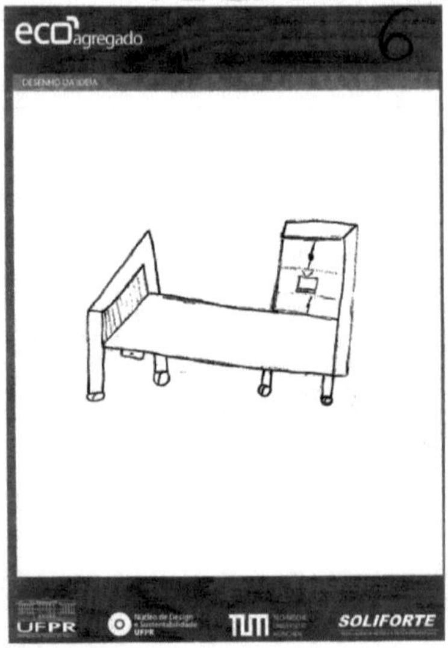

Idea 6 – Foldable chair

Description by creator: *This is a foldable chair which turns into a little box when it is folded – the legs of the chair turn into the sides of the box – and the cushioned part of the chair is at the top.*

The winning ideas address most of these patterns identified above:

- **Wardrobe built into ceiling (idea 27)**: The first place in the competition was won by the idea that aimed to optimize the use of vertical space: a wardrobe built into the ceiling. The participant observed that people tend to store their belongings in wardrobes placed on the floor, leaving the whole space under the ceiling unused. In his bathroom, which measures only one square meter (1 m²), there was no possibility of putting a piece of furniture on the floor. Thus, he suggested building a wardrobe into the ceiling, which would have wheels or rails so that it could be pulled down easily. This solution could not only be used in small rooms (such as a bathroom) but also in every other room where a storage solution is needed. The idea convinced the judges mainly because of its originality, but also its utility.
- **Foldable wardrobe (idea 29)**: The second winning idea – a foldable wardrobe – aimed to better utilize space and also offered multifunctional use. The wardrobe can be pushed against the wall, and it looks like a normal piece of furniture. However, it

is accessible from all sides. It has handles that can separate the wardrobe in the middle, where the two parts are joined by a hinge, so that it can be folded into a right angle. Thus, it creates a space behind it, where the user can get dressed. Besides being a smart solution for creating a space to store belongings, the solution addresses the need for privacy when sharing only one or two rooms with various family members. The idea convinced the judges mainly because of its originality, but also its utility.

- **Room divider (idea 10):** The room divider made by the third place winner divides the living and sleeping areas of a room, which are often in one room due to lack of space in many dwellings. The room divider has functional features on both sides. From the side of the bed, it can be transformed into a wardrobe with eight doors, together with a bed. The creator pointed out that this solution economizes a lot on materials by being used from both sides and by integrating various pieces of furniture. The idea addresses most trends identified: optimal use of space and materials, multifunctionality, and customized storage solutions. The idea convinced the judges mainly due to its utility.

Figure 28: Winning ideas of case study I

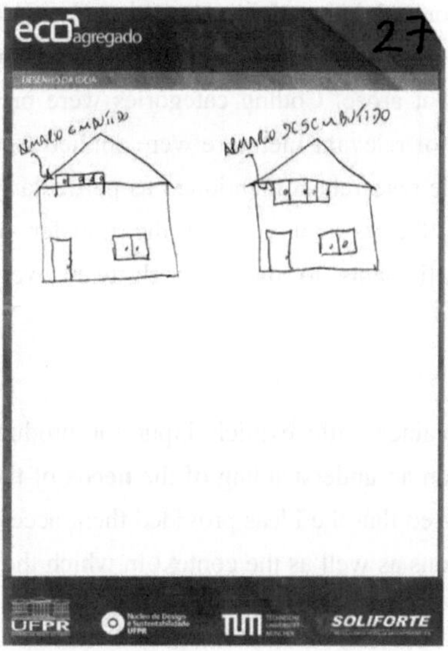

1st Place: Wardrobe built into ceiling (idea 27)

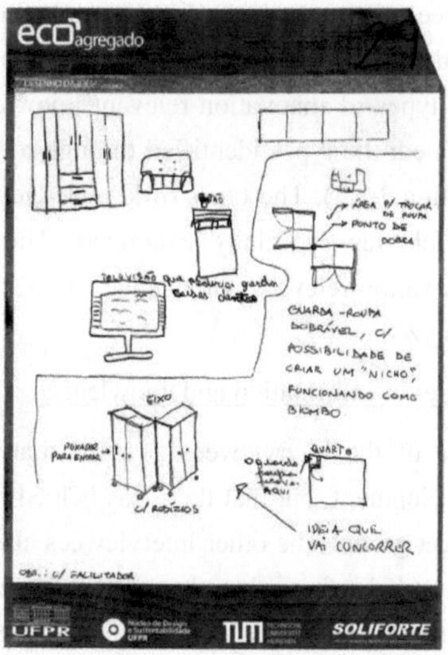

2nd Place: Foldable wardrobe (idea 29)

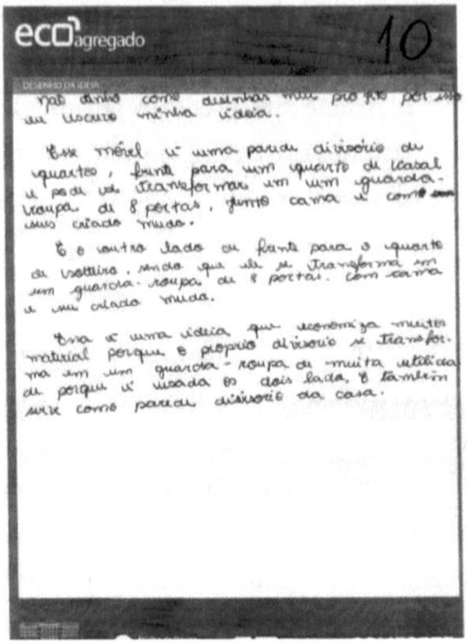

3rd Place: Room divider (idea 10)

Innovation-relevant knowledge obtained throughout the process

Three of the researchers who took part in organizing and implementing the idea competitions were interviewed. The transcripts of the interviews were coded based on the types of innovation-relevant knowledge that arose. Coding categories were pre-defined; the types identified through a review of relevant literature were applied (see section 2.3.4). The types of knowledge that the researchers mentioned as particularly useful was especially examined. Then, the factors that enabled the transfer of innovation-relevant knowledge from the participants to the research team were analyzed.

<u>Types of information and knowledge</u>

One of the interviewees stressed that he obtained little explicit input for product development, but that the ideas helped him gain an understanding of the **needs** of the target group. The other interviewees also stressed that the ideas provided them access to needed information about people's perceptions as well as the context in which they live.

We used the ideas a lot as input for the concept development of the products, as they show real needs.

Some ideas might not provide so much insight for a product concept, but rather support the identification of user requirements.

[The technique] is an excellent strategy to obtain a more profound understanding of people's perception regarding their actual problems and concerns.

(selected responses)

Second, the interviewees stated that they had gained **solution-related information** from their target group. They claimed that the results and the solution-oriented approach were a benefit of the technique. They stressed that this information helped them to see potential solutions through the eyes of the consumer. This points to the fact that the **tacit knowledge** obtained through being exposed to a variety of user-generated solutions was most useful to them. This tacit knowledge proved more useful than any particular solution.

Through the designs, we can understand how participants view their problems and how they suggest solving them. This gives the designer the possibility of designing a product with more direction.

A benefit is that the method generates input from those who need a solution to a problem. There is no one who knows better what they need than the consumers themselves; and it is better to make them think about the solution than to think just about the problem. […] Most of the time, the solutions are in front of our eyes, [...] and we cannot see them because they're not our needs, they're somebody else's needs.

(selected responses)

<u>Enabling factors of knowledge transfer</u>

According to three interviewees, the information and knowledge obtained did not only arise from the analysis of the ideas. Rather, they stressed that they greatly benefited from the **personal, direct contact** they had with the target group: On the one hand, this contact helped to gain the trust of the community, making residents more comfortable to reveal information. On the other hand, it helped the designers gain a better understanding of the target group.

People seem to feel more comfortable and more likely to submit ideas with a face-to-face interaction.

The method also seems to be a good strategy to build relationships between researchers and the community.

> *[My] understanding [of the reality, problems, and needs of the target group] is a result of the direct contact with people.*
>
> (selected responses)

All interviewees pointed out the importance of **giving people a role** during the innovation process, which elevated the self-esteem of participants. Feeling valued and listened to may have made them more inclined to share their ideas and insights:

> *I believe that having the feeling that they are part of the process was a very positive experience for the participants. They could see that they are an important part of society.*
>
> *I believe that the fact of having researchers truly concerned about listening to them and valuing their ideas contributes to improving their self-esteem."*
>
> *I think they feel like the designers and companies are willing to hear what they have to say. And this makes them feel important in some way in the whole process of product development.*
>
> (selected responses)

However, not only the target group benefited from the participatory process. The interviewees pointed out that their participation in the competition helped them see low-income communities in a more positive way. They began by seeing such communities as objects of their research or even people who needed help; then through the competition, they experienced that they can learn and benefit from the interaction with these communities.

> *I believe that one of the major insights I could draw from this research technique is that often, the "object" of the research has more to contribute than we think. This is because the ideas are generated in their specific user context and are, in most cases, a direct response to real problems of real people who are living them.*
>
> *[Low-income consumers] are a reservoir of creativity that is underestimated by designers.*
>
> *I thought they just wanted to get products with the best value for money. But after the idea competition, I could see that what they really want is to have a more equal and fair market.*
>
> (selected responses)

Table 29 provides an overview of the types of information and knowledge as well as the factors that enabled knowledge transfer mentioned by each interviewee.

Table 29: Results of interviews with product designers in case study I

Case study I	Interviewee A	Interviewee B	Interviewee C	
Types of information and knowledge				
Need-related information	✓	✓	✓	100%
Solution-related information	✓	✓	X	66.6%
Tacit knowledge	✓	✓	✓	100%
Explicit knowledge	✓	X	✓	66.6%
Enabling factors of knowledge transfer				
Personal interaction	✓	✓	✓	100%
Trust	X	X	✓	33.3%
Participatory process	✓	✓	✓	100%
Elevated self-esteem	✓	✓	✓	100%
Change in perspective	✓	✓	✓	100%

Source: created by author

Note: a check mark [✓] was used to code when the type of information and knowledge or the enabler was mentioned by the interviewee, and an X when it was not mentioned.

4.2 Case Study II: Project "Amana"[135]

4.2.1 Setting: Topic, target community, and partners

While the north of Brazil suffers from water scarcity, the problem is the opposite in the south: the dwellings of communities in risk areas (i.e., close to rivers) are highly affected by inundations. The governmental housing program "Minha Casa Minha Vida" aims to provide appropriate and safe shelter to Brazilian low-income families. Thus, the housing agency Companhia de Habitação do Paraná (COHAPAR) is tasked with resettling people from these areas, offering them a new, subsidized house.[136] Most of the households on the bank of the river live on illegal property, and the resettlement provides them the opportunity to become legal residents and get connected to the grid and to the water and sewage systems. Many families then pay for these services for the first time, as they previously often had illegal or shared connections, and thus have little idea of how much they consume. Households can receive a consumption subsidy if they earn under half of the minimum salary available per person and consume less than 2.5 m^3 of water per person per month. Consumption above this limit is charged at the normal rate. Thus, their incentive to save water is high. COHAPAR is thus preoccupied with creating awareness about how to effectively manage water consumption to avoid high costs.

Topic: Saving water

Water collection saves water costs for low-income households, but can also reduce the risk of inundation in the communities. However, there is currently no low-cost and low-tech solution on the market that would be suitable for low-income houses. Thus, the objective of the idea competition was to collect ideas to "create a product to collect rainwater."

---

135 The word "Amana" means rain in Tupí-Guaraní – a language spoken by Brazilian Indians.

136 The size of a single house is 40 m^2 with a kitchen, a small living room, a bathroom with a shower, two separate bedrooms (each around 10 m^2), and a service area in the back. The cost of the house for COHAPAR is R$35,000 (around €13,348) – the family only pays around R$9,000 (around €3,432), without interest rates (Internal data from COHAPAR, 2010). The families usually pay about R$60–70 (around €22–27) per month for a period of about 145 months (12 years). The exchange rate is from May 2013. For further information, see website of the housing program: http://www.minhacasaminhavida.mt.gov.br, accessed May 1, 2013.

The community: Jardim Boa Vista, Campo Magro

The community selected for case study II was "Jardim Boa Vista" in Campo Magro, which is situated in the metropolitan region of Curitiba. COHAPAR has divided the community into four areas, each of which has around 350 families. According to internal data from COHAPAR, the composition of the families varies greatly, with an average of 3.62 people per family. Eighty-nine percent of the families have a household income of up to three minimum salaries and thus belong to the low-income classes D and E.

Around 400 households of the community live at the waterside on the river Passaúna. The river frequently overflows, causing precarious living conditions, including humidity and a prevalence of insects and animals in the house, which can cause illnesses. Due to inundations and landslides, many residents suffer damages to furniture or their houses; sometimes their houses are destroyed completely. At the time of the competition, COHAPAR was in the process of building 388 houses in this community, in an area further away from the bank of the river – an investment of R$13 million. All in all, 139 families had already moved or were moving into their new houses during the time of the idea competition.[137]

The project partners: NDS, FINEP, Tigre and COHAPAR

The case study was conducted as part of the field research phase of the research project "Projeto Amana." The project was initiated and led by the NDS, which set up the project team composed of two coordinators, a team of junior researchers, and a professor for quality assurance. The objective of the research project was to develop a rain-water collector that is easy to assemble, use, and maintain. FINEP funded the project.

To assure the practical relevance of the end-product as well as its feasibility, the project also had a partner from the private sector. The company Tigre is the Brazilian market leader for PVC pipes and fitting solutions for water management systems. The company also produces other construction accessories. Despite the fact that its products are behind walls and under floors, Tigre has a very strong brand.[138] Tigre

[137] Source: Internal data from COHAPAR, 2010.

[138] According to the "Top of Mind 2009" survey from the Brazilian market research institute Datafolha, 74% of consumers refer to Tigre when asked about a company that produces pipes and fittings (Datafolha 2009).

Group sales were R$2.3 billion in 2009.[139] The company has an increasing interest in the low-income market, as the sales in so-called "mom and pop" stores represent a big share of their revenue. The role of Tigre in the project was to provide input as well as expertise throughout the product-development process.

COHAPAR supports the implementation of the federal housing program "Minha Casa Minha Vida" in the state of Paraná. In that capacity, COHAPAR is responsible for building a considerable amount of houses in low-income communities and identifying beneficiaries. The choice of the housing agency as a project partner had two objectives. First, having worked in low-income communities in the Metropolitan area of Curitiba for around 20 years, COHAPAR proved a suitable partner to gain access to the target group. Also, COHAPAR is a potential client for the end product. In addition, the organization has an interest in creating awareness for sustainable consumption in the communities. COHAPAR's contributions to the idea competition were twofold: During the promotional phase, the social assistant of COHAPAR responsible for the community in Campo Magro supported the team in distributing flyers and posters and assisted with contacting potential multipliers in the community. Furthermore, the competition was held at the COHAPAR office.

4.2.2 Ideas: Creativity of ideas

To determine the creativity of the ideas submitted, the CAT was applied. The jury of the CAT workshop to assess the ideas of the second idea competition consisted of an academic specialized in new product development, a designer of the company Innove with experience designing for low-income households, a representative of the company Tigre, and two NGO representatives. The requirements of the CAT were fulfilled (see section 3.2.3). Furthermore, the minimum ICC level ($ICC > 0.7$) was reached for all dimensions (see table 30).

To determine the level of creativity, a creativity score (CS) was calculated ranging from 1 to 5 (5-point Likert scale).[140] The scores of each dimension as well as the score of the CS fulfill the requirements $p > 0.05$ of the Kolmogorov-Smirnov goodness-of-fit

---

[139] See company website www.tigre.com.br for further information.

[140] Every idea was assessed by five experts, applying the four dimensions on a five point Likert Scale and adding the score of each dimension. Thus, every idea could reach a minimum creativity score (CS_{min}) of 20 points and a maximum creativity score (CS_{max}) of 100 points. To make the scores comparable to other case studies, they were adjusted by dividing them through the number of judges and creativity dimensions.

test, which means that the variables are normally distributed. The CS for all ideas (n = 37) is on a continuum between very low and very high degrees of creativity.

Table 30: Inter-rater reliability in case study II

Dimensions	ICC	Cronbach's Alpha
Originality	0.746	0.811
Utility	0.752	0.816
Degree of elaboration	0.827	0.893
Feasibility	0.760	0.817

Source: created by author.

The arithmetic mean refers to the average degree of originality, elaboration, utility, and feasibility of the pool of ideas. The means of each CAT dimension are slightly below center scale (see table 31). The CAT dimension that received the highest score is utility, followed by feasibility. This means that most ideas were regarded as useful for the target group, as well as feasible. The mean of the aggregated creativity score also lies below center scale ($CS_{mean,adjusted}$ = 2.55).[141] The highest absolute creativity score reached is 3.55 points, the lowest 1.1 points.

Table 31: Assessment of normality distribution of the CAT dimensions in case study II

Case study II	Originality	Utility	Elabo-ration	Feasibility	CS
Mean	2.45	2.74	2.41	2.58	2.54
Std. deviation	0.73	0.74	0.82	0.74	0.69
Kolmogorov-Smirnov Z	0.574	0.771	0.823	0.645	0.779
Asymp. sig. (2-tailed)	0.897	0.592	0.507	0.800	0.578

Source: created by author.

The ideas can be divided into creative ideas (CS_{high}), defined as those with a value equal to or higher than center scale ($CS_{high} \geq 3$), and less creative ideas ($CS_{low} < 3$). The latter accounts for two-thirds of the ideas (62.2% | n = 23), while the former accounts for just over one-third of the ideas (37.8% | n = 14).

141 The mean of the creativity score (CS_{mean}) is 50.9 points. The adjusted mean was divided by the number of experts and the number of dimensions (see previous footnote).

Those ideas that obtained a high creativity score (CS_{high}) were mostly regarded as useful by the experts (on average, they were ranked 3.41 on a 5-point Likert scale). Originality is above center scale for CS_{high}, but slightly lower compared to the other dimensions.

A comparison of the creativity dimensions of the two groups reveals that the mean of CS_{high} is significantly higher for each dimension. Creative ideas were ranked slightly above center scale, and less-creative ideas below center scale (see figure 29). An independent sample t-test shows that the differences between the means of the two groups are highly significant for each creativity dimension (p=0.000***). The dimension that distinguishes both groups most is the degree of elaboration (delta = 1.25) (see figure 29). This means that creative ideas were elaborated more.

Figure 29: Comparison of creativity groups in case study II

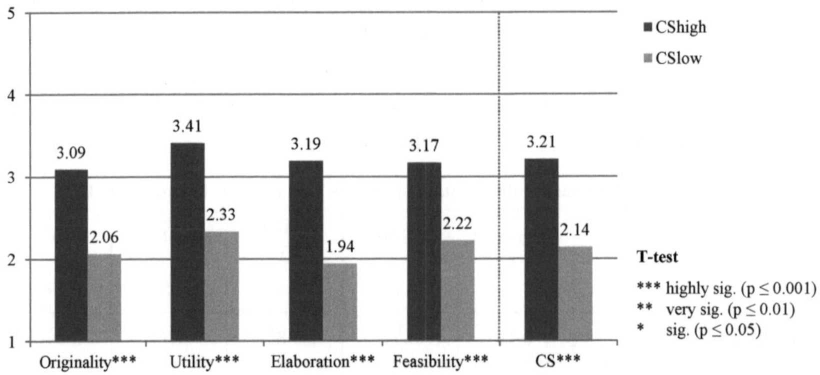

Source: created by author.

Furthermore, Cohen's *d* was calculated (Cohen 1971, 22ff.). For each creativity dimension, it shows a value above 0.8, which indicates a large effect (see table 32).

Table 32: Comparison of means and effect sizes of creativity dimensions – case study II

Case study II	CS_{high}	Std. deviation	CS_{low}	Std. deviation	Cohen's *d*
Originality	3.09	0.49	2.06	0.55	1.97
Utility	3.41	0.35	2.33	0.59	2.23
Elaboration	3.19	0.40	1.94	0.63	2.36
Feasibility	3.17	0.45	2.22	0.65	1.70
CS	3.21	0.19	2.14	0.55	2.62

Source: created by author.

4.2.3 Participants: Analysis of characteristics

In the community of "Jardim Boa Vista," in Campo Magro, 35 participants handed in 37 ideas.[142] The community comprises around 800 people. However, only an estimated 400 people could be addressed through the promotional activities. Thus, an estimated return rate of 9.25% can be regarded as satisfactory.

Socioeconomic characteristics of participants

22 ideas (63%) were handed in by women, and 11 ideas (31%) were handed in by men. The gender of the remaining idea owners was not registered.

The average age of the participants is 30.3 years (n = 31) and the median age 29. The lowest age is 11 and the highest 67. The Kolmogorov-Smirnov statistic shows that age is normally distributed ($p_{age} = 0.15$). Participants from all age groups were represented (except for participants between 9 and 10 and those over 70). The age group 11–20 years of age showed the highest participation (see figure 30).

---

142 Three people handed in two ideas and two people jointly handed in one idea.

Figure 30: Age groups in case study II

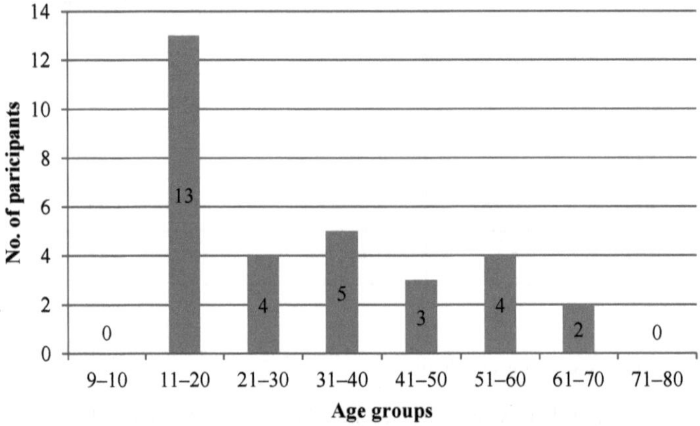

Source: created by author.

The data for years of education ranges from one to 11. Average education of the participants is 6.3 years (n = 29). Thirty-five percent of participants had eight years of schooling (see figure 31). The Kolmogorov-Smirnov statistic shows that education is normally distributed ($p_{education} = 0.185$).

Thirteen ideas (39%, n = 33) stemmed from students and six from homemakers (18%). The owners of the remaining ideas had various professions – for example, day laborer, shop assistant, electrician, mason, teacher, or gardener.

The average family income of the participants is R$1,264 (€550) (n = 24). The highest family income is R$6,500 (€2,828), the second highest R$3,000 (€1,305) and the lowest R$250 (€109).[143] The average number of persons per family is 4.6. All participants were from the lowest income classes D and E except for the participant with the highest income, who belonged to the income class C according to the IBGE.

[143] The exchange rate is from May, 2010, the time when the interviews took place (1 Brazilian Real = 0.435 Euro).

Figure 31: Level of education of participants in case study II

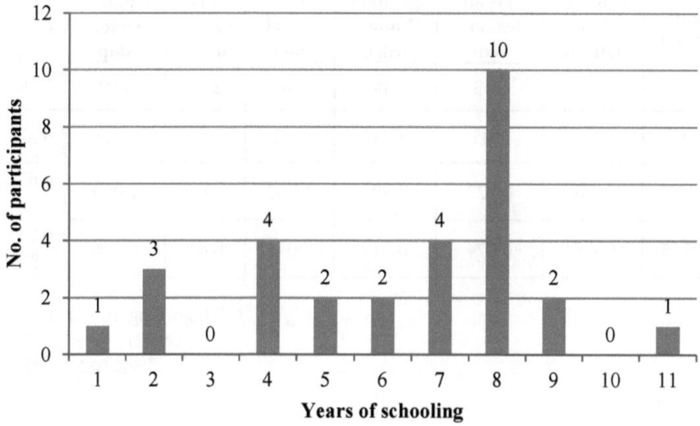

Source: created by author.

Quantitative analysis of lead-user characteristics

To obtain insights on the lead userness of participants, the results from all lead-user interviews were analyzed. To ensure comparability, results were first quantified (see section 3.4) by two different raters. Inter-rater reliability was achieved.[144]

Lead-user interviews were conducted with 28 participants. The aggregated lead-user score is normally distributed. However, not all individual characteristics are normally distributed (see table 33).

The average lead-user score is LUS = 2.19, i.e. it is below the center scale of 3.0 points. The mean of each dimension shows that opinion leadership was the most prevalent characteristic amongst participants. It is the only characteristic with a score slightly above center scale. Trend leadership and involvement are ranked second. The lowest value can be observed for the characteristic *innovative activity*.

[144] The inter-rater reliability – measured with the two-way mixed, unadjusted Intra-Class-Correlation coefficient (ICC) – is above 0.7 for all dimensions of the lead-user score, except for the criterion involvement. However, with a value of 0.541 it is still acceptable. To see the exact values for inter-rater reliability (ICC) of each dimension, please see annex IV.

Table 33: Assessment of normality distribution of the lead-user characteristics in case study II

Case study II	Dissatis-faction	Innova-tive activity	Trend leader-ship	Product know-ledge	Use experi-ence	In-volve-ment	Opinion leader-ship	LUS
Mean	1.80	1.23	2.73	2.00	1.80	2.73	3.02	2.19
Std. deviation	0.94	0.57	1.05	0.90	0.82	0.59	1.29	0.52
Kolmogorov -Smirnov Z	1.423	2.539	0.722	0.992	1.767	1.312	1.089	0.671
Asymp. sig. (2-tailed)	0.035*	0.000***	0.674	0.279	0.004**	0.64	0.186	0.758

*** highly sig. ($p \leq 0.001$)
** very sig. ($p \leq 0.01$)
* sig. ($p \leq 0.05$)

Source: created by author.

Figure 32: Incidence of lead-user characteristics of participants in case study II

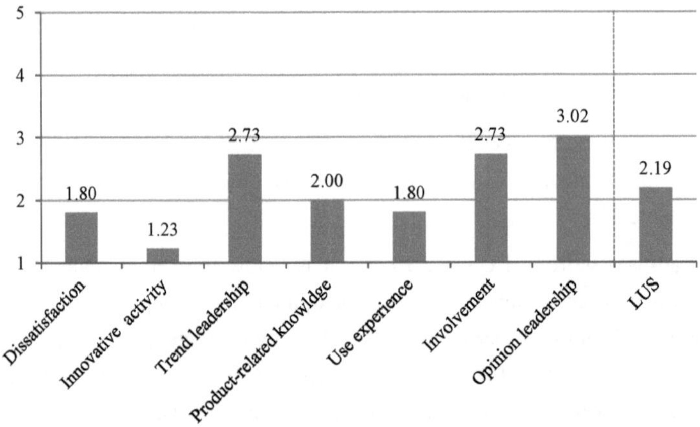

Source: created by author.

By relating each lead-user characteristic to the creativity scores of participants, it can be found that participants with a creativity above average also achieved higher aggregated lead-user scores. In regards to each characteristic, participants with a CS_{high} ranked higher for dissatisfaction, trend leadership, product-related knowledge, involvement, and opinion leadership. The group that produced less creative results ranked slightly higher (delta 0.04) for innovative activity and use experience.

According to the Mann-Whitney U test[145], these differences are significant for the characteristics of dissatisfaction, trend leadership, and involvement. They are also significant for the aggregated lead-user score. This corresponds to the results achieved when applying Cohen's *d* to measure the effect sizes between the LUS achieved by CS_{high} and CS_{low} (see table 34).

Table 34: Comparison of creativity groups along lead-user characteristics in case study II

Case Study II	Dissatis-faction	Inno-vative activity	Trend leader-ship	Product know-ledge	Use experi-ence	Involve-ment	Opinion leader-ship	LUS
CS_{high} (n = 12)	2.38	1.21	3.25	2.13	1.79	3.00	3.29	2.43
Std. deviation	1.00	0.40	1.06	0.93	0.40	0.64	1.30	0.47
CS_{low} (n = 16)	1.38	1.25	2.34	1.91	1.81	2.53	2.81	2.00
Std. deviation	0.62	0.68	0.89	0.90	1.05	0.46	1.28	0.49
Difference	1.00	0.04	0.91	0.22	0.02	0.47	0.48	0.43
p	0.005**	0.531	0.021*	0.485	0.511	0.044*	0.343	0.036*
Cohen's *d*	1.20^{+++}	-0.07	0.93^{+++}	0.24^{+}	-0.03	0.84^{+++}	0.37^{+}	0.89^{+++}

Mann-Whitney U test
*** highly sig. ($p \leq 0.001$)
** very sig. ($p \leq 0.01$)
* sig. ($p \leq 0.05$)

Cohen's *d*
$^{+++}$> 0.8: large effect
$^{++}$> 0.5: medium effect
$^{+}$> 0.2: small effect

Source: created by author.

It is striking that only one participant (idea 7) reached a lead-user score above center scale ($LUS_{adjusted}$ = 3.1). This participant also reached one of the highest creativity scores ($CS_{adjusted}$ = 3.4) and is thus one of the winners of the idea competition.[146] All other participants reached lead-user scores below center scale (see figure 34).

---

[145] The Mann-Whitney U test was selected as not all characteristics are normally distributed (Bühl 2008, 268, 346). For normally distributed variables, a two-independent-samples t-test would be appropriate. However, the Mann-Whitney U test was selected for all characteristics, as it is the stricter measure.

[146] Consequently, it was not possible to build a group of consumers with a high lead userness and a group with low lead userness, as the first group would only comprise one individual.

Figure 33: Comparison of creativity groups along lead-user characteristics in case study II

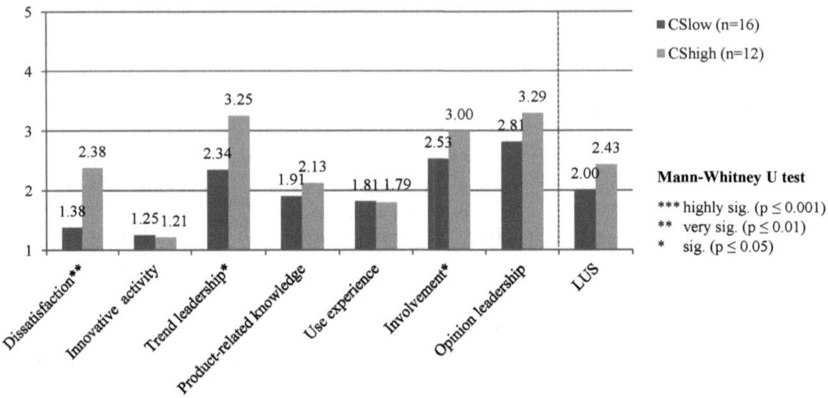

Source: created by author.

Figure 34: Creativity and lead-user characteristics of CS_{high} in case study II

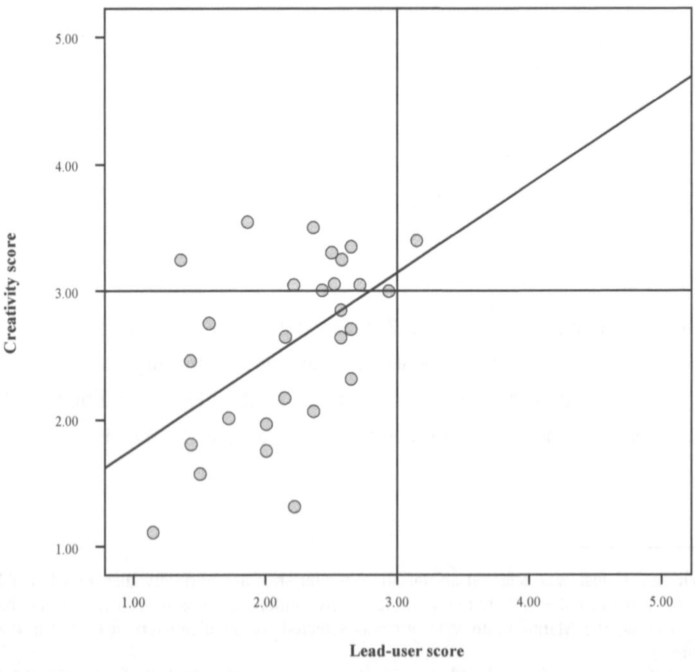

Source: created by author.

Qualitative analysis of lead-user characteristics

The creator of idea 7 – the third-place winner – was the only participant with a lead-user score above average. During the in-depth interview, it was revealed that although the idea was described and developed by the entrant, her father had discussed it with her and helped her refine it: "When she has to do something for school, we always sit together to discuss things. In the case of the competition, she had the idea – and we jointly discussed it." While the lead-user interview was primarily conducted with the daughter, responses from the father were also captured to complete the picture of the two "co-creators." The interview aimed to identify whether the participant can be regarded as a lead user.

<u>Dissatisfaction</u>

The creator of idea 7 stated that she disliked the fact that rainwater just "falls from the sky" without being used. The entrant and her father claimed to be highly dissatisfied with the fact that there is – to their knowledge – no mechanism available to collect rainwater that would suit the context in which they live. The girl stated that the only solutions she knew of were high-end solutions, which were not adapted to her living situation and not affordable to them.

<u>Innovative activity and trend leadership</u>

The creator of idea 7 stressed that the inspiration for all ideas she creates is founded in necessity. As rainwater leaks through their roof, she thought of a way to capture the rainwater: "The idea was natural. The idea, in fact, was born out of something that we suffer from." She made clear that the family would benefit greatly from implementing the idea she submitted to the competition – "otherwise, the rainwater falls on our roof and we don't make use of it." Furthermore, she explained that she had also developed other solutions to collect rainwater for several purposes; however, these solutions had a more improvised character in comparison to the idea submitted. For example, she showed an installation to collect rainwater for the plants the family had in their garden. Furthermore, she showed another installation that collects rainwater to wash clothes: "Not collecting rainwater would be a waste!"

In addition to the ideas to collect rainwater, the entrant had developed other ideas to improve the housing situation of the family – most of them together with her father: "I have already invented a couple of things." Her father, who was a mason, confirmed that in order to deal with the resource constraints they faced on a daily basis, they relied on their innovative abilities to improve their housing situation: "There is always something we can do. We invent all the time."

Product-related knowledge and use experience

Both the entrant and her father seemed to have acquired knowledge of materials through constructing the house, the roof of the house, and other objects. When commenting on the idea that was created for the competition, the entrant gave many details – for example, which construction materials to use. She mentioned that the tube through which the water runs down could be made of transparent acrylic or plastic, so that it would become a decorative element which could "look like a waterfall inside the house." As she had put several ideas in practice together with her father, they confirmed their ability to develop the idea further and put it in practice: "If someone asks me to implement it, I'll do it exactly as we designed it." However, the father stressed that the idea could still be improved: "This idea was just a beginning – it is an incomplete work." Instantaneously, they provided ideas about what could be changed to make the rainwater collector work better and they showed a high willingness to further explore the functionalities of such a solution.

Both the daughter and father also showed use experience, due to the fact that they had created improvised solutions to collect rainwater for watering plants and washing clothes. The girl stated that "by collecting rainwater – for example, to wash the floor – we avoid wasting tap water. We have done this since I was in school – I always help to collect rainwater."

Involvement

Their willingness to improve the idea further showed how involved both father and daughter were. Furthermore, the daughter seemed to research regularly on the Internet. She stated that she had also researched about rainwater collectors on the Internet but only found high-end solutions that were not applicable to her living situation.

Opinion leadership

Opinion leaders make their decisions based on their expertise and independently of their social environment (see section 2.2.1). In the case of the creator of idea 7, it was clear that she was highly inclined to thinking independently and making independent judgments. For example, she stated that she did not like having the same things as her friends or colleagues:

I don't like to copy other people; everybody should have their own things. I don't buy the same things out of envy; I don't like that. My friend always asks: "Does my hair look bad like this? Somebody told me it was ridiculous...!" Then I always tell her that if she likes her hair like that, the opinion of others doesn't matter. What matters is if you like it!

She vividly stressed how she prefers to have her own opinion – even if that meant disrespecting hierarchies – that is, the opinion of her teacher or parents. Furthermore, she related that she was regarded as the "leader" of her group of friends. She stated that she had tried to encourage her friends to take part in the idea competition and to "*at least try.*" She quoted her teacher who had told her, "[a]t 13 years old, you are already an example for people your age!" The attitude seemed to be something she had learned from her father, who encouraged her to "never be ashamed for being poor – but to be proud of what they have achieved." Also, the father seemed to have characteristics of an opinion leader – for example, he would give his ideas and influence people at his workplace on how to implement construction plans, and he stated that he was frequently asked for advice.

Characteristics of creative participants

To gain insights on the participants whose ideas obtained a creativity score equal to or above center scale (group CS_{high}), nine interviews were conducted (see table 35). As a control group, four participants whose ideas obtained a very low creativity score (group CS_{low}) were interviewed as well. It was more difficult to schedule interviews with participants who obtained a low creativity score, which explains the discrepancy between the two groups.[147]

Table 35: Overview of interview participants in case study II

CS_{high}			CS_{low}		
Interview no.	**Idea no.**	**CS**	**Interview no.**	**Idea no.**	**CS**
1	2	3.00	**10**	20	1.10
2	5	3.05	**11**	30	1.95
3	6	3.55	**12**	31	1.80

[147] The small sample size was mainly due to the difficulty of conducting research in low-income environments. For further explanation, see footnote 132 in section 4.1.3.

4	7	3.40	**13**	32	2.45
5	13	3.05			
6	18	3.50			
7	21b	3.30			
8	27a	3.00			
9	27b	3.20			

Source: created by author.

The following clusters of characteristics could be identified amongst the group CS_{high}. There was no evidence of these characteristics in the control group CS_{low}.

High problem-solving ability

The CS_{high} participants claimed to perform creative activities that solve their most pressing needs and problems. They showed an ability to simply put things into practice without having to think too much or make a major effort. The solutions they came up with were related to many topics beyond those in focus in the idea competition. For example, to contribute to the family income, one participant (idea 7) stated that she created and sold flowers out of cloth. Another participant had seen his kids studying in the garden – due to lack of space in the house. Since they were exposed excessively to sunlight, he created an umbrella made of straw and with a tiled table underneath (surrounding the pole). He related that in the house, he wanted to create a "table without table legs," which would facilitate cleaning and provide more space, and which could be adjusted to the height of the kids. He stated that "there is always something we can do. We invent all the time. In fact, we did not have the time nor the money to elaborate all our ideas!" Another participant (idea 21b) was employed in a workshop that manufactured rattan furniture. He stated that demands from customers were sometimes difficult to execute with the material, but that he approached the task creatively and always found a solution.

> *The customers come with an idea, a design, and we have to execute. However, sometimes, the furniture designs are also based on my own ideas. […] Sometimes problems arise when executing the designs. Then, I have to quickly come up with good ideas of how to address or work around them. Otherwise, my boss does not pay…!*

The creator of idea 2a mentioned that she frequently helped her father solve problems related to the construction of a bar, which the family intended to run. She stressed that she and her friends lacked toys to play with, which led her to invent toys or games with materials she found – for example, PET bottles. Her mother said the following about her: "She has every kind of idea… She invents a lot of crazy things – things we don't think are possible but then work surprisingly well in the end." Also, the creator of idea 5 stated that she created various things from PET bottles, like toys, curtains, or bags to earn some money on the side.

Curiosity and positive attitude towards change

Another characteristic that could be strongly observed among CS_{high} participants was extreme curiosity as well as a positive reaction to things that were new to them. For example, one participant (idea 7) stated, "I look at everything." According to her mother she liked to explore things, participated in activities at school – like competitions and projects – and even researched on the internet about the topic of the idea competition: "My daughter is a little shy, but very curious and interested; she wants to know about and understand things." The mother of another participant said, "[d]o you see how curious she is? She always says she wants to go to university!" Other participants whose ideas obtained a high creativity score were so curious about the competition that they stayed around the house where the competition took place (i.e., where ideas were collected) for the whole day (e.g., idea 27b).

Curiosity is not only reflected in a willingness to get to know things, but also in a willingness to learn. For example, the creator of idea 27a had bought a computer against her husband's wish – as she was curious to learn how it worked. She explained how she had opened it up to learn how the pieces were put together, and that afterward she was able to repair it on her own. The investment made also showed her positive attitude towards change. "When I bought the computer," she said, "I did not know how to operate it. […] It all paid off."

Ambition, dedication, and self-confidence

Ambition, dedication, and self-confidence are also characteristics that distinguished the two groups. Those students who contributed creative ideas reported to be "the best in their class." The participant who produced rattan furniture (idea 21b) is "the best employee of the workshop," according to his mother and his boss, who were informally interviewed when doing the house visit and a visit to the work place.

Another participant (idea 13) explains her ambition to get a job: "I want to find a good job. I do not mind if I have to work on the weekend or on holidays. I want to achieve something in life, to contribute something at home." Another participant (idea 2a) explained how she tried to motivate her friends to participate, who stated that they were not interested or able to do so. Similarly, the creator of idea 7 said, "I told them [my friends]: 'if you never try, you will never succeed! At least try!' […] My father taught me to never give up." Another participant stated how being self-confident and ambitious is part of their family culture: " 'I can't' or 'I don't know' are expressions that don't exist in our family. You always can and you always know." The parents of the participants whose ideas were assessed as creative are generally preoccupied with the future of their children and encourage them to strive for a better life. This is also reflected in the future plans of the children: The younger participants explained that they were eager to study and that they strove to become, for example, a lawyer or a veterinarian. This was also reflected in their great ambition to realize ideas: "I have to put all the ideas I have on paper into practice, said one participant, "because one day I will be in 'another world'; and if there they don't have any plants, for example, I will never be able to realize what I have planned."

Ability to think and act independently

Often, participants from the more creative group were also entrepreneurs. They enjoyed the autonomy and independence this type of job provided. The creator of idea 27a, for example, who had bought a computer on credit against her husband's wish, claimed to be proud of having acted independently regardless of his opinion. She had learned to use and apply the software Photoshop to restore old pictures (idea 27a). She then started arranging old pictures for people from the community. The money she earned from doing so had already offset the investment she had made in a scanner. Her daughter, whose idea also obtained a high creativity score, related that she wanted to open up her own business (idea 27b). Her idea was to take care of kids during festivities. Many female participants of this group mentioned that they made and sold handicrafts. For example, they sold handmade flowers or shawls. CS_{low} participants did not state that they performed any entrepreneurial activities, nor did they show a desire to act independently.

Another common characteristic amongst CS_{high} participants was their position as a leader either in their family or circle of friends (or both), which showed their independence of thought and action. For example, one participant talked about her group of friends and made clear that she was the "creative head" of the group – that is, that she had the ideas, for example, for new toys or things they could do together, and the others merely went along (idea 2a).

Environmental consciousness

Two CS_{high} participants developed a product that moves away from individual usage to consider collective use (ideas 6 and 21b): a rainwater collector that would benefit the whole community. However, these ideas were not only motivated by environmental consciousness. Both creators also considered the social benefits. Also, practical considerations were made, as not every house would have space for an individual rainwater collector. None of the participants of group CS_{low} had a comparable idea.

The creator of idea 13 presented a rainwater collector which was made entirely out of recycled materials – mainly PET bottles. "When working on the idea," she stressed, "I thought that it was great that it helps the environment, and helps you to save as well." Also, the creator of idea 2a spoke about various ideas that she had realized using recycled materials. The creator of idea 2 vividly stressed that not collecting rainwater would be a waste, not only for her family's pocket but also for the environment. The creator of idea 5 stated, "I think that today, I can waste a lot of water. But what about tomorrow? And the future of our children? We have to think about the future as well."

Family unity and support

The support that CS_{high} participants received from their families seemed to be extremely high. Most of them reported having been incentivized by a family member to participate in the competition. Others were even supported by family members when brainstorming ideas or putting them on paper (e.g., ideas 6 and 18). Others were supported by family members who brought their ideas to the location of the competition, as they had to work or go to school: "My daughter always likes to participate," said one mother, "and I support her."

The control group CS_{low} did not show evidence of the characteristics outlined above. For the most part, the commentaries of CS_{low} participants contrasted starkly with the reports from those with a high CS. For example, the creator of idea 30 said, "I actually don't like to create things." The creator of idea 31 reported, "[b]efore the competition, I never created an idea on my own." In addition, CS_{low} participants seemed to have a less positive attitude towards change. For example, one participant, who was living in a risk area close to a river which frequently flooded, was offered a new house by the government. She related that at first she did not want to move, as she was afraid of the changes and uncertainties it would bring. Furthermore, CS_{low} participants showed a rather high level of resignation and seemed to be complacent with their lives. In their descriptions of how they spent their free time, idleness predominated. They did not report any ambitions or tasks that they were passionate about, but rather seemed to spend their time at home, watching TV or talking with family and friends. The creator of idea 20, for example, said, "I stay at home the whole week." The creator of idea 31 claimed, "[m]y favorite activity is watching TV!" Furthermore, CS_{low} participants generally reported that they had difficult family situations – for example, divorce or the recent death of a family member. Family unity and support seemed to be fairly low. For example, the creator of idea 20 reported that her mother was always at work. She said, "[m]y brothers never help with anything. […] I have another sister, but I don't even know her."

Table 36: Overview of characteristics of creative participants in case study II

Characteristics of creative participants	**Idea no.**								
	2a	**5**	**6**	**7**	**13**	**18**	**21b**	**27a**	**27b**
High problem-solving ability	✓	✓	✓	✓	✓	✓	✓	✓	✓
Curiosity, positive attitude towards change	✓	✓	X	✓	✓	✓	X	✓	✓
Ambition, dedication, and self-confidence	✓	✓	✓	✓	✓	✓	✓	✓	✓
Ability to think and act independently	✓	✓	X	✓	X	X	✓	✓	✓
Environmental consciousness	✓	✓	✓	✓	✓	X	✓	X	X
Family unity and support	✓	✓	✓	✓	X	✓	✓	✓	X
% of characteristics encountered per person	100.0%	100.0%	66.6%	100%	66.6%	66.6%	83.3%	83.3%	66.6%

Source: created by author.

Note: a check mark [✓] was used to code when the characteristic was present, and an X when it was absent.

4.2.4 Process: Identification and transfer of innovation-relevant knowledge

To explore what types of information and knowledge can be obtained from the process of idea competitions, the content of the submitted ideas was analyzed to identify patterns and trends that give insights into consumer requirements (i.e., what functions a rainwater collector would need to have) and consumers' associations with the product (i.e., whether a rainwater collector is a desirable product for them). Second, the transcripts of the interviews with the research team were analyzed to understand what relevant types of information and knowledge were acquired by the researchers and how they were transferred.

Innovation-relevant knowledge obtained from the ideas

As the ideas submitted were quite similar, the content analysis focused on the details of each idea – that is, on the quality of the product, where it was placed in relation to the house, which functions it provided, and what other, more contextual aspects were conveyed through the idea. The observations could be grouped by functional and semantic characteristics (see table 37, in their order of frequency).

The **functional analysis** of the ideas shows what functions and qualities consumers envision for the product. It revealed that almost half of the participants designed a solution situated on the ground (e.g., ideas 5 and 13, figure 35; idea 6, figure 36). The other half of the solutions were elevated, to take advantage of gravity (e.g., idea 2a, figure 35; ideas 7 and 18, figure 36). The latter solutions were mostly designed to be integrated into the structure of the house (e.g., by taking advantage of the roof and the rain gutter). However, in most cases, the reservoir was designed to be a visible, cubic construction (e.g., idea 5, figure 35). Apparently, the participants did not care about the visual change of the dwelling that the installation of a rainwater collector would cause.

An important finding was that most participants were able to communicate through their designs that they were aware that rainwater is not potable. This was mostly indicated through designating external uses for the rainwater collected (e.g., ideas 5 and 13, figure 35; ideas 6 and 7, figure 36). A few ideas even foresaw a water filter as part of the construction (e.g., idea 2a, figure 35). This insight was of high relevance to the research team, which – prior to the competition – was unsure whether the target group would be aware of the issue of water quality.

Although most collectors were designed for individual use, three ideas opted for collective use (e.g., idea 21b, figure 35; idea 6, figure 36), and three ideas were designed to allow both.

The **semantic analysis** showed what the product meant to the consumer, and how they perceived it. From the drawings, it became obvious that the rainwater collector was perceived as a rather complex technical artifact with many details (e.g., idea 18, figure 36). At the same time, participants colored the collectors or used organic forms to make the product appear friendlier. This alerted the designers to the need of making the product look simple and friendly – and thus accessible to the consumer.

Many ideas for rainwater collectors were not only highly visible but often designed as disproportionally large in relation to the house (e.g., ideas 5 and 13, figure 35; idea 6, figure 36). This may indicate that people would like to show off the installation, and that it could potentially be regarded as a status symbol.

Furthermore, it can be deduced from the drawings and their descriptions that environmental and economic aspects of the product are widely understood and highly welcome among consumers. Many designs express a certain valorization of the environment by visualizing the water-saving aspect of the product, including natural elements in the drawing (flowers, green grass), referencing environmentally correct behavior (such as recycling), or referring to future generations in the descriptions. One idea, for example, was named "Blue consciousness" by the creator. Another idea proposes that PET bottles be recycled to form a rainwater gutter (see, e.g., idea 13, figure 35). The project team derived that economic and environmental benefits of the product were regarded as an important feature, which could be made visible in the design.

Figure 35: Exemplary ideas in case study II[148]

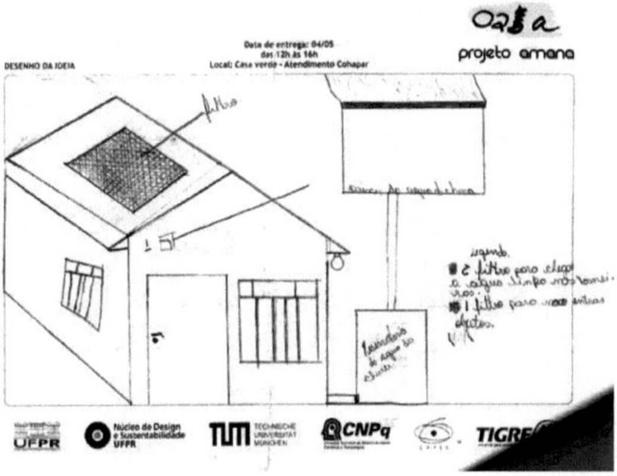

Idea 2a: Project to save water

Description by creator: *The idea is to open the roof, install a filter, and have a reservoir below [see reservoir on the right]. There will be two water reservoirs under the roof – one provided by Sanepar [the local water utility] and the rainwater collector. The reservoir from Sanepar can be accessed depending on additional water needs.*

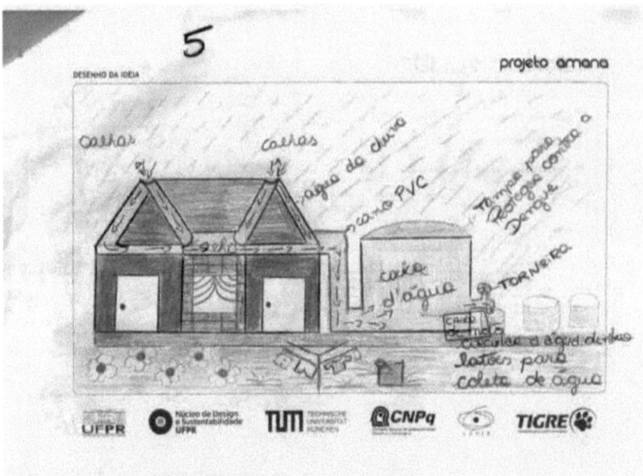

Idea 5: Don't waste water! Use it correctly!

Description by creator: *The water falls on the roof and is directed to the reservoir. The reservoir needs to be covered to protect it against dengue. The reservoir has a tap – this water can be used to wash clothes, the street, for the toilet, for the plants, to wash the car. If it is used to take a shower, it needs to be boiled. Using rainwater, we will save water and help the environment!*

---

148 Ideas were numbered according to the order in which the research team received them. The numbers do not state any sort of ranking.

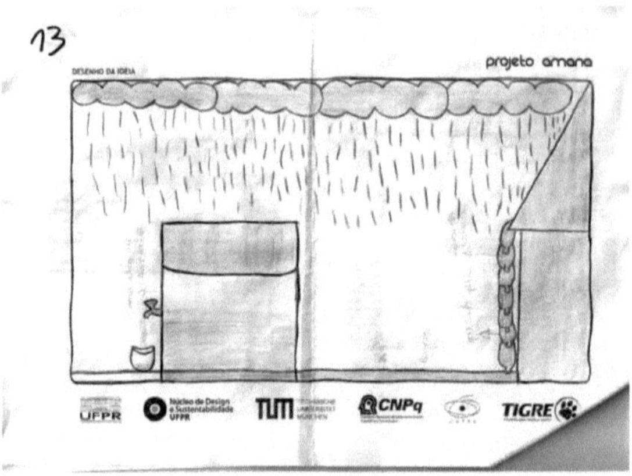

Idea 13: Using PET water bottles as rainwater gutter

Description by creator: *By putting PET bottles together to form a rainwater gutter, water can be collected. The water can be directed to a reservoir.*

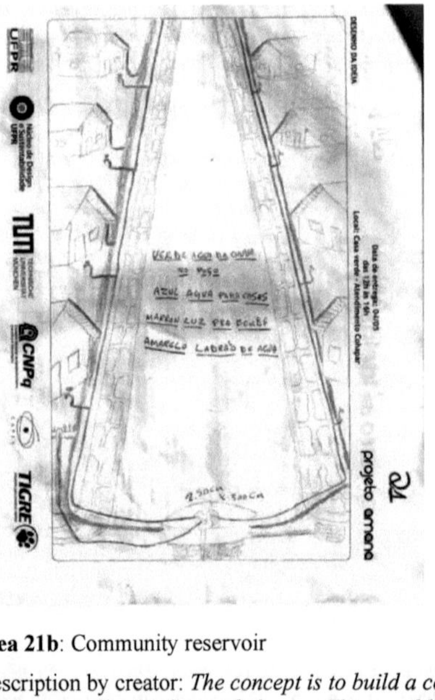

Idea 21b: Community reservoir

Description by creator: *The concept is to build a collective reservoir for a street – instead of building a rainwater collector for each house. This would save material and would be more suitable to the financial conditions of the people. The pipes would run through the street so that each house would have an individual access point and would not have to fetch water at a central point. This collector is particularly designed for the context of the governmental housing project, where little space is left between each house*

Table 37: Frequency of content clusters identified – case study II

Cluster	Subcategories	Frequency *(absolute)*	Frequency *(in percent)*
	Functional requirements		
Ownership	Individual use: 31 Collective use: 3 Both: 3	37	15.61
Type and position of reservoir	Underground: 5 Elevated: 13 On the ground: 17	35	14.77
Size of reservoir in relation to house	Smaller: 24; Larger: 11	35	14.77
Collection of water	Water drips into reservoir: 10 Water drips onto roof first: 24	34	14.35
Visibility of installation		28	11.81
Form of reservoir	Funnel-shaped: 2 Cubical: 16 Cylindrical: 1	19	8.02
Use	Internal: 1 External: 12	13	5.49
	Semantic requirements		
Personal values	Status: 5 Hygiene and health: 3 Valorization of environment: 11 Individualism vs. collectivism: 12 Harmony: 2 Idealism: 3	36	15.19

Source: created by author.

The winning ideas only partly corresponded to the patterns observed through the functional and semantic analysis.

- **"House of rainwater" for the community (idea 7):** The first place winner was one of the few participants who designed an idea for collective use. Her idea is that the local government should build a "house of rainwater," where water would be collected for the whole community. She explains that the water would be collected and stored in tanks, and that it would be made available for low-income households of the community, who don't have the conditions to build an individual rainwater collector for their house. The idea was convincing as it was regarded as very useful and original by the experts (see figure 36).

- **Rainwater collector with underground system (idea 18)**: The second place idea was the most specific design handed in, which considered technical details such as a filter. It specified each part of the collector and where it should best be put. In contrast to most ideas handed in, it has a hidden and integrated system placed underground. The idea convinced the judges due to its degree of elaboration and feasibility, but it lacked originality, as such systems are already available on the market, albeit not adapted to the needs of low-income houses (see figure 36). In fact, the winner mentioned having seen the system at the house of her school principal and having copied it from there.
- **Roof that collects rainwater (idea 7)**: The third place idea envisioned collecting water with a roof in the shape of a funnel. In the subsequent interview, the contestant explained that the water would run from the roof through a tube, which could also stand like a pillar in the middle of the house. The tube should be made of plastic or acrylic, so that the water running through would look like a waterfall. The rainwater collector would thus also become a decorative element for the inside of the house. The idea convinced the jury due to both its originality and usefulness (see figure 36).

Figure 36: Winning ideas of case study II

1st place: "Casa da chuva" ("House of rainwater") (idea 6)

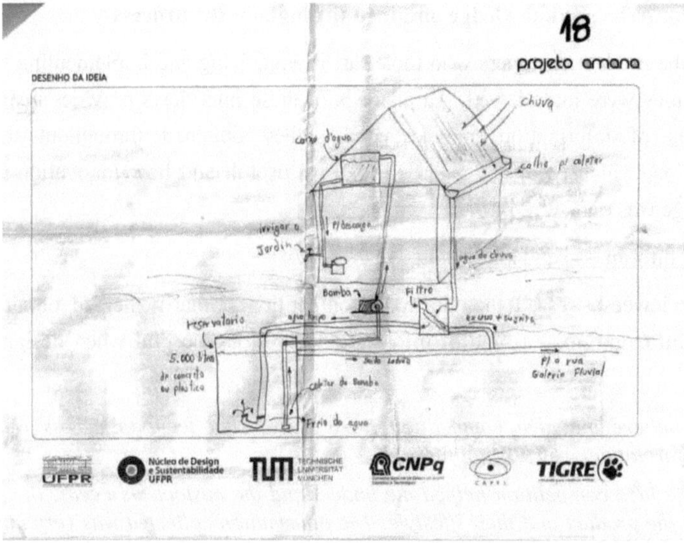

2nd place: Rainwater collector with underground system (idea 18)

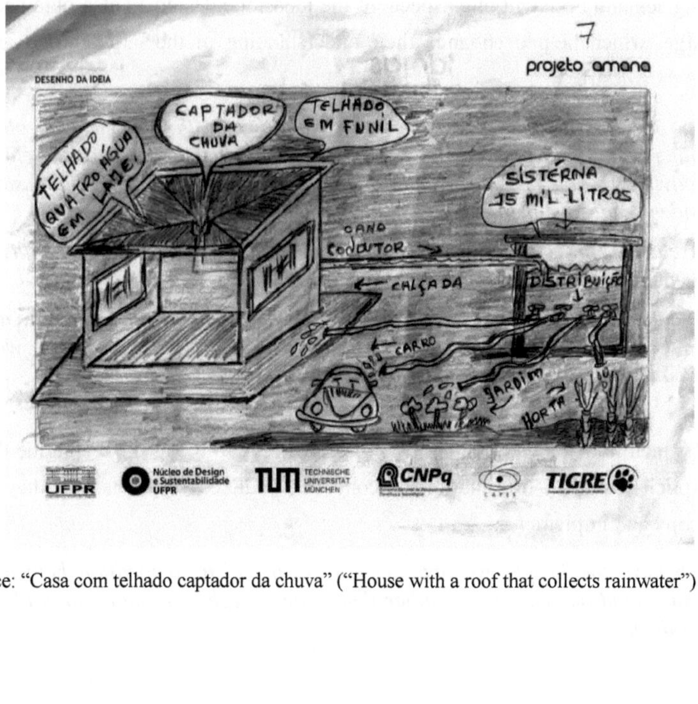

3rd place: “Casa com telhado captador da chuva” (“House with a roof that collects rainwater”) (idea 7)

Innovation-relevant knowledge obtained throughout the process

Four of the product designers who took part in organizing and implementing the idea competitions were interviewed. An analysis of these interviews provides insight into the types of information and knowledge they obtained throughout the idea competition, which type was regarded as most useful, and how innovation-relevant knowledge was transferred.

Types of information and knowledge

All interviewees stressed that the idea competition primarily helped obtain **need-related information** – a type of information they found useful when designing the product:

> *I believe the idea competition helps the design team to access real need information, which is not filtered.*
>
> *The idea competition helped me understand the customer's needs, their vision of the product and their lifestyle. The information collected was very important to define the product requirements and the project strategy.*
>
> (selected responses)

Regarding semantic or symbolic aspects of the ideas, the designers also obtained **tacit knowledge**, which helped enhance their understanding of the target group and the solutions they desire:

> *The ideas produced at the competition have given the design team plenty of material to define the product's aesthetic and functional features. Before this activity, we had just vague and mostly misleading ideas about the customers' understanding of the product we were designing.*
>
> *I realized the richness of semantic elements that [are] inherent in the ideas [generated by users].*
>
> *The ideas were essential to determine aesthetic, symbolic and semantic aspects of the product, i.e., information about the user context, familiarity with the product or the motivations to use it."*
>
> (selected responses)

While the tacit knowledge obtained was of great value to them, the technique did not yield explicit technical information or concrete, finalized solutions that they could simply copy and implement:

> *I believe the insight we obtained during the idea competition helped us to understand our customers rather than provide technical information about the product.*

It was not possible to directly apply participants' ideas to the final solution. Nevertheless, we got insights into the subjective perception of users on the [rainwater collector] system that we are supposed to develop, and those impressions guided us throughout the project.

(selected responses)

Enabling factors of knowledge transfer

The researchers stressed that the offline idea competition – in contrast to other techniques – helped to establish a direct and **personal contact** with the target group, which in turn helped to gain access to innovation-relevant knowledge:

Through [the] idea competition, it becomes possible for the designers to get closer to the people who will actually use the designed systems, increasing the chances of reaching suitable solutions.

Establishing close contact with our target customers has made me realize that the typical market research used in most of the product design projects leaves a lot of important information out of the process. Asking the people about their expectations, dreams, and lives has given us a chance to develop a product that was really user-centered and user-focused.

(selected responses)

The technique required the research teams to visit the communities several times over the different stages (promotion, collection of ideas, awarding). This direct and repeated contact contributed to creating **trust** – which in turn was viewed as an enabler for the exchange of information and knowledge between the participants and the research team:

In my opinion, the biggest benefit is that the method enables the creation of trust between participants and designers, which facilitates the information exchange.

To effectively involve low-income consumers in a process like the idea competition, it is necessary to create an environment of solid trust. It requires time and investment. We realized that the higher the involvement with the community from the beginning [...], the more people participate.

(selected responses)

Furthermore, integrating the community into the innovation process enhanced people's **self-esteem**, which was viewed as a trigger for their participation and ultimately unleashed their creative potential:

Most of them feared that their ideas were not good [...]. By the end of the competition, it was possible to see that they felt important because we were

> *really interested in what they had to say, and that they were happy for giving ideas to a product that was being developed for them.*
>
> *During the competition, it seemed to me that participants felt valued, motivated, and happy to be listened to. I believe that it might have contributed – even if in a subtle and indirect way – to improving their self-esteem and that this triggered their potential to be innovative.*
>
> *The participants got a feeling of recognition. They saw a team of professionals working in a project where they were the target audience.*
>
> (selected responses)

In fact, the interviewees pointed out that they were surprised with the creativity and **knowledge of the target group**. They learned through the idea competition that users can actually play a role in the innovation process:

> *Besides getting to know the method itself, I learned that we should not underestimate the potential benefits of including users in the design process. [...] [Before the idea competition] I believed that participants would have trouble in understanding the proposal and in developing and in representing original ideas. After the competition, I realized that many people in the community had a lot of knowledge and will to create new things – all they needed was a little incentive.*
>
> *After the idea competition I came to the conclusion that they are really participative and creative, it is just a matter of finding the right way of approaching them.*
>
> (selected responses)

For some researchers, the insights about the roles users can play also **changed the way they thought about the target group.** This altered and more positive view of the target group seemed to have made them more inclined to "absorb" the information and knowledge received from them:

> *What surprised me the most was finding out that low levels of education and proficiency did not influence the quality of the solution proposed. I unfortunately have to confess that before the idea competition, I doubted that the ideas could be useful for the project. My inexperience did not allow me to realize the richness of semantic elements that would be inherent in the ideas. After the idea competition, it became clear that the user has a perspective which is as good as that of the designer or the engineer. To explore ideas [created by users] is an obvious path, but rarely practiced to obtain a successful end product.*
>
> (selected response)

Table 38 provides an overview of the types of information and knowledge obtained as well as the enablers of knowledge transfer mentioned per interviewee.

Table 38: Results of interviews with product designers in case study II

Case study II	**Interviewee A**	**Interviewee B**	**Interviewee C**	**Interviewee D**	
Types of information and knowledge					
Need-related information	✓	✓	✓	✓	100%
Solution-related information	✓	✓	X	X	50%
Tacit knowledge	✓	✓	✓	✓	100%
Explicit knowledge	✓	✓	X	X	50%
Enabling factors of knowledge transfer					
Personal interaction	✓	✓	X	✓	75%
Trust	✓	✓	X	✓	75%
Participatory process	✓	✓	✓	✓	100%
Elevated self-esteem	X	✓	✓	✓	75%
Change in perspective	✓	✓	✓	✓	100%

Source: created by author.

Note: a check mark [✓] was used to code when the type of information and knowledge or the enabler was mentioned by the interviewee, and an X when it was not mentioned.

4.3 Case Study III: Project "LED"

4.3.1 Setting: Topic, target community, and partners

Brazilian citizens benefit from extensive electricity coverage. According to Hammond et al. (2007, 85), coverage amongst low-income consumers who earn less than 500 USD purchasing power parity (PPP) per year is 85%. However, high coverage also means high costs: The 6.5 million rural low-income households spend $661.3 million a year on energy, or $102 per household, while the 25.3 million urban low-income households spend $10.1 billion, or $397 per household on energy (Hammond et al. 2007, 79). Lighting accounts for about 20% of the total electricity consumption of a low-income household (ADEME and WEC 2010, 7).

One of the major energy issues in urban slums is illegal tapping of connections, which is estimated to represent around 25% of electricity consumption for residential customers in the poorest regions (ADEME and WEC 2010, 4). Furthermore, it often causes power outages for the whole community. To avoid illegal tapping, the Brazilian government created a subsidized rate for electricity, which benefits around 37% of residential consumers (or around 18 million consumers). The eligibility for this subsidized rate varies from state to state and is mainly based on consumption levels, connection type, and registration for other social benefits (ADEME and WEC 2010, 3). The subsidized rate in the state of Paraná, provided by the utility Companhia Paranaense de Energia (COPEL), grants a discount to low-income households on their energy bills up to a consumption level of 220 kWh.[149] Households that earn less than half a minimum salary per person qualify for the subsidized rate (COPEL 2013).

Topic: Saving energy

Many households in communities that are being regularized by COHAPAR pay their electricity bills for the first time. At first, they benefit from the subsidized rate. However, if they exceed the consumption level of 220 kWh, they have to pay normal rates. Many households fall into this trap, as they are not aware how much energy they consume. Most have old household goods, such as old and highly inefficient refrigerators, electrical water heaters, or incandescent light bulbs, all of which have a high impact on energy consumption. COHAPAR is thus preoccupied with creating

[149] A report by the World Energy Council (WEC) states that the average electricity consumption per household is around 780 kWh per year for Brazilian low-income households (ADEME and WEC 2010, 7).

awareness for saving energy amongst the households that are being legalized, mainly by supporting them in keeping their consumption levels low, so that they can benefit from the subsidized rate. As an additional benefit of the subsidized rate, energy theft also decreases with low energy costs.

Consequently, the idea competition aimed to inspire the target community to think about how to improve their lighting situation – and at the same time save energy. The topic of the competition was thus to "create a product that lights up your house and saves energy."

The community: Vila Zumbi dos Palmares

Figure 37: Map of Vila Zumbi

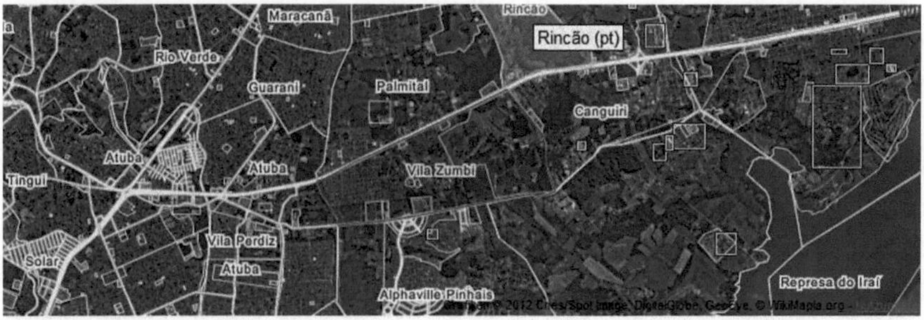

Source: Wikimapia 2012.

The "Vila Zumbi dos Palmares"[150] is one of the biggest irregular occupations of the metropolitan area of Curitiba. It is located in the city of Colombo, at the waterside of the Palmital River. The community Vila Zumbi dos Palmares started to form in 1991. The first residents were from rural areas or other cities who came to Curitiba searching for job opportunities. They built their houses with few resources and on unauthorized land. The community used to be regarded as one of the most violent and poor communities of the metropolitan area of Curitiba. According to reports in newspapers (e.g., Silveira 2009), daily murders – most of them related to drug trafficking – were commonplace in the community, especially during its inception. COHAPAR has been present in the Vila Zumbi dos Palmares for more than 10 years.

150 The name of the community refers to the last leader of the "Quilombo dos Palmares," a self-sustaining fugitive settlement of former slaves who had fled from plantations, located in Bahia in the northeast of Brazil.

Today, around 1,790 families (or around 6,000 inhabitants) are estimated to live in Vila Zumbi dos Palmares.[151] Most of the families have been there for more than five years in masonry or wood constructions. The only socioeconomic data that could be found on the community report that in 2003, the average household income in the village was between one and three minimum wages, and mostly achieved through informal work. Fifteen percent of the inhabitants were unemployed and 5.3% considered to be living in absolute poverty (Agência Estadual de Notícias 2003). In 2004, COHAPAR started regulating the area. The government has since built streets, improved sanitation and electricity, and extended public transport as well as its housing program to this area. Yet many problems remain, including lack of pavement, improper sanitation, improvised dwellings and violence.[152]

The project partners: NDS, FINEP, and COHAPAR

The idea competition was conducted as a preparatory research phase for the "Projeto LED." The project aimed to develop lighting solutions that apply energy efficient LED lamps. However, before starting the project, the research team – which consisted of a project coordinator and a team of junior researchers – aimed to find out what lighting options low-income communities currently use and are aware of, how they perceive their current lighting situation, and what ideas they have for improving lighting and saving energy.

Again, the project was initiated and led by the NDS and funded by FINEP. COHAPAR provided access to the target community. The housing agency also supported the project in promoting and implementing the idea competition, which was held at the local COHAPAR premises.

4.3.2 Ideas: Creativity of ideas

To determine the creativity of the ideas submitted, the CAT was applied. The jury consisted of two product designers – one with expertise in lighting solutions, two

---

[151] Source: Internal data from COHAPAR 2010.

[152] The fact that an affluent gated community named "Alphaville" was built in the neighborhood of Vila Zumbi benefited the settlement, as private social programs were extended to the community, such as professional trainings for electricians and masons, child care, care for elderly and support for entrepreneurs. Furthermore, "Alphaville" created job opportunities for the masons and electricians trained as well as for, e.g., doormen and domestic help. Local initiatives have been growing in Vila Zumbi, such as Coopzumbi and Zumbi Art, which are cooperatives that work with recycled materials.

academics in the areas of social innovation and design, and an NGO representative. The requirements of the CAT were fulfilled (see section 3.2.3). Furthermore, the minimum ICC level (ICC > 0.7) was reached for all dimensions except feasibility and utility (see table 39). However, the value ICC > 0.5 for both dimensions can still be considered acceptable (Wirtz and Casper 2002, 25).

Table 39: Inter-rater Reliability in case study III

Dimensions	ICC	Cronbach's Alpha
Originality	0.751	0.746
Utility	0.588	0.583
Degree of elaboration	0.774	0.783
Feasibility	0.657	0.659

Source: created by author.

To determine the degree of creativity, a creativity score (CS) was calculated, ranging from 1 to 5 (5-point Likert scale).[153] The scores of each dimension as well as the score of the CS fulfill the requirements $p > 0.05$ of the Kolmogorov-Smirnov goodness-of-fit test, which means that the variables are normally distributed (see table 40). The creativity scores for all ideas ($n = 12$) are on a continuum between very low and above average degrees of creativity.

Table 40: Assessment of normality distribution of the CAT dimensions in case study III

Case study III	Originality	Utility	Elaboration	Feasibility	CS
Mean	2.68	3.00	2.53	3.07	2.82
Std. deviation	0.79	0.71	0.75	0.77	0.59
Kolmogorov-Smirnov Z	0.508	0.671	0.484	0.369	0.700
Asymp. sig. (2-tailed)	0.958	0.759	0.973	0.999	0.711

Source: created by author.

[153] Every idea was assessed by five experts, applying the four dimensions on a 5-point Likert scale and adding the score of each dimension. Thus, every idea could reach a minimum creativity score (CS_{min}) of 20 points and a maximum score (CS_{max}) of 100 points. To make the scores comparable to other case studies, they were adjusted by dividing them by the number of judges and creativity dimensions.

The arithmetic mean refers to the average degree of originality, elaboration, utility, and feasibility of the pool of ideas. The mean of each CAT dimension is equal to or slightly above center scale for utility and feasibility and below center scale for originality and elaboration. The mean of the CS also lies below center scale ($CS_{mean,adjusted}$ = 2.82). [154] The highest absolute creativity score reached is 3.25, the lowest 1.5 points.

The ideas can be divided into creative ideas (CS_{high}) and less creative ideas (CS_{low}). The latter are ideas that are below center scale ($CS_{low} < 3$); they account for 58.3% of the ideas (n = 7). The CS_{high} ideas are those that achieve a value equal to or higher than center scale ($CS_{high} \geq 3$). They account for 41.7 % of the ideas (n = 5).

The CS_{high} ideas were mostly regarded as useful by the experts; on average, they were ranked 3.46 on a 5-point Likert scale. Originality and feasibility are above center scale for CS_{high}, while degree of elaboration is slightly lower.

A comparison of the creativity dimensions of the two groups shows that the mean of CS_{high} is higher for each dimension. Creative ideas were ranked slightly above center scale on all measures except for elaboration; less creative ideas fell below center scale. An independent sample t-test shows that the differences between the means of the two groups are significant, except for the dimension of feasibility (see figure 38). The dimensions that distinguishes both groups most are utility (delta = 1.1), originality (delta = 0.97), and degree of elaboration (delta = 0.91). This means that creative ideas were regarded as more useful and original and that they were elaborated more.

---

[154] The mean of the creativity score (CS_{mean}) has 50.9 points. The adjusted mean is divided by the number of experts and the number of dimensions (see previous footnote).

Figure 38: Comparison of creativity groups in case study III

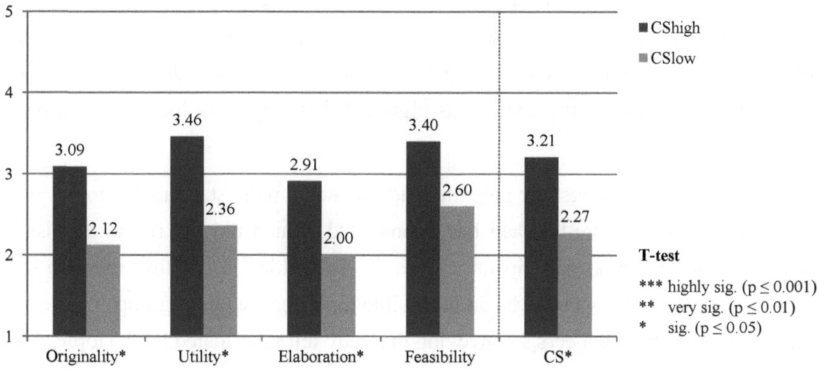

Source: created by author.

Furthermore, Cohen's *d* was calculated (Cohen 1971, 22ff.). For each creativity dimension, it shows a value above 0.8, which indicates a large effect (see table 41).

Table 41: Comparison of means and effect sizes of creativity dimensions– case study III

Case study III	CS_{high}	Std. deviation	CS_{low}	Std. deviation	Cohen's *d*
Originality	3.09	0.69	2.12	0.64	1.51
Utility	3.46	0.28	2.36	0.64	2.23
Elaboration	2.91	0.55	2.00	0.68	1.48
Feasibility	3.40	0.65	2.60	0.73	1.15
CS	3.21	0.13	2.27	0.54	2.41

Source: created by author.

4.3.3 Participants: Analysis of characteristics

The idea competition held in "Vila Zumbi" on lighting products that save energy only yielded ideas from 12 participants. The community has an estimated size of 1,400 inhabitants, with an estimated 500 people reached through the promotion of the competition. The return rate of 2.4% can still be regarded as satisfactory.

The low participation in this case is due to two factors. First, most people in the community are connected to the grid. When asked about their lighting solutions during the promotion of the idea competition, many expressed that they were satisfied with this solution. There was also an obvious lack of knowledge about better solutions. When asked, most people did not seem to be able to name lighting solutions other than bulbs, and they generally showed little interest in the topic. Only a few people commented that their energy spend was high and that they were looking for ways to reduce it.

Second, difficulties amongst the potential participants in understanding the topics were observed. Although a pre-test had been conducted, which did not reveal any issues with the topic, potential participants expressed difficulties in creating ideas to save energy. Energy did not seem to be an accessible topic for the target group – some said that it was "stuff for engineers," conveying that they felt intimidated by the topic. They commented that the topic required technological knowledge to be able to propose something new.

Furthermore, the community members of the "Vila Zumbi" were less receptive and less motivated than the people in the other case study communities. They claimed they were unwilling to bring ideas to the COHAPAR office – where ideas were collected – which was situated only a few minutes on foot (four blocks) from the center of the community. A low level social cohesion could be observed in this rather huge and supposedly dangerous community.

Socioeconomic characteristics of participants

On the day of the competition, 12 participants handed in 12 ideas. 4 ideas (33%) were handed in by women, 8 ideas (67%) by men.

The average age of the participants is 27.5 years (n = 12). The highest age is 56, the lowest 9, and the median age 21. All age groups between 9 and 60 are represented (see figure 39). The Kolmogorov-Smirnov test shows that age is normally distributed ($p_{age} = 0.782$).

Figure 39: Age groups in case study III

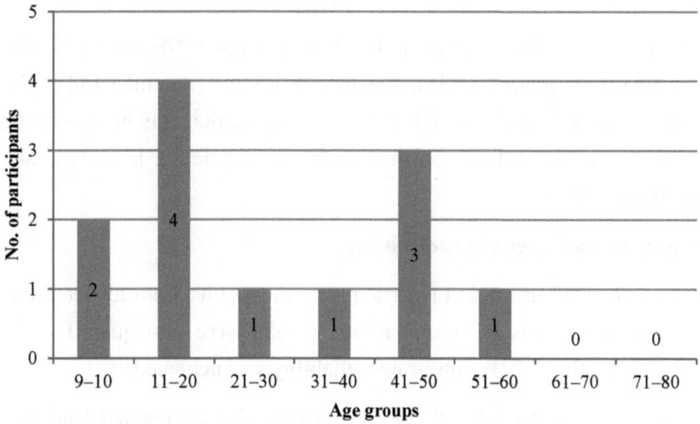

Source: created by author.

The data for years of education ranges from one to 11 years. The average amount of education of the participants is 5.92 years (n = 12). A third of the participants have an education of 8 years – all others have attended school for less than 8 years (see figure 40). The Kolmogorov-Smirnov test shows that education is normally distributed ($p_{education} = 0.691$).

Figure 40: Level of education of participants in case study III

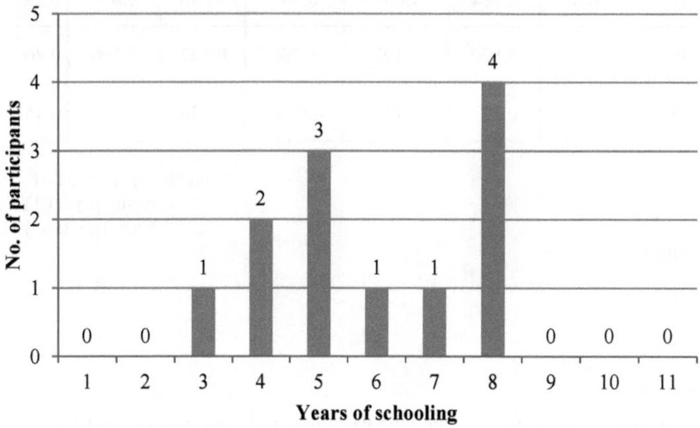

Source: created by author.

A third of the participants are students. Others have various professions, such as waiter or craftsman. One participant is self-employed, one retired, and two are unemployed.

The average family income of the participants is R$641 (around €279) (n = 12). The highest income is R$1,000 (around €435), the lowest R$400 (around €174). The average number of persons per family is 4.7 (n = 11).[155] All participants belong to the lowest income class E, composed of families with an income of less than two minimum salaries (IBGE 2010).

Quantitative analysis of lead-user characteristics

To obtain insights on the lead userness of participants, the results from all lead-user interviews were analyzed. To ensure comparability, results were first quantified by two different raters (see section 3.2.3). Inter-rater reliability was achieved.[156]

Lead-user interviews were conducted with 12 participants. The aggregated lead-user score is normally distributed. Also, the scores for all lead-user dimensions – except innovative activity and use experience – are normally distributed (see table 42).

Table 42: Assessment of normality distribution of the lead-user characteristics in case study III

Case study III	Dissatis-faction	Inno-vative activity	Trend leader-ship	Product know-ledge	Use experi-ence	Involve-ment	Opinion leader-ship	LUS
Mean	2.17	1.41	2.08	2.25	2.42	**2.67**	**2.96**	2.28
Std. deviation	1.231	1.164	1.184	1.034	0.764	1.030	1.054	0.691
Kolmogorov-Smirnov Z	0.849	1.639	0.820	1.197	1.584	0.547	1.100	0.860
Asymp. sig. (2-tailed)	0.467	0.009**	0.513	0.114	0.013*	0.926	0.178	0.451

*** highly sig. ($p \leq 0.001$)
** very sig. $p \leq 0.01$)
* sig. ($p \leq 0.05$)

Source: created by author.

155 The exchange rate is from May 2010 – i.e., the time when the interviews took place (1 Brazilian Real = 0.435 Euro).

156 The inter-rater reliability – measured with the two-way mixed, unadjusted intra-class-correlation coefficient (ICC) – is above 0.7 for all dimensions. To see the exact values for inter-rater reliability (ICC) of each dimension, please see annex V.

The average lead-user score is $LUS_{adjusted} = 2.28$. It is below center scale. The mean of each dimension shows that opinion leadership is the most prevalent characteristic amongst participants. It is the characteristic which is closest to center scale. Involvement is ranked second. The lowest value can be observed for the characteristic of innovative activity (see figure 41).

Figure 41: Incidence of lead-user characteristics of participants in case study III

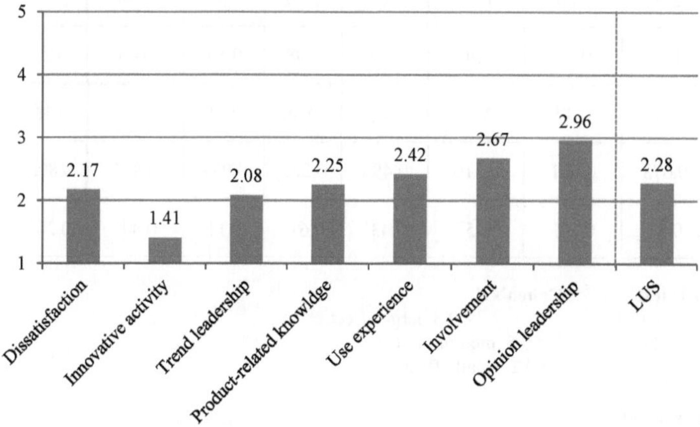

Source: created by author.

Relating each lead-user characteristics to the creativity scores of participants, it can be found that participants with a CS above average also achieved a higher LUS. The group that produced more creative ideas has higher scores for the lead-user characteristics of innovative activity, trend leadership, product-related knowledge, involvement and opinion leadership. Only for the characteristics of dissatisfaction and use experience did CS_{low} score higher. However, according to the Mann-Whitney U test,[157] the differences between groups are not significant. They are also not significant for the aggregated lead-user score. Cohen's delta shows a medium effect size between the scores achieved by CS_{high} and CS_{low} for the characteristics of trend leadership and use experience (see table 43).

[157] The Mann-Whitney U test was selected as not all characteristics are normally distributed (Bühl 2008, 268, 346). For normally distributed variables, a two-independent samples t-test would be appropriate. However, the Mann-Whitney U test was selected for all characteristics, as it is the stricter measure.

Table 43: Comparison of creativity groups along lead-user characteristics in case study III

Case study III	Dissatisfaction	Innovative activity	Trend leadership	Product knowledge	Use experience	Involvement	Opinion leadership	LUS
CS_{high} (n = 7)	2.00	1.57	2.36	2.43	2.21	2.71	3.14	2.35
Std. deviation	1.19	1.51	1.1	1.27	0.57	1.32	1.35	0.91
CS_{low} (n = 5)	2.40	1.20	1.70	2.00	2.70	2.60	2.70	2.19
Std. deviation	1.39	0.45	1.30	0.61	0.98	0.55	0.45	0.21
Difference	-0.40	0.37	0.66	0.43	-0.49	0.11	0.44	0.16
p	0.673	0.901	0.310	0.486	0.285	0.934	0.863	0.806
Cohen's *d*	-0.31^{+}	0.33^{+}	0.55^{++}	0.43^{+}	-0.61^{++}	0.11	0.44^{+}	0.24^{+}

Mann-Whitney U test
*** highly sig. ($p \leq 0.001$)
** very sig. ($p \leq 0.01$)
* sig. ($p \leq 0.05$)

Cohen's *d*
$^{+++}$> 0.8: large effect
$^{++}$> 0.5: medium effect
$^{+}$> 0.2: small effect

Source: created by author.

Figure 42: Comparison of creativity groups along lead-user characteristics in case study III

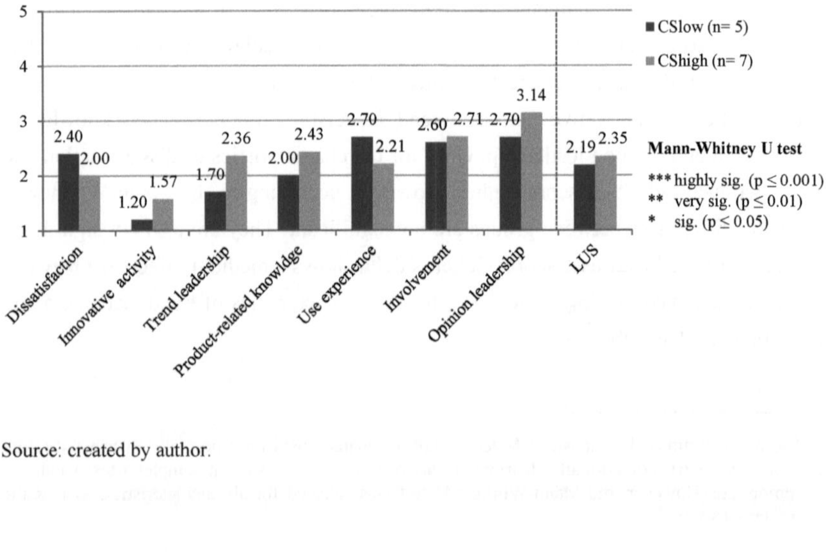

Source: created by author.

Figure 43: Creativity and lead-user characteristics of CS_{high} in case study III

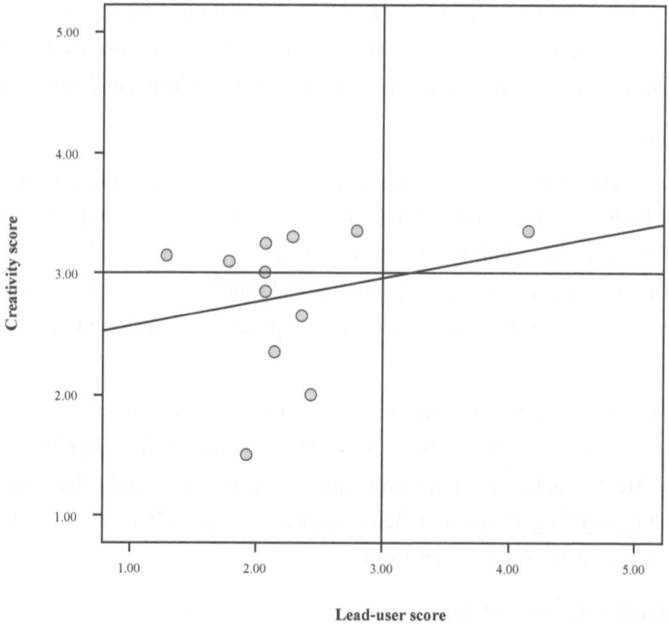

Source: created by author.

It is striking that only one participant (idea 2) reached a lead-user score above center scale ($LUS_{adjusted}$ = 4.14). This participant also reached one of the highest creativity scores ($CS_{adjusted}$ = 3.35) and is thus one of the winners of the idea competition.[158] All other participants reached a lead-user score below center scale (see figure 43).

[158] Consequently, it was not possible to build a group of consumers with high lead userness and a group with low lead userness, as the first group would comprise merely one individual.

Qualitative analysis of lead-user characteristics

The second-place winner of the idea competition was the only participant to show a lead-user score above average. To find out if he can really be regarded as a lead user, an in-depth interview on his lead-user characteristics was conducted and analyzed.

Dissatisfaction

The creator of idea 2 stated that "to save energy, there is no solution that satisfies my needs." He further stressed that he was highly unsatisfied with existing lighting solutions. However, he admitted, "I have not done a proper analysis regarding available solutions. But I read a lot of promotional material." He stated that he had continuously tried to lower his expenses for energy, as he regarded his bills as too high.

His dissatisfaction is in direct contrast with the opinion of other contestants as well as other people of the community, who were approached during the promotion of the competition. Most people were even unwilling to participate, stating that they were satisfied with the lighting situation in their houses as well as with their electricity bills, which may be due to government subsidies.

Innovative activity and trend leadership

The creator of idea 2 took the lighting situation into consideration when building his house: "I built my house thinking about light and how to best take advantage of natural light." He placed windows so that the sun could enter properly, and tried to find the best way to distribute the natural light throughout the house using glass bricks for interior walls as well as mirrors. He commented, "[h]ere, wherever possible, things [walls, ceilings] are made of glass to gain light." Moving away from a product-focused perspective towards a more structural perspective can be regarded as innovative. This structural solution can be regarded as ahead of trend, as no solution of that kind is available in low-income markets.

Product-related knowledge and use experience

The creator of idea 2 stated, "I have always been fond of architecture!" – which may explain his systemic perspective on the lighting situation of his house. He used to frequently go to the library to read about architecture as well as topics related to technology. He had gathered product-related knowledge by "making new things out of old ones." For example, he designed interior walls made from recycled glass or plastic to take advantage of natural light in adjacent rooms with windows. His main concern when doing that was to take advantage of natural light. He stated that building his house as well as furniture out of recycled material was his hobby. However, he also stressed that he simply liked to study and read in his free time. "I read a lot and it interests me."

Involvement

He had a great interest in solutions that save energy, "because it directly impacts your pocket." With the solutions he came up with, he had aimed to reduce the energy consumption in his house. He actively collected information on the subject, had magazines and books at home and took folders with him whenever he saw something of interest. "I like to investigate and inform myself," he said, "I want to know about facts and results." He further emphasized that "when it comes to building a house, you have to think about the question of light. I have put a lot of thought into this and researched a lot."

Opinion leadership

Due to his economic situation, he was not the first to buy new products, but he investigated a lot about new solutions. "I am curious but cautious," he said. The idea he submitted was very spontaneous. However, he stressed that he liked to suggest and share ideas and see results.

> *I already told you that I like architecture. Space requires a lot of creativity. I show initiative in that sense. […] An architect suggests things that are not practical, as he works with measures. I work with space. An architect designs, but so many things happen in practice that he cannot think of – for example, what happens with the people and the objects inside the house. I make suggestions for how these things can be improved.*

He stressed that he mainly shared ideas at work:

> *People ask me about ideas at work.* […] *I have not had time to share ideas in the community. But I do have ideas and I have shared them to create things. But sometimes I lack time to develop an idea, and the idea goes away when you don't have an opportunity to put it into practice. I have had many ideas. I saw reports from engineers and I talked with many people. […] I already had ideas which I thought I should give it to people who know how to make them a reality.*

Characteristics of creative participants

To gain insights on the CS_{high} participants – whose ideas obtained a creativity score equal to or above center scale – two interviews were conducted (see table 44). As a control group, two participants whose ideas obtained a low creativity score (CS_{low}) were interviewed as well.

Only four interviews were conducted due to the difficulties conducting research in this particular community. It turned out that it was too dangerous for the research team to hold interviews in individual houses. To conduct the four interviews, the team was guided by two social workers from COHAPAR for security reasons.

Table 44: Overview of interview participants in case study III

CS_{high}			CS_{low}		
Interview no.	**Idea no.**	**CS**	**Interview no.**	**Idea no.**	**CS**
1	2	3.35	**3**	9	2.35
2	12	3.35	**4**	11	1.50

Source: created by author.

The following clusters of characteristics could be identified amongst the group CS_{high}. There was no evidence of these characteristics in the control group.

<u>High problem-solving ability</u>

The interview with the creator of idea 2 was conducted at his house, which was being built by him and was still under construction. As he had little money to buy furniture, he built almost all the furniture in his house from recycled materials. According to his wife, "he has always been creative." Some of the furniture was integrated into the construction of the house. For example, he had built a closet into the wall and a bed out of brick and steel pieces, from which curtains hung. Both solutions seemed to be inspired by furniture he had seen on TV and tried to imitate: "It's a closet for poor people. I know this does not have the finishing touches other houses have, but at least I can build everything I want with my creativity." Also, some installations were very forward looking. To reach the second floor of his house, he did not build stairs, but a ramp: "One day I will be old, and I won't be able to climb stairs anymore," he told the team. He acknowledged that it was his necessity that pushed him to solve problems creatively. "If you are creative, you achieve things! If I weren't creative, I would not have achieved what I have."

The creator of idea 12 also showed the ability to solve problems creatively. "I like to invent things – I am like a child…a little bit crazy," she said. She related that her house had burnt down and how she managed to reconstruct it by approaching the issue with a problem-solving attitude: "I know there is always a way!" Furthermore, like the creator of idea 2, she related that she copied things she could not afford and made them herself. However, she also shared that she had had ideas but could not realize them due to lack of finances.

Curiosity and positive attitude towards change

The creator of idea 2 seemed to be a highly curious person. He related that he had started frequenting the public library in Curitiba when he was 13 years old:

> *When I was working as an office boy, I always went to the library in my lunch break to read, which was close to the office I worked at. […] I started reading about psychology and architecture.*

He showed a high desire to learn and to become familiar with things: "You have to get to know the world! You come back with a lot of information." In general, he seemed to think positively and liked to convey this spirit to others: "People have many doubts, many questions. We realize that there are many people who lack direction. Often, I have the impulse to help these people. I know there is always a way!"

The creator of idea 12 also showed herself to be highly curious. For example, she related her interest in law and her dream to become a lawyer. Furthermore, she showed an extremely high curiosity to learn about the idea competition. Telling the story of her house that had once burned down – and which she had reconstructed – she vividly showed her positive attitude towards change: "I can't complain [that my house burnt down]. New possibilities always arise and I have to thank God!"

Ambition, dedication, and self-confidence

The wife of the creator of idea 2 said that "he is eager to learn, he always likes to study things." However, he did not only have an eagerness to study, but also to put things into practice. His wife related that when they started to build their house, "he did not know how to put one stone on top of the other." But he was creative, ambitious, and self-confident enough to not only learn how to do things but also to add his own creative abilities when putting things into practice. "We are privileged because we have space," he said. "I worked two years without weekends or holidays to build this [house] with the money I earn. If I had not worked so much, I wouldn't have earned the money to do this."

The creator of idea 12 was also highly ambitious and did not give up easily: "I am a widow. I can't stand still – I have to work." Although poor, she was very positive and thankful for the possibilities she had: "I can't complain. […] I have to thank God!" She dreamt that if she were younger, she would study and become a judge. She related that her youngest daughter had wanted to be a lawyer since she was five. She encouraged her in her ambition and opened an account where she saves money every month for her. "We are poor – we can't pay for university. We have to do it this way. If she later works and saves money as well, maybe it will work out."

Ability to think and act independently

From the conversation with the creator of idea 2, it became obvious that he was someone who always did things his own way – not caring that others told him it was impossible. Most obviously, he built his own house without any knowledge about how to do it and pursued his goals independently of what others thought about him.

The creator of idea 12 was a single mother who also took care of her own mother. In the interview, she stressed that she was proud of being independent. Her entrepreneurial skills helped her make ends meet. She owned a little shop where she sold second hand goods and clothes. She obtained them from church bazaars or markets, where she collected or bought the goods and arranged them.

Environmental consciousness

Both the creators of ideas 2 and 12 showed high environmental consciousness. The creator of idea 2 was the only participant who considered natural light as a source for lighting and mentioned more structural solutions for saving energy, like leaving out interior walls to make use of natural light. He was also the only participant to mention solar energy during the interview. He complained that "there are people who are not able to understand that you can have energy without electricity." Recycling was a recurring theme with him, and he stressed that he cared about the sustainability of the solutions he came up with: He would recycle and reuse material he bought from so-called "casas de demolição" (demolition houses), which offer all kinds of materials from demolished houses. He mentioned individual benefits of recycling – saving costs – but also social benefits, like protecting the environment: "This is all glass to gain light. All this is made out of recycled materials and thus sustainable."

The creator of idea 12 stressed that she liked the topic of the competition and mostly emphasized social benefits: "I think it is great. People need to know how to save energy, how to reuse things that they do not use. [...] Besides the fact that the competition was a great idea of yours, it will help people learn how to save and be conscious. If many people give an idea, maybe one works out!" Furthermore, she stated, "I am very conscious about energy costs. We don't only save for ourselves, but it is good for everybody – not only for me, but for all." The creator of idea 12 regarded recycling also as a business opportunity. As mentioned above, she owned a little shop, where she sold recycled clothes and other goods.

Family unity and support

When interviewing the creators of idea 12, the whole family was present, providing support. During the interview of the creator of idea 2, his wife frequently complemented the comments made by her husband. She claimed to be proud of him and his creations: "My husband is very smart. What he wants to do he does."

Table 45: Overview of characteristics of creative participants in case study III

Characteristics of creative participants	**Idea no.**	
	2	**12**
High problem-solving ability	✓	✓
Curiosity, positive attitude towards change	✓	✓
Ambition, dedication, and self-confidence	✓	✓
Ability to think and act independently	✓	✓
Environmental consciousness	✓	✓
Family unity and support	✓	✓
% of characteristics encountered per person	100%	100%

Source: created by author.

Note: a check mark [✓] was used to code when the characteristic was present, and an X when it was absent.

In contrast to the CS_{high} responses, the interviews with the control group CS_{low} did not provide evidence for the characteristics mentioned above. For example, the participants interviewed from the CS_{low} group did not report any creative activity in general and stated that they had developed the ideas only for the competition. The creator of idea 11 stated, “I participated in the competition because I happened to be at the Telecentro that day [where the competition took place]. Usually, I am not a person who likes to create things.” In the interviews and through the observations of the CS_{low} group, no findings indicated high curiosity or a positive attitude towards change. The interviews with the creators of ideas 9 and 11 showed that they were both shy and self-conscious. The creator of idea 11 reported that she had quit school; she seemed to have little ambition in life. When asked about what she did in her free time, she reported that she “like[d] to talk to her friends.” Furthermore, CS_{low} participants did not mention a particular drive for being independent. Regarding the characteristic of environmental consciousness, the creator of idea 11 (from group CS_{low}) showed herself to be aware of issues but not proactive in solving them. She stated that “if every person would give more value to the environment, things would be better. Energy is very important for everybody, and we should value it more.” However, as opposed to the creators of ideas 2 and 12 (from group CS_{high}), she did not take action to recycle things herself or create things from recycled material. The creator of idea 9 showed limited knowledge regarding environmentally friendly solutions. Furthermore, both the creators of idea 9 and 11 did not provide any indication of high family unity and support. They were interviewed on their own, and the creator of idea 11 commented that she did not even mention her participation in the idea competition to her family.

4.3.4 Process: Identification and transfer of innovation-relevant knowledge

To explore which types of information and knowledge can be obtained from the process of idea competitions, the content of the submitted ideas was analyzed to identify patterns and trends that give insights on consumer requirements regarding lighting solutions. Second, the transcripts of the interviews with the research team were analyzed to understand which relevant types of information and knowledge were acquired by the researchers and how they were transferred.

Innovation-relevant knowledge obtained from the ideas

Although only a very small number of ideas were submitted, three thematic clusters could be identified:

- **Natural light**: Three ideas suggested saving energy through taking better advantage of natural light. These ideas are innovative in regards to house construction. They suggest, for example, transparent ceilings for central rooms, fewer room divisions that hinder sunlight dispersion, or windows at strategic points in the construction.

- **Better dispersion of light**: Three ideas focus on dispersing light from a certain source (e.g., a bulb) using mirrors.
- **New designs**: Four ideas merely present new designs for lamps or lamp shades.

In general, participants showed a certain awareness about saving energy – which could be related to environmental consciousness or simply economic constraints. However, besides the ideas that aimed to make use of natural light, only one idea made use of an alternative energy source: water power. None of the ideas made use of solar energy. It seems that using natural light is easier for participants to grasp than solar energy – which involves technical knowledge.

A surprising fact was that most ideas did not focus on lamps as a product, but more on generating light as a concept (e.g., through using natural light). It seems that the participants were not very familiar with alternative lighting solutions (e.g., lanterns, lamps, lamp shades, torches) and different ways to generate electricity. Overall, the ideas of the third case study can be regarded as less innovative. They were simple but very practical.

Table 46: Frequency of content clusters identified – case study III

Cluster	Frequency *(absolute)*	Frequency *(in percent)*
Efficient use of light/energy	7	41.18
New designs of lamps or lamp shade	4	23.53
Use of natural light (through house construction)	3	17.65
Better dispersion of light	3	17.65

Source: created by author.

The winning ideas only partly corresponded to the patterns identified:

- **Reusing energy (idea 2)**: The idea that won the competition suggested a system that makes use of the heat dispersed by a light bulb to light up another one. The objective was to save energy. The idea convinced the jury due to its utility and originality, compared to the other ideas. In the interview, the winner shared a variety of his ideas related to lighting solutions – one of them being to build houses in a way that makes most use of natural light (see section 4.3.3).

- **Water energy (idea 12)**: The second-place idea aimed to use water power to produce electricity to light up the house of the idea owner, which was situated close to a river. Although it was not regarded as original, the idea convinced the jury due to its utility and feasibility.
- **Micro-energy (idea 5)**: The third-place idea was inspired by traffic lights. The contestant stated that the main feature of traffic lights is that the light can be seen from far away and is very bright. He aimed to re-use the bulbs of traffic lights for household use. The idea was convincing due to the degree of elaboration with which it was presented.

Figure 44: Winning ideas of case study III

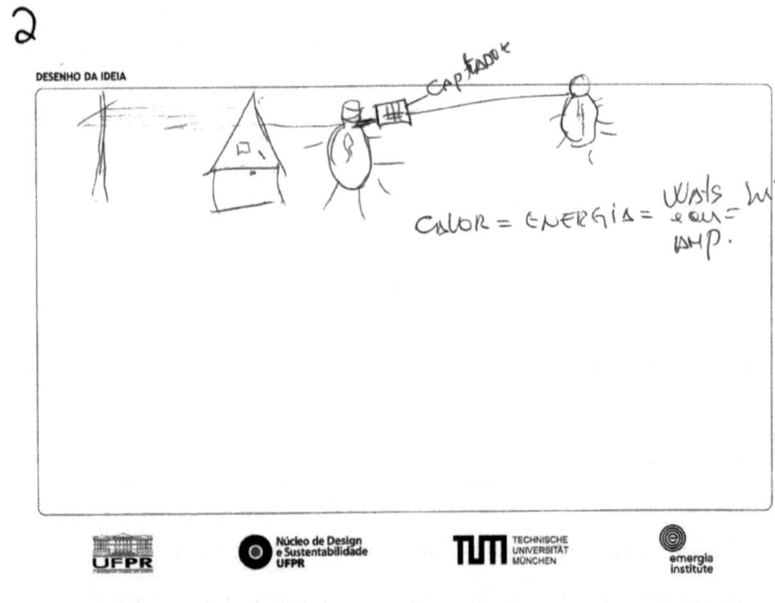

1st place: "Reaproveitamento da energia produzida pelas lâmpadas"
("Reusing the energy produced by bulbs") (idea 2)

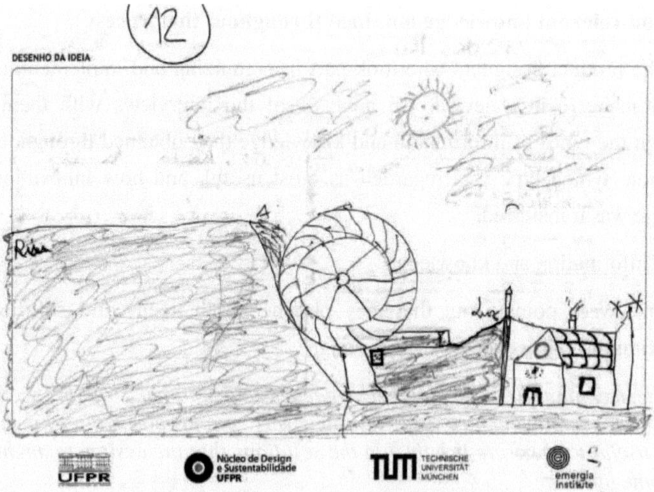

2nd place: “Gerando energia através da roda de agua”
(“Generating energy with a water wheel”) (idea 12)

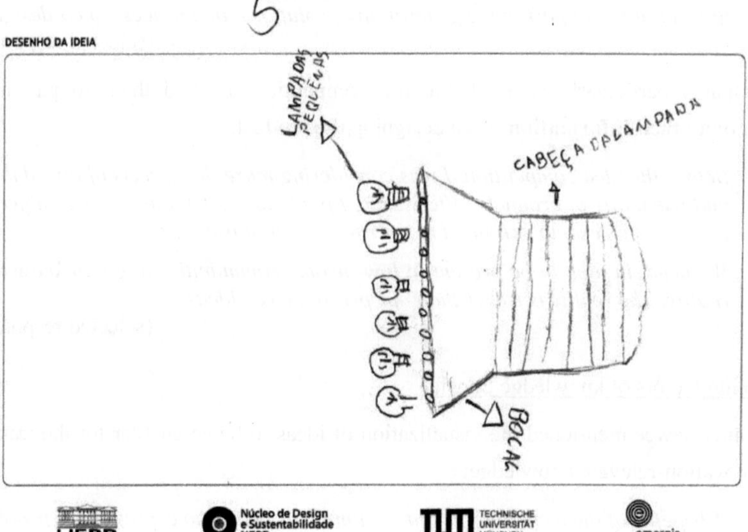

3rd place: “Micro energia” (“micro-energy”) (idea 5)

Innovation-relevant knowledge obtained throughout the process

Two of the product designers who took part in organizing and implementing the idea competitions were interviewed. An analysis of the interviews with them provides insights on the types of information and knowledge they obtained throughout the idea competition, which type was regarded as most useful, and how innovation-relevant knowledge was transferred.

Types of information and knowledge

The interviewees pointed out that they obtained both **need- and solution-related information** through a process of "co-design":

> *The technique is useful to get a deeper understanding of the needs of low-income people and how they view their very own problems. [...] Furthermore, it is useful to generate insights on the solutions that the designers might not have come up with.*
>
> *Amongst the benefits, I would stress that primarily the target group develops a viable solution for themselves, and the designer then continues that process, translating the idea, refining, and improving it – transforming the initial ideas into attractive and feasible solutions. With this, the target group perceives itself to be an integral part in the generation of solutions, in a process of co-design.*
>
> (selected responses)

Participants particularly stressed that the competition directed them to pay more attention to **tacit information** when designing the product.

> *Before the idea competition, I was considering more the aspects of affordability and durability of products. Afterwards, I paid more attention to more subjective aspects – for example, related to the use context of products.*
>
> *We need, in fact, to be present in low-income communities to get to know their reality. The reality is richer than our preconceived ideas.*
>
> (selected responses)

Enabling factors of knowledge transfer

One interviewee mentioned the visualization of ideas to be an enabler for the transfer of innovation-relevant knowledge:

> *A benefit [of the technique] is that it stimulates people to express their problems and necessities using drawings, since many of these people may have difficulties in verbalizing or writing about this.*
>
> (selected response)

Both interviewees further mention that the participatory approach of the method raised the **self-esteem** of participants – which in turn facilitated the transfer of information.

> *I think [through the idea competition] many of them realized how creative they are when it comes to finding solutions to their problems – and that they can and should be active agents in creating these solutions.*
>
> *One participant said to me: "I am learning to be humble with you. You well-educated people come to this poor community to learn from us." The idea competition really elevated their self-esteem.*
>
> (selected responses)

For the designers, the **participatory approach** also offered benefits: it helped them to be empathic with their target group and thus create more appropriate products.

> *I believe the idea competition widened my perception about the real needs of low-income consumers, and it helped me to practice more empathy towards them.*
>
> *This method offers real contact with the user and allows building a relationship based on empathy.*
>
> (selected responses)

A key insight of the interviewees was the realization of the **potential of low-income consumers to be creative**, as well as the ease and ingenuousness with which they create ideas. Again, this learning may have contributed to the openness and receptivity of the researchers towards new information, ultimately enabling the transfer of relevant information and knowledge.

> *One of my major lessons was verifying to that low-income consumers can be (and are) extremely creative if they think about solutions for their very own problems. To respect and use this creativity is an important part of the design process.*
>
> *We could observe the capacity to suggest ideas with ease, without being restricted too much by the real possibilities. We also observed a certain ingenuousness, which is positive.*
>
> (selected responses)

Table 47 provides an overview of the types of information and knowledge as well as the enablers of knowledge transfer mentioned per interviewee.

Table 47: Results of interviews with product designers – case study III

Case study III	**Interviewee A**	**Interviewee B**	
Types of information and knowledge			
Need-related information	✓	X	50%
Solution-related information	✓	X	50%
Tacit knowledge	✓	✓	100%
Explicit knowledge	✓	X	50%
Enabling factors of knowledge transfer			
Personal interaction	✓	✓	100%
Trust	X	X	0%
Participatory process	✓	✓	100%
Elevated self-esteem	X	✓	50%
Change in perspective	✓	✓	100%

Source: created by author.

Note: a check mark [✓] was used to code when the type of information and knowledge or the enabler was mentioned by the interviewee, and an X when it was not mentioned.

5 Cross-case analysis and discussion

According to Yin (2003, 133ff.), a pre-condition for cross-case analysis is that each case study is first treated as a separate study. The previous chapter analyzed the findings from the three case studies individually, in stand-alone sections. The purpose of this chapter is to make the link between these individual case studies, identifying patterns and discussing them.

The chapter is divided into three main sections addressing the three objectives of idea competitions, as suggested by the literature (see chapter 2): (5.1) the generation of creative ideas; (5.2) the identification of lead users and creative consumers, and (5.3) the identification and transfer of innovation-relevant knowledge. Through the cross-case analysis and discussion of data, the main research questions in table 48 are answered.

Each main section of this chapter follows a similar approach:

(1) Cross-case analysis: In the first sub-section of each of the three main sections, the data of the individual case studies are compared to one another. This cross-case analysis is done separately for each research question (resulting in five sections: 5.1.1, 5.2.1, 5.2.3, 5.3.1 and 5.3.2). All qualitative and quantitative information gathered as part of the case studies feed into this analysis. Furthermore, the analysis is complemented by using the author's own expert knowledge about the discourse on the topic and by addressing major rival interpretations where appropriate (Yin 2003, 34, 133ff.; Punch 2005, 254–255).

(2) Discussion: In a final step, the findings of the cross-case analysis are discussed – again, for each research question separately (resulting in five discussion sections: 5.1.2, 5.2.2, 5.2.4, 5.2.5 and 5.3.3). Where possible and suitable, they are triangulated with findings from similar studies to enhance validity (Yin 2003, 34). To close the discussion sections, hypotheses are drawn from these findings where suitable. Although findings from case studies are not generalizable to populations, they may support the articulation of hypotheses, which can be tested in future studies (Yin 2003, 10).

Table 48: Research questions

Objective of the idea competition	Research question	Unit of analysis	Method	Section
(1) Generation of creative ideas	(1) To what extent can offline idea competitions generate **creative ideas** from low-income consumers?	Ideas	CAT	5.1
(2) Identification of lead users and creative participants	(2a) To what extent can offline idea competitions identify low-income consumers with **lead-user** characteristics?	Participants	Content analysis of LU interviews; quantitative analysis of LU scores	5.2
	(2b) What are the common **characteristics** of low-income consumers who produce creative ideas in offline idea competitions?	Participants	Content analysis of interviews	5.2
(3) Identification and transfer of innovation-relevant information and knowledge	(3a) What **types** of information and knowledge can be obtained through idea competitions conducted in low-income contexts? (3b) What types of information and knowledge are most **useful** for innovation processes geared towards developing solutions for low-income consumers?	Ideas, process	Content analysis of ideas, interview protocols, and field notes	5.3
	(3c) What factors **enable** the transfer of innovation-relevant knowledge from participants to designers/developers during offline idea competitions in low-income contexts?	Process	Content analysis of interview protocols and field notes	5.3

Source: created by author.

5.1 Generation of creative ideas

Innovation processes commonly start with the generation of creative ideas. As Kristensson et al. (2004, 4) put it: "Creative ideas may offer a successful start to innovation." Particularly when innovating for low-income contexts, creative solutions are needed which solve or find ways around the challenges of the specific use context (see chapters 1 and 2). Idea competitions are a technique that leverages the creativity and knowledge of consumers and enables them to contribute to the fuzzy front end of innovation processes. However, as most studies in the area of innovation research have applied the technique online with middle- to high-income consumers,[159] it remains unclear whether idea competitions serve to generate creative ideas with low-income consumers.

To find answers, the Consensual Assessment Technique (CAT) was applied. It served to assess the level of creativity of the ideas submitted to each idea competition. Results across case studies are described in section 5.1.1. Through applying the CAT, patterns regarding certain creativity dimensions can be observed. They are discussed and put into context in section 5.1.2.

5.1.1 Cross-case analysis: Creativity of ideas

The three idea competitions produced 83 ideas, which were handed in by 73 participants (see table 49). In analyzing the creativity of these ideas, it stands out that the mean creativity score is fairly low: it is at center scale in case study I ($mean_{cs\text{-}I}$ = 3.01), and slightly below center scale in case studies II and III ($mean_{cs\text{-}II}$ = 2.82; $mean_{cs\text{-}III}$ = 2.82) (see figure 45).

Table 49: No. of ideas and participants

	Case study I	Case study II	Case study III	Total
No. of participants	26	35	12	73
No. of ideas	34	37	12	83

Source: created by author.

[159] Only one idea competition from the literature could be identified that was conducted in low-income settings. However, the study is only published as a whitepaper by company professionals and lacks further investigation (see Jung and Chipchase 2008).

Taking a look at the different dimensions of the creativity score, the jury of experts (see section 3.2.3) rated the ideas highest along the criteria *utility* and *feasibility*. In each case study, both dimensions reached means that are close to (for case study II) or slightly above center scale (for case studies I and III) (see figure 45). The lowest scores in all three cases can be observed for the criterion *degree of elaboration*.

Figure 45: Creativity of ideas

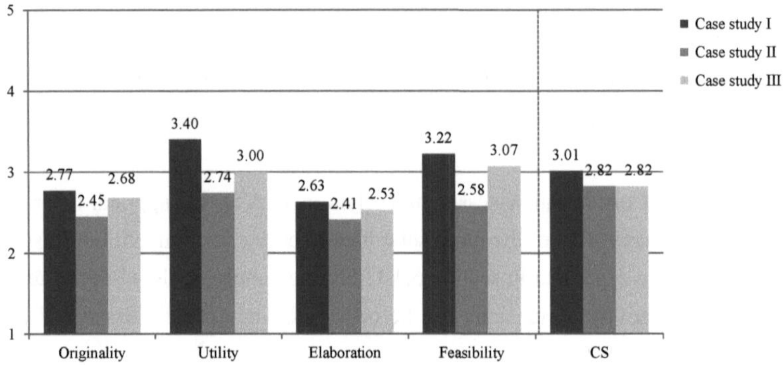

Source: created by author.

To get a sense of the distribution of the data across case studies, the percentage frequency was visualized (see figure 46). The curves for the creativity dimensions of utility and feasibility are slightly skewed to the left (negative skew), with the most frequent ratings of 4 points. In contrast, the curves of the dimensions *originality* and degree of elaboration are skewed to the right (positive skew); they were most frequently rated with 2 points.

Figure 46: Percentage frequency of CAT dimensions

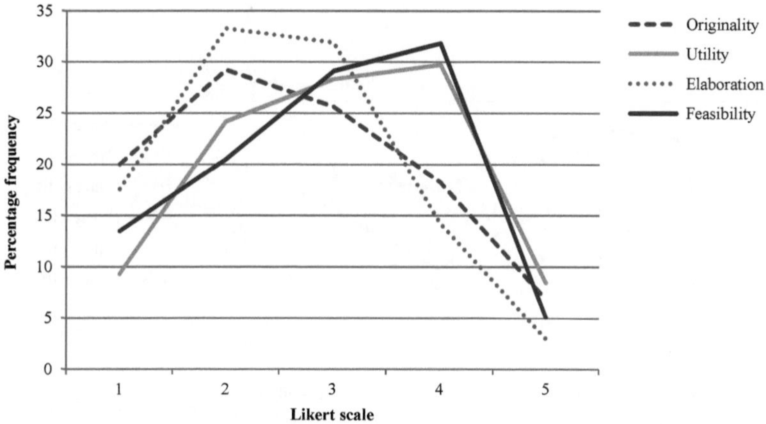

Source: created by author.

Creativity groups

To compare creative ideas with less creative ones, they were arranged into two groups: CS_{high} and CS_{low}. The share of ideas that received a creativity score equal to or above 3 (i.e., CS_{high}) is fairly high in case study I at 55.9%. For case studies II and III, the share of CS_{high} is around 40%. The latter result is similar to the results of Silvertant's study (2011, 206ff.), in which a third of all ideas submitted fall into the group CS_{high}. The similar results may be an indicator for the share of creative ideas one can expect from idea competitions.

Figure 47 visualizes the mean scores of the two groups for each creativity dimension. In all three case studies, the curves of the group CS_{high} are above center scale (except for the dimension degree of elaboration in case study III); the curves are also consistently above the curves of CS_{low}. Furthermore, all curves follow a similar pattern with two peaks – one for the dimension utility and one for feasibility (except CS_{high} in case study II). According to an independent sample t-test, all criteria distinguish significantly between CS_{high} and CS_{low} – with the exception of the criterion feasibility in case study II. Also, the effect sizes between the values of CS_{high} and CS_{low} consistently indicate a large effect (see chapter 4).

Figure 47: Differences between creativiy groups across case studies

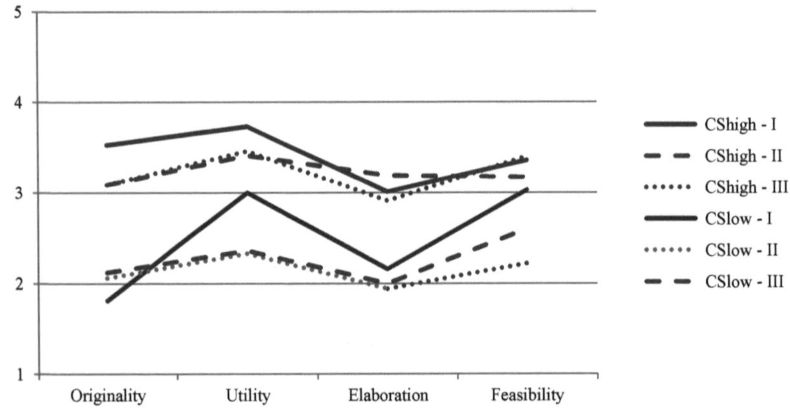

Source: created by author.

Table 50: Creativity groups

	Case study I			Case study II			Case study III		
	CS_{high} (n = 19)	CS_{low} (n = 15)	difference	CS_{high} (n = 14)	CS_{low} (n = 23)	difference	CS_{high} (n = 5)	CS_{low} (n = 7)	difference
% of ideas	55.9%	44.1%	---	37.8%	62.2%	---	41.7%	58.3%	---
Originality	3.53	1.81	**1.72*** **	3.09	2.06	1.03***	3.09	2.12	0.97*
Utility	**3.73**	**2.98**	0.75**	**3.41**	**2.33**	1.08***	**3.46**	2.36	**1.10***
Elaboration	3.01	2.16	0.85***	3.19	1.94	**1.25*** **	2.91	2.00	0.91*
Feasibility	3.36	3.03	0.33*	3.17	2.22	0.95***	3.4	**2.60**	0.8
CS	3.41	2.50	0.91***	3.21	2.14	1.07 ***	3.21	2.27	0.94*

Source: created by author.

T-test

* significant ($p \leq 0.05$)
** very significant ($p \leq 0.01$)
*** highly significant ($p \leq 0.001$)

Note: Numbers in bold represent the highest values in that category and underlined numbers lowest values.

An analysis of the ideas of the first-place winners (i.e., those who obtained the highest creativity scores) provides a slightly different – albeit consistent – picture across cases. Scores are mostly above average (with the exception of idea 2 in case study III for the dimension feasibility). Also, the three ideas rank highest for originality and utility (see figure 48).

Figure 48: Creativity of the ideas of the first-place winners

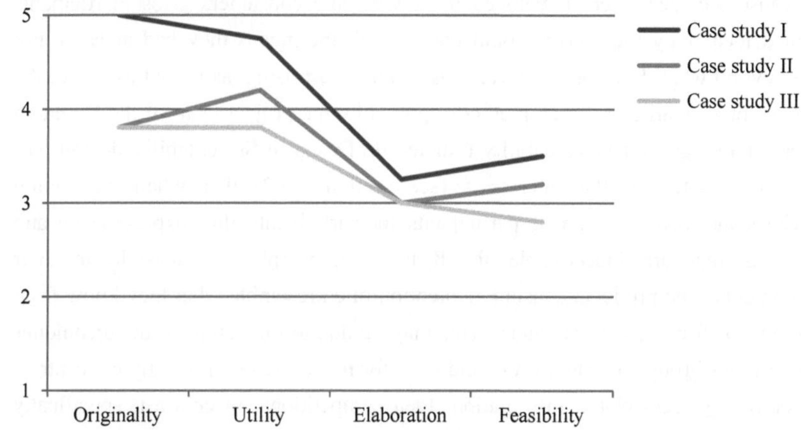

Source: created by author.

5.1.2 Discussion: Idea competitions as a technique to generate creative ideas

The creativity analysis provides insights into the level of creativity of the pool of ideas. The results of the cross-case analysis provide an answer for research question 1: Three idea competitions with low-income consumers showed that the technique serves to generate averagely creative ideas, with means around center scale ($mean_{cs\text{-}I} = 3.01$; $mean_{cs\text{-}II} = 2.82$; $mean_{cs\text{-}III} = 2.82$).[160] Furthermore, ideas were mostly rated as *feasible* and *useful*.

Values for CS_{high} are consistently above center scale, while values for CS_{low} are consistently below center scale – with a few exceptions. However, what stands out is the linearity of results across creativity dimensions and groups. In each case study,

[160] This is particularly true when taking into consideration that participants "selected themselves," rather than being selected (see section 2.1.6), which could imply that creative people may be more likely to participate than those who usually lack creative ideas.

both groups achieve highest values for utility and feasibility. This is particularly surprising as the case studies had different topics and as experts were asked to assess creativity within each case – that is, only comparing the ideas with one another within each case study. The results demand a closer look at the different creativity dimensions interpreted within the context the case studies.

The high **feasibility** ratings of ideas indicate that they are easy to implement. This may be because the ideas were developed by low-income consumers. Most participants designed ideas they themselves could realize with the means they had at hand, not going beyond what they could afford. This result is surprising, as it contrasts with the results of other market research methods applied by the project team of the Research Center for Design and Sustainability (Núcleo de Design e Sustentabilidade [NDS]): Researchers stated in the interviews (see section 5.3.2) that when conducting interviews and focus groups with participants, the participants often express wants and aspirations that are inaccessible for them – or simply not feasible in their environments. The products consumers mention often resemble what they know from TV shows or from advertisements.[161] This may be due to the nature of the techniques applied: focus groups or interviews conducted for market research mostly concentrate on identifying need-related information. Idea competitions, in contrast, specifically encourage users to find a solution for their needs – which may make suggestions much more likely to be pragmatic and down-home.

The high **utility** of the ideas can be viewed as a natural benefit of their being generated by the users themselves. Ideas were created by users sitting in the kitchen or living room of their own house. They not only had the use context in mind, but were directly surrounded by it. Thus, it seems evident that the ideas generated address a real need and that the evaluators perceived them as useful for the target group.

This finding can also be confirmed by studies conducted in middle- to high-income contexts. Magnusson (2009) finds that ordinary users are experts regarding user needs and thus produce ideas that are useful. Kristensson et al. (2004, 11) come to a similar conclusion comparing the ideas of ordinary users with those of company professionals. Magnusson explains that while ideas from ordinary users are generally more useful, they cannot be viewed as "ready-made solutions." Rather, they serve as "an inspiration for the innovation process." However, other authors warn that ordinary users only

[161] Source: Interviews with researchers of NDS.

provide ideas that are useful in the present; their capability to provide insights into future needs is regarded as limited. As von Hippel (1986, 791) writes, "[u]sers steeped in the present are [...] unlikely to generate novel product concepts which conflict with the familiar."

This may explain why, on average, ideas were not rated as original ($mean_{orig} = 2.63$) by the experts – which is in contrast to the ideas of the winners of the idea competition (see figure 48). The low overall **originality** of ideas may be due to the context in which the ideas were generated: Given the daily struggle to satisfy needs and solve problems – such as a lack of water, energy, or living space – the originality of solutions may not be the main focus of these problem-solvers. Rather, they may look for solutions that work and are useful and easy to implement.[162] Nonetheless, the winners were obviously able to generate original ideas. Moreover, a variety of practical examples show that particularly original products developed for low-income contexts – such as adapted solar lamps or new information technologies – have spread rapidly in low-income markets due to their ability to overcome market barriers and solve pressing problems (so-called disruptive innovations; see section 2.1.2 for examples). Thus, originality is definitely a relevant dimension of creativity when developing products for low-income markets, even though the results of this study indicate that idea competitions may not be most suitable method to yield a pool of original ideas. Rather, originality can be expected from only a few, very creative individuals who can be identified through the competition (see section 5.2).

The **degree of elaboration** of ideas was also rated as below average across cases ($mean_{elab} = 2.52$); most ideas lacked technical specifications regarding, for example, the materials to be used or construction details. In fact, most ideas were handed in as simple sketches with a brief description. It seems that participants particularly lacked technical knowledge, which may be due to the low level of education of participants (see sections 4.2.3 and 4.3.3). The latter is again congruent with the findings of Magnusson (2009, 591), which show that ordinary users have high use knowledge –

[162] For the results of case study II, it also needs to be taken into account that the product "rainwater collector" was unknown to most participants. During the promotion of the competition, the research team often had to explain the product to potential participants. In addition, there are currently no solutions for rainwater collection available for low-income households. Consequently, it does not come as a surprise that most submitted ideas seemed rather conventional and were thus regarded as less creative. However, from the perspective of the participants (i.e., the low-income consumers), many ideas suggested can be regarded as (at least incremental) innovations, as they are new to the market.

making their ideas useful – but that they lack the technological knowledge required to develop the ideas further or implement them.[163]

As mentioned above, the winners of each idea competition produced ideas that were rated as original and useful (see figure 48, section 5.1.1). Being able to develop ideas that diverge from the familiar is a quality attributed particularly to lead users. The question remains whether the individuals identified through the competitions can even be considered lead users. This will be explored in the next section (5.2).

5.2 Identification of lead users and creative participants

The previous section discussed to what extent offline idea competitions serve to identify creative ideas (section 5.1). This section focuses on the **individuals** who generate creative ideas. They are known as **lead users** and are said to be able to contribute the most relevant information and knowledge to innovation processes. More concretely, the section aims to find out to what extent idea competitions with low-income consumers serve to identify lead users. A literature review identified characteristics commonly found in lead users in the consumer-goods industry (see section 2.2.6). The first part of this section (5.2.1) thus investigates the (overall) incidence of these lead-user characteristics amongst participants across cases (see figure 49: left side, quadrants I and IV). Then, the section takes a closer look at the few participants who show a high incidence of lead-user characteristics and whose ideas achieved a high creativity score – namely, the winners of the competitions (see figure 49: right side, quadrant I). Section 5.2.2 discusses the results of this analysis.

[163] However, in contrast to this study, Kristensson et al. (2004) and Magnusson (2009) find that ordinary users in high-income markets are also able to produce ideas that are more original than the ideas of company professionals.

Figure 49: Graphical representation of research question 2

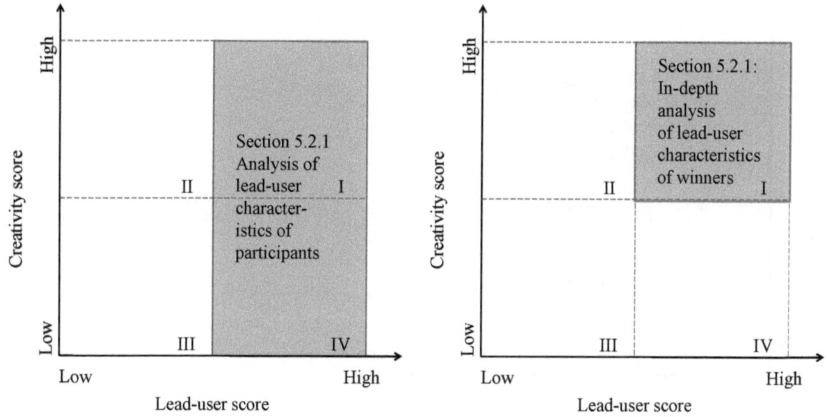

Source: created by author.

Consumers who produce creative ideas but do not show lead-user characteristics may still be able to make valuable contributions to innovation (Silvertant 2011; Schrader and Belz 2012, 345ff.). Also, being able to distinguish these consumers from those who are merely motivated to contribute to innovation but not creative may significantly improve the efficiency of consumer integration into innovation (Schrader and Belz 2012, 345ff.). Consequently, this study inductively identifies **characteristics** that distinguish idea-competition participants who produce ideas with a creativity score above average (i.e., the group named CS_{high}; see quadrants I and II in figure 50) from those with a creativity score below average (CS_{low}) as a control group (see quadrants III and IV in figure 50). For that purpose, section 5.2.3 compares the results of qualitative, in-depth interviews and participant observation across cases. Section 5.2.4 discusses these results and triangulates them with findings from other studies. Based on these findings, hypotheses about the characteristics of CS_{high} are developed. The final section (5.2.5) then systematically compares CS_{high} participants with lead users.

Figure 50: Graphical representation of research question 3

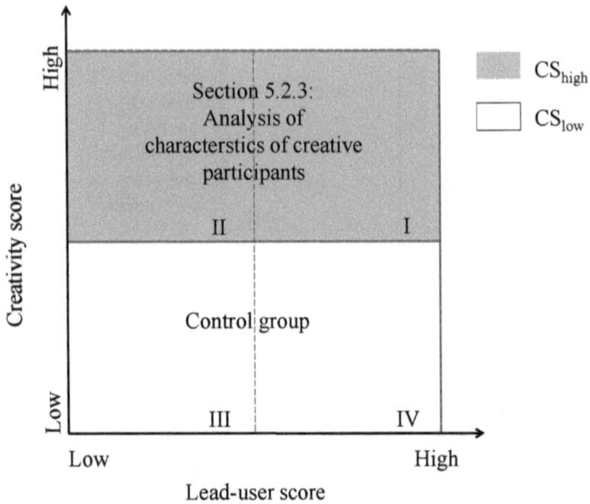

Source: created by author.

5.2.1 Cross-case analysis: Lead-user characteristics of participants

In all three case studies, aggregated lead-user scores (LUS) were calculated for those participants who agreed to take part in a lead-user interview (case study I: n = 5; case study II: n = 28; case study III: n = 12). The means of the average aggregated LUS are below center scale for case studies II and III ($mean_{LUS\text{-}II}$ = 2.19; $mean_{LUS\text{-}III}$ = 2.27), and slightly above center scale in case study I ($mean_{LUS\text{-}I}$ = 3.51). Thus, the overall lead userness of participants can be assessed as low.

Figure 51 shows the mean LUS for each lead-user characteristic. Here, a low incidence can be observed for case studies II and III. Case study I can be regarded as an exception: the high values of the aggregated scores are due to the low number of participants interviewed (n = 5). Two of these interviewees in case study I were the winners of the competition. Figure 51 further shows that *trend leadership* and *opinion leadership* as well as *involvement* are the characteristics that rank highest. The lowest means in all three case studies can be observed for the characteristic *innovative activity*.

Figure 51: Lead-user characteristics of all participants

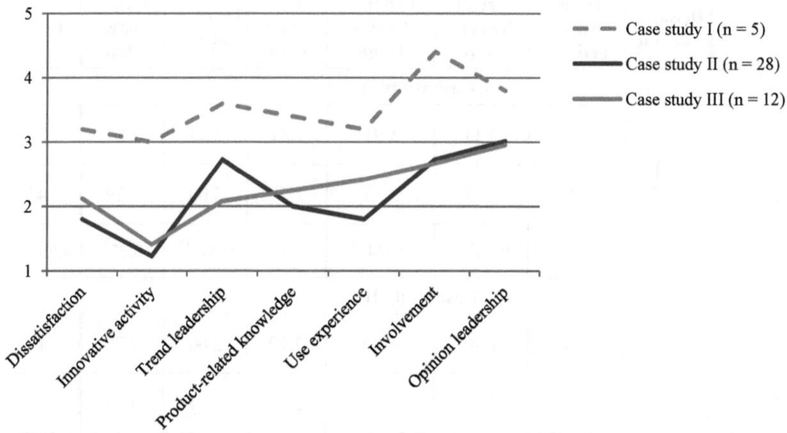

Source: created by author.

In case studies II and III, enough data were available to compare the lead-user scores of those participants with a high creativity score (CS_{high}) to those with a low one (CS_{low}). However, results are not strong enough to allow deriving clear findings. While in case study I, the differences between the scores are significant for some characteristics (i.e. dissatisfaction, trend leadership, involvement as well as the overall lead user score), they are not significant in case study III. This is most probably due to the small sample of case study III (n = 12). Measuring Cohen's *d*, mostly small effect sizes between the scores of CS_{high} and CS_{low} can be found in both cases for the characteristics dissatisfaction, trend leadership, product-related knowledge, opinion leadership and the aggregated LUS (see table 51, bold results).

Table 51: Comparison of creativity groups along lead-user characteristics applying Cohen's *d*

	Dissatis-faction	Inno-vative activity	Trend leader-ship	Product know-ledge	Use experi-ence	Involve-ment	Opinion leader-ship	LUS
Case study II								
CS_{low} (n = 16)	1.38	1.25	2.34	1.91	1.81	2.53	2.81	2.00
CS_{high} (n = 12)	2.38	1.21	3.25	2.13	1.79	3.00	3.29	2.43
Cohen's *d*	**1.20**$^{+++}$	-0.07	**0.93**$^{+++}$	**0.24**$^{+}$	-0.03	0.84^{+++}	**0.37**$^{+}$	**0.89**$^{+++}$
Case study III								
CS_{low} (n = 5)	2.40	1.20	1.70	2.00	2.70	2.60	2.70	2.19
CS_{high} (n = 7)	2.00	1.57	2.36	2.43	2.21	2.71	3.14	2.35
Cohen's *d*	**-0.31**$^{+}$	0.33^{+}	**0.55**$^{++}$	**0.43**$^{+}$	-0.61^{++}	0.11	**0.44**$^{+}$	**0.24**$^{+}$

Cohen's *d*
$^{+++}$> 0.8: large effect
$^{++}$> 0.5: medium effect
$^{+}$> 0.2: small effect

Figure 52: Lead-user characteristics and creativity of ideas

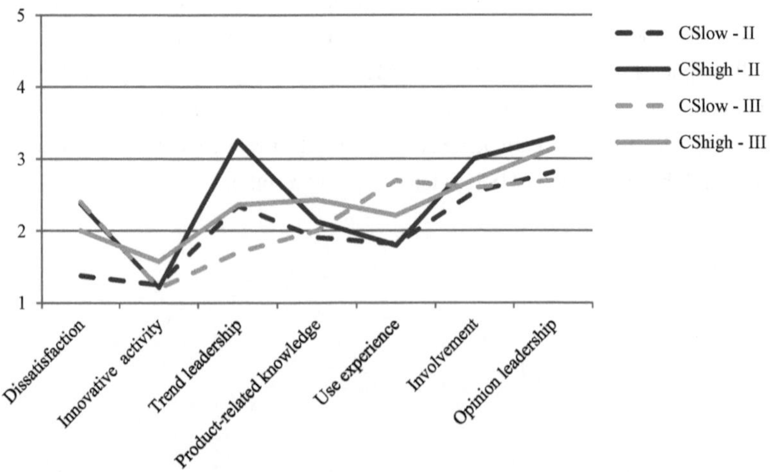

Source: created by author.

What stands out across cases is that four individuals reached both a lead-user score and a creativity score above center scale (two participants in case study I and one participant in each of the case studies II and III; see figure 54). In fact, they are amongst the three winners of each competition, having created ideas which reached (at least the third) highest CS of all participants. The high originality of their ideas (see figure 48, section 5.1.1) further points towards the innovative potential of these participants when it comes to creating solutions for the low-income context – in contrast to the remaining participants, who only reached below average scores for originality (see section 5.1). Furthermore, the above average usefulness of their ideas indicates their high use knowledge. Hence, these individuals were portrayed in depth in the individual case studies (see sections 4.1.3, 4.2.3, and 4.3.3). The following elaboration looks at patterns across these portraits, which are again structured along the lead-user characteristics.

Figure 53: Scatter plots: Lead-user score and creativity score

Case study I

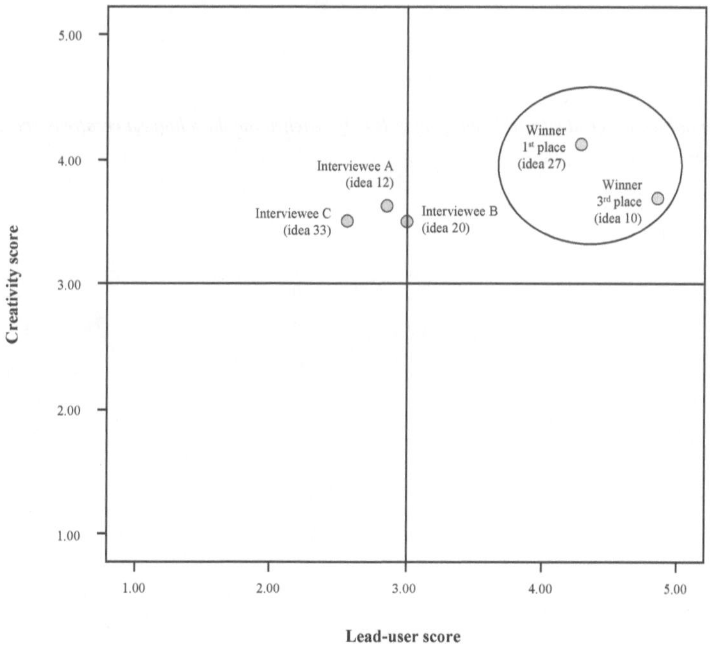

Case study II

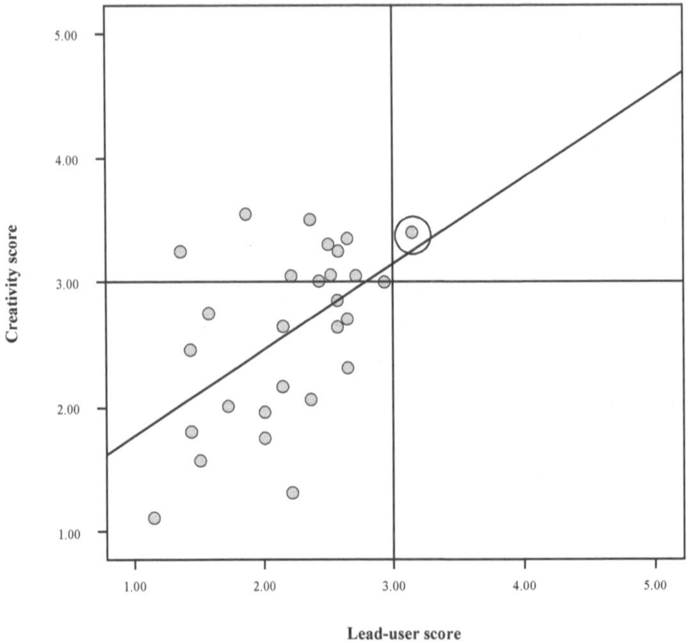

Note: The potential lead user identified in case study II only reached the third highest creativity score (see figure above).

Case study III

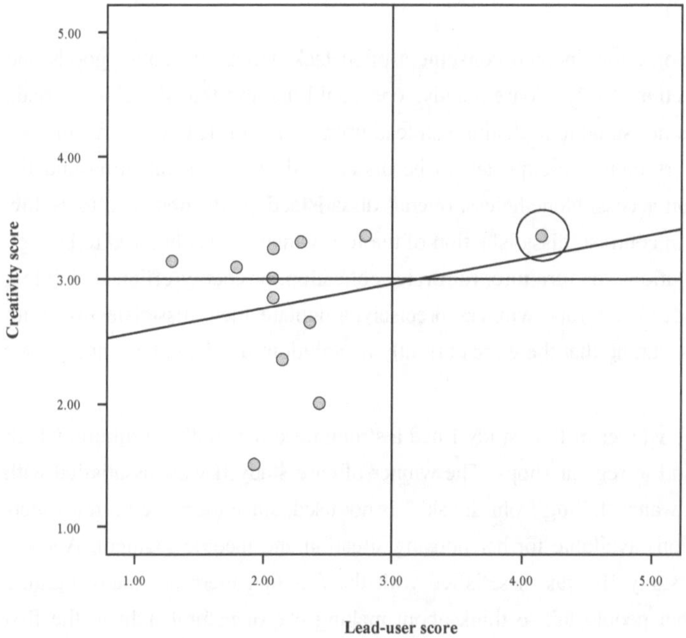

Source: created by author.

In depth analysis of lead-user characteristics of winners

Dissatisfaction

For various reasons, low-income consumers often lack access to quality goods and services (see section 2.1.2). Consequently, one could assume that the characteristic *dissatisfaction* is not suitable to distinguish lead users from non-lead users, as all low-income consumers could be expected to be dissatisfied with their situation and the products they can access. Nonetheless, overall dissatisfaction was observed to be low (see figure 52). In contrast, dissatisfaction of the four winners was observed to be high in regards to solutions for furniture, rainwater collection, or energy-efficient lighting, respectively. Indeed, all four winners precisely articulate their dissatisfaction with current products, stating that there are currently no solutions available that satisfy their needs.

For example, the winner of case study I had a strong need for quality furniture, which she could not find in regular shops. The winner of case study II was dissatisfied with the fact that the water "falling from the sky" is not used, since there are no rainwater-collection solutions available for her housing situation and income segment. And the winner of case study III was dissatisfied with the fact that there are many lighting solutions, but that people fail to think about making use of natural light in the first place.

Table 52: Selected quotes on dissatisfaction

Case study I	Case study I	Case study II	Case study III
Idea 10	Idea 27	Idea 7	Idea 2
Score: 5	Score: 5	Score: 3	Score: 4
There are so many things to improve – the pieces of furniture they sell in the shops occupy too much space. In the shops, everything is big. These products don't fit into a small house. And I like to have space!	*Every piece of furniture is big. They do not work in small houses. And the things that are available for small houses are things you do not want. They are simpler. No, I am definitely not satisfied.*	*Dissatisfaction with the fact that rainwater is wasted when it just "falls from the sky" and is not used: "Not collecting rainwater would be a waste!"*	*To save energy, there is no solution that satisfies my needs.*

Source: interviews conducted by author.

Innovative activity

Comparing the LUS of all participants, figure 52 shows that innovative activity was the characteristic ranked lowest. In the case of the winners of case studies I and III, however, innovative activity ranks between 4 and 5 points on a 5-point Likert scale (see table 53).

As lead users benefit significantly from a solution to their unaddressed needs, they are willing to devote significant resources to obtain a new solution – be it time or money. Von Hippel states (1986, 797) that "users able to obtain the highest net benefit from the solution to a given new product (or process or service) will be the ones who have devoted the most resources to understanding it." Previous studies have found dissatisfaction to be a trigger for innovative activity (Lüthje 2000, 33ff.; Lüthje 2004, 686; Urban and von Hippel 1988, 570).

This was also the case in this study: The creator of idea 10 (case study I) had already put many of her ideas for improved furniture pieces into practice, as the solutions sold in the shops did not fit into her house and or match her expectations regarding the quality of the material. For example, she refurbished and adapted old furniture pieces to make them suit her needs. She also had some of her ideas custom-made by a carpenter. These were more complex designs for which machinery was needed, which she lacked. She seemed to be a true expert when it came to creating furniture solutions for her specific context (i.e., low-income houses) – in particular those that make use of idle space like corners. Similarly, the creator of idea 2 built his whole house with the aim of creating an optimal lighting situation, taking advantage of natural light in particular. Consequently, he showed that he had thought about the topic "lighting solutions" in a way that was not only product-based but also structural and holistic. In fact, he liked architecture and sought solutions to save light through the architecture of the house. The innovative activity of the creator of idea 7 was rated low (score 1), as she had not created a rainwater collector yet. However, she had developed creative ideas in other areas (see table 53). Regardless, the idea she submitted to the competition was triggered by her family's living situation – a leaky roof.

All four interviewees stated that their innovative activity was driven by financial constraints – a trigger which may distinguish low-income and high-income lead users. The creator of idea 10, however, also stated that her family's financial constraints impeded her from implementing more ideas, as she simply could not afford to do so.

Table 53: Selected quotes on innovative activity

Case study I	Case study I	Case study II	Case study III
Idea 10	Idea 27	Idea 7	Idea 2
Score: 5	Score: 4	Score: 1	Score: 5
I like things that do not exist! [...] I am designing my own dinner table with chairs, as I want it to be different – I don't want the normal things they sell in the shops. That is why I design my furniture and have the pieces made by the carpenter.	*I like to create something new and original.*	*The idea was natural. The idea, in fact, was born out of something that we suffer from.* *I have already invented a couple of things [but not related to rainwater collection] [...] When there is not much to do here, I draw things or put ideas on paper.*	*Here, wherever possible, things [walls, ceilings] are made of glass to gain light.*

Source: interviews conducted by author.

Trend leadership

To identify their level of trend leadership, all participants of the lead-user interviews were asked, "[i]f there is a new (lighting, furniture, or rainwater collection) solution available on the market, are you one of the first people to know about the novelty and/or buy it? The winners of case studies I and II (ideas 10, 7, and 27) vividly affirmed that they would be among the first buyers, as they would have a high expected benefit from such an improved solution. The participant of case study III was hesitant to confirm, as his needs were not related to a certain product solution. Rather, he looked for structural solutions (i.e., in the architecture of the house). However, having implemented such solutions himself, he can be seen as a trend leader.

Also, the other interviewees created trends through the products they developed. For example, the winner of case study I emphasized that many people also wanted to have the shelf she created for corner spaces. In addition, she related that the carpenter – where she had her ideas for furniture solutions custom-made – always made two versions of the products she commissioned, because "they sell." The creator of idea 27 stated that he often had ideas that he much later saw put into practice – making him regret that he had not implemented the ideas when he had first had them.

Table 54: Selected quotes on trend leadership

Case study I	Case study I	Case study II	Case study III
Idea 10	Idea 27	Idea 7	Idea 2
Score: 5	Score: 5	Score: 5	Score: 2
A lot of people saw the solution I implemented to use the space in the corners of the house, a triangle shelf. Some people copied this idea.	*I have had ideas that I much later saw realized somewhere else.*	Teacher's comments about her: *At 13 years, you are already an example for people your age!*	*I built my house thinking about light and how to best take advantage of natural light.*

Source: interviews conducted by author.

Product-related knowledge and use experience

People in low-income environments lack access to certain quality products and services. The knowledge consumers have regarding such products (*product-related knowledge*) or the experience they have using them (*use experience*) may thus be rather low, depending on the type of product or solution in focus. This can be partly confirmed by this study. The low overall incidence of both criteria may also be due to low levels of education, which also influence the level of, for example, technical knowledge related to a product.

Nonetheless, the winners of the idea competitions showed average to high levels of product-related knowledge and average levels of use experience (see table 55). As shown in the interviews, this can be attributed to their hobbies and occupational observations. Through hobbies, the winners could experiment with materials. Through their occupations, they were exposed to materials they usually could not afford or access. Indeed, both hobbies and occupational experiences have been discussed in literature as an indicator for use experience as well as product-related knowledge in a certain field (see, e.g., Lüthje 2000; Lüthje 2004[164]; Silvertant 2011[165], Nair et al. 2012).

164 Lüthje shows that a high share of the innovative customers identified in his study have technical professions, in comparison to non-innovative customers (2000, 68). In his study on outdoor products, he finds that 64% of the innovators have a technical job or hobby (2004, 690).

165 Silvertant (2011) also assumes that recreational activities related to the topic of an idea competition can have a positive influence on the quality of the idea submitted. Her study shows that people who submit creative ideas in an idea competition have a creative hobby or job, or have some kind of creative training.

The creator of idea 10 stated that her hobby was designing furniture – a hobby closely related to the topic of the idea competition. She seemed to spend all her leisure time thinking about and developing solutions to improve the use of space. She had created various pieces of furniture already and commented on material quality and design. Furthermore, she claimed to have high use experience due to spending a lot of time at home, using the furniture solutions as well as cleaning and re-arranging them. The winner of case study II (idea 2) was a waiter. He said he had acquired knowledge of architecture by frequenting the library and researching about it. He claimed to be self-taught, having built his house on his own and including several innovations in it. He had acquired knowledge of materials through recycling, for example, glass, mirrors, plastic, or wood, and had a variety of ideas to give them new functions.

Table 55: Selected quotes on product-related knowledge and use experience

Case study I	Case study I	Case study II	Case study III
Idea 10	Idea 27	Idea 7	Idea 2
$Score_{prod.-know.}$: 4	$Score_{prod.-know.}$: 5	$Score_{prod.-know.}$: 3	$Score_{prod.-know.}$: 5
$Score_{use-exp.}$: 5	$Score_{use-exp.}$: 3	$Score_{use-exp.}$: 2	$Score_{use-exp.}$: 5
When you have things custom-made, they are oftentimes cheaper. I spend much less having things made, and I can select good materials – for example, high-quality timber. That way the furniture can be used by my great-grandchildren!	*I have put together furniture and know about materials through my job as a construction worker.*	*Collecting rainwater – for example, to wash the floor – we avoid wasting tap water. We have done this since I was in school – I always help collect rainwater [with a bucket].*	*Making new things out of old ones [is my hobby].* *I have always been fond of architecture! [...] I read a lot and it interests me.*

Source: interviews conducted by author.

Involvement

Across participants, involvement was the characteristic that showed the second highest (case studies II and III) or highest (case study III) means across cases. As low-income consumers, by definition, only have a very low household income to spend, each purchasing decision must be carefully thought through. If they buy a good that serves their needs, they may not be able to invest in an alternative. Thus, it can be assumed that low-income consumers are naturally more involved.

The four winners showed a very high incidence of involvement (with values between 4 and 5): They stated that they spent a lot of time seeking information to find the solution that best suited their needs. As assumed above, this high involvement is driven by the economic situation of these individuals – they aim to get the best value for their money. The creators of ideas 27 and 7 said that they researched on the internet to find the best offers. The latter, when talking about rainwater collectors, commented on products she had seen online which were tailored to high-end markets and do not exist for her housing situation. The creator of idea 2 actively collected information by reading books and magazines and frequenting the library.

Table 56: Selected quotes on involvement

Case study I	Case study I	Case study II	Case study III
Idea 10	Idea 27	Idea 7	Idea 2
Score: 5	Score: 5	Score: 4	Score: 4.5
I look in catalogues, I go to shops, I talk to other people. I always go to shops to take home flyers and catalogues. […] When I want to buy something new, I wait up to a year as I research until find an affordable solution.	*I look up a lot of things online. It is good to research things – I always take a look.*	*I researched on the internet about rainwater collectors.*	*When it comes to building a house, you have to worry about the question of light. I have put a lot of thought into this and researched a lot.*

Source: interviews conducted by author.

Opinion leadership

Opinion leadership ranked high across all participants with values close to or above center scale (see table 51). This may be because all competitions were held in small communities, where a vivid exchange between the community members could be observed – be it related to personal topics or experiences with certain products.

A particularly high incidence of the opinion leadership could also be observed amongst the winners of the idea competitions (see table 57). In comparison to the other participants, winners stood out as they expressed a clear need and motivation to express their opinion. Also, they confirmed that they were sought after by others: The creator of idea 27 was the shiest of the four winners. He stated that he did not frequently pass ideas on to people he did not know closely. However, he confirmed that he had many ideas and that his friends asked him for advice and help.

The creators of ideas 10 and 7 affirmed that they enjoyed sharing ideas and were sought after by their friends, families, neighbors, or coworkers for creative advice. The creator of idea 10 stated that she did not understand why some people are not interested in improving their living situation; she would often spread her ideas with the motivation of "converting" them. The creator of idea 7 claimed to have a leadership position in her group of friends, who always ask her for advice. While others merely copy, she stressed that having her own, independent opinion was important to her – which is characteristic for opinion leaders (see section 2.2.1). Her father – a construction worker – stated that he raised his daughter encouraging her to have an opinion of her own. The creator of idea 2 also confirmed that he shared ideas with his colleagues at work.

Table 57: Selected quotes on opinion leadership

Case study I	Case study I	Case study II	Case study III
Idea 10	Idea 27	Idea 7	Idea 2
Score: 5	Score: 3	Score: 4	Score: 5
People asked me about the shelf for the corners. And I have the contact to the carpenter who puts it into practice.[...] Also, the carpenter often asked me for my advice. Once, he had a client who wanted to get stairs custom-made. I developed an idea which allows creating storage room under the stairs.	*Some friends sometimes come over to ask what I think.*	*I don't like to copy other people; everybody should have their own things. I don't buy the same things out of envy; I don't like that.*	*I like architecture. Space requires a lot of creativity. I show initiative in that sense. [...] An architect suggests things that are not practical [...] An architect designs, but so many things happen in practice that he cannot think of [...]. I make suggestions for how these things can be improved.*

Source: interviews conducted by author.

Figure 54 provides an overview of the lead-user scores of these four individuals. It shows that the means of the lead-user scores are above center scale for almost every characteristic, with three exceptions (circles).

Exception 1& 2: The winner of case study II shows means below center scale for the characteristics of innovative activity and use experience. As explained above, little use experience was evident since a rainwater collector for low-income households did not yet exist on the market. Also, the participant showed high innovative activity in general in the qualitative interview – but not related to rainwater collection, which explains the low value. The idea developed for the competition was the first rainwater collector the participant had developed.

Exception 3: Similarly, the winner of case study III shows a value below center scale for trend leadership. In the lead-user interview, the question to observe this characteristic was, "[i]f there is a new lighting solution available on the market, are you one of the first people to know about the novelty and/or buy it?" As explained above, the participant was hesitant to confirm this, as his needs were not related to a certain product solution. Rather, he was the only participant who looked for structural solutions: his lighting concept was related to the architecture of the house – namely, the best way to build a house to make use of natural light. Thus, while his thinking was indeed "ahead of trend," his self-assessment during the interview did not point in this direction.

Figure 54: Lead-user characteristics of winners

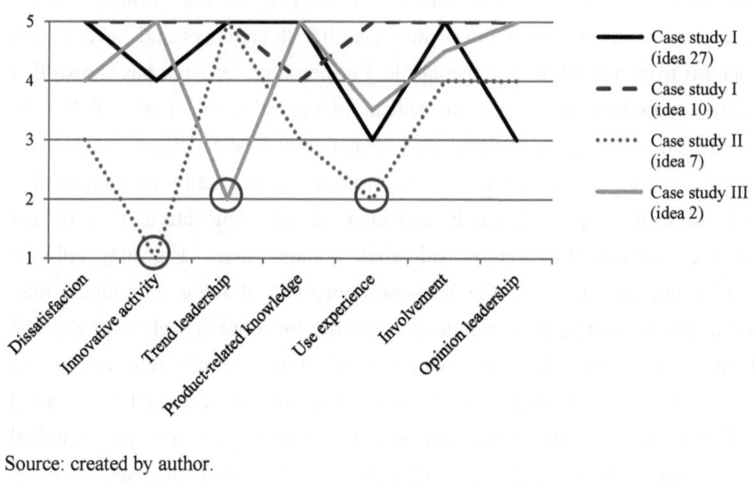

Source: created by author.

Note: The circles in the figure indicate the exceptions mentioned above.

All three exceptions do not necessarily indicate that the performance of the winners in terms of the given characteristic was low. Rather, the exceptions show that the **operationalization of the lead-user characteristic** may have to be improved to better suit the realities of low-income markets.

5.2.2 Discussion: Identifying BoP lead users

The previous section presented a cross-case analysis of the four participants identified as having an **above average incidence of lead-user characteristics.** These participants were also amongst the winners of each idea competition, having submitted ideas that were amongst the three **most creative ideas** of each competition (see figure 53). Their ideas were primarily rated as **original and useful** (see section 5.1.1), indicating that they were able to create ideas for products that experts considered valuable and suitable for these contexts. The high originality of their ideas further points to the potential of these participants to innovate for their particular use context. During the in-depth interviews, they also showed that they expected great benefits from their innovations: they were highly dissatisfied with existing products and apt to create their own inventions that would address their needs.

However, it can still be questioned whether the individuals identified are actual "lead users" in the term's original sense put forth by von Hippel (see, e.g., 1986/1988). He stated that these consumers sense future needs earlier than others and have a high expected benefit from a solution to those needs. Furthermore, research has shown that they are able to produce ideas that are radical in nature (Lettl et al. 2008). The individuals identified in this study developed ideas that can be considered as new for their particular use context or market. For example, the construction of a house that makes the best use of natural light can be considered as very innovative, if not radical for low-income markets. However, outside their context, their ideas may only be perceived as conventional. Thus, the lead-user potential of these individuals may "only" be relevant for this particular context – and not for more upscale markets. The identified individuals are likely to address needs that become relevant in the marketplace of the future. However, their innovative potential cannot be compared with that of lead users in high-income contexts, who usually possess higher technical knowledge. Consequently, the individuals identified may be called lead users for base-of-the-pyramid markets, or ***BoP lead users***. Companies that seek to develop products for low-income markets can learn from these BoP lead users how to adapt their products to this particular use context.

Moreover, idea competitions are not the only way to identify lead users. In fact, there may be even more innovative "BoP lead users" who did not attend the competition. However, the identified winners can serve as a starting point in the search for other individuals with a similar or even a higher potential to innovate in the specific search field. In fact, von Hippel et al. (2009, 1397) point out that "people having a strong interest in a given attribute […] will tend to know of people who know more about […] that attribute than they themselves do."

To find BoP lead users, the cross-case analysis above (5.2.1) indicates that the **operationalization** of lead-user characteristics may have to be adapted to low-income markets. Section 3.2.3 presented how the items were operationalized in comparable studies. Based on these items, the present study developed an interview questionnaire (see section 3.2.3). The discussion below provides suggestions for how the questionnaire should be adapted when aiming to identify BoP lead users.[166] These suggestions are summarized in table 58. Future research may further refine these suggestions (see chapter 6).[167]

When assessing the expected benefit to individuals from a certain product or solution, most studies measure their **dissatisfaction** with current products/solutions (Franke et al. 2006, 315; Soll 2006, 129; Silvertant 2011, 285ff.). Similarly, the lead users interviewed for this study expressed high dissatisfaction with existing goods and services. It stood out that there is a great desire for solutions that are useful in their context. For example, pieces of furniture are too big for their small houses, occupying too much space while not storing enough. The dissatisfaction they expressed, however, was not usually based on use experience with the respective product or solution – that is, rarely had they actually bought the product and been dissatisfied with its functionalities. Rather, they were unsatisfied with the market offer. Consequently, the operationalization chosen for this characteristic can be validated, as the question asked about their dissatisfaction with the market offer and not with products they possessed (see table 58).

[166] Besides being more tailored to the target group, the adapted questionnaire may require an increased number of items, a practice generally recommended for questionnaire designs. In this study, the number of questions asked was limited to ensure feasibility of the interviews and limit the response burden – since all lead user interviews per case study had to be conducted on the same day, the day of the collection of ideas. However, support questions were asked whenever the interviewer perceived that questions were not clear.

[167] For example, future studies could specifically identify innovators in low-income contexts and study their characteristics. For further elaborations, see chapter 6.

Trend leadership is mostly operationalized through assessing the "time of adoption" – that is, how soon the individual buys products that are new on the market in the respective field of interest. While some participants stated in the interviews that they liked to be the first to buy a new product, they also often pointed towards their financial constraints. Thus, time of adoption may not be the right measure for trend leadership. From the in-depth interviews, however, it became obvious that the individuals identified as lead users often copy new products they see on the market but cannot afford, or set trends through the products they create. For example, the creator of idea 2 (case study III) had copied innovations he had seen on the market and could not afford when building his house. The creator of idea 10 (case study I) had created a solution that was copied by a carpenter and by others from the community. Consequently, the following questions to gauge trend leadership may be more appropriate:

Have you copied products related to ___ that had been recently launched on the market?

Have you developed products related to ___ that others have copied?

Innovative activity was high among the participants identified as potential BoP lead users. They often innovated to address a strong, unsatisfied need. This need existed either because there was no solution available on the market or because the solution available was not adapted to their context, which left them unsatisfied. As mentioned above, another trigger for their innovative activity were financial constraints. The creator of idea 10 (case study I) created furniture solutions specifically designed for the needs of low-income houses. Due to high electricity costs, the creator of idea 2 (case study III) looked for ways to make use of natural light. Thus, he adapted the construction of his house in a way that allowed natural light to enter. Doing so, he recycled glass, plexiglass, and mirrors. In their study of grassroots innovators, Nair et al. (2012) come to a similar conclusion regarding innovative activity: They find that the trigger for innovation in Indian low-income markets is often the result of an unfulfilled need in addition to financial constraints.[168] Thus, interview questions could more specifically address this aspect.

---

[168] For example, the invention of a low-cost harvesting and threshing machine created by a smallholder farmer in a rural Indian village was triggered by a shortage of labor and the high cost of normal machines (Nair et al. 2012).

Financial constraints are not only a trigger for innovative activity – sometimes, they also impede innovators from realizing their ideas. For example, the interviewees of the present study stated that they sometimes could not afford the necessary materials. Also, many of them had more than one job to be able to make a living; one worked, for example, as a cleaning lady during the day and as a night guard. Thus, some stated to simply lack time to realize their ideas. Consequently, a BoP lead-user questionnaire could consider this by also asking about ideas they have had but were not able to implement:

Have you created products or solutions related to ___ because you could not afford a suitable item on the market? If yes, what product/solution?

Have you adapted an existing product or solution related to ___ to your needs because no suitable solution was available on the market? If yes, what product/solution?

What ideas for new products have you had related to ___ that you were not able to implement – for example, due to financial or time constraints?

Through the cross-case analysis, it was found that **product-related knowledge and use experience** was rather low – especially for products that are not yet available in low-income markets, such as rainwater collectors. Nevertheless, the in-depth interviews with the potential lead users show that they did have some degree of knowledge on the functions or the materials of a certain solution – for example, through having seen it in their job environment or because they had a hobby related to the field of interest. The study conducted by Nair et al. (2012), which examines grassroots innovators in India, also finds that 19% of the innovations in their sample were triggered by a "hobby" as well as an "occupational observation." For example, they cite the case of a potter who came up with several innovations related to or made from clay, such as a pan and a water filter. They also found that the most radical grassroots innovations occur when an innovator applies the skills gained through a hobby or a profession to another (analogous) product category. For example, the innovator of a harvesting and threshing machine was a rice farmer who transferred his knowledge of farming to the domain of auto repair. Although this had been observed in previous studies – such as that of Lüthje (2000, 68[169]) – these findings are often not considered when operationalizing product-related knowledge and use experience. Consequently, the following questions are suggested for BoP lead-user questionnaires:

[169] Lüthje (2000, 68) showed that a high proportion of the innovative consumers identified in his study had technical professions, in comparison to non-innovative consumers.

What products/solutions related to ___ do you use at home?

What products/solutions related to ___ do you use as part of a hobby or at your workplace? How often do you use them and in what situations?

Do you know about the materials and functions of products related to __?

Do you work with these materials as part of a hobby or at work? What materials and products do you use in your hobbies or at work?

To operationalize **involvement**, studies ask about participants' level of interest in the topic, which is also viable in low-income markets. Additional questions, however, could ask where the individual obtains relevant information – which may be quite different in low-income markets. This may show the effort individuals are willing to make to inform themselves, and thus give an idea of the real interest a person has. For example, the creator of idea 7 (case study II) did not have internet access at home; however, she had previously informed herself about existing rainwater collection systems to see if there was a solution suitable for her house. As access to Internet in low-income contexts is often expensive or only available in the next city or village, people who invest time and money to obtain information may show higher involvement in comparison to those who inform themselves merely by looking at shops they walk by on a daily basis.

How interested are you in products/solutions related to ___?

What information sources do you consult to inform yourself about such products/solutions?

How frequently do you consult these sources of information?

How much effort are you willing to make to get access to information on products/solutions related to ___?

Opinion leadership was found to be strong, not only amongst the potential lead users but also amongst other participants. This is because the operationalization of the characteristic asks if the person shares experiences on the topic with others and/or is asked for recommendations or advice. Particularly in small communities, where social cohesion is strong, exchanging information with friends and neighbors is the norm rather than the exception. Weidner et al. (2010, 559) explains that

> *a noteworthy characteristic of these [low-income] marketplaces is the one-to-one interaction between small neighborhood storeowners and local consumers [...]. These strong social relationships in subsistence marketplaces create interdependency among members, thus elevating the role of powerful group influences and word of mouth communications.*

Nonetheless, not all the people who vividly exchange information can actually be regarded as opinion leaders. Rather, opinion leaders tend to have a higher level of knowledge about the product or solution in question (Trommsdorff 1993, 217). In addition, they form their opinions independently and are able to sense and influence the opinions of people in their environment (Lazarsfeld et al. 1944; King and Summers 1970, 43; Granovetter 1985; Childers 1986, 184; Soll 2006, 109; Walcher 2007, 189ff.). However, previous questionnaires have not considered these findings. Asking more specified questions for opinion leadership may be particularly relevant in low-income contexts, where there is usually a vivid exchange between community members. Thus, the questionnaire to identify BoP lead users could ask the following questions:

Do others consider you an expert regarding products/solutions related to ___? If yes, why?

To what extent is your opinion influenced by other people regarding ___?

Do others ask you for advice or recommendations regarding products/solutions related to ___?

To what extent do you influence the opinion of others regarding products/solutions related to ___?

Table 58: Suggestions for BoP lead-user questionnaires

Charac-teristic	Questions asked in this study	Suggestions for how to adapt the questions
Dissatis-faction	Are you unsatisfied with the products/ solutions currently available on the market related to ___ ? If yes, to what degree and why? Do you have needs related to ___ which are not covered by the products currently on the market?	*No changes suggested.*
Trend leadership	If there is a new solution related to ___ available on the market, are you one of the first people to know about the novelty and/or buy it? If yes, why?	Have you copied products related to ___ that had been recently launched on the market? Have you developed products related to ___ that others have copied?
Innovative activity	Had you had ideas before the competition related to ___? If yes, what were they? Please describe the idea and whether/how you developed it.	Have you created products or solutions related to ___ because you could not afford a suitable item on the market? If yes, what product/ solution?

		Have you adapted an existing product or solution related to ___ to your needs because no suitable solution was available on the market? If yes, what product/solution? What ideas for new products have you had related to ___ that you were not able to implement – for example, due to financial or time constraints?
Product-related knowledge	Do you know existing products or solutions related to ____? If yes, what are they? Please describe (e.g., functions, materials).	Do you know about the materials and functions of products related to __? Do you work with these materials as part of a hobby or at work? What materials and products do you use in your hobbies or at work?
Use experience	What products/solutions related to ___ do you use? How often do you use them and in what situations?	What products/solutions related to ___ do you use at home? What products/solutions related to ___ do you use as part of a hobby or at your workplace? How often do you use them and in what situations?
Involvement	How interested are you in products/solutions related to ___ ? Why? With what frequency do you look for information on the subject?	How interested are you in products/solutions related to ___? What information sources do you consult to inform yourself about such products/solutions? How frequently do you consult these sources of information? How much effort are you willing to make to get access to information on products/solutions related to ___?
Opinion leadership	Do you share your experiences with others regarding products/solutions related to ____ ? Do others ask you for recommendations about how to use new products/solutions related to ___ ?	Do others consider you an expert regarding products/solutions related to ___? If yes, why? Do others ask you for advice or recommendations regarding products/solutions related to ___? To what extent is your opinion influenced by other people regarding ___? To what extent do you influence the opinion of others regarding products/solutions related to ___?

Source: created by author.

5.2.3 Cross-case analysis: Characteristics of creative participants

Most participants who submitted an idea with a high creativity score (CS_{high}) do not show lead-user characteristics. Also, considering the quality of their ideas and related innovative activity, they cannot be considered lead users. Nonetheless, their ideas were regarded by the product developers as valuable input for the fuzzy front end of the innovation process (see section 5.3). Previous studies refer to these consumers as "creative mainstream consumers" (Silvertant 2011, 256ff.) or "interested, creative non-lead users" (Schrader et al. 2012, 345ff.). However, to the author's best knowledge, no studies in innovation research have investigated this group further.

To find out which characteristics identify them, they are contrasted to those participants who obtained a low creativity score (CS_{low}). Qualitative in-depth interviews were conducted with representatives from both groups.[170;171] Through qualitative content analysis, a series of characteristics could be identified for CS_{high} participants. These characteristics could not be found amongst any of the CS_{low} interviewees.[172]

The inductively identified characteristics for CS_{high} could be grouped into five clusters: They (1) show a high ability to solve problems; (2) are ambitious, dedicated, and are self-confident; (3) think and act independently; (4) are curious and have a positive attitude towards change; and (5) are environmentally conscious.[173] Furthermore, a sixth cluster points towards an enabling condition for creativity – namely, (6) family unity and support.

---

170 In case study I, four representatives of CS_{high} were interviewed along with two representatives of CS_{low} – as a control group. In case study II, nine representatives of CS_{high} were interviewed and four from CS_{low}. In case study III, two representatives of each group were interviewed. Generally, it was more difficult to find volunteers from CS_{low} for the interviews.

171 This is in accordance with Yin, who suggests selecting extreme examples ("polar types") through "theoretical sampling" (Yin 2003; Eisenhardt and Graebner 2007, 27).

172 For further explanation, see footnote 133 in chapter 4.1.3.

173 Strictly speaking, the clusters "high problem-solving ability" and "ability to think and act independently" are rather abilities than personality traits, as they may be acquired over time. A characteristic is defined as a distinguishing trait, quality, or property (see Merriam-Webster Dictionary, http://www.merriam-webster.com/ dictionary/characteristic – accessed May 1, 2013). Traits are usually seen as something that one possesses by nature – while abilities can also be acquired. However, in some cases it cannot clearly be distinguished if the trait identified is entirely possessed by nature or learned and trained over time. The purpose here is to be able to distinguish CS_{high} from CS_{low}. As abilities may also serve this purpose, further discussion on this distinction is outside of the scope of this study. Nonetheless, this may be the subject of future studies, since in the area of lead-user research, this distinction has not been made.

(1) High problem-solving ability

All representatives of the group CS_{high} showed themselves to be good problem solvers. They approached problems they encountered in their everyday lives with the attitude that they could be solved. Their creativity always helped them work around problems, be they related to the construction of the house or a lack of toys. One participant (case study I) related that a wardrobe her husband bought did not fit into her house. Thus, she cut it in half and made two commodes out of it. A participant from case study II worked at a rattan furniture factory where pieces are custom-made. He said it was sometimes difficult to implement the ideas of customers, but that his creativity always helped him to find a way to solve this challenge.

In the interviews, financial constraints were often stated to be a trigger for creative activity: People create what they cannot afford with the materials they encounter – which often involves recycling or re-using old materials. For example, one participant related that she had created a sofa out of PET bottles covered by fabric. However, participants also stated that financial constraints impeded them from putting some of their ideas into practice. Younger participants related that problem solving was a way to spend their time. Some of them also claimed to have learned to create – or to regularly co-create – solutions with their parents.

Table 59: Selected quotes on high problem-solving ability

Case study I	Case study II	Case study III
I always look around. The neighbors throw a lot of things away that can be re-used or re-combined. […] For example, when people throw away clothes, I always take out the buttons, zippers, pieces of the cloth – and I create new clothes. […] I would have been able to develop 30 ideas for the competition. *I have so many ideas that sometimes, I don't even remember all of them.*	*There is always something we can do. We invent all the time. In fact, we did not have the time nor the money to elaborate all our ideas!* Mother of a participant: *She has every kind of idea… She invents a lot of crazy things – things we don't think are possible but then work surprisingly well in the end.*	*If you are creative, you achieve things! If I weren't creative, I would not have achieved what I have.* *I like to invent things – I am like a child… a little bit crazy.* *I have already had many ideas about how to create things. But I often lack the means to develop them further – and then I forget them.*

Source: interviews conducted by author.

(2) Curiosity and a positive attitude towards change

Representatives of CS_{high} were highly curious individuals. They had broad interests and a high willingness to learn, explore, and understand new things. For example, one participant of case study II related that she had dissembled a whole computer to find out how it worked, and put it together again. She stated that she was then even able to repair it on her own.

Their curiosity was also reflected in the interviews: They welcomed the research team to conduct the interviews and to find out more about the background of the competition. Closely related to their curiosity was their positive attitude towards change. Change did not scare them but rather sparked their interest and drove them. In fact, they experimented with new things and formats out of curiosity to see results. For example, one participant (case study I) enjoyed changing the interior of her house by rearranging things frequently; another participant (case study I) – the leader of the community – wanted to create change for the community; he organized meetings and parties to create greater unity and to move things forward. Being open and positive towards the future, they also seemed to be more resilient and to interpret external change positively. One participant, for example, related that her house had burnt down. With her ambitious attitude and her entrepreneurial skills, she rebuilt it.

Table 60: Selected quotes on curiosity and positive attitude towards change

Case study I	Case study II	Case study III
We have to change – if not, we get sick of the same things. *I always pay attention to new things.*	*When I bought the computer, I did not know how to operate it. [...] It all paid off.* Mother of a participant: *Do you see how curious she is? She always says she wants to go to university!*	*When I was working as an office boy, I always went to the library in my lunch break to read. [...] I started reading about psychology and architecture.* *I can't complain [that my house burnt down]. New possibilities always arise and I have to thank God! [...] I know there is always a way!*

Source: interviews conducted by author.

(3) Ambition, dedication, and self-confidence

What set the participants of CS_{high} apart from others was their ambition and dedication. They vividly stated how they are willing to grow and fight to achieve a better life. They were often the best in their class at school or the best employees. Of course, this ambition was also put towards putting their ideas in practice. Furthermore, they had ambitious dreams: one participant dreamt of building a factory, another had ambitious goals for his community, and yet another spoke about wanting to realize all his ideas before he died.

Moreover, participants interviewed showed strongly that they believed in their abilities and self-confidently relied on them. Participants with kids cared about the future of their children, and encouraged them to strive for a better life. The younger participants revealed their ambitions and self-confidence in their dreams of becoming, for example, a doctor or a lawyer.

Table 61: Selected quotes on ambition, dedication, and self-confidence

Case study I	Case study II	Case study III
There are people who do not want to get ahead in life – but I want to grow a lot! *I did not have the chance to study – thus, I need to work hard today. When you study, you can be somebody. I tell you, if I had gone to school, I would already be rich!*	*I can't' or 'I don't know' are expressions that don't exist in our family. You always can and you always know.* *I do not mind if I have to work on the weekend or on holidays – I want to achieve something in life, contribute something at home.*	*I worked two years without weekends or holidays to build this [house] with the money I earn. If I had not worked so much, I wouldn't have earned the money to do this.* *I am a widow. I can't stand still – I have to work.*

Source: interviews conducted by author.

<u>(4) Ability to think and act independently</u>

The interviews conducted with CS_{high} participants showed that they were highly autonomous and independent. They seemed uninfluenced by the opinions of others. Rather, they liked to make their own judgments and stood by them: "*I don't like to copy other people; everybody should have their own things*!" Some female participants make clear that they set the tone at home: "*In our house, there is no 'machismo'*!"

The independent personalities of CS_{high} also clearly showed leadership and entrepreneurial skills. Some CS_{high} participants acted as leaders in their circles of friends, or even in the community. For example, one participant in case study I was the president of the local residents' association. He showed entrepreneurial skills – for example, through organizing fundraising events for the community – but also through the fact that he had his own business running a little garage. In fact, many participants of CS_{high} showed themselves to be true entrepreneurs. One resident had opened a second-hand shop, while others spoke about small businesses they had or used to have on top of their regular jobs. For example, one participant restored old pictures by scanning them and touching them up through the program Photoshop. With the income, she financed the loan she took to buy the scanner. When asked about what she wanted to do in the future, one of the younger participants interviewed made clear that she wanted to have her own business, and she presented her business idea for a childcare facility she aimed to build.

Table 62: Selected quotes on ability to think and act independently

Case study I	Case study II	Case study III
I have a grocery shop – it is next to my house. There, I also sell lunch boxes. Previously, I also made handicraft, sew carpets or made table cloths. How many things I do and have done! […]. I did everything to make ends meet – except steeling! *I run a little garage where I repair car wheels. I have developed my own technique of developing car wheels, which is very effective.*	*When I bought the computer, I did not know how to operate it. We did not even have a sofa by then – but I bought it against the will of my husband. He said: 'For what do we need a computer?' […] I also bought a scanner. It all paid off. I learned Photoshop by myself – now, I restore old pictures for people and they pay me. Like that, the investment has already been amortized.*	*I run a little second hand shop. I go to bazaars, by clothes, re-arrange them and re-sell them!*

Source: interviews conducted by author.

<u>(5) Environmental consciousness</u>

CS_{high} participants also showed environmental consciousness. They claimed to be annoyed at seeing others pollute or waste resources such as water or materials that could still be used. Some participants of case studies II and III even mentioned that had they learned about recycling materials at school or at their jobs – and that they liked the topic of the competition due to its connection to sustainability. A few created forward-looking ideas that consider collective use of products/services (such as a rainwater collector for the whole community) or of natural resources (such as interior lighting with natural light).

Nonetheless, it should be stressed that the participants had a very obvious reason to care about the environment: they were often the ones most affected by the pollution of water and air or by accumulated waste. Moreover, their willingness to recycle materials was often not driven by their urge to preserve the planet, but rather by the scarcity of resources, like water and energy, as well as by financial constraints. For example, blackouts and interruptions in the water supply are quite commonplace in low-income environments.

Table 63: Selected quotes on environmental consciousness

Case study I	Case study II	Case study III
Throwing things away is extravagance! […] People prefer to buy new things – I, in contrast, value every material and recycle it. *Our country is poor because people don't know how to make use of things; if they knew, our country would be rich.*	*I think that today, I can waste a lot of water. But what about tomorrow? And the future of our children? We have to think about the future as well. It will be very important.* *When working on the idea, I thought that it was great that it helps the environment, and helps you to save as well.*	*This is all glass to gain light. All this is made out of recycled materials and thus sustainable.* *I am very conscious about energy costs. We don't only save for ourselves, but it is good for everybody.* *My idea is environmentally sustainable – I am just not sure if it is feasible!*

Source: interviews conducted by author.

(6) Family unity and support

Family unity and support are not characteristics of participants as such. Rather, they describe an enabling condition. Because these participants received support from their families, they could dedicate time or even resources to their creative activities and put their ideas into practice. In one case, the husband of a participant supported her in the household so that she could focus on realizing her creative activities. In another case, the father actively encouraged his daughter to pursue her creative activities.

Ultimately, it clearly stood out that creative participants came from functioning families that supported them. For example, some ideas of the CS_{high} group were handed in by a family member – either because the actual contestant could not make it on the day of the competition (case study I), or because the family member believed in the creative abilities of the participant and had encouraged him or her to take part (case study II). Some family members also accompanied CS_{high} participants when handing in their ideas or were present during the interviews conducted with them, showing their pride and support. In some families, this family support even led to co-creation activities. Jointly creating ideas seemed to be part of the family culture. As one participant mentioned, "[w]e [our family] often come together to create ideas for problems we face."

Table 64: Selected quotes on family unity and support

Case study I	Case study II	Case study III
It was my wife who motivated me to participate! *In my house, there is no 'machismo'!*	*The family members cooperate by helping each other.* *My daughter always likes to participate – and I support her.*	Wife about participant: *My husband is very smart. What he wants to do he does. He did not know how to build a house, but he did it.*

Source: interviews conducted by authors.

As table 65 shows, each participant demonstrated at least two-thirds of the characteristics identified (a check mark [✓] was coded when the characteristic was present, and an X when it was absent). This could mean that some characteristics may be necessary to qualify as a creative person, while other characteristics may be supplementary but not essential. For example, all interviewees of the group CS_{high} showed a high capacity for problem-solving along with ambition, dedication, and self-confidence. The remaining characteristics were only shown by some participants.

Alternatively, like lead-user characteristics, the characteristics of creative people may lie on a spectrum rather than being dichotomously present or lacking. In this case, a compensatory approach could be applied to determine the creative nature of a participant. Similar to building a lead-user score, the incidence of each characteristic could be rated on a Likert scale. An aggregated score could attest to the creativity level of the person (Jokisch 2007; Jeppesen and Laursen 2009). Further research is needed to clarify the questions raised here.

Table 65: Characteristics of creative participants

Case study	Idea no.	Characteristics (✓ = Presence of characteristic) (X = Absence of characteristic)					Enabling condition	
		High problem-solving ability	Curiosity and positive attitude towards change	Ambition, dedication, and self-confidence	Ability to think and act independently	Environmental consciousness	Family unity and support	% by person
Case study I	10	✓	✓	✓	✓	✓	✓	100.0%
	12	✓	✓	✓	✓	✓	✓	100.0%
	20	✓	✓	✓	X	X	X	50.0%
	27	✓	✓	✓	X	X	✓	66.6%
Case study II	2a	✓	✓	✓	✓	✓	✓	100.0%
	5	✓	✓	✓	✓	✓	✓	100.0%
	6	✓	X	✓	X	✓	✓	66.6%
	7	✓	✓	✓	✓	✓	✓	100.0%
	13	✓	✓	✓	X	✓	X	66.6%
	18	✓	✓	✓	X	X	✓	66.6%
	21b	✓	X	✓	✓	✓	✓	83.3%
	27a	✓	✓	✓	✓	X	✓	83.3%
	27b	✓	✓	✓	✓	X	X	66.6%
Case study III	2	✓	✓	✓	✓	✓	✓	100.0%
	12	✓	✓	✓	✓	✓	✓	100.0%
% by characteristic		100.0%	86.6%	100.0%	66.6%	66.6%	80.0%	

Source: interviews conducted by author.

5.2.4 Discussion: Identifying creative consumers

This study makes a first step in inductively investigating the characteristics of "creative mainstream consumers" (Silvertant 2011, 256ff.) or "creative, interested non-lead user[s]" (Schrader et al. 2012, 345ff.), who were identified through idea competitions. In a cross-case analysis, it was found that these consumers indeed show common abilities and personality traits, summarized in table 65. It should be stressed, however, that the characteristics identified were derived inductively from a very small sample of participants (CS_{high}: n = 15; CS_{low}: n = 8). Although patterns could be identified regarding their abilities and traits, they cannot be generalized to populations. Additional research is needed to investigate these characteristics further. Nonetheless, the present findings may be used to phrase tentative hypotheses about the group of creative participants, which could be further refined and tested in future studies (Yin 2003, 10).

As already mentioned, innovation literature has noted that this type of consumer exists, but has not explored the characteristics that set this consumer apart from others (Silvertant 2011, 256ff.; Schrader et al. 2012, 345ff.). In contrast, the field of psychology – creativity research in particularly – closely examines people regarded as creative. However, the overlaps of literature in the field of psychology/creativity and innovation research regarding lead users or creative mainstream consumers remain underexplored. This study makes a first attempt to bridge this gap by triangulating the findings of this study – grounded in innovation research – with findings from literature in the field of psychology / creativity research. This triangulation was primarily done on the basis of meta-analyses as well as articles and handbooks that provide an overview of the state of the art in creativity research.[174] An in-depth literature review was beyond the scope of this study, which is already based on two literature streams – namely open innovation / customer integration and BoP literature (see chapter 2).[175] Nonetheless, a high degree of agreement is apparent when comparing the results of the studies conducted in the field of creativity research to the results of this study.

[174] To identify these articles, a literature research was conducted via Databases (applying EBSCO), using key words such as "creative personality" and "meta-analysis."

[175] Consulting additional literature to explain findings that occur at later stages of a qualitative research process is a valid approach. For further elaboration, see for example Kelle (1997, 22) or Reichertz (2004, 159 ff.).

Triangulation with findings from creativity research

As found in a meta-analysis by Rhode, creativity research in the field of psychology hinges on four categories: Person, Product, Process and Press[176] (Rhode 1987). However, Guilford (1950, 444) stresses that creativity research ultimately always comes back to studying the **characteristics of people**: "In its narrow sense, creativity refers to the abilities that are most characteristic of creative people. [...] In other words, the psychologist's problem is that of creative personality." In the "Handbook of Creativity," Glover, Ronning and Reaynolds (1989) find that no cognitive abilities reliably distinguish creative from non-creative people. Rather, personality traits provide the distinction. Indeed, a variety of studies single out personality traits of creative people, or investigate the relationship between single personality traits and creativity.[177] In his meta-analysis of creativity in artists and scientists, Feist (1998, 299) concludes that "in general, a **'creative personality'** does exist and personality dispositions do regularly and predictable relate to creative achievement in art and sciences."[178] The results of the present study show strong similarities to the meta-analysis of Feist (1998). Other studies also point towards similar findings (see table 66).

High problem-solving ability

To create ideas that solve a problem, one needs to be creative. Guilford (1976, 98) thus insists that creativity and problem-solving are not so different: "Problem solving is creative."[179] Similarly, Hirschmann (1980, 286) also states that "expertise at problem solving [...] is one of the central operational measures of creativity."[180] Runco (1994, xi) also points to the fact that both are closely related: "Many individuals studying problem solving tend to look at creativity as merely a special type of problem solving.

[176] Press refers to the environment of the person, the product or the process. It is concerned with the environmental variables that may affect creativity.

[177] For example, studies examine the relationship between creativity and intelligence (see, for example, Subotnik and Arnold 1994; Sternberg 1995).

[178] Note that the bold font in quotations in this section has been added by the author.

[179] In his later study (Guilford 1977, 161), he elaborates on this relationship, stating that "creative thinking produces novel outcomes, and problem solving involves producing a new response to a new situation, which is a novel outcome. Thus we can say that problem solving has creative aspects."

[180] Based on this finding, she develops the construct of "consumer creativity," which she defines as "problem solving capability possessed by individuals that may be applied towards solving consumer related problems" (Hirschmann 1980, 285).

Conversely, many individuals studying creativity view problem solving as a special type of creative performance."

The findings of this study correspond with the findings of creativity research. Whether the characteristic *problem-solving ability* indeed serves to identify consumers who can contribute creative ideas to the fuzzy front end of innovation processes needs to be determined. Future studies could test this. Consequently, the following hypothesis is developed:

> *H 1: A person's* ***ability to solve problems*** *positively influences his or her ability to generate creative ideas.*

Curiosity and a positive attitude towards change

The present study finds that participants who produce creative ideas are curious and have a positive attitude towards change or new things. Also Kashdan and Fincham (2002, 374) point towards the fact that "curiosity and creativity resonate as interrelated constructs." They further clarify that high curiosity does not lead directly to high creativity, "but that high curiosity is necessary, though not sufficient, for creativity." While other studies do not use the term curiosity or positive attitude towards change, they describe characteristics of creative people that are very closely related.

A variety of studies take the "Five Factor Model (FFM)" as a basis for studying creativity. The model narrows personality traits down to five core traits (for a comprehensive overview, please see Feist 1998, 303–304).[181] The reason for the popularity of the FFM is that a variety of researchers have independently conducted a factor analysis on different samples and arrived at very similar conclusions. "Openness to experience" is the factor of the FFM with most empirical support in relation to creativity (McCrae 1987). Also, a more recent meta-analysis by Guastello (2009) comes to the same conclusion. Feist (1998, 300) explains openness to experience as follows:

---

[181] Feist (1998) conducted a meta-analysis of these studies which relate the five factors to creative personality. The resulting factors are (1) openness to experience (inventive/curious vs. consistent/cautious) (2) conscientiousness (efficient/organized vs. easy-going/careless) (3) extraversion (outgoing/energetic vs. solitary/reserved) (4) agreeableness (friendly/compassionate vs. cold/reserved) and (5) neuroticism (sensitive/nervous vs. secure/confident). Each of these factors has a cluster of correlated (sub-)traits and can be described by various adjectives (see, for example, Feist 1998, 293).

> *Openness is closely related to [...] being able to think "outside the box" and not being tied to any one perspective (functional fixedness). Openness and flexibility in turn are related to having the imagination to think of how things could be, not just how they are. By being receptive to different perspectives, ideas, people, and situations, open people are able to have at their disposal a wide range of thoughts, feelings, and problem-solving strategies, the combination of which may lead to novel and useful solutions or ideas.*

This passage precisely describes the characteristic found in the people interviewed in this study. Due to their curiosity, they were open to think of alternative solutions (thinking "outside the box") and pro-active in approaching problems. Being open to "thinking how things could be," they were also open to change and new things.

Similarly, Barron and Harrington (1981, 453) find that, amongst other criteria,[182] "**broad interests, attraction to complexity**, [...] and a firm sense of oneself as 'creative' continue to emerge as correlates of creative achievement and activity in many domains." A study by Puccio and Grivas (2009, 247) explores the relation between individuals' expressed preferences for stages within the creative process and their personality traits. They find that "those who express strong preferences for the idea generation stage of the creative process are likely to show such traits as willingness to challenge prevailing thought, **need for change and attraction to variety**."

The characteristics found in this study and those identified in literature are similar, but not identical. However, they all fit under the trait "openness to experience" identified by Feist in applying the FFM. Thus, this characteristic is used for hypothesis development.

*H 2: A person's **openness to experience** positively influences his or her ability to generate creative ideas.*

Ambition, dedication, and self-confidence

This study found that creative participants are highly ambitious, dedicated, and self-confident. Indeed, studies have pointed towards the fact that the ability to be creative is not enough – individuals also have to have a drive to be creative. Feist (1998, 300)

[182] The other characteristics they name are "high energy, **independence of judgment, autonomy**, intuition, **self-confidence, ability to resolve antinomies** or to accommodate apparently opposite or conflicting traits in one's self concept." The bolded characteristics could also be confirmed by this study (see the following sub-sections).

finds that "creative people in general tend to be motivated by ambition and a need to work and do well." In his meta-analysis, he confirms that creative people are more **autonomous, self-accepting, self-confident, driven, and ambitious** – all of which are characteristics in the cluster "extraversion."[183]

Similarly, a study of Glover et al. (1989) finds that highly creative people[184] show a "**devotion to work.**" Also Barron and Harrington (1981, 453) name "self-confidence" as a trait of creative people. In her study "In Search of the Creative Personality," Helson (1996, 295) finds that creative individuals share "**high aspirations.**"

A high level of ambition, dedication, and self-confidence seems to be common among creative people. Consequently, the following hypothesis is developed:

> *H 3: A high **level of ambition, dedication, and self-confidence** positively influences a person's ability to generate creative ideas.*

<u>Ability to think and act independently</u>

This study found that creative people often think and act independently. This is shown in the way they behave in relation to others or in how they are seen by others. For example, they are often seen as leaders in their family, circle of friends, or community. The fact that they often run their own business may also show their desire to act independently.

Again, this finding corresponds to findings from creativity research. For example, Feist (1998, 300ff.) writes that "the tendency to **question social norms** and to be relatively **independent of group influence** are social dispositions commonly found in creative people. […] [I]ndependence in creative people goes along with sticking to one's beliefs in the face of doubt and skepticism by others." Feist finds that creative people **lack agreeableness** – they are more dominant and hostile, as they place their own opinion and independence of thought above getting along with others (Feist 1998, 300ff.).

Similarly, the study by Puccio and Grivas (2009, 247) finds that individuals with a preference for the idea generation stage of the creative process often show a

---

183 For the purpose of his study, Feist (1998, 293) divided "extraversion" into the two sub-dimensions "confidence" and "sociability," as "[b]eing sociable and outgoing is often accompanied by confidence and leadership qualities."

184 Note that the study investigates scientists specifically.

"**willingness to challenge prevailing thought.**" In fact, most of the previously mentioned studies find independence to be a part of the creative character: Glover et al. (1989) find that creative scientists show an "**independence of thought and action**"; Barron and Harrington (1981, 453) name "**independence of judgment**" and "**autonomy**" as characteristics of creative people; also Helson (1996, 295) confirms independence as a personality trait.

It seems that creative people like to form their opinions independently from what others think and that they act according to their own convictions. Consequently, the following hypothesis can be proposed:

H 4: A person's ***ability to think and act independently*** *positively influences his or her ability to generate creative ideas*

Environmental consciousness

In addition to the characteristics related above, most individuals of CS_{high} in this study showed high environmental consciousness. No corresponding finding could be identified in creativity research.[185] As pointed out in the cross-case analysis (5.3.2), a rival explanation may be that the characteristic labeled "environmental consciousness" is partly the result of unintentional behavior: low-income consumers use recycled materials for the things they create because they cannot afford the original product or simply are not familiar with other materials. Nonetheless, this still puts them in an excellent position to come up with creative ideas that are environmentally friendly. Indeed, this thought has been put forth by Gupta (2010/2013) and Nair et al. (2012). Gupta (2010, 137) argues that a "lack of material resources spurs knowledge-intensive innovation by common people from the informal sector and thus provides a basis for sustainability by reducing entropy." He cites various examples, such as herbal pesticides – to replace chemical ones – developed by rural farmers in India.[186] He

[185] The only exception found is a study in the field of innovation research. Belz et al. (2012) suggest that lead users who bring about particularly sustainable innovations set themselves apart by sensing not only a high individual benefit but also a high social benefit from the innovation. For example, innovators of electric cars or bikes not only care about the benefit they have from inventing such a product, but also care about the benefits for society. However, the characteristics discussed here focus on creative consumers and not on lead users.

[186] Further examples cited by Gupta include the case of a person from an Indian village who had invented a cycle that can generate energy, and an Indian inventor who developed a frying pan "with a ribbed bottom to conserve energy" due to its increased thermal efficiency (Gupta 2010, 143).

claims that it is highly unlikely that these "grassroots innovations," as he calls them, would have emerged "in an environment of material abundance." Rather, "[s]uch frugal innovations [...] will emerge only in an environment where knowledge is maximized and materials economized." However, the relationship between a lack of resources and creativity was not investigated in this study. As this question needs further research, no corresponding hypothesis was phrased.

Family unity and support

Family unity and support are not characteristics of creative people – but rather enabling conditions: receiving support from their family helped participants unfold their creativity. While few studies could be identified that examine this relationship, studies were found that examine the influence of a person's work environment on their creative performance. A study by Madjar, Oldham and Pratt (2002), which builds on findings from Amabile (1996), confirms a relation between creative performance and support from supervisors and co-workers as well as from family and friends outside of the workplace. In their longitudinal field study, Amabile et al. (2004) find that perceived team leader support is positively related to the creativity of individuals working on creative projects. Also, Lee and Tan (2012, 984) sustain the finding that support by people closely related to the creative employee can be crucial: In their meta-analysis they find that "high quality relationships between the employee and his/her supervisor" positively influence employee creativity and performance. They further find that psychological empowerment by supervisors contributes to creativity.

Consequently, it can be assumed that family unity and support helps creative consumers to unfold their creative potential. Consequently, the following hypothesis can be developed:

> *H 5: **Family unity and support** positively influence an individual's ability to unfold his or her creative potential.*

It may even be assumed that, as an enabling condition, family union and support positively influences the development of the traits that characterize creative consumers. It that case, it could be seen as a moderator, as it affects the strength of a relationship between two variables (Baron and Kenny 1986; Jose 2013). However, this relationship needs to be further explored to enable hypotheses-development. The findings of the cross-case analysis (section 5.3.2) and the findings from creativity research are summarized in the table below (see table 66).

Table 66: Triangulation of characteristics of creative people

Characteristic identified in this study	Characteristic identified in creativity research	Authors
High problem-solving ability	Problem-solving ability	Hirschmann (1980, 285) Runco (1994, xi) Guilford (1976, 98; 1977, 161)
Curiosity and a positive attitude towards change (rephrased as "openness to experience")	Curiosity	Kasdan and Fincham (2002)
	Openness to experience	Feist (1998, 300) Guastello (2009)
	Broad interests; attraction to complexity	Barron and Harrington (1981, 453)
	Need for change and attraction to variety	Puccio and Grivas (2009, 247)
Ambition, dedication, and self-confidence	Autonomous, self-accepting, self-confident, driven and ambitious	Feist (1998, 300 ff.)
	Devotion to work	Glover et al. (1989)
	Self-confidence	Barron and Harrington (1981, 453)
	High aspirations	Helson (1996, 295)
Ability to think and act independently	Extraversion: questioning of norms, independence from group influence, sticking to one's beliefs; lack of agreeableness	Feist (1998, 300ff.)
	Independence of thought and action/judgment; autonomy	Glover et al. (1989) Barron and Harrington (1981, 453)
	Willingness to challenge prevailing thought	Puccio and Grivas (2009, 247)
Family unity and support	Support from supervisors and co-workers as well as non-work sources (e.g., family and friends)	Madjar et al. (2002) Amabile et al. (2004) Lee and Tan (2012, 984)

Source: created by author.

The table shows that all characteristics identified inductively by interviewing creative participants from low-income markets could be triangulated with findings from the field of psychology or, more concretely, creativity research. It should be noted that the studies discussed here did not have a specific focus on low-income environments. This may indicate that the findings on the characteristics of creative mainstream consumers are not context-specific and that a generalization may be possible across various socioeconomic contexts.

Even so, this result should be taken with caution. As already mentioned, the inductively identified characteristics in this study are based on a small sample[187] of low-income consumers, and only overview articles from creativity literature (such as handbooks, meta-analyses, etc.) were consulted for triangulation purposes. Nevertheless, the congruence of findings can be seen as a valuable and interesting contribution upon which future studies can build. Certainly, it is advisable that future studies in the area of innovation management and customer integration consult the knowledge base of creativity research more systematically and consider a deductive approach (see chapter 6 for further details). The hypotheses developed in this study, which are summarized in figure 55, may provide a good starting point.

Figure 55: Hypotheses 1–5 on characteristics of creative consumers

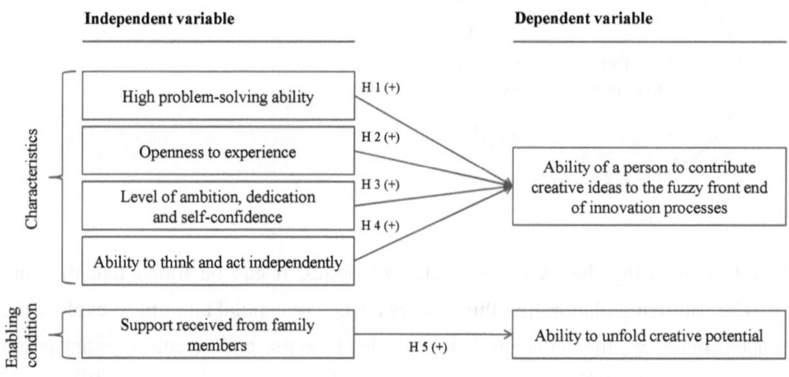

Source: created by author.

[187] The small sample size was mainly due to the difficulty of conducting research in low-income environments. For example, the communities were difficult to access, as they are situated in the outskirts of the metropolitan area of Curitiba. Thus, private transport had to be arranged. Security was also an issue when visiting people in their homes rather than at a safer location like the community center or the COHAPAR office. Furthermore, participants with jobs could only be interviewed at night, when it was especially dangerous to access the communities. Lastly, it was difficult to localize the interviewees, as some of them did not have a proper address or phone number.

5.2.5 Discussion: Identifying and distinguishing lead users and creative consumers

To date, it is unclear whether lead users can be accurately distinguished from creative mainstream consumers. In the case of this study, participants who showed above average lead-user and creativity scores belong to the group CS_{high}. This means that the characteristics of CS_{high} outlined above were also based on the interviews with those participants identified as potential lead users. The following distinction should, therefore, be highlighted:

- The lead users identified also show the characteristics attributed to creative participants.
- The remaining creative participants identified do not show an above average incidence of lead-user characteristics.

Figure 56: Intersection of characteristics of lead users and creative mainstream consumers

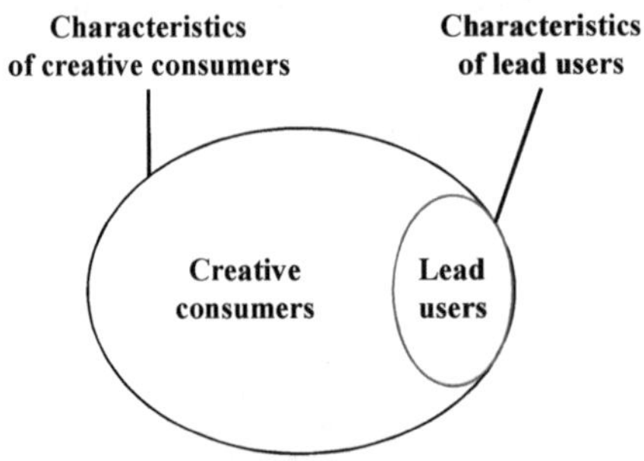

Source: created by author.

By directly comparing the two sets of characteristics, it can be found that they are related. The following elaboration thus makes a first conceptual attempt to explore the differences between the characteristics of lead users and creative mainstream consumers. The main difference that stands out is that creative consumers show **more general characteristics** (see table 67), while lead users – in addition – show a specific **expertise and interest** in a certain **field or sector**.

- Creative consumers have a high ability to solve problems. Doing so, they apply their creativity to various fields, mostly without a specific focus. While lead users may also be creative in various fields, they additionally have a high commitment to and deep technical expertise in one specific field or sector. Consequently, they have "lower innovation-related costs" (Lüthje 2004, 686, 693) and are thus more likely to innovate only in this particular field or sector.

- Creative consumers think and act independently, which makes them more inclined to question what others regard as given. They are also more likely to state their dissatisfaction with things. However, their independent thinking and lack of agreeableness are general traits, and not targeted towards a specific field of interest. In the case of lead users, their dissatisfaction – the trigger for their innovative activity – is particularly geared towards a certain field, sector, or product.
- Creative consumers value forming their opinions independently and reacting autonomously – thus influencing others, who may regard them as "leaders." Lead users are also considered to be opinion leaders. While creative people may be regarded as independent thinkers in general, lead users may be particularly sought after for advice in their specific domain of expertise.
- Creative consumers are curious and react positively to new things. Furthermore, they are generally very dedicated and ambitious people. All these characteristics point towards a general high degree of involvement. In addition, lead users may show a particularly high involvement in their field of expertise.
- Creative consumers seem able to apply their creativity in a rather general way. Lead users in consumer goods industries, in contrast, have high product-related knowledge and use experience in a specific field or regarding specific products or solutions (Lüthje 2000/2004).

The latter finding that lead users have a very specific expertise and interest in a particular field – as opposed to creative consumers, who apply their creativity more "generally"– is actually inherent in the definition of lead users: they are said to be ahead of a certain trend. Usually, this trend is in a particular field or industry. Indeed, most studies conducted in lead-user research focus on a particular field or sector. This is consistent with the phenomenon of "bounded rationality," which explains that users tend to stick to a domain in which they are already proficient (Bilgram et al. 2008, 433ff.).[188]

[188] The concept was originally proposed by Herbert A. Simon. For further information, see Simon (1991).

Table 67: Comparison between characteristics of creative participants and lead users

<table>
<tr><th>Characteristics of creative participants</th><th>Characteristics of lead users</th></tr>
<tr><td>High problem-solving ability (in general)</td><td>Innovative activity
(in the respective sector/field)</td></tr>
<tr><td rowspan="2">Ability to think and act independently (in general)</td><td>Dissatisfaction
(regarding a solution in a specific sector/field)</td></tr>
<tr><td>Opinion leadership
(in a certain sector/field)</td></tr>
<tr><td>Curiosity and a positive attitude towards change (in general)</td><td rowspan="2">Involvement (in a certain sector/field)</td></tr>
<tr><td>Ambition, dedication and self-confidence (in general)</td></tr>
<tr><td>Family unity and support</td><td>No correspondence</td></tr>
<tr><td>No correspondence, as field specific</td><td>Product-related knowledge
(regarding a certain product/solution)</td></tr>
<tr><td>No correspondence, as field specific</td><td>Use experience
(with a certain product/solution)</td></tr>
</table>

Source: created by author.

This focused interest of lead users is also made explicit in studies on methods that serve to identify them. For example, building on the lead-user definition, the lead-user method first identifies current trends in a particular field or sector, and then seeks lead users who are working towards a solution to a need related to these trends (Herstatt and von Hippel 1992; Lüthje and Herstatt 2004). Pyramiding is another proven method to identify lead users which assumes that people with a certain level of expertise know or may be able to point to others with a similar or higher level of expertise (von Hippel et al. 2009). Von Hippel et al. (2009, 1397) provide the following example: "[i]f an individual is an expert heart surgeon, pyramiding assumes that individual will know of others who are still more expert in that field." Consequently, lead users identified can only be regarded as lead users for a particular sector or field. Lüthje (2004, 685) confirms this claim:

> *We assume that the motivation and qualification for innovation in a product field can only be understood in the context of that particular product field. Consequently, we propose that a user who might initiate the development of new products in one market is not necessarily innovating in other product fields.*

In his study on characteristics of innovative users in a consumer goods field, Lüthje thus focuses on "independent variables that are linked to the market for which innovating and non-innovating users are to be differentiated" (Lüthje 2004, 685). Nonetheless, some lead users are found to be able to apply their field-specific expertise to an analogous industry (Hienerth et al. 2007). However, the analogous field still needs to be related to the lead user's field of expertise. For example, a makeup artist may be able to contribute her knowledge of the human skin to the development of a surgical drape (von Hippel et al. 1999)

In addition to the fact that lead users are specialists in a certain field – while creative consumers apply their creativity more generally – additional differences between the two types of consumers can be extrapolated from the empirical findings of this study. However, it needs to be noted that they are merely based on preliminary considerations (see table 68 and elaboration below).

Table 68: Differences between creative participants and lead users

	Creative participants	Lead users
Characteristics	General personality traits	Deep expertise and interest in a certain field or sector
Direction of needs	Concerned with current needs and everyday problems; solutions do not necessarily require a high level of (technical) expertise	Concerned with solutions to future needs, which often require a high level of (technical) expertise
Direction of thinking	Divergent thinking	Divergent and convergent thinking
Stage in innovation process	Idea generation	Idea generation; concept and prototype development; testing

Source: created by author.

By definition, lead users sense **future needs** earlier than any other people (von Hippel 1986, 796). In contrast, no evidence could be found in literature that reveals whether the needs of creative people are directed towards the future or the present. However, considering the outcomes of the idea competitions of this study, it can be assumed that they are more concerned with solutions to **everyday problems**.

Creative participants have a high predisposition to **divergent thinking**[189] – the ability to generate multiple and diverse answers to a given problem (Guilford 1967; Amabile 1989). They apply their creativity to create multiple solutions to a problem, which may serve as an inspiration for the innovation process (Magnusson 2009, 591). Thus, their abilities may be particularly fruitful for opening up innovation processes ("ideation"). Along these lines, Kristensson et al. (2004, 12) write that professional developers rarely think outside of what is technically possible. "Ordinary" or "mainstream" consumers, in contrast, are more likely to "be able to generate divergent ideas." They are not bound by what is technically feasible simply because they lack technical knowledge (see also Magnusson 2010, 306). Thus, they may inspire product developers particularly in this early phase and help them to think "outside the box" (see figure 57).[190]

Lead users may be equally able to engage in divergent thinking. However, their core competency lies in applying their deep expertise to **converge** their wealth of insights into the *one* relevant future need, and thus create a specific **solution** for this need. Due to their expertise and technical knowledge, they are not only suitable partners for developing a solution, but also for either developing or evaluating a prototype. Thus, they can be engaged at all stages of the innovation process (see figure 57).

Based on the findings above, the following hypotheses can be inductively developed (see box below). Since they are based on preliminary conceptual considerations, future studies could further refine and eventually test them (see chapter 6).

*H 6: Lead users differentiate themselves from creative consumers by their **higher level of expertise** in a specific field or sector.*

*H 7: Lead users differentiate themselves from creative consumers by their greater ability to **create solutions for future needs** (as opposed to everyday problems).*

*H 8: Lead users differentiate themselves from creative consumers by their greater ability to engage in **convergent thinking** (as opposed to only divergent thinking).*

*H 9: Lead users differentiate themselves from creative consumers by their greater ability to make a valuable contribution to **all stages of the innovation process** (as opposed to only the early stages).*

---

189 Many creativity tests use divergent thinking as a measure for creativity. See, e.g., the Torrance Test of Creative Thinking (Torrance 1974).

190 See also studies by Kristensson et al. (2002, 59ff.), Magnusson (2009, 587ff.), Magnusson et al. (2010, 306ff.), Kristensson and Magnusson (2010, 155) and Ramakrishnan (2011, 172ff.).

Figure 57: Strengths of lead users and creative mainstream consumers

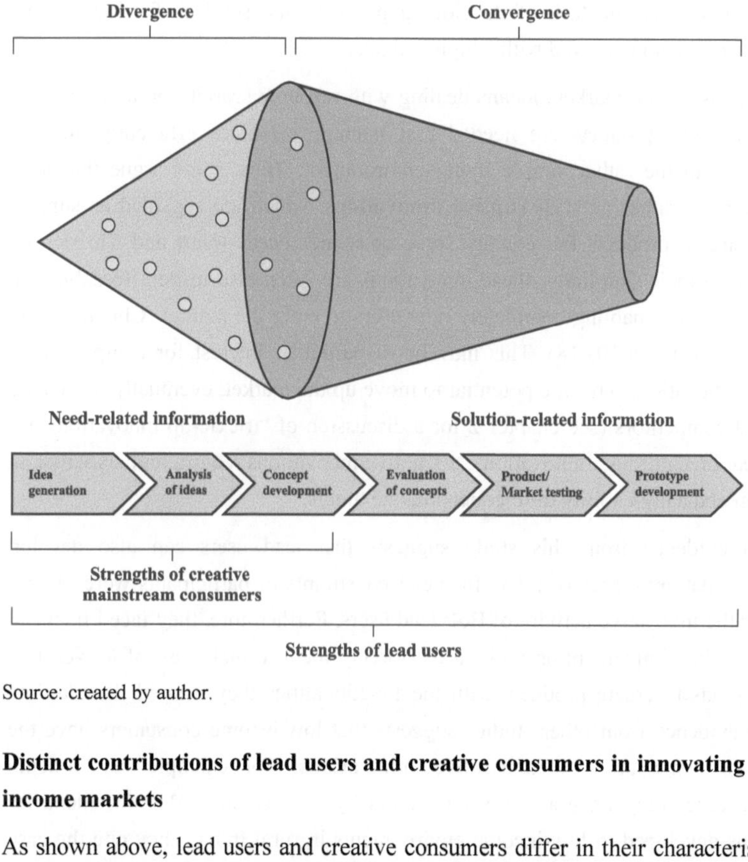

Source: created by author.

Distinct contributions of lead users and creative consumers in innovating for low-income markets

As shown above, lead users and creative consumers differ in their characteristics and abilities. Considering these finding as well as the theoretical and empirical findings from other studies, a first conceptual attempt is made here regarding the ways in which these two types of consumers can contribute to innovation for low-income markets.

Lead users are said to produce ideas that will be relevant in the future (see, e.g., von Hippel 1986, 796). This, as well as their very specific technical expertise, makes them able to generate ideas that are **radical** in nature (see, e.g., Lettl et al. 2008). However, companies that aim to innovate for a certain target group may not always aim for radical innovations. Although such innovations promise high profits when they succeed, they are risky. They often also require considerable investment from the company side (Tidd et al. 2005). This may not be suitable for smaller companies or for innovation endeavors with low budgets. In particular, business units of larger companies that have the task of developing products and services for low-income markets are often not endowed with a high budget.

Living in low-income markets means dealing with resource scarcity on a daily basis. In these markets, products are needed that manage resources efficiently and are compatible with the rather simple living environment. Thus, some argue that low-income markets rather need **disruptive innovations**, which are regarded as simpler than mainstream products but equally serve consumer needs (Hart and Christensen 2001). Due to their simplicity, these innovations are often also more affordable and less complex, thus enabling completely new users to enter the market (Christensen et al. 2001; Ahlstrom 2010, 18). This may be of particular interest for companies, as disruptive innovations have the potential to move up the market, eventually displacing established competitors (see chapter 2 for a discussion of "trickle-up innovations").[191] Like radical breakthrough innovations, disruptive innovations require high expertise in the domain and a high ability to re-conceptualize things.

Anecdotal evidence from this study suggests that lead users can also develop innovations that are disruptive: The financial constraints of participants were often a trigger for the innovative activity of BoP lead users. Furthermore, they faced financial constraints when implementing their ideas, forcing them to make use of low-cost or recycled goods to create products with the functionalities they desired. In addition, anecdotal evidence from other studies suggests that low-income consumers have the potential to come up with **disruptive innovations**. For example, an in-depth qualitative case study on grassroots innovators by Nair et al. (2011, 48) identifies innovations developed in low-income environments in rural India. They cite the case of a potter who invented a machine that makes Teflon-like, non-sticky clay pans that last longer than common clay pans, which must be replaced every 15 days. The same potter also invented a clay water filter that exploits the porosity of clay, and a clay chiller that utilizes the material's thermal characteristics. These inventions are adapted to the context of low-income markets, as they require materials that are locally available, work with minimal resources, and are affordable. They can also be regarded

[191] For example, General Electric's healthcare division developed an affordable mobile ECG machine designed for low-income environments. As healthcare systems in developed markets are also under pressure to reduce costs, the device ultimately tackled a bigger target group than previously envisioned (India Knowledge@Wharton 2010).

as disruptive. However, Nair et al. (2011) do not address the question of whether these individuals show lead-user characteristics. Future research could more specifically explore the capacity of lead users to develop disruptive innovation (see chapter 6).

Nonetheless, there may not always be a need to come up with disruptive or radical solutions when innovating for low-income markets. Often, adapting existing products to local market conditions – that is, **creating incremental innovations** – may suffice. This may require knowledge of the context, of what works and what does not. Nair et al. (2011, 23) use the term "grassroots innovations" for "products developed by the economically poor […] through the creative deployment of their indigenous skills and local knowledge." They state that these innovations "are mostly minor or incremental changes to existing technological products making them better suited for local adaptation." Also, the Economist (2010b) calls for rethinking innovation in that regard, as "many of the most important innovations consist of incremental improvements to products and processes aimed at the middle or the bottom of the income pyramid."

To develop these innovations, companies may not have to undergo the effort of identifying the rare breed of lead users.[192] Rather, creative consumers may be the right innovation partners. Indeed, the ideas suggested by creative consumers (CS_{high}) in this study were ranked highest for the dimensions of utility and feasibility (see section 5.1), meaning that these consumers have the ability to develop products that bring value to and are viable in low-income markets. Furthermore, their capacity to "diverge" in their thinking enables them to provide a variety of ideas as input for the fuzzy front end of innovation processes. This ability may partially replace expensive market research efforts that are geared towards innovation. Companies that aim to innovate for low-income environments particularly lack market information, and for them to conduct market research in these contexts is difficult and cumbersome (see section 2.2). Thus the information obtained from creative consumers may be of particular value. In conclusion, low-income consumers who are creative and motivated to contribute their ideas may be ideal partners in coming up with incremental innovations. The present study can be seen as a first step in this direction, as it identifies characteristics by which these individuals can be found (see section 5.2.3–4). However, since the

[192] Studies have shown that lead users are particularly rare. For example, for his lead user study in the consumer goods industry, Lüthje (2000) used screening methods. He contacted 2,043 consumers. Only 1.1% (22) were found to be lead users for the innovation projects in focus (game development and public transportation) (see also von Hippel et al. 2009).

findings are only based on a small sample, these characteristics need further investigation (see chapter 6).

The present study further found that some consumers prove to be motivated to participate in techniques, such as idea competitions, that integrate them into innovation processes. However, they do not have the creative capabilities to transfer their need information into solutions. Silvertant (2011, 256ff.) calls these consumers “interested and motivated mainstream consumers.” Due to their lacking ability to come up with their own ideas, they are not well positioned to contribute to innovation. At best, these consumers have input on how to enhance products that are already available in the marketplace. Due to their high motivation, they may also be likely to share this knowledge. For example, they may suggest product improvements (not innovations), like improvements in the color or shape of a product. Thus they are the typical target group of **mainstream market research**.

It can be concluded that researchers and practitioners should more clearly distinguish between innovation projects, which require lead users, and innovation projects, in which inputs from creative consumers may suffice. Furthermore, being able to clearly distinguish the different types of consumers through certain characteristics could significantly enhance the efficiency and results of consumer integration (Schrader and Belz, 2012, 345ff.). The hypotheses developed above are a first step in this direction.

Figure 58: Types of lead users and non-lead users and types of innovations

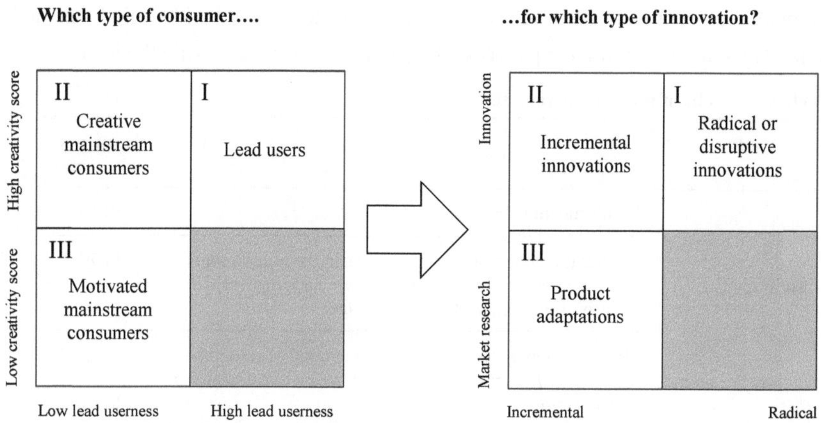

Source: created by author.[193]

5.3 Identification and transfer of innovation-relevant knowledge

Quite obviously, idea competitions produce ideas. Only occasionally, however, one breakthrough solution may emerge amongst these ideas. Nonetheless, the information and knowledge inherent in the pool of ideas collected is usually valuable. When developing ideas, the creators combine "principles and elements of knowledge and insights that have not been connected before" (Ekvall 1997, 195). However, the mere analysis of the outcome of the idea competitions (i.e., the ideas) does not suffice. Rather, innovation-relevant knowledge is also exchanged between the participants and the research team throughout the process of the competition.

Consequently, two analyses are presented here: First, the ideas as well as the field notes from the research team are analyzed to identify common patterns and, thus, the types of information and knowledge they convey. Second, an analysis of the semi-structured interviews with the research team reveals the most useful types of information and knowledge obtained and how they were transferred throughout the process of the competition.

[193] The fourth quadrant in the figure (in grey) was left empty as no consumers could be identified who show high lead userness and low creativity. They likely do not exist as both constructs seem closely related.

5.3.1 Cross-case analysis: Types and usefulness of information and knowledge

Through a content analysis of ideas, a variety of clusters could be identified (see table 69).[194] The clusters capture the patterns which emerged from analyzing the ideas.

Table 69: Results of the content analysis

Case study	**Cluster**	**Frequency** *(in percent)*
Case study I	Multifunctionality	38.10
	Better utilization of existing spaces in the house/rooms	35.70
	Customized organization and storage	19.00
	Reduction in materials used and recycling of resources	7.10
Case study II	Ownership	15.61
	Personal values	15.19
	Type and position of reservoir	14.77
	Size of reservoir in relation to house	14.77
	Ways of collecting water	14.35
	Visibility of installation	11.81
	Form of reservoir	8.02
	Internal/external use	5.49
Case study III	Efficient use of light/energy	41.18
	New designs of lighting solutions	23.53
	Use of natural light (through construction of house)	17.65
	Better dispersion of light	17.65

Source: created by author.

194 These clusters are presented in detail and separately for each case study in chapter 4. Besides considering the ideas themselves, the analysis also factored in field notes which encompass relevant observations regarding the creators of the ideas and the context they lived in (see section 3.2.4).

Need- and solution-related information

Looking at these clusters across case studies, it becomes evident that they provide two **types of innovation-relevant information**: First, they reveal information about the **needs** of participants. Second, when developing their ideas, participants had to transform this need information into concrete solutions, yielding **solution**-related information.

Table 70: Results of the analysis of ideas

	Case study I	Case study II	Case study III
Need-related information	• Need for more space • Need for storage solutions that use existing space better • Need for solutions that allow storage of different types of belongings • Information on meaning of product (associated with quality of life)	• Need for alternative solutions in case of failure/shortage of urban water supply • Need for solutions that help alleviate inundations • Need for status symbols	• Need for low-cost energy solutions (alternatives to urban energy supply and illegal tapping) • Need for solutions that better disperse light or make use of natural light • High value of natural light within dwellings
Solution-related information	• Multifunctionality • Customization of solutions • Foldable solutions (that occupy less space)	• Type, position, and size of reservoir • Visibility of installation • Internal and external use	• Solutions that better disperse light • New designs of lamps
Explicit knowledge	• Product features (e.g., multifunctionality)	• Product features (e.g., type and size of reservoir)	• Product features (e.g., better dispersion of light)
Tacit knowledge	• High acceptance of recycling and re-use of material • Desire to live in an organized dwelling	• High cultural relevance of water • Personal values connected to collecting water: status, hygiene and health, stewardship of the environment, harmony with nature • Acceptance of options for shared use within neighborhood or community	• High value of natural light within dwelling

Source: created by author.

- Need-related information: In the first case study, participants stated a strong need for more space. As they had limited resources to increase the space of their dwellings (e.g., through an outbuilding), they had a need to better utilize existing space. Furthermore, due to limited space for furniture, they needed to store different types of belongings in one piece of furniture (e.g., clothes and domestic appliances). The second case study revealed a need for alternative solutions for accessing water. Participants reported that urban water supply often failed, leaving them without water for personal hygiene or cooking for some time. They also stressed their various uses for "greywater," rather than costly tap water – for example, in watering plants or cleaning the outside of the house. In the case of the third competition, there was an evident need for solutions that better disperse interior light. Here the desire for solutions that take advantage of natural light was clear. These predominant needs may be attributed to the high grid-energy costs.

  However, needs beyond basic physiological or safety needs were also identified. Esteem needs, as classified by Maslow, were revealed (Maslow 1954). For example, in the competition of the second case study, most ideas stressed the visibility of the rainwater collector. Prior to the competition, the research team had sought discreet solutions that integrated the reservoir well into the house or underground. However, the visibility of the reservoir was identified as an important user requirement. Participants likely regarded the product as a status symbol.

- Solution-related information: The drawings and related descriptions suggest concrete product features that the users regarded as important. For example, in the case of the first competition, the need for more space or better utilization of space was solved through multifunctional products. Participants also suggested customized products that could be adapted to the size or the conditions of the house. As most houses in low-income communities are built by the proprietor or by family and friends – and not by a trained architect or mason – their ceiling heights vary, which makes it difficult to use or design standard products for this context. Customized solutions could help bridge this lack of standards. To ensure that occasionally needed pieces of furniture can be stored easily, other participants suggested foldable solutions, such as a chair that transforms into a box or a wardrobe that transforms into a changing cubicle. Some ideas in the second competition provided details not only about a variety of features, like the size or placement of the rainwater collector, but also about the product's business model –

that is, if it should be owned by an individuals or the community. In the case of the third competition, it was found that rooms often have only one power outlet and one light bulb in the middle of the room. Thus participants made suggestions about how to better disperse light – for example, through mirrors and other reflective materials. Another recurrent suggestion was to make better use of natural light through glass ceilings or translucent interior walls.

Explicit and tacit knowledge

Knowledge was conveyed in two different forms, i.e. as explicit and tacit knowledge.

- Explicit knowledge: Participants largely suggested specific features the designed products should have. For example, in the first competition, multifunctional solutions were explicitly suggested. In the second competition, product features were designed or described in detail with regard to the form or size of the reservoir, the use of the roof to collect water, or the use of filters. During the third competition, participants suggested product features that would create a better dispersion of light – be it artificial or natural.
- Tacit knowledge: The analysis of ideas and field notes also conveyed a wealth of information about what the designed artifact actually meant to the participants and what values, attitudes, aspirations, and feelings were connected to it. For example, many entrants proposed a product that could be made of recycled material. This reveals that recycling may be a common activity for low-income consumers, and that recycled products are accepted and valued. Otherwise, participants could have suggested using brand new materials, as there were no restrictions in this regard. In the case of the second competition, the designs revealed that water is regarded as a precious and highly valued resource. The ideas strongly conveyed personal values connected to the product, such as hygiene, stewardship of the environment and nature, as well as the importance of clean water. Furthermore, the solutions proposed in the second case study indicated that the use contexts of low-income communities – with their strong social ties amongst community members – might allow for shared use of products. In addition, the ideas of the third case study revealed that participants particularly valued natural light – perhaps because their houses were often small and crowded, with small or no windows.

Usefulness of information and knowledge for the product development process

To complement the findings of the content analysis of the ideas, they can be triangulated with the analysis of the interviews with the team of designers. In total, nine interviews were conducted, in which the researchers pointed out that one major benefit of the idea competition was that they obtained different types of information and knowledge. Although researchers did not use the terms need- and solution-related information or explicit and tacit knowledge, the types of information and knowledge they described did fit into these categories well. Thus, these categories served as codes when analyzing the content of the interview transcripts.

The cross-case analysis of the interviews reveals that researchers found both need- and solution-related information useful for the subsequent product development process. Need-related information was mentioned most often in the interviews (see table 71). However, the researchers stressed the identification of **solution-related information** to be a unique characteristic of idea competitions: Participants who had a clear idea about how the solution should look like explicitly visualized or described it. This is in contrast to other market research methods such as surveys or observations, whose results are usually limited to information about needs. Nonetheless, the researchers further stressed that these solutions did not provide concrete and usable technical information. Rather, they served as an inspiration for the researchers and helped them get an idea of the consumers' vision of the product (see selected quotes in table 72).

Table 71: Incidence of types of innovation-relevant knowledge

Case study	Case study I			Case study II				Case study III		Fre-quency
Interviewee	A	B	C	A	B	C	D	A	B	
Need-related information	✓	✓	✓	✓	✓	✓	✓	✓	X	100.0%
Solution-related information	✓	✓	X	✓	✓	X	X	✓	X	66.6%
Tacit knowledge	✓	✓	✓	✓	✓	✓	✓	✓	✓	100.0%
Explicit knowledge	✓	X	✓	✓	✓	X	X	✓	X	55.6%

Source: created by author.

Note: a check mark [✓] was coded when the type of information and knowledge was mentioned by the interviewee, and an X when it was not mentioned.

Tacit knowledge is generally considered difficult to tap (see chapter 2), as it is often unconscious and "deeply ingrained in people" (Nonaka/Takeuchi 1995; Nonaka et al. 1996) – people are not aware of the information they possess nor that it could be valuable to others. However, precisely this information was tapped through the competitions. Researchers could derive information on the participants' values and attitudes. This helped the designers understand what the product meant for the participants and what needs it should address beyond its obvious functions (e.g., rainwater collection as a status symbol) (see selected quotes in table 72).

Table 72: Selected quotes on the types of information and knowledge obtained by researchers

Case study I	Case study II	Case study III
[The technique] is an excellent strategy to obtain a more profound ***understanding of people's perception*** *regarding their actual problems and concerns.*	*The idea competition helped me* ***understand the customer's need, their vision of the product, and their lifestyle.***	*The technique is useful to get a deeper understanding of the* ***needs*** *of low-income people and* ***how they view their very own problems.***
Some ideas might not provide so much insight for a product concept, but rather support the ***identification of user requirements.***	*It was not possible to directly apply participants' ideas to the final solution. Nevertheless, we got* ***insights into the subjective perception of users*** *on the [rainwater collection] system in development, and those impressions guided us throughout the project.*	*I believe the insight we obtained during the idea competition helped us to understand our customers rather than provide technical information about the product.*

Source: interviews conducted by author.

Concluding, it can be found that the interviews revealed relationships between the different types of information and knowledge. Two relationships were strongest: Solutions-related information was most often explicitly visualized or described; need-related information, in turn, was mostly conveyed as tacit knowledge, i.e. in the form of values and attitudes (see figure 59).

Figure 59: Relationship between different types of innovation-relevant knowledge

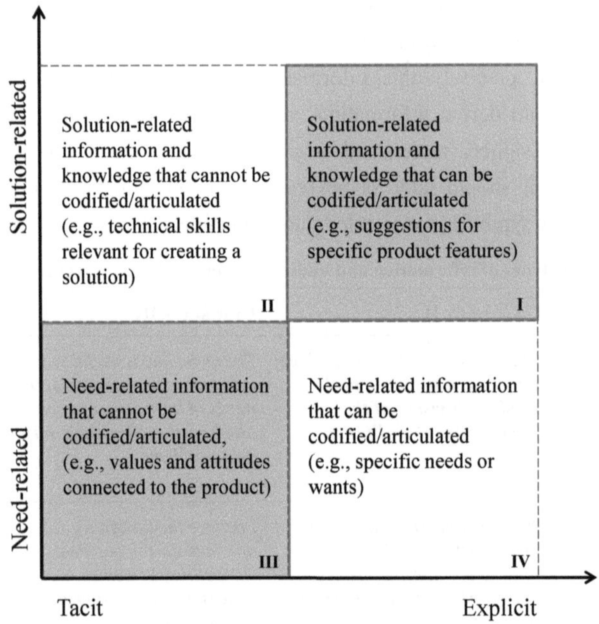

Source: created by author.

Note: The boxes marked in grey show which trends were strongest in this study.

5.3.2 Cross-case analysis: Enabling factors of knowledge transfer

The interviews consistently uncovered a variety of factors that enabled the transfer of information and knowledge from the participants to the product designers (see table 73). Coding the interviews inductively revealed that **direct contact and repeated and positive interaction** and the resulting creation of **trust** were regarded as enablers. Furthermore, the design of the idea competitions as a **participatory process** created the basis for transferring knowledge: On the one hand, it increased the **self-esteem** of the target group, who felt heard and valued. This, in turn, made them aware that they had something to contribute and more inclined to share it. On the other hand, the participatory process allowed the research team to get to know the people in the low-income community and **change their perspective** on their lifestyle. This enhanced understanding of the target group and ultimately also enabled the transfer of information and knowledge.

Table 73: Enablers of knowledge transfer

Case study	Case study I			Case study II				Case study III		Frequency
Interviewee	A	B	C	A	B	C	D	A	B	
Personal interaction	✓	✓	✓	✓	✓	X	✓	✓	✓	88.9%
Trust	X	X	✓	✓	✓	X	✓	X	X	44.4%
Participatory process	✓	✓	✓	✓	✓	✓	✓	✓	✓	100.0%
Elevated self-esteem	✓	✓	✓	X	✓	✓	✓	X	✓	77.8%
Change in perspective	✓	✓	✓	✓	✓	✓	✓	✓	✓	100.0%

Source: created by author.

Note: a check mark [✓] was coded when the enabler was mentioned by the interviewee, and an X when it was not mentioned.

Repeated personal interaction and creation of trust

The content analysis of ideas (see section 5.3.1) confirmed that the information researchers obtained was partly **accessed through the ideas**. Through the drawings, the target group transformed tacit into explicit information. Interviews with the project team confirmed this finding. As one researcher stated, "[the technique] stimulates people to express their problems and necessities using the drawings – as many of these people may have difficulties to verbalize or write about this."

However, the drawings alone could be misinterpreted by the researchers. Yet, the offline idea competition gave researchers the opportunity to gather additional information and knowledge through **repeated direct contact** with their target group, which complemented the insights obtained through the drawings. The repeated interaction took place at all stages of the idea competition:

- **Promotion**: The initial purpose of this step was to promote the idea competition and recruit participants through putting up posters, distributing flyers, and telling people about the competition. More importantly, however, it also served to collect a wealth of insights. In total, the researchers went 2-3 times to the target communities to promote the idea competitions. By asking for permission to put up posters at central points in the community, such as bars, internet cafes, or schools, or handing out flyers to individuals, the research team engaged in informal conversations. Going house-to-house, they were often invited inside the dwelling to explain their offer.

- **Collection of ideas and awarding**: Both the collection of ideas and the awarding took place in the communities. This allowed the researchers to collect further information about the context in which their target group lived, which helped them verify the observations made during the promotion phase. The ideas were collected in the building of a local organization. Preparing the location for the collection of ideas and spending a day there gave the research team another opportunity to feel part of and to socialize with the community. In some cases, the prizes that participants received were brought to the house of the winner, allowing even more personal observation.

All stages of the idea competition offered opportunities for participant observation, which is defined as "the process of learning through exposure to or involvement in the day-to-day or routine activities of participants in the research setting" (Schensul et al. 1999, 91). By organizing the competition, the researchers participated in and experienced the target group's everyday context.

The interviews with the research team revealed that precisely the information regarded as most valuable by the researchers – namely tacit knowledge – was accessed through the **continuous personal interaction** described above (see table 74). However, in such research there is no guarantee that the target group will share tacit knowledge – particularly not low-income consumers, amongst whom mistrust is usually strong. As one researcher stated, "[they] usually don't get a lot of attention and are not used to having people ask them about their ideas and opinions – apart from politicians during campaign time." The social worker of COHAPAR, one of the partner organizations of the idea competition, confirmed this: "Much has been promised to these communities by different organizations – be they private, public, or non-governmental ones." Many of these promises are not followed by action, which is why skepticism prevails. Consequently, the researchers stressed that building **trust** was essential. Many researchers emphasized that trust grew through their repeated visits in the community.

Table 74: Selected quotes on repeated personal interaction as an enabler for knowledge transfer

Case study I	Case study II	Case study III
*The main benefit of the technique is the **direct contact** with participants and their realities.* *[My] understanding [of the reality, problems, and needs of the target group] is a result of having **direct contact** with people.*	*Through [the] idea competitions, it becomes possible for the designers to **get closer to the people** who will actually use the designed systems, increasing the chances of reaching suitable solutions.* *A major aspect was **trust**. [...] We realized that the higher the involvement with the community from the beginning [...] [through personal contact], the more people participate.*	*The method offers **real contact** with the user and a relationship of empathy. It achieves **getting the best out of participants**, as it stimulates the involvement of the user.*

Source: interviews conducted by author.

Participatory process and creation of self-esteem

The idea competition is a technique that allows participants to create ideas as input for a product development process. During the promotion of the competition, the participants' role as "co-creators" was clearly communicated. Having a role in a product development process was a unique experience for the community. As one researcher stressed, "the participants [...] don't have many opportunities to express themselves, because our society doesn't recognize their potential and creativity." Being asked for their opinion and encouraged to make a contribution made participants **feel empowered and raised their self-esteem.**

Thus, it can be concluded that the participatory process empowers participants. This empowerment, in turn, created the basis for a relationship of mutual appreciation and **trust**, which ultimately enabled the transfer of information and knowledge from the participants to the researchers.

Table 75: Selected quotes on participatory process as enabler for knowledge transfer

Case study I	Case study II	Case study III
*I believe that having the feeling that they are **part of the process** was a very positive experience for the participants.*	*In my opinion, the biggest benefit is that the method enables the **creation of trust** between participants and designers, which facilitates the information exchange.*	*Amongst the benefits, I would stress that primarily, the target group develops a viable solution for themselves, and the designer then continues that process, translating the idea, refining and improving it [...]. With this, the target group*

		perceives itself to be an ***integral part*** *in the generation of solutions, in a process of co-design.*
I believe that the fact of having researchers truly concerned about listening to them and valuing their ideas contributes to improving their ***self-esteem****.*	*During the competition, it seemed to me that participants felt valued, motivated and happy to be listened to. I believe that it might have contributed (even if in a subtle and indirect way) to improving their* ***self-esteem*** *and that this triggered their potential to be innovative.*	*I think [through the idea competition], many of them realized how creative they are when it comes to finding solutions to their problems, and that they can and should be* ***active agents*** *in creating these solutions.*

Source: interviews conducted by author.

Change in perspective

Only a few members of the team of product designers had had prior knowledge of the low-income segment before the idea competition – many of them had not even been to a *favela* (i.e., slum) before. Several visits to the low-income community were part of the process of the idea competition. The designers spent time there during the promotion, the collection of ideas, and the awarding ceremony. The period between visits provided team members enough time to reflect on the experiences gathered and discuss them with each other. This made the team members question their assumptions about the low-income community. For example, low-income consumers are often criticized for possessing a TV, rather than using their money to satisfy basic needs like a water filter. Nonetheless, by visiting the community, one researcher found why it might make sense to have a TV: "The community is very violent. For the family, it made sense to possess a TV. This way, they were able to keep their children at home while the parents are at work – instead of having them stroll through the streets."

Before the competition, the views the researchers had of low-income consumers certainly shaped their thinking about their abilities (and inabilities) to contribute to innovation. Amongst many researchers, prejudices prevailed rather than enthusiasm about getting input from low-income communities. The experience of immersing themselves into the low-income context and being confronted with another way of seeing things changed these perceptions. One particularly fruitful question put to researchers was, "What did you, as a co-organizer and product designer of the idea competition, learn from conducting the idea competitions?" Many researchers replied that they learned that **people from low-income environments *can* indeed play a valuable, integral role in the innovation process**. In fact, various researchers admitted having underestimated the potential of low-income users in coming up with ideas (see table 76).

These insights about the target group resulted in a change in perspective on the side of the researchers. Instead of viewing them as poor, uneducated, and incapable, the product designers started viewing the target group as creators of ideas and as potential innovators – prejudices turned into insights. In fact, the participatory process changed the frame of reference of the information gathered, which increased the researchers' openness towards information from participants and can thus be viewed as an enabler for the transfer of information and knowledge.[195]

Table 76: Selected quotes on changed perspective of the researchers

Case study I	Case study II	Case study III
I believe that one of the major insights I could draw from this research technique is that often ***the "object" of the research has more to contribute than we think****. This is because the ideas are generated in their specific user context and are, in most cases, a direct response to real problems of real people who are living them.*	*The idea competition* ***opened my eyes regarding the role the user can play in the development of solutions*** *[...]. By suggesting products and sharing experiences which solve their own needs, the user gives us insights for the project which often will disrupt paradigms or limitations that the designer imposed.*	*One of my major lessons was verifying that* ***low-income consumers can be (and are) extremely creative*** *if they think about solutions for their very own problems. To respect and use this creativity is an important part of the design process.*
Low-income consumers are a ***reservoir of creativity that is underestimated*** *by designers.*	*Before the idea competition, I unfortunately have to confess, I doubted that the ideas could be useful for the project. [...] After the idea competition, it became clear that the* ***user has a perspective which is as good as that of the designer or the engineer****.*	*I believe the idea competition* ***widened my perception about the real needs*** *of low-income consumers, and it helped me to practice* ***more empathy*** *towards them.*

Source: interviews conducted by author.

195 On the side of the participants, a similar learning process may have taken place. However, the interviews conducted with participants did not focus on this aspect. Further research is needed.

5.3.3 Discussion: Idea competitions as a tool for identifying and transferring innovation-relevant knowledge

The cross-case creativity analysis (section 5.1.1) suggests that idea competitions can yield averagely creative ideas. Equally important as the quality of the ideas seems to be their quantity: Idea competitions are rarely conducted to identify *the one* specific solution. Rather, the objective at the fuzzy front end of innovation processes is to "diverge." A quantity of ideas is required to nurture this divergence. From the quantity of ideas, information and knowledge can be extracted that are relevant for the new product development process – or as Ekvall (1997, 195) puts it: "The larger the set of skills, information and knowledge at hand, the more numerous are the alternatives available for producing something new."

However, this study shows that the competitions' final ideas themselves were only a small part of the information and knowledge transferred from the consumers to the product designers. Rather, innovation-relevant knowledge was transferred throughout the whole process of the offline idea competitions.

Consequently, this section first discusses the trends in the innovation-relevant knowledge transferred. Based on the insights gained through the cross-case analysis, it further identifies the factors that enable the transfer of innovation-relevant knowledge. The identified factors are triangulated with the results from other studies, which were conducted in both low- and middle- to high-income contexts.[196] Key relationships between variables are captured as hypotheses, which merit further research (see chapter 6).

Identification of innovation-relevant knowledge

Literature on idea competitions suggests that they serve to identify **trends** (Belz et al. 2009, 16). Indeed, the thematic clusters identified through the cross-case content analysis of ideas correspond to trends in previous research on low-income markets. Two examples illustrate this point:

(1) Case study I identified "multifunctionality" as a trend across ideas. Also Viswanathan and Sridharan (2012, 62) point towards this trend. In their words, "it seems that products for low-income markets will also need to be innovative by being

---

[196] The fact that results could actually be triangulated with studies from other income contexts points towards the potential of generalizing these results (see chapter 6 for further elaboration).

multifunctional and contextually malleable." Along the same lines, Gupta (2010, 139) states that

> *most cultures in developing countries are multi-functional in their orientation. When goods and services are well designed, multiple functions are considered. The skills, resources and tools for multi-functional design are quite different from those needed for highly specialized and single function goods and services.*

Both authors point towards the skills needed to design appropriate, multifunctional products, and consulting consumers for input may be one way of acquiring these skills.

(2) Similarly, in case study II, the rainwater collector was identified as a symbol of status through the content analysis of ideas. Also here, evidence can be found that this is a trend beyond the findings of this study – that is, in other low-income markets. For example, Subramanyan and Gomez-Arias (2008, 408) states that "individuals who cannot fulfill their primary needs, especially regarding self-esteem or self-actualization, would compensate for its lack by alternative means [...]." She refers to the "compensatory consumption theory," explaining how "[i]t predicts that low-income households, or those facing racial or ethnic discrimination, will spend heavily on socially visible products to make up for their lack of status in society" (Subramanyan and Gomez-Arias 2008, 408–409). Also, Tiwari and Herstatt (2012c, 7) find that "despite income constraints, [low-income consumers] seek sophisticated products that do not carry the stigma of being a poor people's product."

In an effort to more systematically categorize these trends in low-income markets, research question 4a asks what **types of information and knowledge** idea competitions in low-income environments yield. The cross-case analysis (see section 5.3.1) showed that idea competitions serve to create four types of information and knowledge: (1) need-related information as well as (2) solution-related information – which are transferred as (3) explicit knowledge or (4) tacit knowledge.

BoP literature indicates that all four types are relevant when innovating for low-income markets: Halme and Paton (2007) argue towards "bringing the **needs** of the poor into the BoP debate." Viswanathan and Sridharan (2012, 60) also stress the importance of identifying "critical" or "basic" needs as well as "key aspirational needs" (i.e., needs that help one gain status and/or transcend social classes) when developing products for low-income markets: "Making the identification of such critical basic life needs a key product development objective may be an important success factor in BoP markets."

Simanis, Hart, and Duke (2008, 59) advocate for moving "beyond basic needs strategies" by tapping low-income consumers' **solution-related information**. Recapitulating the approach of the BoP Protocol, they say the following about their own findings: "The active participation of the poor in the design and implementation of solutions had empowering effects of its own, and ensured that solutions were 'appropriate' for the local context." Other authors have also strongly advocated for getting input on solutions from low-income consumers (see, e.g., Prahalad 2005/2006; Simanis et al. 2008; Gupta 2010/2013).

While there is little mention of explicit knowledge, authors particularly stress the value of **tacit knowledge** when innovating for low-income contexts. For example, Viswanathan et al. (2011, 567) state the following:

> *Most important perhaps, when compared to product development in relatively resource-rich contexts that managers can relate to, is the need for deep listening and understanding of customer needs. […] Issues, such as latent needs and cultural sensitivities, that managers are not familiar with, take on importance in subsistence marketplaces.*

All the above-mentioned types of information and knowledge are stressed in innovation literature as crucial for innovation processes. However, the latter – namely tacit knowledge – is seen as particularly relevant (Senker 1993[197]). According to Nonaka, "[m]any dimensions of customer needs take the form of tacit knowledge that an individual customer or other market participants cannot articulate by themselves" (Nonaka 1994, 23). Cooper et al. (2004, 49) further confirm that the "identification of customers' or users' real or unarticulated needs and their problems is considered fundamental […] and should be a key input to product design."

Indeed, when asked about relevant information and knowledge obtained through the idea competitions, product designers across cases primarily valued having obtained **tacit knowledge**. Certainly, it can be assumed that tacit knowledge is particularly important when innovating for low-income markets. Information on low-income

[197] In her paper on "The contribution of tacit knowledge to innovation," Senker (1993, 2012) states that "both scientific and technological inputs to innovation embody a considerable tacit component, which can only be acquired by practical experience."

consumers, their behavior, values, and beliefs is frequently lacking (see chapter 2) – and thus uncertainty is high at the fuzzy front end of innovation processes.

Nonetheless, the fact that the research team obtained tacit knowledge through the idea competition is particularly surprising, as tacit knowledge is usually difficult and costly to obtain and codify, as it "sticks" to the information holder (von Hippel 2005, 67). This can be seen as a direct outcome of the fact that the idea competitions were conducted offline: Researchers not only had the ideas as a basis for analysis, but they also had the chance to get in direct contact with the target group at various stages of the process (i.e., during the promotion of the competition or the collection of ideas).

Based on the explanation above, the following first hypothesis can be formulated:

H1: Offline participatory idea generation processes positively influence the transfer of innovation-relevant knowledge from consumers to product designers.

Figure 60: Hypothesis 1

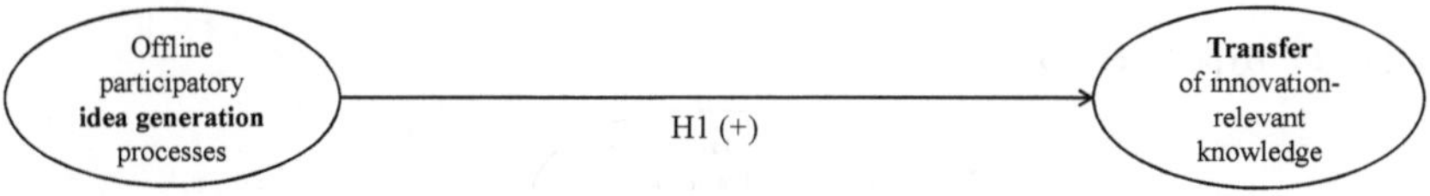

Source: created by author.

Enabling factors of knowledge transfer

The cross-case analysis in section 5.3.2 concluded that trust can be created as part of a participatory idea generation process, and that trust, in turn, positively influences the transfer of innovation-relevant knowledge. This finding, obtained in the low-income context, can be triangulated with findings from other researchers.

For example, Nonaka finds trust to be the **basis for creating a dialogue** between individuals. Only after establishing trust can individuals share experiences and create a common understanding of a subject (Nonaka 1994, 22). Other authors come to a similar finding, although their studies have organizations as a unit of analysis. Sawhney and Prandelli (2000, 261–262), for example, regard trust in the organization that invites participants to co-create as an indispensable antecedent to cooperation. Becerra et al. (2008, 693) point out that "for the successful exchange of knowledge to take place in cooperative relationships, it is presumably necessary to have a trusting relationship." They examine the role of trustworthiness in company alliances and find that "the transfer of tacit knowledge [is] highly related to perceptions of the partner's trustworthiness" (ibid., 707). Similarly, other researchers find that the willingness of organizational members to share tacit knowledge depends on the extent to which co-workers are trusted (see, e.g., Holste and Fields 2005).

In conclusion, it can be supposed that trust mediates between the two variables "offline participatory idea generation processes" and "transfer of innovation-relevant knowledge." Since without trust the relationship between the two variables would not exist, it can be seen as a full mediator between the variables (Baron and Kenny 1986; Jose 2013). Thus, the following hypotheses are phrased:

H2: Offline participatory idea generation processes positively influence the creation of ***trust*** *between participants and organizers.*

H3: ***Trust*** *between participants and organizers of offline participatory idea generation processes positively influences the transfer of innovation-relevant knowledge.*

Figure 61: Hypotheses 1–3

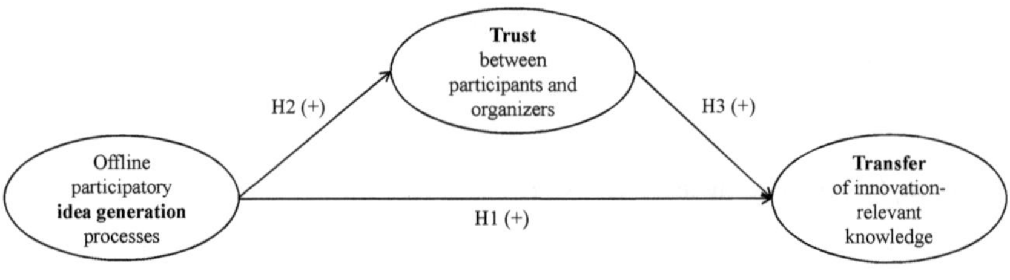

Source: created by author.

If trust positively influences the transfer of innovation-relevant knowledge, the question arises as to whether there are additional factors that foster this. Ebner et al. (2009, 347) stress the importance of integrating trust-supporting instruments into the design of an idea competition. However, they do not examine how trust is built and how trust-building can be enhanced. The findings of the present study provide insights in this regard. According to the cross-case analysis (see section 5.3.1), two variables positively influence the creation of trust:

(1) The degree of **perceived empowerment** of participants as part of the participatory process

(2) The **frequency and quality of contact** between the research team and the participants

With regard to the first variable (1), this study shows that the participatory process creates trust: The idea competition granted participants the ability to contribute their ideas. Throughout the process (i.e., the promotion of the competition and the collection of ideas), the team conveyed to participants that their ideas would be seriously taken into account in the subsequent product development process. Feeling valued and listened to elevated their self-esteem and created a feeling of empowerment, which motivated them to participate and share their ideas and insights.

Similarly, a study by Barki and Parente (2010, 11) on the behavioral characteristics of BoP consumers in Brazil indicates that they have "a stronger need to compensate for a dignity deficit and low self-esteem, a stronger preference for personalized relationships [and] a high aspiration to feel socially included in society." Hahn regards the right to self-esteem as a subcategory of human dignity (Hahn 2012, 49). He argues that human dignity (and thus self-esteem) can be enhanced through including the poor "as a resource" along the value chain – for example, in the research and development stage (Hahn 2012, 52, 56). Participatory processes may, therefore, positively influence a feeling of empowerment on the side of the included individual.

The relationship between participatory processes, empowerment, and trust is shown more clearly in a study by Füller et al. (2009, 81) on virtual co-creation tools. They cite the definition of trust from Moorman et al. (1992, 315) who define trust as "a willingness to rely on an exchange partner in whom one has confidence." Through empirical research, Füller et al. confirm that perceived empowerment (through co-creation processes) positively influences trust in the empowering organization. Consequently, they suggest that empowerment is an antecedent of trust: "Trust achieved through meaningful and information-rich interactions [….] leads to the establishment of positive community-company relationships […]. Therefore, consumers participating in virtual NPD [new product development] who feel empowered will develop increasing trust in the cooperating firm" (Füller et al. 2009, 80). Accordingly, the following hypotheses can be formulated:

H4: Offline ***participatory idea generation*** *processes positively influence participant's perceived feeling of empowerment.*

H5: Perceived ***empowerment*** *of participants positively influences the creation of* ***trust*** *between the empowering organizers of the participatory idea generation process and participants.*

Figure 62: Hypotheses 1–5

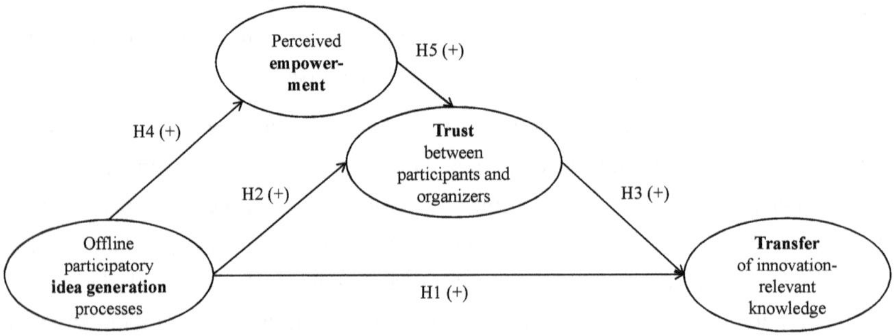

Source: created by author.

(2) Low-income consumers grow up in – or are socialized in – rural villages or urban slums. While growing up in this environment, they acquire knowledge about their needs – what works in their everyday contexts and what does not – as well as their values, beliefs, and mental models. As this knowledge is tacit, they are unlikely to share it with others, as they may have limited awareness of the usefulness of this kind of information to others and/or they may have difficulties in expressing it (see, e.g., Holste and Fields 2005).

However, tacit knowledge was shared as part of the idea generation process (see cross-case analysis in section 5.3.1). To explain how the sharing of tacit knowledge was enabled, Nonaka's description of the way knowledge is created provides valuable insights ("SECI model" in Nonaka 1994; see section 2.1.6). He explains that information and knowledge can be transferred from one individual to the other (or, respectively, one organization to the other) via socialization and externalization. **Socialization** describes the transfer of tacit knowledge in its tacit form through direct personal contact: "We use the term socialization to emphasize that tacit knowledge is exchanged through joint activities – such as being together, spending time, living in the same environment – rather than through written or verbal instructions" (Nonaka and Konno 1998, 42). They thus clarify that the transfer of tacit knowledge does not necessarily require the use of language. Rather, "physical, face-to-face experiences are the key to conversion and transfer of tacit knowledge" (Nonaka and Konno 1998, 46).

Indeed, it seems that the product designers in this study accessed the tacit knowledge of their target group by immersing themselves into their living environment and by socializing with them. At all stages of the idea competitions (i.e., the promotion, collection of ideas, and awarding ceremonies), the product designers had repeated direct contact with the target group. As Nonaka (1994, 21–22) describes, "individuals accumulate tacit knowledge through direct 'hands-on' experience." He emphasizes that, when developing new products, "the use of judgment and knowledge [is] formed through interaction with customers – and by personal bodily experience rather than by 'objective', scientific conceptualization" (Nonaka 1994, 21–22). The low-income consumers did not have to express what they knew, but rather the research team gradually gained an understanding of how the low-income context looks, smells, and feels, and thus they also started learning about the context, what works there and what does not. Nonaka and Konno (1998, 42) theorize this idea as follows:

> *Tacit knowledge can only be shared if [...] we empathize with our [...] customers, rather than sympathizing with them. [...] In practice, socialization involves capturing knowledge through physical proximity. The process of acquiring knowledge is largely supported through direct interaction with [...] customers.*

Other authors also find **personal contact and interaction** to be enablers of information and knowledge transfer (see, e.g., Cohen and Levinthal 1990). Senker (1993, 217) writes that "personal contact is used to gain supporting information of a tacit nature." Similarly, Mascitelli (2000, 189) states that

> *tacit-to-tacit exchange is greatly enhanced by close personal contact: indwelling with others, sharing common emotions and experiences, and coaxing forth an occasional deep insight. Thus, my final recommendation is that physical co-location and face-to-face interaction can be an important catalyst for breakthrough innovation.*

Viswanathan and Sridharan (2012, 56) sent student teams to Indian slums as part of a course on product concept and prototype development targeted towards BoP markets. They report that "actual experience of the context invariably brought a dimension to the process not replicable through virtual means. It enabled participants to 'connect the dots' in powerful and unpredictable ways." In their paper, published in the *Journal of Product Innovation Management*, they cite one of their students who reports the following: "We were really only able to find useful ideas from having a chance to listen to individuals who live in the rural BoP market [...] and from seeing their life context first hand" (Viswanathan and Sridharan 2012, 57). They further stress that repeated visits of the students were vital for the end result (Viswanathan and Sridharan 2012, 59): "[N]ot only the technology but the use it is subjected to and the usage situation itself were shaped by iterative exposure to the BoP context – something that would be unachievable through merely logical processes conducted in labs."

However, knowledge transfer through socialization can be inhibited by a lack of trust in whomever seeks the information. The personal contact or interaction must be positive to encourage the sharing of ideas, experiences, or emotions. Koskinen et al. (2003, 289) studied tacit knowledge acquisition and sharing in a project context, stressing that **trust** is "a significant facilitator of successful tacit knowledge acquisition and sharing" when a project team can interact face-to-face with each other. If personal contact and interaction is positive, it contributes to building trust. Koskinen et al. stress (2003, 288) that "trust builds incrementally and [...] accumulates." Thus not only one-time personal contact but rather repeated interactions may be required to build trust.

Based on the findings from the cross-case analysis as well as the triangulation with studies from both low- and middle- to high-income environments, the following hypotheses can be formulated:

*H6: Offline **participatory idea generation** processes positively influence socialization between the participants and organizers through enabling repeated personal interaction.*

*H7: **Socialization through repeated and positive personal interaction** between participants and organizers of offline participatory idea generation processes positively influences the **trust** of participants in the organizers.*

*H8: **Socialization through repeated and positive personal interaction** between participants and organizers of offline participatory idea generation processes positively influences the transfer of innovation-relevant knowledge.*

Figure 63: Hypotheses 1–8

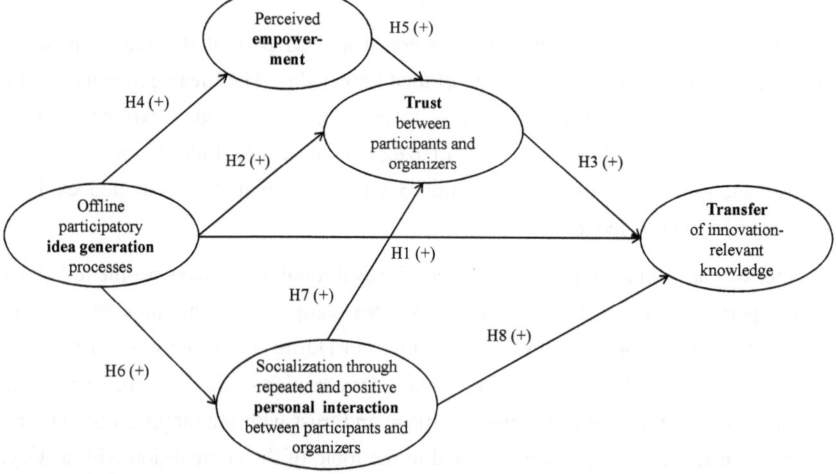

Source: created by author.

From the discussion above, it becomes clear that socialization positively influences the transfer of tacit knowledge in its tacit form (tacit-to-tacit). Through repeated personal interaction, the product designers internalize the tacit knowledge obtained from the target group, which they can then apply when developing the products for the target group.

However, innovation-relevant knowledge may also arise and be transferred in its explicit form (see section 2.3.4). The advantage is that explicit (or codified) knowledge can be shared more easily – not only between the target group and the product designers, but also amongst product designers – as it can be written down or at least verbalized.

To share knowledge in its explicit form, the tacit knowledge inherent in participants needs to be "externalized," – that is, converted into explicit knowledge. Nonaka and Konno state that "dialogue, listening and contributing to the benefit of all participants strongly supports externalization" (Nonaka and Konno 1998, 44). Furthermore, Nonaka suggests applying **figurative language and metaphoric images** to facilitate converting tacit knowledge into explicit knowledge (Nonaka 1994, 18ff.). Also Goffin and Koners (2011, 315) demonstrate that metaphors and stories are often used to transfer tacit knowledge. Likewise, Hernández-Serrano et al. (2002, 55) find that people are able to make tacit knowledge explicit through a **story**, which may be "tantamount to going through the experience oneself."

In this study, both images and stories were shared as part of the idea generation process, supporting the externalization of tacit knowledge. The **ideas** generated by the target group can be viewed as one way to make tacit knowledge explicit, as they appear in figures and images instead of behavior or words. Indeed, the cross-case content analysis of the ideas (see section 5.3.1) shows that they provided explicit, solution-related knowledge.

Another way tacit knowledge was transferred was through the **stories** people tell about their experiences related to the topic of the idea competition. This took place at all stages of the idea competitions in this study: (1) During the promotion of the idea competitions, researchers engaged in informal conversations, which can be seen as the beginning of establishing a common language and trust with the target group. During these conversations, many people reacted to the topic of the competition with a story. For example, during the second competition on water collection, people told stories about how they had dealt with failures or shortages in the urban water supply by using rainwater they had collected in a bucket. Others showed constructions they had built for that purpose already. (2) During the collection of the ideas, the participants were engaged in a brief and informal interview to verbally describe their submitted ideas. These conversations helped transform the tacit knowledge inherent in the ideas into explicit information. In most cases, the verbal description of the ideas was provided as a **story or analogy**. For example, in the first idea competition, a participant told the story of a bed that was delivered to her house but that did not fit into the small room where her three children slept. She then had to cut the bed into smaller pieces of furniture that gave the three children a place to sleep and created additional space for storage. Her idea for the competition was based on that solution. (3) Awarding the winners provided the research team with another opportunity to engage in a dialogue with participants and listen to their stories.

Building on these findings, the following hypotheses can be concluded:

*H9: **Trust** between participants and organizers of offline participatory idea generation processes positively influences the externalization of information and knowledge through the creation of **ideas** and through **storytelling**.*

*H10: **The externalization of information and knowledge through ideas and storytelling** by participants in offline participatory idea generation processes positively influences the transfer of innovation-relevant knowledge.*

Figure 64: Hypotheses 1–10

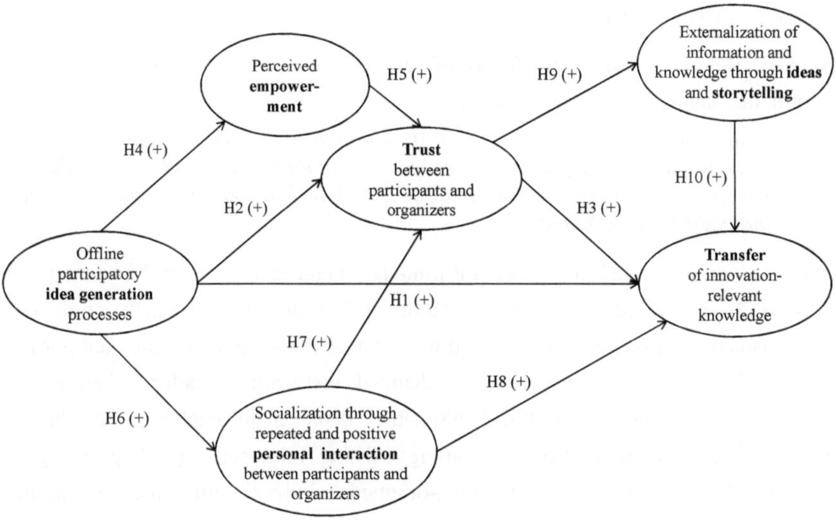

Source: created by author.

Building trust enables the transfer of innovation-relevant knowledge. However, repeated personal interaction also helps the research team become acquainted with the research context – the living environment of low-income consumers.

Styhre (2004, 178) suggests that knowledge "only become[s] useful in a social, contextual and holistic setting and **must therefore be examined within such a setting.**" With each visit, the researchers were also able to familiarize themselves with the new context. During the first visit, they gathered information and knowledge which helped them contextualize new information during subsequent visits. This process is described by a variety of authors.

For example, Cohen and Levinthal (1990, 128–129) find that "knowledge may be nominally acquired but not well utilized subsequently because the individual [does] not already possess the **appropriate contextual knowledge** necessary to make the new knowledge fully intelligible."[198] Zahra and George (2002, 189) explain that if this contextual knowledge is missing, the information and knowledge gathered in the field may not be well understood, as they "may embody heuristics that differ significantly from those used by the firm [or individual]." [199] They further elaborate that "ideas and discoveries that fall beyond a firm's search zone are overlooked because the firm cannot easily comprehend them."

Nonaka (1994, 17) finds that a **frame of reference** is needed to recognize pieces of information and knowledge as valuable:

> *Man cannot grasp the meaning of information about his environment without some frame of value judgment. The meaning of information differs according to what a particular system aims to do [...] and the broader environment in which that system exists (context).*

In their study on "transforming **mental models** on emerging markets," Dhanaraj and Khanna (2011, 692) come to a similar finding: "Often one's mind-set is the product of concepts and contexts one has grown up with and developed over a significant portion of one's life. [...] Shifting mental models demands that learners challenge their mental models, [...]." In their article (2011, 689), they depict major challenges that hinder students and executives from overcoming existing mind-sets regarding emerging markets. They report that a "problem-oriented mind-set" often prevails, seeing "emerging markets as a problem to be solved rather than as an opportunity to be leveraged." They claim that "for veteran businessmen, these markets are a destination for charity and not active candidates for businesses. [...] Yet, the same countries are also the breeding ground for dynamic entrepreneurs and innovators [...]." They call executives to open their minds to the opportunities in these markets. To shift mental models, they call for "experiential learning opportunities, so that there is learning by doing" (Dhanaraj and Khanna 2011, 693). Learning to see the target group not only as poor, uneducated, and incapable, but as creators of ideas and as potential innovators,

---

[198] Note that the bold font in quotations in this section has been added by the author.

[199] While Zahra and George make these observations for firms, it can be assumed that they are equally valid for individuals or teams.

prejudices turn into insights. This change in perspective may powerfully help companies absorb information and knowledge from this context.

The researchers cited above all use different terms – for example, mental models or frame of reference – to describe the same phenomenon. Cohen and Levinthal (1990) introduce yet another term called "**absorptive capacity**." Relating these terms, one might say that enhanced absorptive capacity influences the mental models or frame of reference of an individual. The term absorptive capacity is used in the following hypotheses, as it is widely used in business and particularly in innovation literature,[200] and thus seems most appropriate for the findings presented here.

Cohen and Levinthal (1990, 129) further describe antecedents of absorptive capacity – namely, direct personal contact (in the form of verbal or non-verbal communication) and prior knowledge:

> *The ability to evaluate and utilize outside knowledge is largely a function of the level of prior related knowledge. At the most elemental level, this prior knowledge includes basic skills or even a shared language – but may also include knowledge on the most recent scientific or technological developments in a given field. Thus, prior related knowledge confers an ability to recognize the value of new information, assimilate it and apply it to commercial ends. (Cohen and Levinthal 1990, 129)*

Through the process of the idea competitions, the researchers repeatedly visited the low-income communities. Through each visit, the research team acquired and connected new pieces of information and knowledge about the low-income community. Building on this gradually acquired knowledge helped them to recognize and process new relevant information.

As stated in hypothesis 5, repeated and personal interaction with low-income consumers positively influences the transfer of innovation-relevant knowledge. In addition, the following hypotheses can be phrased:

H11: Repeated and positive personal contact between participants and organizers of offline idea generation processes positively influences the ***absorptive capacity*** *of the research team.*

H12: A higher absorptive capacity positively influences the ***transfer and acquisition of innovation-relevant knowledge****.*

---

[200] See for example the articles by Sawhney and Prandelli (2000, 263), Zahra and George (2002), Lüthje and Herstatt (2004, 558), Lane et al. (2006) or Bilgram et al. (2008, 434).

Figure 65: Hypotheses 1–12

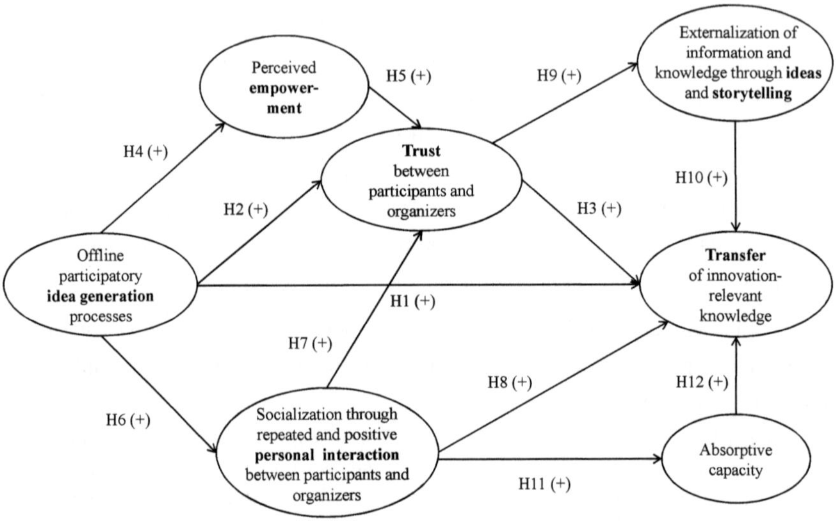

Source: created by author

Instead of treating economically poor people as a sink of public aid, assistance, advice, and corporate goods and services, we should treat them as a source of ideas, innovations [...] Inclusive development requires harnessing the minds on the margin that are not marginal minds. (Gupta 2013)

6 Summary and outlook

When it comes to doing market research for new product development, companies have traditionally seen consumers as a **source of information** who "speak only when spoken to" (von Hippel 1978, 243). The company's role is to capture their needs and preferences, and ultimately to develop appropriate solutions. Over the last decade, researchers and practitioners have realized that consumers can also be a **source of innovation**, helping discover solutions that meet their own needs. As a result, companies have started to actively integrate consumers into innovation processes. At the same time, researchers have begun to empirically explore "why" such integration is desirable and "how" it is possible. However, research thus far has focused only on middle- to high-income segments in the industrialized world (see section 2.1.1).

Nonetheless, companies and practitioners alike are recognizing the business potential in developing and emerging countries. Lately, considerable growth has taken place in these regions; R&D activities are increasingly shifting to these markets and innovations are originating from them (see, e.g. Green 2013; Economist 2010b). Furthermore, more than 80% of the world population lives in developing and emerging countries (ECB 2013; UNFPA 2013), and almost one-third of these individuals still live on less than two USD PPP per day (World Bank 2013). While individual purchasing power is low, the aggregated market is considerable, as are the opportunities to achieve not only financial objectives in these markets but also to contribute to a more sustainable pattern of development that includes the poor (Gradl et al. 2008; UNDP 2008).

Consequently, a variety of researchers have started to study the business opportunities in low-income markets (see chapters 1 and 2). Many studies have corroborated what mainstream innovation research had already put forth: to successfully explore new markets, companies should tap the information and knowledge inherent in consumers by including them in innovation. However, related considerations in the so-called "BoP literature" have remained, for the most part, on a conceptual level.

Furthermore, existing studies have neglected to build on the insights of empirical investigations in the area of innovation management (see section 2.1.2).

The present study has addressed the various research gaps in this area. It had two objectives: First, the study aimed to test if insights from innovation research can be transferred to low-income markets. Second, by extending these insights to a new context, the study aimed to create new findings (see chapter 1).

To give focus to the study, a particular technique for integrating consumers into innovation was selected – namely, idea competitions. This method was selected as it has shown promising results when integrating consumers into the fuzzy front end of innovation processes in other contexts (Walcher 2007; Belz et al. 2009; Silvertant 2011). Furthermore, initial experiences applying the technique in low-income markets exist (Jung and Chipchase 2008). To ensure feasibility, the study had a regional focus, conducting these competitions in three low-income communities in the south of Brazil (see section 3.2.1).

The following section summarizes the extent to which the theoretical objectives of testing and building theory were met. Furthermore, the first section points to the limitations of this study and develops suggestions for further research (section 6.1). The second section explains the relevance of the findings for practitioners (section 6.2).

6.1 Contributions to theory, limitations, and further research

Eisenhardt (1989, 535) points out that case studies can be employed for testing and building theory. Both purposes were pursued in this study. First, the study showed that three objectives can be met by applying idea competitions in low-income environments: (1) to identify creative ideas, (2) to help identify lead users and creative consumers, and (3) to provide access to knowledge which is relevant for the pre-development stage of innovation processes. By applying what is known to a new context, the study further expanded these findings (see research questions 3–5 in section 1.1). As a result, three sets of hypotheses were developed in regards to (1) the characteristics of creative consumers, (2) the differences between lead users and creative consumers, and (3) the factors that enable knowledge transfer between consumers and company professionals. Eisenhardt (1989, 547) concludes that "the final product of building theory from case studies may be [...] modest theories [...]

[which] are likely to be testable, novel and empirically valid [...]. They are essentially theories about specific phenomena [...]." The hypotheses developed here, which explore the specific phenomena encountered as well as their interconnections, can be seen as a contribution to building modest or middle-range theory.

The study has three main limitations. First, the research was conducted in a specific region of Brazil – namely, the metropolitan area of Curitiba. Thus, only urban low-income consumers of a particular region were addressed. Second, the findings only build on evidence from three case studies. Third, each case study only comprises a limited sample of ideas and participants.

Consequently, the results of this research must undoubtedly be replicated in other regions, such as low-income markets in other parts of Brazil or Latin America, or even in Africa or Asia. Additional case studies as well as larger samples may provide further evidence for refining and testing the hypotheses developed.

The following subsections, which are organized along the three main objectives of this study, briefly summarize the findings and main theoretical contributions. Furthermore, each subsection specifies the limitations related to each objective. Most importantly, detailed suggestions for future research are offered.

(1) Identification of creative ideas

First, the idea competitions served to generate creative ideas among low-income consumers. In each competition, 12 to 37 ideas were generated. In total, the three competitions yielded 83 ideas. A creativity analysis conducted by a jury of experts found that on average the ideas can be regarded as creative. They mainly granted high scores for the *utility* and *feasibility* of the ideas in low-income contexts. The ideas of lead users stood out from the generally creative ideas by their particularly high scores for *utility* and *originality*.

A limitation of the study was that the experts who assessed the ideas were from middle- to high-income segments of society. A common practice in innovation research is to have experts assess ideas by taking the perspective of the user (see, e.g., Walcher 2007, 111ff.; Silvertant 2011, 91ff.). Readers may question how these experts are able to put themselves into the shoes of consumers. However, one criterion for selecting the jury was that they should be highly familiar with low-income environments (see section 3.2.1 and 3.2.3). The experts also represented different societal perspectives – from business, academia, and NGOs. Furthermore, the inter-rater reliability between experts was assessed and confirmed (see sections 4.1.2, 4.2.2, and 4.3.2).

Future research could also involve the users themselves in the assessment of ideas (Haller et al. 2009, 5; Haller 2013). Two options for this approach are conceivable, each of which has advantages and disadvantages: (1) A small jury is easier to handle and more feasible. However, it is challenging to find individuals with the relevant expertise to judge the level of creativity. People with a profession in the field of the competition could potentially be considered experts – for example, an electrician, a carpenter, or a plumber for the competitions on lighting, furniture design, or rainwater collection, respectively. (2) A second option would be to tap the "wisdom of the crowd" (Surowiecki 2004) to have as many potential consumers or users as possible rate the ideas. To do this, the ideas could be physically displayed in the community center; people could rate them or vote for the three ideas they consider most creative. Online ratings may also be viable for online competitions.

(2a) Identification of lead users

Four individuals identified through this study exhibited the lead-user characteristics suggested by previous research (see section 5.2.1). They had relevant input for innovation processes targeted towards low-income contexts. They were able to create ideas for new products that are original and useful for their contexts. Their innovative activity was mostly driven by their *dissatisfaction* with existing solutions and their resulting high expected benefit from new solutions.

Nonetheless, their innovative potential cannot be compared with that of lead users in high-income contexts, who usually possess higher technical knowledge due to their education. Thus, they may not be lead users in the term's original sense put forth by von Hippel (see, e.g., 1986/1988/2005). However, a variety of authors find that while technical knowledge can be a source of inspiration, too much expertise may also "inhibit innovators' creativity to the extent that they only suggest ideas that readily conform to existing restrictions" (Kristensson and Magnusson 2010, 155).[201] Furthermore, the individuals identified in this study have deep knowledge of the use context of low-income markets along with the necessary skills to transform their needs into viable solutions that are new to the market in which they live. Their solutions may

[201] See also Kristensson et al. (2002, 59ff.), Kristensson et al. (2004, 10ff.), Magnusson (2009, 587ff.), Magnusson et al. (2010, 306ff.) and Ramakrishnan (2011, 172ff.).

even address needs that will become relevant in that marketplace in the future. Consequently, the study suggests calling them "BoP lead users."

To identify these individuals, the study chose a deductive approach. Participants were interviewed following a questionnaire that was structured along the lead-user characteristics identified through a literature review. However, the study found that while the characteristics do seem to apply, their operationalization needs to be refined to better reflect the realities of low-income contexts. This study made a first step in this direction based on results from qualitative interviews.

Future research could investigate more thoroughly how to adapt the operationalization of lead-user characteristics. In addition, researchers might investigate whether additional characteristics can be found that are specific to BoP lead users. To do so, an inductive approach might work best: Individuals who have come up with innovations could be identified and their characteristics studied in depth through, for example, interviews, participant observation, or even ethnographic studies that include home-stays. BoP lead users might be identified through idea competitions or a *pyramiding* approach. Pyramiding relies on the insight that in strong social networks, lead users can be identified by "asking around." A "snowball effect" then ultimately leads to the most innovative person in the network (see section 2.2.3). In fact, pyramiding seems particularly appropriate for low-income markets due to the tight social networks and cohesion in these contexts (Weidner et al. 2010, 559). Without referring to the technique by name, Gupta (2010, 2013) and his Honey Bee Network applied such an approach to identify "grassroots innovators" in rural India. He and his team essentially walked through rural and urban Indian villages to scout out unique solutions and their inventors.[202] On his website, he stresses that "special effort is made to look for creative knowledge among communities alienated from the mainstream." Researchers could thus build on his findings by studying the innovators he has already identified, or start searching for such innovators themselves.

---

[202] The Honey Bee Network aims to identify and disseminate grassroots innovations, always ensuring that the innovator gets acknowledged. To date, the Network has identified more than 170,000 ideas, innovations, and traditional knowledge practices from 545 Indian districts (Gupta 2013, 19). To support the Network, the Society for Research and Initiatives for Sustainable Technologies and Institutions (SRISTI) was founded, which systematically documents, disseminates, and develops grassroots green innovations, providing intellectual property rights protection and providing venture support to grassroots innovators. For more information, see the websites of the organizations: http://www.sristi.org/hbnew/aboutus.php# and http://www.sristi.org/cms/ – accessed May 1, 2013.

Such a research endeavor is time and resource intensive. However, investing in such research may be rewarding, since identifying BoP lead users may also help address the sustainability challenges the world faces today. For example, Viswanathan et al. (2011) sent engineering and design students to immerse themselves in low-income contexts with the task of developing products for these markets. They conclude that "lessons learned here can also be extended to other radically different contexts, such as future scenarios involving severe energy shortages or climate change consequences." In fact, innovators who live in low-income contexts deal with resource constraints on a daily basis – such as energy or water shortages. The solutions they come up with often particularly address such challenges, as reflected in the names various authors have given these innovations. They are called "disruptive innovations" (Hart and Christensen 2002), "Ghandian innovations" (Prahalad and Mashelkar 2010), "grassroots innovations" (Gupta 2010), or "frugal innovations" (Tiwari and Herstatt 2012a/2012b/2012c). These types of innovations all minimize the use of material resources along value chains, and have positive social impacts by being more affordable and suitable for low-income segments. They may also be referred to as "sustainability innovations" (Belz and Peattie 2009, 137ff.). In conclusion, it seems promising to further explore how BoP lead users can best be identified – and whether their innovations can contribute to tackling sustainability challenges.

(2b) Identification of creative participants and their characteristics

Previous studies have indicated that a type of consumer exists who is able to produce creative ideas but who cannot be considered a lead user (Silvertant 2011, 356ff.; Ramakrishnan 2012, 169ff.; Schrader and Belz 2012, 345ff.). The present study also identified this type of consumer. The ideas of these creative non-lead users were rated as useful and feasible in the idea competitions. Other studies have also concluded that this type of user creates ideas that are particularly valuable (Magnusson 2009, 591; Magnusson et al. 2010, 293; Ramakrishnan 2012, 177ff.). However, as opposed to lead users, who are said to sense future needs earlier, these more "mainstream" consumers rather generate ideas for current needs.

Nonetheless, this does not necessarily make them unsuitable for providing input for innovation. In fact, product developers merely need to be aware of what they can and cannot expect from these consumers. They will certainly not provide input for the radical, breakthrough innovation endeavors of tomorrow. However, their input may help product developers get a better idea of their target group. This may be particularly relevant when innovating for the use context of low-income markets, which is typically quite unfamiliar for product developers. This low-income consumer segment is also generally under-researched, and little market information about it is available. In fact, the product developers interviewed for this study confirmed that gaining access to a pool of creative, user-generated ideas helped them get a better sense of consumers' current needs and wants, and of how they envision useful solutions for their very own problems.

Previous studies had already determined the existence of these creative mainstream consumers and debated their contribution to innovation (Silvertant 2011; Ramakrishnan 2012; Belz and Schrader 2012). This study focused on the characteristics that set this type apart. Hence, the individuals identified here were interviewed in depth to inductively develop hypotheses about their characteristics. Less creative consumers were also interviewed as a control group. It was found that creative mainstream consumers have a high ability to solve problems and a positive attitude towards change. They are curious, ambitious, dedicated, and self-confident, and they think and act independently. The hypotheses developed (see section 5.2.5) can be considered a contribution to research on low-income markets, where this type of consumer may be particularly relevant.

However, the findings need not be confined to low-income contexts. They also contribute to innovation research, which has thus far not addressed the characteristics of creative mainstream consumers. The characteristics identified in this study were triangulated with findings of studies from creativity research, which did not have a regional focus or look at a particular income segment. The compatibility of the findings indicates that the characteristics identified here may be valid beyond the low-income context.

Nonetheless, the limitations of these results must be stressed. The characteristics identified were derived inductively from a small sample of participants from low-income contexts – fifteen interviews were conducted with creative participants and eight interviews with the control group.[203] Furthermore, the triangulation was conducted considering only a limited number of overview articles (such as handbooks and meta-studies). This limited scope was due not only to time and resource

[203] The small sample size was mainly due to the difficulty of conducting research in low-income environments. For further explanation, see footnote 132 in section 4.1.3.

constraints, but also to the fact that this study is not grounded in the field of psychology but rather in business and innovation research. Future studies could thus dive deeper into the body of knowledge of creativity research to test, expand, and refine the hypotheses developed.[204] Confirming these hypotheses would help significantly enhance the efficiency and effectiveness of user integration, as they screen out those participants who – although motivated – do not have skills to contribute to innovation.

In addition to identifying and characterizing lead users and creative consumers, the study systematically compared their characteristics, resulting in initial conceptual considerations on the similarities and difference between these two types of consumers.[205] It was shown that while both lead users and creative consumers can apply their creative skills to a variety of fields, lead users distinguish themselves by showing a high level of expertise in a specific field or sector. Furthermore, both lead users and creative consumers have the ability to engage in divergent thinking and can thus contribute to the idea generation stage of innovation processes. However, as mentioned above, the ideas of lead users are more future-oriented, while those of creative mainstream consumers focus on present needs. Lead users also have a higher ability to engage in convergent thinking: due to their higher technical knowledge, they are more apt to create specific solutions to specific problems. In addition, lead users were found to be able to contribute to the later stages of the innovation process – for example, prototype testing or market introduction.

This comparison of creative mainstream consumers and lead users makes a first step towards clarifying which type companies should look for when innovating. Although the findings are extrapolated from the empirical results of this study, they may also be applicable to innovation endeavors in high-income markets. However, as they only remained on a conceptual level, they require further research.

---

[204] In fact, also scholars in the area of creativity research call for more interdisciplinary research (Hennessey and Amabile 2010, 591, 569).

[205] However, studies could be found that compare lead users and creative consumers along other dimensions. For example, Ramakrishnan (2011, 183ff.) compares the two types of consumers along the creativity dimensions of their ideas. Silvertant (2011, 256ff.) classifies the types of consumers and shows what methods are suitable for integrating them into innovation.

(3) Identification and transfer of innovation-relevant information and knowledge

Previous studies have mostly focused on the **outcomes** of idea competitions. This study assumed that innovation-relevant information and knowledge can also be obtained from the **process** of these competitions. Thus, it examined what types of innovation-relevant knowledge the method yields and how they can be passed over from participants to product developers/designers throughout the process of the competition.

Conducting the idea competitions offline allowed for several interactions between the participants and the product developers – during the setup, realization, and awarding phases. Interviews with the product developers indicated that this interaction primarily granted them access to tacit, need-related knowledge, which they regarded as most useful for defining the product concept (see section 5.3.1). As this type of knowledge "sticks" to the consumer, it is usually hard to obtain (von Hippel 2005, 67). To understand how this knowledge was acquired, this study identified the factors that positively influence the transfer of innovation-relevant knowledge. Gaining more clarity on this question may help future research adapt the design of open innovation methods to low-income markets, ultimately making these methods more effective. One of the main enabling factors of knowledge transfer was the participatory process itself: including participants in innovation empowers them and contributes to creating trust. Furthermore, repeated personal interaction over the course of the process supported the knowledge transfer. Personal interaction also helped the product developers gain a better understanding of the context, which provided the right frame for the information they acquired; in other words, the personal interaction enhanced their "absorptive capacity" (Cohen and Levinthal 1990). These findings were condensed in hypotheses for future research to explore further.

The enabling factors identified are particularly relevant when innovating for low-income contexts, as these markets are generally very unfamiliar for product developers. When they develop solutions for high- to middle-income markets, they often know the use context from being consumers in their private lives as well (Schrader and Belz 2012, 346ff.). Nonetheless, also in markets that are closer to them, they may lack contextual knowledge about the target group for whom they are innovating – for example, when creating solutions for teenage, elderly, or disabled people. Hence, user integration may offer ways to become acquainted with this new target group and use context.

Future studies could thus explore whether the enabling factors identified also support tapping knowledge from other target groups. Since user integration in the early stages of innovation processes is often conducted online, researchers could further explore whether the enabling factors identified here can also be leveraged for online interactions between participants and company professionals.[206] More specifically, researchers might try to mimic the enablers in an online setting. For example, idea competitions could be combined with online communities, where participants and company professionals can interact and exchange information via text messages, pictures, or videos. This exchange could help corporate executives ask participants questions related to the ideas submitted to get a better understanding of them. Furthermore, executives could follow discussions between users and learn from this exchange.[207] *Socialization*, which refers to transferring tacit knowledge from one person to another through shared experience (Nonaka 1994, 19), could be further mimicked by asking users to upload videos of themselves using the product prototypes they developed, which may generate insights into the use context. Also, specific incentives could be set to foster the *externalization* of knowledge – i.e. the conversion of tacit into explicit knowledge (Nonaka 1994, 19) – via an online community. For example, participants who submit an idea could be asked to tell a story related to their product in the online community.

Alternatively, online idea competitions could be deliberately combined with offline interactions that allow further socialization, ultimately leveraging the enablers identified. These offline interactions could happen at very specific, selected points in time to minimize costs. For example, online idea competitions with a clearly delineated target group may be partly promoted offline to allow an initial direct point of contact. Online idea competitions might also be combined with workshops with selected participants – for example, with the most active participants in the online community halfway through the competition, or with the winners at the end of the competition (see also Silvertant 2011, 225ff., 280ff.).

---

[206] In accord with previous research, this study found that empowering participants and building trust are enablers of knowledge transfer. Füller et al. (2011), amongst others, have also concluded that participatory processes empower participants, which positively influences trust in the empowering organization.

[207] Kozinets (2002/2009) named this approach "netnography," referring to ethnography adapted to the study of online communities. "It provides information on the symbolism, meanings, and consumption patterns of online consumer groups" (Kozinets 2002, 61).

The present study focused only on the acquisition of innovation-relevant knowledge. In Nonaka and Takeuchi's model, this refers to the first two phases of the SECI-model, namely *socialization* and *externalization* (see chapter 2.3.4, figure 14). In addition to testing and refining the hypotheses developed in this study, future research could explore what happens once innovation-relevant knowledge has been transferred to product developers – that is, how it is spread and utilized within the organization. This corresponds to the later phases of the SECI-model, referred to as *combination* and *internalization*. Combination means blending external knowledge – obtained through socialization and then made explicit – with an organization's own set of knowledge (Nonaka and Konno 1998, 45). Internalization refers to making use of the combined knowledge by converting it into an individual's or organization's tacit body of knowledge (ibid.). This is important as it ensures that the knowledge actually becomes an asset for the organization.[208]

Additional topic for future research: Integrating local organizations

This study focused on integrating consumers into innovation processes. However, this approach left out a whole range of other "outside innovators" who could contribute valuable input when innovating for low-income contexts, such as representatives of community organizations, non-profit or governmental organizations that operate in the community, or representatives from international donors who work in the field. While the research team cooperated with local organizations to set up, promote, and implement the idea competitions, including them into the innovation process was beyond the scope of the study. However, observations made during the research process indicate that this may be a valuable approach that future research could investigate more closely. For example, the social worker who supported the research team to set up the idea competitions clearly had in-depth knowledge about how the community functioned as well as a comprehensive view of the community members' needs, wants, and aspirations. She may have also gathered relevant solution-related information.

Other studies have made similar observations. For example, Brugmann and Prahalad (2007, 85) found that NGOs "have developed a deep understanding of local cultures and consumption habits." They thus conclude that "when companies and NGOs

[208] See, for example, the work of Pobisch (2010) who did a first attempt to investigate how innovation-relevant knowledge obtained from consumers is spread within organizations and what capacities organizations need to have to absorb this knowledge.

innovate together […], the outcome is often breakthrough" (Brugman and Prahalad 2007, 89). Chesbrough et al. (2006, 56) also suggest that NGOs could incubate new business models that work in low-income contexts, upon which the for-profit sector could then build. Other studies cite examples in which this approach has already worked in practice.[209] Future research could thus consider including key representatives of local organizations into innovation. Their collective view may also contribute to the efficiency of such an open innovation approach. Nonetheless, whether they have equally relevant input for innovation as consumers is yet to be shown, particularly when it comes to creating solutions. Thus future research might opt for an experimental design which compares the input of such organizations with that of users. Also, it needs to be explored whether the different organizational cultures of NGOs and governmental or international organizations are actually compatible with those of companies when it comes to innovating for low-income markets – again a topic which deserves further exploration.

6.2 Contributions to practice

Viswanathan et al. (2011, 558) state that "most product development educational curricula have been focused on relatively resource-rich and literate consumers and markets." Companies that aim to enter low-income markets commonly lack not only information about this market environment but also the skills and tools to gain this information. Product developers and marketers who are unfamiliar with this new market thus find it extremely difficult to create appropriate solutions. Common market research methods are not suitable for these markets, or they must at least be adapted to yield relevant insights (DI 2011). Similarly, new methods that integrate low-income consumers into market research and innovation efforts sound promising to most practitioners, particularly since researchers have promoted them so actively (see chapter 2). However, few studies have offered guidance on how these methods can be implemented.[210] There is also a lack of empirical evidence that shows what outcomes

[209] For example, Seelos and Mair (2007) describe the case of the partnership between the telecommunication provider Telenor and Grameen Bank. To develop their business model, Telenor benefited from the bank's knowledge about providing credit to rural communities and about how to establish functioning payment systems.

[210] As elaborated upon in chapter 2, only two techniques could be identified: immersion and the BoP Protocol. While both seem adequate techniques, they have shortcomings: the former does not give consumers an active role, while the latter is a structured process that takes a considerable amount of time – up to a year or even more.

can and cannot be expected from integrating the target group into innovation. This is particularly relevant for middle managers, who are often the *intrapreneurs* who recognize and promote the opportunities of engaging in low-income markets. These intrapreneurs are also often tasked with exploring opportunities in these new markets but are not equipped with the necessary resources. In both cases, they need top management buy-in – which often requires hard facts.

This study supports practitioners in three ways. First, it conceptually showed the benefits of integrating consumers at the early stages of innovation processes. Second, it provides practitioners with a practical and tested tool to do so – namely, idea competitions. It described the method and its application in detail (see section 3.2.1), thus facilitating its replication. Third, the study explained what outcomes can be expected from the method, laying the ground for the empirical facts that may be necessary to get buy-in from senior management. More specifically, the method provides creative, user-generated ideas, from which practitioners can extract information about needs, wants, and consumer trends. It identifies BoP lead users who can serve as partners in creating solutions with future relevance. The method also serves to identify creative mainstream consumers, whose input may be suitable for incrementally adapting existing products to the context of low-income markets.

More importantly, the study showed that practitioners may benefit greatly by being involved in the actual implementation of open innovation methods – or at least by joining in crucial stages if the initiative is outsourced to a service provider. In this study, the trips to the low-income community during the implementation of the idea competitions were invaluable for practitioners. By immersing themselves into the context, they could feel first hand why consumers have certain needs. This not only granted them access to information, but also provided the proper framework for them to recognize what pieces of information and knowledge obtained from the ideas or the interaction were actually important and relevant. In theoretical terms, it enhanced their "absorptive capacity" (Cohen and Levinthal 1990). The importance of such immersion is often neglected in practice due to time or resource constraints, or simply because the benefits are not clear. The results of this study, however, point towards the effectiveness of such interaction when it comes to innovating for low-income contexts. As the quotes in section 5.3.2 illustrate, the immersion truly created "light bulb moments" for many of the product developers and designers. For example, one of them stated, "The idea competition opened my eyes regarding the role the user can play in the development of solutions [...]. By suggesting products and sharing experiences which solve their own needs, the user gives us insights for the project which many times will disrupt paradigms or limitations that the designer imposed." Most practitioners only began to realize the opportunities of doing business with low-income consumers and including them into innovation after having experienced their immediate context and lives. In conclusion, this study empirically showed that particularly middle managers who drive BoP projects in companies should get to know low-income markets first hand. It showed what results can be expected from involving the target group into innovation – and provides them with a powerful tool for learning and dialogue with the target group.

Finally, this study was written following the open innovation paradigm, which calls for opening up corporate innovation processes to input from customers and other stakeholders – with the ultimate aim of gaining new and richer insights. The study itself found that breaching the boundaries of innovation research to related disciplines, such as creativity research or knowledge management, provides rich insights and a more coherent understanding of the subject. Most importantly, however, the study encourages innovation researchers to look beyond the boundaries of middle- to high-income markets in industrialized countries. The research followed the assumption that applying a tried and tested method in low-income markets may yield new insights. This approach has shown that innovation research may also benefit from innovating its own approaches and rethinking its implicit assumptions. The study was written in the hopes that both researchers and practitioners stop seeing low-income markets as backward and daunting but rather as opportunities for new business and research.

7 APPENDIX ILLUSTRATIONS

ANNEX I: Lead-user questionnaires

Lead-user questionnaire with categories (as basis for coding) in case study I						
Character-istics	**Question**	**Likert Scale**				
		1	**2**	**3**	**4**	**5**
Dissatis-faction	*Are you unsatisfied with the solutions currently available to organize your house? If yes, to what degree and why?*	No, s/he is satisfied with the solutions that s/he knows of.	No, but s/he thinks that solutions s/he knows of could be better.	S/he is a little unsatisfied with the solution s/he knows of.	S/he is unsatisfied with the solution s/he knows of.	S/he is very unsatisfied with the solution s/he knows of.
Innovative activity	*Had you had ideas before the competition (related to organizing your house)? If yes, please describe the idea and whether/how you developed it.*	Never	S/he has created a simple solution.	S/he had already had an innovative idea before the competition (and can specify it).	S/he already had a couple of ideas (and can specify them).	Yes, s/he already had various ideas (and can specify them).
Trend leadership	*If there were a new solution to organize your house, would you be one of the first people to use it or would you let other people try it out first? Please explain why.*	S/he would surely let other people test the product first.	S/he would maybe let other people test the product first.	S/he would probably use it first.	S/he would probably want to be the first person to buy the product.	S/he would definitely like to be the first person to buy the product.
Product-related knowledge	*Do you know of existing products to organize your house? If yes, what are they? Please describe.*	No	S/he has an idea of possible solution (has already seen it on, e.g., TV or internet).	S/he knows of possible solutions and can describe them.	S/he knows of possible solutions and can describe them in detail.	S/he knows of various possible solutions and can describe them in great detail.
Use experience	*How often have you used and/or put together a solution to organize your house?*	No	S/he has used/puts together a simple solution.	S/he used/puts together solutions.	S/he often used/puts together solutions and can describe how s/he uses them in detail.	S/he always used/puts together solutions and can describe how s/he uses them in great detail.
Involve-ment	*How interested are you in solutions to organize your house? (Have you thought about this topic before?)*	No	S/he is only slightly interested but has never actively looked for information	S/he is interested and sometimes looks for information.	S/he is interested and actively and informs him-/herself about solutions.	S/he is very interested and always looks for information on new solutions.

Opinion leadership	*Do you often share with others your experiences related to solutions for organizing your house?*	No, s/he is rather shy and not a very social person.	S/he shares her/his experiences only with my family.	S/he shares her/his experiences with my friends (and family).	S/he shares her/his experiences, but few people ask her/him for her/his opinion.	S/he shares her/his experiences with a lot of people and/becaus e they always ask for her/his opinion.

Lead-user questionnaire with categories (as basis for coding) in case study II						
Character-istics	**Question**	**Likert Scale**				
		1	**2**	**3**	**4**	**5**
Dissatis-faction	*Are you unsatisfied with the solutions currently available to collect rainwater? If yes, to what degree and why?*	No, s/he is satisfied with the solutions that s/he knows of.	No, but s/he thinks that solutions s/he knows of could be better.	S/he is a little unsatisfied with the solution s/he knows of.	S/he is unsatisfied with the solution s/he knows of.	S/he is very unsatisfied with the solution s/he knows of.
Innovative activity	*Had you had ideas before the competition (related to rainwater collection or storing water)? If yes, please describe the idea and whether/how you developed it.*	Never	S/he has used simple solutions (e.g., bucket).	S/he had already had an innovative idea before the competition (and can specify it).	S/he already had a couple of ideas (and can specify them).	Yes, s/he already had various ideas (and can specify them).
Trend leadership	*If there were a new solution to collect rainwater, would you be one of the first people to use it or would you let other people try it out first? Please explain why.*	S/he would surely let other people test the product first.	S/he would maybe let other people test the product first.	S/he would probably use it first.	S/he would probably want to be the first person to buy the product.	S/he would definitely like to be the first person to buy the product.
Product-related knowledge	*Do you know of existing products to collect rainwater? If yes, what are they? Please describe.*	No	S/he knows of simple solutions (e.g., bucket).	S/he knows components.	S/he has an idea of the product (has already seen it on, e.g., TV or internet).	Yes
Use experience	*How often have you used a rainwater collector?*	No	S/he has used a simple solution (e.g., bucket).	S/he used a collector once.	S/he used a collector a couple of times (e.g., at other person's house).	Yes, s/he has a collector at home and always uses it.
Involve-ment	*How interested are you in solutions to collect rainwater (or save water)? (Have you thought about this topic before?)*	No	S/he is only slightly interested but has never actively looked for information	S/he is interested and sometimes looks for information.	S/he is interested and actively and informs him-/herself about solutions.	S/he is very interested and always looks for information on new solutions.

Opinion leadership	*Do you often share with others your experiences related to solutions for rainwater collection (or saving water)?*	No, s/he is rather shy and not a very social person.	S/he shares her/his experiences only with my family.	S/he shares her/his experiences with my friends (and family).	S/he shares her/his experiences, but few people ask her/him for her/his opinion.	S/he shares her/his experiences with a lot of people and/becaus e they always ask for her/his opinion.

Lead-user questionnaire with categories (as basis for coding) in case study III						
Character-istics	**Question**	**Likert Scale**				
		1	**2**	**3**	**4**	**5**
Dissatis-faction	*Are you unsatisfied with the products/solutions currently available on the market to illuminate your house (in an energy-efficient way)? If yes, to what degree and why? (Alternative): Do you have needs related to lighting solutions/products which are not covered by the products currently on the market?*	S/he is satisfied with the products/soluti ons available.	S/he makes do with what is available to him/her.	S/he claims to be unsatisfied, but cannot explain why.	S/he claims to be unsatisfied. S/he can specify at least one product feature that s/he would improve.	S/he claims to be very unsatisfie d. S/he can specify various product features that s/he would improve.
Innovative activity	*Had you had ideas before the competition related to (energy-efficient) illumination of your home? If yes, what were they? Please describe the idea and whether/how you developed it.*	S/he never had any ideas before the competition	S/he has modified/adap ted existing products/solut ions.	S/he had one idea before the competition and can describe it	S/he had more than one idea before the competition and can describe them.	S/he had more than two ideas before the competitio n and can describe them.
Trend leadership	*If there is a new lighting solution available, are you one of the first people to know about the novelty and/or buy it? If yes, why?*	S/he always learns about a new product through other people (friends/family) and/or always lets other people try it out first before buying it.	S/he usually learns about a new product through other people (friends/famil y) and/or lets other people try it out first before buying it.	S/he claims to sometimes be one of the first people to know about a new (energy-efficient) lighting product/solu tion and/or buy it.	S/he claimed to usually be one of the first people to know about a new (energy-efficient) lighting product/solution and/or buy it.	S/he claims to always be one of the first people to know about a new (energy-efficient) lighting product/so lution and/or buy it.

Product-related knowledge	*Do you know of existing products or solutions to illuminate your house (in an energy efficient way)? If yes, what are they? Please describe.*	S/he does not know of any existing products/solutions.	S/he knows of a product/solution but cannot describe it (well).	S/he knows of one existing product/solution and can describe it in detail.	S/he knows of more than one existing product/solution and can describe them in detail.	S/he knows of more than two existing products/solutions and can describe them in detail.
Use experience	*What lighting products/solutions do you use in your house (or other spaces)? Are they energy efficient? How often do you use them and in what situations?*	S/he does not have/use lighting products/solutions.	S/he only uses simple lighting products/solutions (e.g., bulbs).	S/he has various lighting solutions but uses them less frequently.	S/he uses various lighting products/solutions every day. S/he also uses energy-efficient lighting solutions. However, s/he only depends on them for regular / day-to-day activities (e.g., cooking, personal hygiene).	S/he uses various lighting products/solutions every day. S/he also uses energy-efficient lighting solutions. Due to his/her work, studies, or hobbies, s/he depends heavily on lighting products/solutions.
Involve-ment	*How interested are you in lighting products/solutions (that are energy-efficient)? Why? How frequently do you look for information on the subject?*	S/he is not interested in (energy-efficient) lighting products/solutions. S/he claims it to be a boring or unimportant subject.	S/he is interested in (energy-efficient) lighting solutions, but there are other things/products that interest him/her more or are more important.	S/he demonstrates an average interest. S/he claims it to be an important subject, but rarely looks for new information on the subject.	S/he demonstrates an interest. S/he claims it to be an important subject. S/he sometimes looks for new in-formation on the subject.	S/he demonstrates a high interest. S/he claims it to be an important subject. S/he always looks for new information on the subject. S/he can explain/specify the reason for his/her interest (e.g., due to occupation, economic situation).

Opinion leadership	*Do you share your experiences with others related to (energy-efficient) lighting products/solutions?* *Do others ask you for recommen-dations about how to improve the lighting situation in their house or about new products/ solutions?*	S/he does not share experiences (is shy).	S/he shares experiences only with family.	S/he shares experiences only with friends.	S/he likes to share his/her experiences with others, but others rarely ask him/her for advice.	S/he likes to share his/her experienc es with others. Others always ask him/her for advice.

ANNEX II: Lead-user characteristics tested in the consumer goods industry

Source	Product	Tested lead-user characteristic
Lüthje 2000	Outdoor sports, parlor games, public transport	New needs / trend leadership Own idea developed independently Dissatisfaction Use experience Object-related knowledge
Franke and Shah 2003	Outdoor sports	Ahead of trend High benefit from innovation
Lüthje 2004	Consumer outdoor products	New needs Dissatisfaction Expected financial benefit Use experience Product-related knowledge (i.e., know-how concerning Materials, products, and technologies) Fun innovating
Franke et al. 2006	Kitesurfing	Ahead of trend High benefit expected Technical expertise Community-based resources
Bartl 2006	Infotainment	Product-related knowledge Dissatisfaction New needs Involvement
Jeppesen and Frederiksen 2006	Music software	Trend leadership High benefit Prototype testing
Soll 2006	Household appliances	Innovativeness Opinion leadership New needs Latent dissatisfaction* Product involvement*
Schreier et al. 2007	Kitesurfing, technical diving	Leading-edge status Dissatisfaction New needs Trend leadership Opinion leadership
Walcher 2007	Sports shoes	Dissatisfaction Product-related knowledge Application knowledge Trend leadership Opinion leadership Involvement
Schreier and Prügl 2008	Sailing, technical diving, kitesurfing	Consumer knowledge User experience Locus of control Innovativeness Adoption behavior
Magnusson 2009	Mobile phone service	Use experience Technical knowledge
Silvertant 2011	Food and beverages (packaging)	Object-related knowledge Use experience Opinion leadership Trend leadership Involvement Dissatisfaction

Source: adapted from Silvertant 2011, 46.

ANNEX III: Data of the empirical analysis – case study I

Creativity dimensions and score

Descriptive statistics – case study I					
		Originality	Utility	Elaboration	Feasibility
N	Valid	34	34	34	34
	Missing	0	0	0	0
Mean		2.7739	3.3989	2.6342	3.2151
Median		2.7813	3.5000	2.6563	3.2813
Std. Deviation		1.10140	.69869	.66289	.42784
Variance		1.213	.488	.439	.183
Skewness		.033	-.704	-.708	-1.118
Std. Error of Skewness		.403	.403	.403	.403
Minimum		1.00	1.50	1.00	1.81
Maximum		5.00	4.75	3.75	3.81

One-Sample Kolmogorov-Smirnov Test – case study I						
		Originality	Utility	Elaboration	Feasibility	CS
N		34	34	34	34	34
Normal Parameters	Mean	2.7739	3.3989	2.6342	3.0055	3.2151
	Std. Deviation	1.10140	.69869	.66289	.57062	.42784
Most Extreme Differences	Absolute	.084	.210	.134	.112	.219
	Positive	.084	.102	.070	.110	.110
	Negative	-.079	-.210	-.134	-.112	-.219
Kolmogorov-Smirnov Z		.491	1.223	.782	1.279	.655
Asymp. Sig. (2-tailed)		.969	.100	.574	.076	.784

Distribution of the creativity dimension *originality* – case study I					
		Frequency	Percent	Valid Percent	Cumulative Percent
Valid	1.00	2	5.9	5.9	5.9
	1.25	3	8.8	8.8	14.7
	1.31	1	2.9	2.9	17.6
	1.50	1	2.9	2.9	20.6
	1.81	1	2.9	2.9	23.5
	2.06	3	8.8	8.8	32.4
	2.25	1	2.9	2.9	35.3
	2.31	1	2.9	2.9	38.2
	2.56	2	5.9	5.9	44.1
	2.75	2	5.9	5.9	50.0
	2.81	2	5.9	5.9	55.9
	3.00	1	2.9	2.9	58.8
	3.25	2	5.9	5.9	64.7
	3.31	2	5.9	5.9	70.6
	3.56	1	2.9	2.9	73.5
	3.75	4	11.8	11.8	85.3
	4.25	3	8.8	8.8	94.1
	4.50	1	2.9	2.9	97.1
	5.00	1	2.9	2.9	100.0
	Total	34	100.0	100.0	

Distribution of the creativity dimension *utility* – case study I					
		Frequency	Percent	Valid Percent	Cumulative Percent
Valid	1.50	1	2.9	2.9	2.9
	2.00	1	2.9	2.9	5.9
	2.25	1	2.9	2.9	8.8
	2.31	1	2.9	2.9	11.8
	2.50	1	2.9	2.9	14.7
	2.75	1	2.9	2.9	17.6
	2.81	1	2.9	2.9	20.6
	3.25	2	5.9	5.9	26.5
	3.31	6	17.6	17.6	44.1
	3.50	4	11.8	11.8	55.9

	3.56	4	11.8	11.8	67.6
	3.75	4	11.8	11.8	79.4
	3.81	1	2.9	2.9	82.4
	4.00	1	2.9	2.9	85.3
	4.25	3	8.8	8.8	94.1
	4.50	1	2.9	2.9	97.1
	4.75	1	2.9	2.9	100.0
	Total	34	100.0	100.0	

Distribution of the creativity dimension *elaboration* – case study I					
		Frequency	Percent	Valid Percent	Cumulative Percent
Valid	1.00	1	2.9	2.9	2.9
	1.25	2	5.9	5.9	8.8
	1.75	1	2.9	2.9	11.8
	2.00	1	2.9	2.9	14.7
	2.25	3	8.8	8.8	23.5
	2.31	4	11.8	11.8	35.3
	2.50	2	5.9	5.9	41.2
	2.56	3	8.8	8.8	50.0
	2.75	2	5.9	5.9	55.9
	2.81	2	5.9	5.9	61.8
	3.00	2	5.9	5.9	67.6
	3.06	2	5.9	5.9	73.5
	3.25	4	11.8	11.8	85.3
	3.31	2	5.9	5.9	91.2
	3.50	2	5.9	5.9	97.1
	3.75	1	2.9	2.9	100.0
	Total	34	100.0	100.0	

Distribution of the creativity dimension *feasibility* – case study I					
		Frequency	Percent	Valid Percent	Cumulative Percent
Valid	1.81	1	2.9	2.9	2.9
	2.25	1	2.9	2.9	5.9
	2.75	1	2.9	2.9	8.8
	3.00	11	32.4	32.4	41.2
	3.06	2	5.9	5.9	47.1
	3.25	1	2.9	2.9	50.0
	3.31	6	17.6	17.6	67.6
	3.50	2	5.9	5.9	73.5
	3.56	3	8.8	8.8	82.4
	3.75	5	14.7	14.7	97.1
	3.81	1	2.9	2.9	100.0
	Total	34	100.0	100.0	

Distribution of the creativity score – case study I					
		Frequency	Percent	Valid Percent	Cumulative Percent
Valid	1.56	1	2.9	2.9	2.9
	1.94	1	2.9	2.9	5.9
	2.25	1	2.9	2.9	8.8
	2.38	3	8.8	8.8	17.6
	2.56	1	2.9	2.9	20.6
	2.63	3	8.8	8.8	29.4
	2.69	1	2.9	2.9	32.4
	2.81	1	2.9	2.9	35.3
	2.88	3	8.8	8.8	44.1
	3.06	1	2.9	2.9	47.1
	3.13	4	11.8	11.8	58.8
	3.19	5	14.7	14.7	73.5
	3.50	2	5.9	5.9	79.4
	3.56	2	5.9	5.9	85.3
	3.63	2	5.9	5.9	91.2
	3.69	1	2.9	2.9	94.1
	4.06	1	2.9	2.9	97.1
	4.13	1	2.9	2.9	100.0
	Total	34	100.0	100.0	

Comparison between means of CS_{high} and CS_{low} – case study I				
Creativity dimensions	**CS group**	**n**	**Mean**	**Std. deviation**
Originality	CS_{low}	15	1.8125	.67480
	CS_{high}	19	3.5329	.70106
Utility	CS_{low}	15	2.9792	.70341
	CS_{high}	19	3.7303	.49741
Elaboration	CS_{low}	15	2.1625	.61274
	CS_{high}	19	3.0066	.42639
Feasibility	CS_{low}	15	3.0292	.47825
	CS_{high}	19	3.3618	.32581
CS	CS_{low}	15	2.4958	.36935
	CS_{high}	19	3.4079	.32165

Creativity dimensions	Levene's Test for Equality of Variances	F	Sig	T-test Sig. (2-tailed)
Originality	Equal variances assumed	.046	.832	**.000**
	Equal variances not assumed			.000
Utility	Equal variances assumed	3.761	.061	**.001**
	Equal variances not assumed			.002
Elaboration	Equal variances assumed	1.406	.244	**.000**
	Equal variances not assumed			.000
Feasibility	Equal variances assumed	.021	.885	**.022**
	Equal variances not assumed			.030
CS	Equal variances assumed	.016	.899	**.000**
	Equal variances not assumed			.000

ANNEX IV: Data of the empirical analysis – case study II

Creativity dimensions and score

Descriptive statistics – case study II						
		Originality	Utility	Elaboration	Feasibility	CS
N	Valid	37	37	37	37	37
	Missing	0	0	0	0	0
Mean		2.4486	2.7405	2.4108	2.5784	2.5446
Median		2.4000	2.8000	2.6000	2.6000	2.7000
Std. Deviation		.72481	.73615	.82185	.74354	.69170
Variance		.525	.542	.675	.553	.478
Skewness		-.056	-.326	-.107	-.167	-.504
Std. Error of Skewness		.388	.388	.388	.388	.388
Minimum		1.20	1.20	1.00	1.00	1.10
Maximum		3.80	4.20	4.00	4.00	3.55

One-Sample Kolmogorov-Smirnov Test – case study II						
		Originality	Utility	Elaboration	Feasibility	CS
N		37	37	37	37	37
Normal Parameters	Mean	2.4486	2.7405	2.5784	2.5446	2.4108
	Std. Deviation	.72481	.73615	.74354	.69170	.82185
Most Extreme Differences	Absolute	.094	.127	.106	.128	.135
	Positive	.094	.086	.106	.073	.135
	Negative	-.079	-.127	-.096	-.128	-.132
Kolmogorov-Smirnov Z		.574	.771	.823	.645	.779
Asymp. Sig. (2-tailed)		.897	.592	.507	.800	.578

Distribution of the creativity dimension *originality* – case study II					
		Frequency	Percent	Valid Percent	Cumulative Percent
Valid	1.20	4	10.8	10.8	10.8
	1.40	1	2.7	2.7	13.5
	1.60	1	2.7	2.7	16.2
	1.80	1	2.7	2.7	18.9
	2.00	4	10.8	10.8	29.7
	2.20	4	10.8	10.8	40.5
	2.40	6	16.2	16.2	56.8
	2.60	3	8.1	8.1	64.9
	2.80	2	5.4	5.4	70.3
	3.00	4	10.8	10.8	81.1
	3.20	2	5.4	5.4	86.5
	3.40	1	2.7	2.7	89.2
	3.60	3	8.1	8.1	97.3
	3.80	1	2.7	2.7	100.0
	Total	37	100.0	100.0	

Distribution of the creativity dimension *utility* – case study II					
		Frequency	Percent	Valid Percent	Cumulative Percent
Valid	1.20	1	2.7	2.7	2.7
	1.40	2	5.4	5.4	8.1
	1.60	1	2.7	2.7	10.8
	1.80	1	2.7	2.7	13.5
	2.00	4	10.8	10.8	24.3
	2.40	5	13.5	13.5	37.8
	2.60	1	2.7	2.7	40.5
	2.80	4	10.8	10.8	51.4
	3.00	5	13.5	13.5	64.9
	3.20	5	13.5	13.5	78.4
	3.40	3	8.1	8.1	86.5
	3.60	2	5.4	5.4	91.9
	3.80	2	5.4	5.4	97.3
	4.20	1	2.7	2.7	100.0
	Total	37	100.0	100.0	

Distribution of the creativity dimension *elaboration* – case study II					
		Frequency	Percent	Valid Percent	Cumulative Percent
Valid	1.00	1	2.7	2.7	2.7
	1.20	3	8.1	8.1	10.8
	1.40	4	10.8	10.8	21.6
	1.60	3	8.1	8.1	29.7
	2.00	3	8.1	8.1	37.8
	2.20	1	2.7	2.7	40.5
	2.40	2	5.4	5.4	45.9
	2.60	4	10.8	10.8	56.8
	2.80	3	8.1	8.1	64.9
	3.00	5	13.5	13.5	78.4
	3.20	5	13.5	13.5	91.9
	3.60	1	2.7	2.7	94.6
	3.80	1	2.7	2.7	97.3
	4.00	1	2.7	2.7	100.0
	Total	37	100.0	100.0	

Distribution of the creativity dimension *feasibility* – case study II					
		Frequency	Percent	Valid Percent	Cumulative Percent
Valid	1.00	1	2.7	2.7	2.7
	1.40	2	5.4	5.4	8.1
	1.60	3	8.1	8.1	16.2
	2.00	6	16.2	16.2	32.4
	2.20	2	5.4	5.4	37.8
	2.40	2	5.4	5.4	43.2
	2.60	4	10.8	10.8	54.1
	2.80	3	8.1	8.1	62.2
	3.00	3	8.1	8.1	70.3
	3.20	4	10.8	10.8	81.1
	3.40	3	8.1	8.1	89.2
	3.60	3	8.1	8.1	97.3
	4.00	1	2.7	2.7	100.0
	Total	37	100.0	100.0	

Distribution of the creativity score – case study II					
		Frequency	Percent	Valid Percent	Cumulative Percent
Valid	1.10	1	2.7	2.7	2.7
	1.30	2	5.4	5.4	8.1
	1.45	1	2.7	2.7	10.8
	1.55	1	2.7	2.7	13.5
	1.75	1	2.7	2.7	16.2
	1.80	1	2.7	2.7	18.9
	1.90	1	2.7	2.7	21.6
	1.95	1	2.7	2.7	24.3
	2.00	1	2.7	2.7	27.0
	2.05	1	2.7	2.7	29.7
	2.15	1	2.7	2.7	32.4
	2.30	2	5.4	5.4	37.8
	2.45	1	2.7	2.7	40.5
	2.60	1	2.7	2.7	43.2
	2.65	2	5.4	5.4	48.6
	2.70	2	5.4	5.4	54.1
	2.75	1	2.7	2.7	56.8
	2.85	1	2.7	2.7	59.5
	2.90	1	2.7	2.7	62.2
	3.00	2	5.4	5.4	67.6
	3.05	4	10.8	10.8	78.4
	3.20	1	2.7	2.7	81.1
	3.25	2	5.4	5.4	86.5
	3.30	1	2.7	2.7	89.2
	3.35	1	2.7	2.7	91.9
	3.40	1	2.7	2.7	94.6
	3.50	1	2.7	2.7	97.3
	3.55	1	2.7	2.7	100.0
	Total	37	100.0	100.0	

Comparison between means of CS_{high} and CS_{low} – case study II				
Creativity dimensions	**CS group**	**n**	**Mean**	**Std. deviation**
Originality	CS_{low}	23	2.0609	.55082
	CS_{high}	14	3.0857	.48810
Utility	CS_{low}	23	2.3304	.59271
	CS_{high}	14	3.4143	.34609
Elaboration	CS_{low}	23	1.9391	.62794
	CS_{high}	14	3.1857	.40356
Feasibility	CS_{low}	23	2.2174	.65203
	CS_{high}	14	3.1714	.44966
CS	CS_{low}	23	2.1370	.55046
	CS_{high}	14	3.2143	.18752

Creativity dimensions	Levene's Test for Equality of Variances	F	Sig	T-test Sig. (2-tailed)
Originality	Equal variances assumed	.166	.686	**.000**
	Equal variances not assumed			.000
Utility	Equal variances assumed	4.726	.037	.000
	Equal variances not assumed			**.000**
Elaboration	Equal variances assumed	8.421	.006	.000
	Equal variances not assumed			**.000**
Feasibility	Equal variances assumed	1.875	.180	**.000**
	Equal variances not assumed			.000
CS	Equal variances assumed	16.232	.000	.000
	Equal variances not assumed			**.000**

Lead-user score

Inter-rater reliability – case study II		
Lead-user characteristics	**ICC**	**Cronbach's Alpha**
Dissatisfaction (D)	0.926	0.929
Innovative activity (IA)	0.863	0.866
Trend leadership (TL)	0.940	0.941
Product-related knowledge (PK)	0.924	0.913
Use experience (UE)	0.888	0.882
Involvement (IV)	0.541	0.550
Opinion leadership (OL)	0.881	0.879

Descriptive statistics – case study II									
		D	**IA**	**TL**	**PK**	**UE**	**IV**	**OL**	**LUS**
N	Valid	28	28	28	28	28	28	28	28
	Missing	9	9	9	9	9	9	9	9
Mean		1.804	1.232	2.732	2.000	1.804	2.732	3.018	2.1888
Median		1.750	1.000	3.000	2.000	2.000	3.000	3.500	2.2857
Std. Deviation		.9363	.5690	1.0495	.9027	.8203	.5850	1.2873	.52027
Variance		.877	.324	1.102	.815	.673	.342	1.657	.271
Skewness		.913	2.531	-.101	.610	2.153	.317	-.323	-.387
Std. Error of Skewness		.441	.441	.441	.441	.441	.441	.441	.441
Minimum		1.0	1.0	1.0	1.0	1.0	2.0	1.0	1.14
Maximum		4.0	3.0	4.5	4.0	5.0	4.0	5.0	3.14

One-Sample Kolmogorov-Smirnov Test – case study II									
		D	**IA**	**TL**	**PK**	**UE**	**IV**	**OL**	**LUS**
N		28	28	28	28	28	28	28	28
Normal Parameters	Mean	3.018	1.232	2.1888	2.000	1.804	1.804	2.732	2.732
	Std. Deviation	1.2873	.5690	.52027	.9027	.8203	.9363	1.0495	.5850
Most Extreme Differences	Absolute	.206	.480	.127	.187	.334	.269	.136	.248
	Positive	.131	.480	.097	.187	.334	.269	.114	.216
	Negative	-.206	-.342	-.127	-.143	-.237	-.195	-.136	-.248
Kolmogorov-Smirnov Z		2.539	2.539	.722	.992	1.767	1.312	1.089	.671
Asymp. Sig. (2-tailed)		.000	.000	.674	.279	.004	.064	.186	.758

Distribution of lead-user score – case study II					
		Frequency	Percent	Valid Percent	Cumulative Percent
Valid	1.14	1	2.7	3.6	3.6
	1.36	1	2.7	3.6	7.1
	1.43	2	5.4	7.1	14.3
	1.50	1	2.7	3.6	17.9
	1.57	1	2.7	3.6	21.4
	1.71	1	2.7	3.6	25.0
	1.86	1	2.7	3.6	28.6
	2.00	2	5.4	7.1	35.7
	2.14	2	5.4	7.1	42.9
	2.21	2	5.4	7.1	50.0
	2.36	2	5.4	7.1	57.1
	2.43	1	2.7	3.6	60.7
	2.50	2	5.4	7.1	67.9
	2.57	3	8.1	10.7	78.6
	2.64	1	2.7	3.6	82.1
	2.64	2	5.4	7.1	89.3
	2.71	1	2.7	3.6	92.9
	2.93	1	2.7	3.6	96.4
	3.14	1	2.7	3.6	100.0
	Total	28	75.7	100.0	
Missing	System	9	24.3		
Total		37	100.0		

Comparison of creativity groups along lead-user characteristics (Mann-Whitney-U test) – case study II				
Lead-user characteristics	**Creativity group**	**n**	**Mean Rank**	**Sum of Ranks**
Dissatisfaction (D)	CS_{low}	16	10.94	175.00
	CS_{high}	12	19.25	231.00
Innovative activity (IA)	CS_{low}	16	13.94	223.00
	CS_{high}	12	15.25	183.00
Trend leadership (TL)	CS_{low}	16	11.44	183.00
	CS_{high}	12	18.58	223.00
Product-related knowledge (PK)	CS_{low}	16	13.59	217.50
	CS_{high}	12	15.71	188.50
Use experience (UE)	CS_{low}	16	13.72	219.50
	CS_{high}	12	15.54	186.50
Opinion leadership (OL)	CS_{low}	16	13.25	212.00
	CS_{high}	12	16.17	194.00
Involvement (IV)	CS_{low}	16	11.97	191.50
	CS_{high}	12	17.88	214.50
LUS	CS_{low}	16	11.69	187.00
	CS_{high}	12	18.25	219.00

	D	**IA**	**TL**	**PK**	**UE**	**IV**	**OL**	**LUS**
Mann-Whitney U	39.000	87.000	47.000	81.500	83.500	55.500	76.000	51.000
Wilcoxon W	175.000	223.000	183.000	217.500	219.500	191.500	212.000	187.000
Z	-2.827	-.626	-2.312	-.698	-.657	-2.011	-.948	-2.093
Asymp. Sig. (2-tailed)	.005	.531	.021	.485	.511	.044	.343	.036
Exact Sig. [2*(1-tailed Sig.)]	.007	.698	.023	.507	.568	.059	.371	.037

ANNEX V: Data of the empirical analysis – case study III

Creativity dimensions and score

Descriptive statistics – case study III						
		Originality	Utility	Elaboration	Feasibility	CS
N	Valid	12	12	12	12	12
	Missing	0	0	0	0	0
Mean		13.42	15.00	12.67	15.33	56.42
Median		14.00	16.00	13.00	15.50	61.00
Std. Deviation		3.942	3.568	3.725	3.869	11.851
Skewness		.054	-.908	-.584	-.145	-1.268
Std. Error of Skewness		.637	.637	.637	.637	.637
Kurtosis		-1.454	-.337	-.081	.061	.836
Std. Error of Kurtosis		1.232	1.232	1.232	1.232	1.232
Minimum		8	8	5	8	30
Maximum		19	19	17	22	67

One-Sample Kolmogorov-Smirnov Test – case study III						
		Originality	Utility	Elaboration	Feasibility	CS
N		12	12	12	12	12
Normal Parameters	Mean	13.42	15.00	12.67	15.33	56.42
	Std. Deviation	3.942	3.568	3.725	3.869	11.851
Most Extreme Differences	Absolute	.147	.194	.140	.107	.202
	Positive	.147	.131	.122	.083	.186
	Negative	-.142	-.194	-.140	-.107	-.202
Kolmogorov-Smirnov Z		.508	.671	.484	.369	.700
Asymp. Sig. (2-tailed)		.958	.759	.973	.999	.711

Distribution of the creativity dimension *originality* – case study III					
		Frequency	Percent	Valid Percent	Cumulative Percent
Valid	8	1	8.3	8.3	8.3
	9	2	16.7	16.7	25.0
	10	1	8.3	8.3	33.3
	11	1	8.3	8.3	41.7
	14	2	16.7	16.7	58.3
	15	1	8.3	8.3	66.7
	16	1	8.3	8.3	75.0
	17	1	8.3	8.3	83.3
	19	2	16.7	16.7	100.0
	Total	12	100.0	100.0	

Distribution of the creativity dimension *utility* – case study III					
		Frequency	Percent	Valid Percent	Cumulative Percent
Valid	8	1	8.3	8.3	8.3
	10	1	8.3	8.3	16.7
	11	1	8.3	8.3	25.0
	14	1	8.3	8.3	33.3
	15	1	8.3	8.3	41.7
	16	2	16.7	16.7	58.3
	17	1	8.3	8.3	66.7
	18	3	25.0	25.0	91.7
	19	1	8.3	8.3	100.0
	Total	12	100.0	100.0	

Distribution of the creativity dimension *elaboration* – case study III					
		Frequency	Percent	Valid Percent	Cumulative Percent
Valid	5	1	8.3	8.3	8.3
	9	1	8.3	8.3	16.7
	10	2	16.7	16.7	33.3
	12	2	16.7	16.7	50.0
	14	2	16.7	16.7	66.7
	15	1	8.3	8.3	75.0
	17	3	25.0	25.0	100.0
	Total	12	100.0	100.0	

Distribution of the creativity dimension *feasibility* – case study III					
		Frequency	Percent	Valid Percent	Cumulative Percent
Valid	8	1	8.3	8.3	8.3
	11	1	8.3	8.3	16.7
	13	2	16.7	16.7	33.3
	14	1	8.3	8.3	41.7
	15	1	8.3	8.3	50.0
	16	1	8.3	8.3	58.3
	17	2	16.7	16.7	75.0
	18	1	8.3	8.3	83.3
	20	1	8.3	8.3	91.7
	22	1	8.3	8.3	100.0
	Total	12	100.0	100.0	

Distribution of the creativity score – case study III					
		Frequency	Percent	Valid Percent	Cumulative Percent
Valid	30	1	8.3	8.3	8.3
	40	1	8.3	8.3	16.7
	47	1	8.3	8.3	25.0
	53	1	8.3	8.3	33.3
	57	1	8.3	8.3	41.7
	60	1	8.3	8.3	50.0
	62	1	8.3	8.3	58.3
	63	1	8.3	8.3	66.7
	65	1	8.3	8.3	75.0
	66	1	8.3	8.3	83.3
	67	2	16.7	16.7	100.0
	Total	12	100.0	100.0	

Comparison between means of CS_{high} and CS_{low} – case study III				
Creativity dimension	**CS group**	**n**	**Mean**	**Std. deviation**
Originality	**CS_{low}**	5	2.1200	.64187
	CS_{high}	7	3.0857	.64143
Utility	**CS_{low}**	5	2.3600	.63875
	CS_{high}	7	3.4571	.27603
Elaboration	**CS_{low}**	5	2.0000	.67823
	CS_{high}	7	2.9143	.55205
Feasibility	**CS_{low}**	5	2.6000	.73485
	CS_{high}	7	3.4000	.65320
CS	**CS_{low}**	5	2.2700	.53689
	CS_{high}	7	3.2143	.13452

Creativity dimensions	Levene's Test for Equality of Variances	F	Sig	T-test Sig. (2-tailed)
Originality	Equal variances assumed	.026	.876	**.028**
	Equal variances not assumed			.031
Utility	Equal variances assumed	5.657	.039	.002
	Equal variances not assumed			**.015**
Elaboration	Equal variances assumed	.039	.848	**.028**
	Equal variances not assumed			.040
Feasibility	Equal variances assumed	.047	.833	**.075**
	Equal variances not assumed			.087
CS	Equal variances assumed	8.735	.014	.001
	Equal variances not assumed			**.016**

Lead-user score

Inter-rater reliability – case study III		
Lead-user characteristics	**ICC**	**Cronbach's Alpha**
Dissatisfaction (D)	0.891	0.900
Innovative activity (IA)	0.939	0.939
Trend leadership (TL)	0.911	0.908
Product-related knowledge (PK)	0.961	0.965
Use experience (UE)	0.928	0.922
Involvement (IV)	0.921	0.921
Opinion leadership (OL)	0.907	0.913

Descriptive statistics – case study III									
		D	**IA**	**TL**	**PK**	**UE**	**IV**	**OL**	**LUS**
N	Valid	12	12	12	12	12	12	12	12
	Missing	0	0	0	0	0	0	0	0
Mean		2.167	1.417	2.083	2.250	2.417	2.667	2.958	2.2798
Median		2.000	1.000	1.750	2.000	2.000	2.750	3.000	2.1071
Std. Deviation		1.2309	1.1645	1.1839	1.0335	.7638	1.0299	1.0544	.69149
Variance		1.515	1.356	1.402	1.068	.583	1.061	1.112	.478
Skewness		.416	3.142	.601	1.853	1.435	.211	1.247	1.790
Std. Error of Skewness		.637	.637	.637	.637	.637	.637	.637	.637
Minimum		1.0	1.0	1.0	1.0	2.0	1.0	2.0	1.29
Maximum		4.0	5.0	4.0	5.0	4.0	4.5	5.0	4.14

One-Sample Kolmogorov-Smirnov Test – case study III									
		D	IA	TL	PK	UE	IV	OL	LUS
N		12	12	12	12	12	12	12	12
Normal Parameters	Mean	2.167	1.417	2.083	2.250	2.417	2.667	2.958	.08
	Std. Deviation	1.2309	1.1645	1.1839	1.0335	.7638	1.0299	1.0544	.289
Most Extreme Differences	Absolute	.245	.473	.237	.346	.457	.158	.318	.530
	Positive	.245	.473	.237	.346	.457	.158	.318	.530
	Negative	.172	.360	-.180	.154	.293	-.127	-.182	.386
Kolmogorov-Smirnov Z		.849	.849	.820	1.197	1.584	.547	1.100	1.837
Asymp. Sig. (2-tailed)		.467	.467	.513	.114	.013	.926	.178	.002

Distribution of lead-user score – case study III					
		Frequency	Percent	Valid Percent	Cumulative Percent
Valid	1.29	1	8.3	8.3	8.3
	1.79	1	8.3	8.3	16.7
	1.93	1	8.3	8.3	25.0
	2.07	3	25.0	25.0	50.0
	2.14	1	8.3	8.3	58.3
	2.29	1	8.3	8.3	66.7
	2.36	1	8.3	8.3	75.0
	2.43	1	8.3	8.3	83.3
	2.79	1	8.3	8.3	91.7
	4.14	1	8.3	8.3	100.0
	Total	12	100.0	100.0	

Comparison of creativity groups along lead-user characteristics (Mann-Whitney-U test) – case study III				
Lead-user characteristics	**Creativity group**	**n**	**Mean Rank**	**Sum of Ranks**
Dissatisfaction (D)	CS_{low}	5	7.00	35.00
	CS_{high}	7	6.14	43.00
Innovative activity (IA)	CS_{low}	5	6.60	33.00
	CS_{high}	7	6.43	45.00
Trend leadership (TL)	CS_{low}	5	5.30	26.50
	CS_{high}	7	7.36	51.50
Product-related knowledge (PK)	CS_{low}	5	5.70	28.50
	CS_{high}	7	7.07	49.50
Use experience (UE)	CS_{low}	5	7.50	37.50
	CS_{high}	7	5.79	40.50
Opinion leadership (OL)	CS_{low}	5	6.30	31.50
	CS_{high}	7	6.64	46.50
Involvement (IV)	CS_{low}	5	6.40	32.00
	CS_{high}	7	6.57	46.00
LUS	CS_{low}	5	6.80	34.00
	CS_{high}	7	6.29	44.00

	D	**IA**	**TL**	**PK**	**UE**	**IV**	**OL**	**LUS**
Mann-Whitney U	15.000	17.000	11.500	13.500	12.500	17.000	16.500	16.000
Wilcoxon W	43.000	45.000	26.500	28.500	40.500	32.000	31.500	44.000
Z	-.423	-.125	-1.014	-.696	-1.069	-.082	-.172	-.245
Asymp. Sig. (2-tailed)	.673	.901	.310	.486	.285	.934	.863	.806
Exact Sig. [2*(1-tailed Sig.)]	.755	1.000	.343	.530	.432	1.000	.876	.876

8 REFERENCES

A. T. Kearney. *Serving the Low-Income Consumer: How to Tackle this Mostly Ignored Market*, 2007. Accessed May 1, 2013. http://www.atkearney.com/documents/10192/343423c1-7053-45e8-8ab2-0d4b9cedb7a2

Ackoff, R. L. "From Data to Wisdom." *Journal of Applied Systems Analysis* 16 (1989): 3–9.

Adamson, R. E. "Functional Fixedness as Related to Problem Solving: A Repetition of Three Experiments." *Journal of Experimental Psychology* 44, no. 4 (1952): 288–291.

ADEME/WEC. *Measures focused on low-income households. WEC-ADEME Case studies on Energy Efficiency Measures and Policies*, July 2010. Accessed May 1, 2013.
http://www.worldenergy.org/documents/ee_case_study_for_low_income_households.pdf

Ahlstrom, D. "Innovation and Growth: How Business Contributes to Society." *Academy of Management Perspective* 24, no. 3 (2010): 10–23.

Amabile, T. M. *Creativity in Context*. New York: Westview Press, 1996.

Amabile, T. M. *Growing Up Creative: Nurturing a Lifetime of Creativity*. New York: Crown Publishers, 1989.

Amabile, T. M., E. A. Schatzel, G. B. Moneta, and S. J. Kramer. "Leader Behaviors and the Work Environment for Creativity: Perceived Leader Support." *The Leadership Quarterly* 15, no. 1 (2004): 5–32.

Amabile, T. M. "Beyond Talent: John Irving and the Passionate Craft of Creativity." *American Psychologist* 56, no. 4 (April 2001): 333–336.

Anderson, J., and N. Billou. "Serving the World's Poor: Innovation at the Base of the Economic Pyramid." *Journal of Business Strategy* 28, no. 2 (2007): 14–21.

Badry, D. *Multinational Companies in Low-Income Markets: An Analysis of Social Embeddedness in Southeast Asia*. Wiesbaden: Gabler Verlag, 2009.

Barki, E., and J. Parente. "Consumer Behaviour of the Base of the Pyramid Market in Brazil." *Greener Management International* 56 (2010): 11–23.

Baron, R. M., and D. A. Kenny. "The Moderator–Mediator Variable Distinction in Social Psychological Research: Conceptual, Strategic, and Statistical Considerations." *Journal of Personality and Social Psychology* 51, no. 6 (December 1986): 1173–1182.

Barron, F. X., and D. M. Harrington. "Creativity, Intelligence, and Personality." *Annual Review of Psychology* 32 (1981): 439–476.

Bartl, M. *Virtuelle Kundenintegration in die Neuproduktentwicklung*. Wiesbaden: Gabler, 2006.

Bartl, M., H. Ernst, and J. Füller. "Community Based Innovation – Eine Methode zur Einbindung von Online Communities in den Innovationsprozess." In *Produktentwicklung mit virtuellen Communities. Kundenwünsche erfahren und Innovationen realisieren,* edited by H. Herstatt and J. G. Sander, 141–167. Wiesbaden: Gabler, 2004.

Becerra, M., R. Lunnan, and L. Huemer. "Trustworthiness, Risk, and the Transfer of Tacit and Explicit Knowledge Between Alliance Partners." *Journal of Management Studies* 45, no. 4 (June 2008): 691–713.

Bellinger, G., D. Castro, and Mills, A. "Data, Information, Knowledge and Wisdom, Systems Thinking." Last modified 2004. Accessed May 1, 2013. http://www.systems-thinking.org/dikw/dikw.htm

Belz, F.-M., R. Codita, and K. Moysidou. "Driving the Change: Innovating (Lead) Users and Expected Benefits." Paper presented at the EURAM Annual Conference 2012 of the Rotterdam School of Management, Erasmus University, Rotterdam, June 7th, 2012.

Belz, F.-M., and K. Peattie. *Sustainability Marketing: A Global Perspective.* Chichester: John Wiley & Sons, Ltd, 2009.

Belz, F.-M., S. Silvertant, J. Füller, and J. Pobisch. *Ideenwettbewerbe: Konsumenten Involvieren, Ideen Generieren, Lead User Identifizieren.* Freising: Technische Universität München, Professur für Betriebswirtschaftslehre Brau- und Lebensmittelindustrie, 2009.

Belz, F.-M., U. Schrader, and M. Arnold, eds. *Nachhaltigkeitsinnovation durch Nutzerintegration.* Marburg: Metropolis-Verlag, 2011.

Beshouri, C. P. "A Grassroots Approach to Emerging Market Consumers." *The McKinsey Quarterly* 4 (2006): 61–71.

Bilgram, V., A. Brem, and K.-I. Voigt. "User-Centric Innovation in New Product Development – Systematic Identification of Lead Users Harnessing Interactive and Collaborative Online-Tools." *International Journal of Innovation Management* 12, no. 3 (2008): 419–458.

Bogers, M., A. Afuah, and B. Bastian. "Users as Innovators: A Review, Critique, and Future Research Directions." *Journal of Management* 36, no 4 (2010): 857–875.

Bonoma, T.V. "Case Research in Marketing: Opportunities, Problems, and Process." *Journal of Marketing Research* XXIII (May 1985): 199–208.

Booz, Allen & Hamilton. *New Product Management for the 1980s*. New York: Booz Allen & Hamilton, 1979.

Bortz, J., and N. Döring. *Forschungsmethoden und Evaluation für Human- und Sozialwissenschaftler*. 4th ed. Heidelberg: Springer Medizin Verlag, 2006.

Boudon, R. "What Middle-Range Theories Are." *Contemporary Sociology (American Sociological Association)* 20, no. 4 (1991): 519–522.

Brugmann, J., and C.K. Prahalad. "Cocreating Business's New Social Compact." *Harvard Business Review* (February 2007): 80–90.

Bucherer, E., and U. Eisert. "Towards Systematic Business Model Innovation: Lessons from Product Innovation Management." *Creativity and Innovation Management* 21, no. 2 (2012): 183–198.

Bühl, A. *SPSS 16: Eine Einführung in die Moderne Datenanalyse*. 11th ed. München: Pearson Studium, 2012.

Büschken, J., and C. Blümm. "Zur Rolle von Implizitem Wissen im Innovationsprozess." Diskussionsbeiträge der Katholischen Universität Eichstätt, Wirtschaftswissenschaftliche Fakultät Ingolstadt Nr. 142, Wirtschaftswissenschaftliche Fakultät Ingolstadt, Lehrstuhl für Allgemeine Betriebswirtschaftslehre, Absatzwirtschaft und Marketing, Katholischen Universität Eichstätt, Ingolstadt, September 2000. Accessed May 1, 2013. http://www.ub.uni-koeln.de/ssg-bwl/archiv/ei/kuei/marketing/innovation.pdf

Caixa Econômica Federal."Demanda Habitacional no Brasil." República Federativa do Brasil, 2012. Accessed May 1, 2013. http://downloads.caixa.gov.br/_arquivos/habita/documentos_gerais/ demanda_habitacional.pdfconomica

Campbell, A. J., and R. G. Cooper. "Do Customer Partnerships Improve New Product Success Rates?" *Industrial Marketing Management* 28 (1999): 507–519.

Carol, M. "Danone Innovates to Help Feed the Poor." Business Week, Last modified April 28, 2008. Accessed May 1, 2013. http://www.businessweek.com/ globalbiz/content/apr2008/gb20080428_971498.html

Chesbrough, H. W. *Open Innovation: The New Imperative for Creating and Profiting from Technology*. Boston: Harvard Business School Press, 2003.

Chesbrough, H. W. *Open Business Models: How to Thrive in the New Innovation Landscape*. Boston: Harvard Business School Press, 2006.

Chesbrough, H. W. "Business Model Innovation: It's Not Just About Technology Anymore." *Strategy & Leadership* 35, no. 6 (2007): 2–17.

Chesbrough, H. W., S. Ahern, M. Finn, and S. Guerraz. "Business Models for Technology in the Developing World: The Role of Non-Governmental Organizations." *California Management Review* 48, no. 3 (Spring 2006): 48–61.

Chesbrough, H. W., W. Vanhaverbeke, and J. West, eds. *Open Innovation: Researching a New Paradigm*. Oxford: Oxford University Press, 2008.

Chikweche, T., and R. Fletcher. "Revisiting the Marketing Mix at the Bottom of Pyramid (BOP): From Theoretical Considerations to Practical Realities." *Journal of Consumer Marketing* 29, no. 7 (2012): 507–520.

Childers, T. L. "Assessment of the Psychometrie Properties of an Opinion Leadership Scale." *Journal of Marketing Research* 23, no. 2 (1986): 184–188.

Chipchase, J. "Shared Phone Use." Last modified December 21st, 2006. Accessed May 1, 2013. http://janchipchase.com/2006/12/shared-phone-use/ 2006

Christensen, C. M., T. Craig, and S. L. Hart. "The Great Disruption." *Foreign Affairs* 80, no. 2 (2001): 80–95.

Cohen, J. *Statistical Power Analysis for the Behavioural Sciences*. Hillsdale, New Jersey: Lawrence Earlbaum Associates Publishers, 1971.

Cohen, W. M., and D. A. Levinthal. "Absorptive Capacity: A New Perspective on Learning and Innovation." *Administrative Science Quarterly* 35, no. 1 (1990): 128–152.

Cooper, A. "Customer Knowledge Management and Mass Customization." *Internet Business*, H. 4 April 1999.

Cooper, R. G. "New Product Performance and Product Innovation Strategies." *Research Management* 29 (May–June 1986): 17–25.

Cooper, R. G. "Predevelopment Activities Determine New Product Success." *Industrial Marketing Management* 17, no. 2 (1988): 237–247.

Cooper. R. G., S. J. Edgett, and E. J. Kleinschmidt. "Benchmarking Best NPO Practices-III." *Research Technology Management* (November-December 2004): 43–55.

Cooper, R.G., and E. J. Kleinschmidt. "Success Factors in Product Innovation." *Industrial Marketing Management* 16, no. 3 (1987): 215–223.

Cooper, R. G., and E. J. Kleinschmidt. "Screening New Products for Potential Winners." *Institute of Electrical and Electronics Engineers IEEE Engineering Management Review* 22, no. 4 (1994): 24–30.

Crawford, C. M. "New Product Failure Rates: A Reprise." *Research Management* 30, no. 4 (1987): 20–24.

Creswell, J. W. *Research Design. Qualitative, Quantitative, and Mixed Methods Approaches.* Thousand Oaks, California: SAGE Publications, 2009.

Creswell, J. W., and V. L. Plano Clark. *Designing And Conducting Mixed Methods Research.* 1st ed. Thousand Oaks, California: SAGE Publications, 2006.

Dahl, D. W., and P. Moreau. "The Influence and Value of Analogical Thinking During New Product Ideation." *Journal of Marketing Research* 39, no. 1 (2002): 47–60.

Davenport, T. H., and L. Prusack. *Working Knowledge: How Organizations Manage What They Know.* Boston: Harvard Business School Press, 1998.

De Soto, H. *The Mystery of Capital: Why Capitalism Triumphs in the West and Fails Everywhere Else*. New York: Basic Books, 2000.

Dhanaraj, C., and T. Khanna. "Transforming Mental Models on Emerging Markets." *Academy of Management Learning & Education* 10, no. 4 (2011): 684–701.

DI. *Market Creation Toolbox,* 2011. Accessed May 1, 2013. http://di.dk/SiteCollectionDocuments/DIBD/Market%20Creation%20Toolbox.pdf

Duflo, E., M. Greenstone, R. Hanna, and R. Muthiah. "Clean Cookstoves Must Be Rethought so They Actually Get Used in Developing World." *National Geographic*, June 18, 2012. http://newswatch.nationalgeographic.com/2012/06/18/clean-cookstoves-must-be-rethought-so-they-actually-get-used-in-developing-world/

Dul, J. and T. Hak, *Case Study Methodology in Business Research*. Oxford: Butterworth-Heinemann, 2008.

Duncker, K. "On Problem Solving." *Psychological Monographs* 58, no. 5 (1945): i–113.

Ebner, W. "Community Building for Innovations – Der Ideenwettbewerb als Methode für die Entwicklung und Einführung einer Virtuellen Innovations-Gemeinschaft." PhD diss., Technische Universität München, 2008.

Ebner, W., J. M. Leimeister, and H. Krcmar. "Community Engineering for Innovations: The Ideas Competition as a Method to Nurture a Virtual Community for Innovations." *R&D Management* 39, no. 4 (2009): 342–356.

Eisenhardt, K. M. "Building Theories from Case Study Research." *The Academy of Management Review* 14, no. 4 (October 1989): 532–550.

Eisenhardt, K. M., and M. E. Graebner. "Theory Building from Cases: Opportunities and Challenges." *Academy of Management Journal* 50, no.1 (2007): 25–32.

Ekvall, G. "Organizational Conditions and Levels of Creativity." *Creativity and Innovation Management* 6, no. 4 (1997): 195–205.

Ernst, H. "Success Factors of New Product Development: A Review of the Empirical Literature." *International Journal of Management Reviews* 4, no. 1 (2002): 1–40.

Ernst, H. "Virtual Customer Integration. Maximizing the Impact of Customer Integration on New Product Performance." In *Cross-Functional Innovation Management. Perspectives from Different Disciplines*, edited by S. Albers, 191–208. Wiesbaden: Gabler, 2004.

Ernst, H., J. H. Soll, and M. Spann. "Möglichkeiten der Lead-User-Identifikation." In *Produktentwicklung mit Virtuellen Communities. Kundenwünsche Erfahren und Innovationen Realisieren*, edited by C. Herstatt and J.G. Sander, 121–140. Wiesbaden: Gabler, 2004.

Feist, G. "A Meta-Analysis of Personality in Scientific and Artistic Creativity." *Personality and Social Psychology Review* 2, no. 4 (1998): 290–309.

Festinger, L. *A Theory of Cognitive Dissonance.* Stanford, California: Stanford University Press, 1957.

Fisher, R. J. "Social Desirability Bias and the Validity of Indirect Questioning." *Journal of Consumer Research* 20, no. 2 (September 1993): 303–315.

Franke, N., and F. Piller. "Value Creation by Toolkits for User Innovation and Design: The Case of the Watch Market." *The Journal of Product Innovation Management* 21, no. 6 (2004): 401–415.

Franke, N., and S. Shah. "How Communities Support Innovative Activities: An Exploration of Assistance and Sharing Among End-Users." *Research Policy* 32, no. 1 (January 2003): 157–178.

Franke, N., E. von Hippel, E., and M. Schreier. "Finding Commercially Attractive User Innovations: A Test of Lead-User Theory." *The Journal of Product Innovation Management* 23, no. 4 (2006): 301–315.

Freeman, C., and L. Soete. *The Economics of Industrial Innovation*. 3rd ed. London: Pinter, 1997.

Frey, B.S. "How Intrinsic Motivation is Crowded Out and In." *Rationality and Society* 6, no. 3 (1997): 334–352.

Fukushima, N. "Dimensão Social do Design Sustentável: Contribuições do Design Vernacular da População de Baixa Renda." Universidade Federal do Paraná, Curitiba, 2009. Accessed May 1, 2013. http://dspace.c3sl.ufpr.br/dspace/bitstream/handle/1884/20931/Fukushima,N_DSSustentabilidade_PPGDesgin.pdf?sequence=1

Füller, J. "Why Consumers Engage in Virtual New Product Developments Initiated by Producers." *Advances in Consumer Research* 33, no. 1 (2006): 639–646.

Füller, J. "Refining Virtual Co-Creation from a Consumer Perspective." *California Management Review* 52, no. 2 (2010): 98–122.

Füller, J., M. Bartl, H. Mühlbacher, and H. Ernst. "Community Based Innovation - A Method to Utilize the Innovative Potential of Online Communities." Proceedings of the 37th Hawaii International Conference on System Sciences, 2004. Accessed May 1, 2013. http://www.virtual-communities.net/mediawiki/images/7/7a/205670195c.pdf

Füller, J., and C. Dr. Hienerth. "Engaging the Creative Consumer." *European Business Forum* 19 (Autumn 2004): 54–57.

Füller, J., K. Hutter, and R. Faullant. "Cocreation Experience Matters." *R&D Management* 41, no. 3 (June 2011): 259–273.

Füller, J., H. Mühlbacher, K. Matzler, and G. Jawecki. "Consumer Empowerment Through Internet-Based Co-Creation." *Journal of Management Information Systems* 26, no. 3 (Winter 2009–10): 71–102.

Gau, R., H. Jae, and M. Viswanathan. "Studying Low-Literate Consumers through Experimental Methods: Implications for Subsistence Marketplaces." *Journal of Business Research* 6, (2012): 1683–1691.

George, D., and P. Mallery. *SPSS for Windows Step by Step: A Simple Guide and Reference. 11.0 update.* 4th ed. Boston: Allyn & Bacon, 2003.

Gephart, R. P. "From the Editors: Qualitative Research and the Academy of Management Journal." *Academy of Management Journal* 47, no. 4 (2004): 454–62.

Glaser, B.G., and A. L. Strauss. *The Discovery of Grounded Theory: Strategies for Qualitative Research.* Chicago: Aldine Pub. Co., 1967.

Glover, G., R. Ronning, and C. Reynolds. *Handbook of Creativity: Perspectives on Individual Differences*. New York: Plenum, 1989.

Goffin, K., and U. Koners. "Tacit Knowledge, Lessons Learnt, and New Product Development." *Product Development & Management Association* 28, (2011): 300–318.

Goffin, K., U. Koners, D. Baxter, and C. van der Hoven. "Managing Lessons Learned and Tacit Knowledge in New Product Development." *Research Technology Management* 53, no. 4 July–August 2010): 39–51.

Gradl, C. "The Business Model as a Governance Heuristic: An Ordonomic Contribution to the Management of Value Networks." PhD diss., Martin-Luther-Universität Halle-Wittenberg, Halle (Saale), forthcoming.

Gradl, C., A. Gasnier, S. Sobhani, and A. Bootsman. "Understanding the Markets of the Poor – A Market System Approach to Inclusive Business." In *Sustainability Challenges and Solutions at the Base-of-the-Pyramid: Business, Technology and the Poor.* edited by P. Kandachar and M. Halme, Chapt. 1. London: Greenleaf, September 2008.

Granovetter, M. "Economic Action and Social Structure: A Theory of Embeddedness." *American Journal of Sociology* 91, no. 3 (1985): 481–510.

Grant, R. M. "Toward a Knowledge-Based Theory of the Firm." *Strategic Management Journal* 1, Winter Special Issue (1996): 109–122.

Grant, R. M. "The Knowledge-based View of the Firm: Implications for Management Practice." *Long Range Planning* 30, no. 3 (1997): 450–454.

Gravetter, J. F., and L. B. Wallnau. *Essentials of Statistics for the Behavioral Sciences*. 8th ed. California: Wadsworth, 2012.

Greenwald, A. G., and C. Leavitt. "Audience Involvement in Advertising: Pour Levels." *Journal of Consumer Research* 11, no. 1 (1984): 581–592.

Green, A. "Africa's Clinical Trial: Big Pharma Deploys R&D in Africa." *This is Africa* (June/July 2013): 25–27.

Griffin, A., and J.R. Hauser. "The Voice of the Customer." *Marketing Science* 12, no. 1 (Winter 1993): 1–27.

Grosh, M.E., and Glewwe, P. "Household Survey Data from Developing Countries: Progress and Prospects." *The American Economic Review* 86, no. 2 (1995): 15–19.

Gruner, K. E., and C. Homburg. "Does Customer Interaction Enhance New Product Success." *Journal of Business Research* 49, no. 1 (2000): 1–14.

Guastello, S. J. "Creativity and Personality." In *Routledge Companion to Creativity*, edited by T. Rickards, M. A. Runco, and S. Moger, 256–266. Abington, England: Routledge, 2005.

Guba, E. G, and Y. S. Lincoln. "Competing Paradigms in Qualitative Research." In *Handbook of Qualitative Research*, edited by N. K. Denzin, and Y. S. Lincoln, 105–117. London, Thousand Oaks, CA and New Delhi: Sage Publications, 1994.

Guilford, J.P. "Creativity." *The American Psychologist* 5, no. 9 (1950): 444–454.

Guilford, J. P. *The Nature of Human Intelligence*. New York, NY: McGraw-Hill, 1967.

Guilford, J. P. "Intellectual Factors in Productive Thinking." In *Explorations in Creativity,* edited by R. Mooney, and T. Rayik. New York: Harper & Row, 1976.

Guilford, J. P. *Way Beyond the IQ: Guide to Improving Intelligence and Creativity*. Buffalo, NY: Bearly Limited, 1977.

Gupta, A. K. "Grassroots Green Innovations for Inclusive, Sustainable Development." In *The Innovation for Development Report 2009-2010: Strengthening Innovation for the Prosperity of Nations*, edited by A. López-Carlos, 137–146. Palgrave Macmillan: Hampshire, 2010.

Gupta, A. K. "Tapping the Entrepreneurial Potential of Grassroots Innovation." In *Global Perspectives on How Social Innovation Can Promote the Well-Being of Humanity*, edited by Stanford Social Innovation Review, 18–21, 2013. Accessed May 1, 2013. http://www.ssireview.org/articles/entry/tapping_the_entrepreneurial_potential_of_grassroots_innovation

Gwet, K. L. *Handbook of Inter-Rater Reliability*. 2nd ed. Gaithersburg: Advanced Analytics, LLC, 2010.

Hanna, R., E. Duflo, and M. Greenstone. "Up in Smoke: The Influence of Household Behavior on the Long-Run Impact of Improved Cooking Stoves." Working Paper 12–10, Massachusetts Institute of Technology Department of Economics Working Paper Series, Cambridge, April 16, 2012. Accessed May 1, 2013. http://www.povertyactionlab.org/publication/smoke-influence-household-behavior-long-run-impact-improved-cooking-stoves

Hahn, R. "Inclusive Business, Human Rights and the Dignity of the Poor: A Glance Beyond Economic Impacts of Adapted Business Models." *Business Ethics: A European Review* 21, no. 1 (2012): 47–63.

Haller, J. *Open Evaluation. Integrating Users into the Selection of New Product Ideas.* Series: Markt- und Unternehmensentwicklung / Markets and Organisations. Wiesbaden: Springer, 2013.

Haller, J., A. C. Bullinger, and A. K. Neyer. "Beyond the Black Box of Idea Contests." Paper presented at the EURAM Annual Conference, Liverpool, 2009.

Halme, M., S. Lindeman, and P. Linna. "Innovation for Inclusive Business: Intrapreneurial Bricolage in Multinational Corporations." *Journal of Management Studies* 49, no. 4 (2012): 743–784.

Hammond, A. L., W. J. Kramer, R. S. Katz, J. T. Tran, and C. Walker. *The Next 4 Billion – Market Size and Business Strategy at the Base of the Pyramid.* Washington, DC: International Finance Corporate, World Resources Institute, 2007.

Hansen, U., and T. Raabe. "Konsumentenbeteiligung an der Produktentwicklung von Konsumgütern. Ergebnisse einer Empirischen Untersuchung." *Zeitschrift für Betriebswirtschaft* 61, no. 2 (1991): 171–194.

Hanson, M., and K. Powell. *Procter & Gamble PuR Purifier of Water™ (A): Developing the Product and Taking it to Market.* Fountainebleau, France: European Case Clearing House (Case # 706-057-1), 2006.

Hart, S. L. *Capitalism at the Crossroads: The Unlimited Business Opportunities in Solving the World's most Difficult Problems.* Upper Saddle River, New Jersey: Pearson Prentice Hall, 2005.

Hart, S. *Capitalism at the Crossroads: Next Generation Business Strategies for a Post-Crisis World.* 3rd ed. Upper Saddle River, New Jersey: Pearson Prentice Hall, 2010.

Hart, S. L., and C. M. Christensen. "The Great Leap: Driving Innovation from the Base of the Pyramid." *Sloan Management Review* 44, no. 1 (2002): 51–56.

Hart, S. L., and T. London. "Developing Native Capability: What Multinational Corporations Can Learn From the Base of the Pyramid." *Stanford Social Innovation Review* 3 (2005): 28–33.

Hart, S. L., and S. Sharma. "Engaging Fringe Stakeholders for Competitive Imagination." *Academy of Management Executive* 18, no. 1 (2004): 7–18.

Haupt, S., and A. Krämer. *Bringing Medicines to Low-Income Markets – A Guide to Creating Inclusive Business Models for Pharmaceutical Companies.* Edited by GIZ and BMZ. Bonn and Eschborn, Berlin, 2012. Accessed May 1, 2013. http://www.medicines-for-bop.net/fileadmin/user_upload/publications/_BringingMedicinesToLIM_Final_20120301.pdf

Hauschildt, J., and S. Salomo, S. *Innovationsmanagement.* 4th ed. München: Vahlen, 2007.

Helson, R. "In Search of the Creative Personality." *Creativity Research Journal* 9, no. 4 (1996): 295–306.

Hennessey, B. A., and T. M. Amable. "Creativity." *Annual Review Psychology* 61 (2010): 569–98.

Hernandez, R., and Y. Mugica. *What Works: Prodem FFP's Multilingual Smart ATMs for Microfinance. Innovative Solutions for Delivering Financial Resources for*

Rural Bolivia. World Resources Institute, August 2003. Accessed May 1, 2013. http://pdf.wri.org/dd_prodem.pdf

Hernandez-Serrano, J., S. E. Stefanou, L. F. Hood, and B. L. Zoumas. "Using Experts' Experiences through Stories in Teaching New Product Development." *The Journal of Product Innovation Management* 19 (2002): 54–68.

Herrndorf, M. "Stories of Microinsurance: Strategy Processes for the Base of the Pyramid in Multinational Companies and Their Network." PhD diss., University of St. Gallen, School of Management, Economics, Law, Social Sciences and International Affairs, forthcoming.

Herstatt, C., and E. von Hippel. "From Experience: Developing New Product Concepts Via the Lead User Method: A Case Study in a 'Low Tech' Feld." *Journal of Product Innovation Management* 9, no. 3 (1992): 213–221.

Herstatt, C. "Theorie und Praxis der frühen Phasen des Innovationsprozesses." *io Management* 68, no. 10 (1999): 72–81.

Hienerth, C., M. Pötz, and E. von Hippel: "Appropriability, Proximity, Routines and Innovation. Exploring Key Characteristics of Lead User Workshop Participants: Who Contributes Best to the Generation of Truly Novel Solutions." Paper presented at the DRUID Summer Conference, Copenhagen, CBS, Denmark, June 18–20, 2007.

Hirschmann, E.C. "Innovativeness, Novelty Seeking and Consumer Creativity." *Journal of Customer Research* Vol. 7, no. 3 (1980): 283–95.

Holste, J. S., and D. Fields. "The Relationship of Affect and Cognition Based Trust with Sharing and Use of Tacit Knowledge." Academy of Management Best Conference Paper, 2005.

Hutter, K., J. Hautz, J. Füller, J. Mueller, and K. Matzler. "Communitition: The Tension Between Competition and Collaboration in Community-Based Design Contests." *Creativity and Innovation Management* 20, no. 1 (2011): 3–21.

IDB. "Latin America and the Caribbean Face Large and Growing Housing Deficit, IDB Study Says." May 14, 2012. Accessed May 1, 2013. http://www.iadb.org/en/news/news-releases/2012-05-14/housing-deficit-in-latin-america-and-caribbean,9978.html

IEA. *World Energy Outlook.* Paris Cedex: OECD/IEA, 2012.

ITU. "ICT Facts and Figures: The World in 2013." Accessed May 1, 2013. http://www.itu.int/en/ITU-D/Statistics/Documents/facts/ICTFactsFigures2013.pdf

Jaiswal, A. K. "Fortune at the Bottom of the Pyramid: An Alternate Perspective." Working Paper No. 2007–07–13, Indian Institute of Management Ahmedabad, India, September 2007.

Jeppesen, L.B. "User Toolkits for Innovation: Consumers Support Each Other." *The Journal of Product Innovation Management* 22, no. 4 (2005): 347–362.

Jeppesen, L.B., and L. Frederiksen. "Why Do Users Contribute to Firm-Hosted User Communities? The Case of Computer-Controlled Music Instruments." *Organization Science* 17, no. 1 (January–February 2006): 45–63.

Jeppesen, L.B., and K. Laursen. "The Role of Lead Users in Knowledge Sharing." *Research Policy* 38, no. 10 (Dec 2009): 1582–1589.

Jokisch, M. *Active Integration of Users Into the Innovation Process of a Manufacturer. The BMW Customer Innovation Lab.* München: Dr. Hut, 2007.

Jose, P. E. *Doing Statistical Mediation and Moderation.* New York: Guilford Press, 2013.

Jung, Y., and J. Chipchase. "Nokia Open Studio: Engaging Communities." Accessed May 1, 2013. http://janchipchase.com/content/essays/nokia-open-studios/

Kandachar, P., and M. Halme, eds. *Sustainability Challenges and Solutions at the Base-of-the-Pyramid: Business, Technology and the Poor.* London: Greenleaf, 2008.

Karnani, A. "The Mirage of Marketing to the Bottom of the Pyramid: How the Private Sector Can Help Alleviate Poverty." *California Management Review* 49 (2007a): 90–111.

Karnani, A. "Doing Well By Doing Good – Case Study: 'Fair and Lovely' Whitening Cream." *Strategic Management Journal* 28 (2007b): 1351–7.

Karnani, A. "Romanticizing the Poor." *Stanford Social Innovation Review* 7, no. 1 (Winter 2009): 38–43.

Kashdan, T. B., and F. D. Fincham. "Facilitating Creativity by Regulating Curiosity." *American Psychologist* 57, no. 5 (May 2002): 373–374.

Katz, R., and T. J. Allen. "Investigating the Not Invented Here (NIH) Syndrome: A Look at the Performance, Tenure and Communication Patterns of 50 R&D Projects." *R & D Management* 12, no. 1 (1982):7–20.

Kaufmann, J. C., and J. A. Sternberg, eds. *The Cambridge Handbook of Creativity.* New York: Cambridge University Press, 2010.

Kelle, U. *Empirisch Begründete Theoriebildung: Zur Logik und Methodologie Interpretativer Sozialforschung. Status Passages and the Life Course.* 2nd ed. Weinheim: Dt. Studien-Verlag, 1991.

Khurana, A., and S. R. Rosenthal. "Integrating the Fuzzy Front End of New Product Development." *MIT Sloan Management Review,* January 15, 1997.

Kim, J., and D. Wilemon. "Focusing the Fuzzy Front–End in New Product Development." *R&D Management* 32, no. 4 (September 2002): 269–279.

King, C.W., and J. O. Summers.O. "Overlap of Opinion Leadership Across Consumer Product Categories." *Journal of Marketing Research* 7, no. 1 (1970): 43–50.

Klein, M. H. "Poverty Alleviation Through Sustainable Strategic Business Models. Essays on Poverty Alleviation as a Business Strategy." PhD diss, Erasmus

Research Institute of Management (ERIM), RSM Erasmus University / Erasmus School of Economics, 2008.

Koen, P. A., M. J. Heidi, and I. R. Elsum."The Three Faces of Business Model Innovation: Challenges for Established Firms." *Research Technology Management,* May–June 2011.

Kohlbacher, F. "The Use of Qualitative Content Analysis in Case Study Research." *Forum Qualitative Sozialforschung / Forum: Qualitative Social Research* 7, no. 1, Art. 21, 2006. Accessed May 1, 2013. http://nbn-resolving.de/urn:nbn:de:0114-fqs0601211

Koskinen, K. U., P. Pihlanto, and H. Vanharanta. "Tacit Knowledge Acquisition and Sharing in a Project Work Context." *International Journal of Project Management* 21, no. 4 (May 2003): 281–290.

Kotler, P., and G. Armstrong. *Principles of Marketing*. Upper Saddle River NJ: Prentice Hall, 2004.

Kozinets, R. V. "The Field Behind the Screen: Using Netnography for Marketing Research in Online Communities." *Journal of Marketing Research* 39, no. 1 (February 2002): 61–72.

Kozinets, R. V. *Netnography – Doing Ethnographic Research Online*. London: Sage Publications Ltd., 2010.

Krämer, A., and F.-M. Belz. "Consumer Integration in Innovation Processes - A New Approach for Creating and Enhancing Innovations for the Base-of-the-Pyramid (BoP)?" In *Sustainability Challenges and Solutions at the Base-of-the-Pyramid: Business, Technology and the Poor*, edited by P. Kandachar and M. Halme, Chap. 13. London: Greenleaf, 2008.

Kratzer, J., and C. Lettl. "A Social Network Perspective of Lead User and Creativity: An Empirical Study among Children. *Creativity and Innovation Management 17,* no. 1 (2008): 26–36.

Kristensson, P., A. Gustafsson, A, and T. Archer. "Harnessing the Creative Potential Among Users." *Journal of Product Innovation Management* 21, no. 1 (2004): 4–14.

Kristensson, P., P. R. Magnusson, and J. Matthing. "Users as a Hidden Resource for Creativity: Findings from an Experimental Study on User Involvement." *Creativity and Innovation Management* 11, no. 1 (2002): 55–61.

Kuhn, T. *The Structure of Scientific Revolutions.* International Encyclopedia of Unified Science, vol. 2, no. 2, 2nd ed. enlarged. Chicago: University of Chicago Press, 1970.

Labaree, R. V. "The Risk of 'Going Observationalist': Negotiating the Hidden Dilemmas of Being an Insider Participant Observer." *Qualitative Research* 2, no. 1 (April 2002): 97–122.

Landrun, N. E. “Advancing the ‘Base of the Pyramid’ Debate.” *Strategic Management Review* 1, no. 1 (2007): 1–12.

Lane, P. J., B. Koka, and S. Pathak. “The Reification of absorptive Capacity a Critical Review and Rejuvenation of the Construct.” *Academy of Management Review* 31, no. 4 (2006): 833–863.

Lawton, L., and A. Parasuraman. “So You Want New Product Planning to Be Productive.” *Business Horizons* 1 (December 1980): 29–34.

Lazarsfeld, P., B. Berelson, and H. Gaudet. *The People's Choice*. New York: Columbia University Press, 1944.

Leonard-Barton, D. “Synergistic Design for Case Studies: Longitudinal Single-Site and Replicated Multi-Site.” Paper presented at the National Science Foundation Conference on Longitudinal Research Methods in Organizations, Austin, 1988.

Lettl, C., C., Hienerth, H.G. Gemuenden. “Exploring How Lead Users Develop Radical Innovation: Opportunity Recognition and Exploitation in the Field of Medical Equipment Technology.” In *IEEE Transactions on Engineering Management 55*, no. 2 (2008): 219–233.

Li, M., and F. Gao. “Why Nonaka Highlights Tacit Knowledge: A Critical Review.” *Journal of Knowledge Management Studies* 7. no. 4 (2003) 6–14.

Lilien, G. L., P. D. Morrison, K. Searls, M. Sonnack, and E. von Hippel. “Performance Assessment of the Lead User Idea-Generation Process for New Product Development.” *Management Science* 48, no. 8 (August 2002): 1042–1059.

Lincoln, Y. S., and E. G. Guba. *Naturalistic Inquiry.* Beverly Hills, CA: Sage Publications, 1985.

Lee, L.-Y., and E. Tan. “The Influences of Antecedents on Employee Creativity and Employee Performance: A Meta-Analytic Review.” *Interdisciplinary Journal of Contemporary Research in Business* 4, no. 2 (2012): 984–996.

London, T. “A Base-of-the-Pyramid Perspective on Poverty Alleviation.” Working Paper, The William Davidson Institute & Ross School of Business, University of Michigan: Ann Arbor, 2007.

London, T. “The Base of the Pyramid Perspective: A New Approach to Poverty Alleviation.” William Davidson Institute & Ross School of Business University of Michigan, 2008.

London, T. “Making Better Investments at the Base of the Pyramid.” *Harvard Business Review* 87, no. 5 (2009): 106–113.

London, T., and S. L. Hart. “Reinventing Strategies for Emerging Markets: Beyond the Transnational Model.” *Journal of International Business Studies* 35 (2004): 350–370.

London, T., A. Ravi, and S. Sheth. "Creating Mutual Value with Base of the Pyramid Procedures." William Davidson Institute & Ross School of Business University of Michigan: Ann Arbor, 2009.

Lüthje, C. *Kundenorientierung im Innovationsprozess. Eine Untersuchung der Kunden-Hersteller Interaktion in Konsumgütermärkten*. Wiesbaden: Deutscher Universitäts-Verlag, 2000.

Lüthje, C. "Characteristics of Innovating Users in a Consumer Goods Field: An Empirical Study of Sport-Related Product Consumers." *Technovation* 24, no. 9 (2004): 683–695.

Lüthje, C., and C. Herstatt. "The Lead User Method: an Outline of Empirical Findings and Issues for Future Research." *R&D Management* 34, no. 5 (2004): 553–568.

Lüthje, C., C. Herstatt, and E. von Hippel. "User-Innovators and 'Local' Information: The Case of Mountain Biking." *Research Policy* 34, no. 6 (2005): 951–965.

Lynn, G.S., and A. E. Akgün. "Innovation Strategies under Uncertainly: A Contingency Approach for New Product Development." *Engineering Management Journal* 10, no. 3 (1998): 11–17.

Madjar, N., G. R. Oldham, and M. G. Pratt. "There's No Place Like Home? The Contributions of Work and Non-Work Creativity Support to Employees Creative Performance." *Academy of Management Journal* 45, no. 4 (2002): 757–767.

Magnusson, P. R. "Exploring the Contributions of Involving Ordinary Users in Ideation of Technology-Based Services." *Journal of Product Innovation Management* 26, no. 5 (2009): 578–593.

Magnusson, P. R., and P. Kristensson. "Tuning Users' Innovativeness During Ideation." *Creativity and Innovation Management* 19, no. 2 (2010): 147–159.

Magnusson, P. R., P. Kristensson, and C. Hipp. "Exploring the Ideation Patterns of Ordinary Users: The Case of Mobile Telecommunications Services." *International Journal of Product Development* 11, no. 3–4 (2010): 289–309.

Manning, K.C., W. O Bearden, and T. J. Madden. "Consumer Innovativeness and the Adoption Process." *Journal of Consumer Psychology* 4, no. 4 (1995): 329–345.

Mascitelli, R. "From Experience: Harnessing Tacit Knowledge to Achieve Breakthrough Innovation." *Journal of Product Innovation Management* 17, no. 3 (2000): 179–193.

Maslow, A. *Motivation and Personality*. New York: Harper, 1954.

Mayring, P. "Qualitative Inhaltsanalyse." *Forum Qualitative Social Research* 1, no. 2, Art. 20, June 2000a. Accessed May 1, 2013. http://www.qualitative-research.net/index.php/fqs/article/view/1089/2383

Mayring, P. "Qualitative Inhaltsanalyse." In *Qualitative Forschung. Ein Handbuch*, edited by U. Flick, E. von Kardorff and I. Steinke, 468–475. Reinbeck bei Hamburg: Rowohlt, 2000b.

Mayring, P. *Qualitative Inhaltsanalyse: Grundlagen und Techniken.* 8th ed. Weinheim; Basel: Beltz, 2003.

McCrae, R. R. "Creativity, Divergent Thinking and Openness to Experience." *Journal of Personality and Social Psychology* 52, no. 6 (June 1987): 1258–1265.

McKinsey & Company. *'And the Winner Is...': Capturing the Promise of Philanthropic Prizes*, 2009. Accessed May 1, 2013. http://www.mckinseyonsociety.com/downloads/reports/Social-Innovation/And_the_winner_is.pdf

Meffert, H., C. Burmann, and M. Kirchgeorg. *Marketing: Grundlagen Marktorientierter Unternehmensführung. Konzepte - Instrumente – Praxisbeispiele*. 9th ed., 2000 reprint. Wiesbaden: Gabler, 2005.

Mendoza, R.U. "Why do the Poor Pay More? Exploring the Poverty Penalty Concept." *Journal of International Development* 23, no. 1 (2011): 1–28.

Mendoza, R.U., and N. Thelen. "Innovations to Make Markets More Inclusive for the Poor." *Development Policy Review* 26, no. 4 (2008): 427–458.

Merton, R. K. *Social Theory and Social Structure.* Enlarged ed. New York: Free Press, 1968.

Midgley, D.F., and G. R. Dowling. "Innovativeness: The Concept and its Measurement." *Journal of Consumer Research* 4, no. 2 (1987): 229–242.

Miles, M., and M. Hubermann. *Qualitative Data Analysis. An Expanded Sourcebook.* 2nd ed. Thousand Oaks, Calif.: Sage Publications, 1994.

Miles, M., M. Hubermann. *Qualitative Data Analysis. An Expanded Sourcebook.* 2nd ed. 1994. Reprint, Thousand Oaks, Calif.: Sage Publications, 2005.

Mills, A. J., G. Eurepos, and E. Wiebe, ed. *Encyclopedia of Case Study Research.* Vol. 2. Thousand Oaks: Sage Publications, 2010.

Mittal, B. "A Comparative Analysis of Four Scales of Consumer Involvement." *Psychology & Marketing* 12, no. 7 (1995): 663–682.

Mohr, J. J., S. Sengupta, and S. F. Slater. "Serving Base-of-the-Pyramid Markets: Meeting Real Needs Through a Customized Approach." *Journal of Business Strategy* 33, no. 6 (2012): 4–14.

Moorman, C., G. Zaltman, and R. Desphande. "Relationship Between Providers and Users of Market Research: The Dynamics of Trust Within and Between Organizations." *Journal of Marketing Research* 29, no. 3 (August 1992): 314–328.

Morgan, G., and L. Smircich. "The Case for Qualitative Research." *Academy of Management Review* 5, no. 4 (1980): 491–500.

Morrison, P. D., J. H. Robberts, and E. von Hippel. "Determinants of User Innovation an Innovation Sharing in Local Markets." *Management Science* 46 (December 2000): 1513–1527.

Morrison, P.D., and J. H. Roberts, and D. F. Midgley. "The Nature of Lead Users and Measurement of Leading Edge Status." *Research Policy* 33, no. 2 (2004): 351–362.

Möslein, K. M., J. B. A. Haller, and A. C. Bullinger. "Open Evaluation: Ein IT-Basierter Ansatz für die Bewertung Innovativer Konzepte." *HMD Sonderheft: IT-basiertes Innovationsmanagement*, 2010.

Nair, A. K., R. Tiwari, and S. Buse. "Emerging Patterns of Grassroot Innovations: A Conceptual Study Based on Selected Case Studies from India." Working Paper No. 70, May 2012. Accessed May 1, 2013. http://www.tuhh.de/tim/downloads/arbeitspapiere/Workingpaper_71.pdf

Nambisan, S. "Designing Virtual Customer Environments for New Product Development: Toward a Theory." *Academy of Management Review* 27, no. 3 (2002): 392–413.

Narver, J. C., and S. F. Slater. "The Effect of a Market Orientation on Business Profitability." *Journal of Marketing* 54, no. 4 (1990): 20–35.

Narver, J. C., S. F. Slater, and D. L. MacLachlan. "Responsive and Proactive Market Orientation and New-Product Success." *Journal of Product Innovation Management* 21, no. 5 (2004): 334–347.

Neal, D. K. "Goodness of Fit Tests for Normality." *Mathematical Education Research* 5, no. 2 (1996): 23–30.

Neale, M. B., and D. B. Corkindale. "Co-Developing Products: Involving Customers Earlier and More Deeply." *Long Range Planning* 31, no. 3 (1998): 418–425.

Nederhof, A. J. "Methods of Coping with Social Desirability Bias: A Review." *European Journal of Social Psychology* 15, no. 3 (1985): 263–280.

Neyer, A.-K., A. C. Bullinger, and K. M. Möslein. "Integrating Inside and Outside Innovators: A Sociotechnical Systems Perspective." *R&D Management* 39, no. 4 (2009): 410–419.

Nokia. "Inform, Involve, Empower – Nokia's Service Mantra for Emerging Markets with Nokia Life Tools." Last modified November 4, 2008. Accessed May 1, 2013. http://press.nokia.com/2008/11/04/inform-involve-empower-nokias-service-mantra-for-emerging-markets-with-nokia-life-tools/

Nonaka, I. "The Knowledge-Creating Company." *Harvard Business Review* 69 (November – December 1991): 96–104.

Nonaka, I. "A Dynamic Theory of Organizational Knowledge Creation." *Organization Science* 5, no. 1 (1st February 1994): 14–37.

Nonaka, I., and T. Hirotaka. *The Knowledge Creating Company: How Japanese Companies Create the Dynamics of Innovation.* New York: Oxford University Press, 1995.

Nonaka, I., and N. Konno. "The Concept of '*Ba*': Building a Foundation for Knowledge Creation." *California Management Review* 40, no. 3 (Spring 1998): 40–54.

Nonaka, I., K. Umemoto, and D. Senoo. "From Information Processing to Knowledge Creation: A Paradigm Shift in Business Management." *Technology in Society* 18, no. 2 (1996): 203–218.

OECD. *Oslo Manual: Guidelines for Collecting and Interpreting Innovation Data*. 3rd ed., Luxembourg: Statistical Office of the European Communities, 2005.

Olson, E.H., and G. Bakke. "Implementing the Lead User Method in a High Technology Firm. A Longitudinal Study of Intensions versus Actions." *Journal of Product Innovation Management* 18 (2001): 388–395.

Paton, B., and M. Halme. "Bringing the Needs of the Poor into the BOP Debate." *Business Strategy and the Environment* 16 (2007): 585–586.

Patton, M.Q. Qualitative evaluation and research methods. Newbury Park, California: Sage Publications, 1990.

Piller, F., and D. Walcher. "Toolkits for Idea Competitions. A Novel Method to Integrate Users in New Product Development." *R&D Management* 36, no. 3 (2006): 307–318.

Pitta, D. A., R. Guesalaga, and P. Marshall. "The Quest for the Fortune at the Bottom of the Pyramid: Potential and Challenges." *Journal of Consumer Marketing* 25, no. 7 (2008): 393–401.

Pobisch, J. *Konsumentenorientierte Produktinnovationen: Erfolgreiche Generierung, Verbreitung und Verwertung von Konsumentenwissen*. Hochschulschriften Band 130. Marburg: Metropolis-Verlag, 2010.

Pobisch J., S. Eckert, and W. Kustermann. "Konsumentenintegration in Nachhaltigkeitsinnovationen: Ein Beitrag zur Unternehmerischen Verbraucherbildung?" Consumer Science, Diskussionsbeitrag no. 12. Freising: TU München. Fakultät für Wirtschaftswissenschaften, Professur für Betriebswirtschaftslehre, Brau- und Lebensmisttelindustrie.

Poetz, M.K., and M. Schreier. "The Value of Crowdsourcing: Can Users Really Compete with Professionals in Generating New Product Ideas." Conference Paper: DRUID Summer Conference, Denmark, June 17–19, 2009.

Polanyi, M. *Personal Knowledge: Towards a Post-Critical Philosophy*. Chicago: University of Chicago Press, 1958.

Polanyi, M. *The Tacit Dimension.* London: Routledge (Chicago: University of Chicago Press), 1966, reprint 2009.

Popper, K. *Conjectures and Refutations.* London: Routledge, 1963.

Prahalad, C. K. *The Fortune at the Bottom of the Pyramid: Eradicating Poverty Through Profits*. Wharton School Publishing, 2004.

Prahalad, C. K. “The Innovation Sandbox.” *Strategy+Business* (Autumn 2006): 62–71.

Prahalad. C. K. “The Big Picture.” In *Next Generation Business Strategies for the Base of the Pyramid: New Approaches for Building Mutual Value*, edited by T. London and S. Hart, xxvi-xxxiii. Upper Saddle River, New Jersey: Pearson Education Inc., 2010.

Prahalad, C. K., and A. L. Hammond. “Serving the World's Poor, Profitably.” *Harvard Business Review* (September 2002): 4–11.

Prahalad, C. K., and S. L. Hart. “The Fortune at the Bottom of the Pyramid.” *Strategy+Business 26* (2002): 54–67.

Prahalad, C.K., and K. Lieberthal. “The End of Corporate Imperialism.” *Harvard Business Review* 76, no. 4, (1998): 68–79.

Prahalad, C. K., and R. A. Mashelkar. “Innovation’s Holy Grail.” *Harvard Business Review,* July–August 2010.

Prahalad, C. K., and V. Ramaswamy. “Co-Opting Customer Competence.” *Harvard Business Review,* January–February 2000.

Price, L. L., and N. M Ridgeway. “Development of a Scale to Measure Use Innovativeness.” In *Advances in Consumer Research* Vol. 10, edited by R. P. Bagozzi and A. M. Tybout, 679 – 684. Ann Arbor, MI: Association of Consumer Research, 1983.

Prügl, R., and M. Schreier, M. “Learning From Leading-Edge Customers at the Sims: Opening Up The Innovation Process Using Toolkits.” *R&D Management* 36, no. 3 (2006): 237–250.

Puccio, G., and C. Grivas. “Examining the Relationship Between Personality Traits and Creativity Styles.” *Creativity and Innovation Management* 18, no. 4 (2009): 247–255.

Punch, K. F. *Introduction to Social Research–Quantitative & Qualitative Approaches*. London: Sage Publications, 2005.

Ramakrishnan, S. “Aktive Konsumentenintegration im Kontext Konsumtiver Mobilitätsdienst-leistungen: Eine Empirische Analyse der Teilnahmebereitschaft und Teilnahmeleistung von Konsumenten mit hoher bzw. niedriger Lead-Userness bei Innovationsprojekten im Öffentlichen Personennahverkehr.” PhD diss., Technische Universität München, 2012.

Reichwald, R., A. Meyer, M. Engelmann, M., and D. Walcher. *Der Kunde als Innovationspartner. Konsumenten integrieren, Flop-Raten reduzieren, Angebote verbessern.* 1st ed. Wiesbaden: Gabler, 2007.

Reichwald, R., and F. Piller. *Interaktive Wertschöpfung. Open Innovation, Individualisierung und neue Formen der Arbeitsteilung.* Wiesbaden: Gabler, 2006.

Rhode, S. M. "An Analysis of Creativity." In *Frontiers of Creativity Research: Beyond the Basics*, edited by S. G. Isaksen, 216–222. *Buffalo*, NY: Bearly Ltd., 1987.

Ricart, J. E., M. J. Enright, P. Ghemawat, S. L. Hart, and T. Khanna. "New Frontiers in International Strategy." *Journal of International Business Studies* 35 (2004): 175–200.

Rickards, T., M. A. Runco, and S. Moger, eds. *The Routledge Companion to Creativity (Routledge Companions* in *Business*, *Management* and *Accounting*). Oxford: Routledge, 2008.

Ritchie, J., and J. Lewis. *Qualitative Research Practice: A Guide for Social Science Students*. London: SAGE, 2003.

Rivera-Santos, M., and C. Rufín. "Global Village vs. Small Town: Understanding Networks At the Base of the Pyramid." *International Business Review* 19, no. 2 (April 2010): 126–139.

Robertson, T. S. *Innovative Behaviour and Communication*. New York: Holt, Rinerhart and Winston, 1971.

Robertson, T. S., J. Zielinski, and S. Ward. *Consumer Behaviour*, *Glenview*, IL: Scott, 1984.

Rogers, E.M. *Diffusion of Innovations*. New York: The Free Press, 1995.

Rogers, E. M., and F. F. Shoemaker. *Communication of Innovations*. New York: The Free Press, 1971.

Rothwell, R., C. Freeman, A. Horsley, V. Jervis, A. Robertson, and J. Townsend. "SAPPHO Updated – Project SAPPHO Phase II." *Research Policy* 3, no. 4 (1974): 258–291.

Runco, M. A. *Problem Finding, Problem Solving and Creativity*. Norwood, New Jersey: Greenwood Publishing Group, 1994.

SadreGhazi, S. "Product Innovation for Low-income Markets: Beyond Making Cheap Goods." In *Global CSR Case-book: Business and Poverty*, edited by ICEP, CODESPA, 59–65. ICEP: Vienna, 2008.

Sánchez, P., J. E. Ricart, and M. Á. Rodríguez. "Influential Factors in Becoming Socially Embedded in Low-Income Markets." *Greener Management International* 5 (2007) 19–38.

Sawhney, M., and E. Prandelli. "Beyond Customer Knowledge Management: Customers as Knowledge Co-Creators." In *Knowledge Management and Virtual Organization*, edited by Y. Malhotra, 258–281. Hershey: Idea Group Publishing, 2000.

Schensul, S. L., J. J. Schensul, and M. D. LeCompte. *Essential Ethnographic Methods: Observations*, Interviews, *and Questionnaires,* Book 2 in Ethnographer's Toolkit. Walnut Creek, CA: AltaMira Press, 1999.

Schilling, J. "On the Pragmatics of Qualitative Assessment." *European Journal of Psychological Assessment* 22, no. 1 (2006): 28–37.

Schmidt, T., and W. Sofka. "Lost in Translation: Empirical Evidence for Liability of Foreignness as Barriers to Knowledge Spillovers." Discussion Paper No. 06-01, Centre for European Economic Research (ZEW), Mannheim, Germany, 2005. Accessed May 1, 2013. http://ftp.zew.de/pub/zew-docs/dp/dp0601.pdf

Scholz, R. W., and O. Tietje. *Embedded Case Study Methods. Integrating Quantitative and Qualitative Knowledge*. Thousand Oaks, CA: Sage Publications, 2002.

Schrader, U., and F.-M. Belz. "Involving Users in Sustainability Innovations." In *The Nature of Sustainable Consumption and How to Achieve it: Results from the Focal Topic 'From Knowledge to Action: New Paths towards Sustainable Consumption'*, edited by R. Defila, A. DiGiulio and R. Kaufmann-Hayoz, 335–353. München: oekom Verlag, 2012.

Schrage, M. "My Consumer, My Co-Innovator." *Strategy+Business* 43, Summer 2006, Last modified May 30th, 2006. Accessed May 1, 2013. http://www.strategy-business.com/article/06216?pg=all

Schreier, M., S. Oberhauser, and R. Prügl. "Lead Users and the Adoption and Diffusion of New Products: Insights from Two Extreme Sports Communities." *Market Lett* 18, no. 1 (2007): 15–30.

Schreier, M., and R. Prügl. "Extending Lead User Theory: Antecedents and Consequences of Consumers' Lead Userness." The *Journal of Product Innovation Management* 25, no. 4 (2008): 331–346.

Schumpeter, J. *The Theory of Economic Development: An Inquiry into Profits, Capital, Credit, Interest, and the Business Cycle*. Cambridge: Harvard University Press, 1912.

Scott, W. R. *Institutions and Organizations*. Thousand Oaks, CA: Sage Publications, 1995.

Seelos, C., and J. Mair. "Profitable Business Models and Market Creation in the Context of Deep Poverty: A Strategic View." *Academy of Management Perspectives* 21, no. 4 (2007): 49–63.

Sen, A. *Development as Freedom*. Oxford: Oxford University Press, 1999.

Senker, J. "The Contribution of Tacit Knowledge to Innovation." *AI & Society* 7, no. 3 (1993): 208–224.

Shah, S. "Sources and Patterns of Innovation in a Consumer Products Field: Innovations in Sporting Equipment." Working Paper Nr. 4105, MIT Sloan School of Management, Cambridge, Massachussetts, 2000. Accessed May 1, 2013. http://users.tkk.fi/u/phannuka/articles/Shah_2000 _Sources_and_Patterns.pdf

Shaw, B. "The Role of the Interaction between the User and the Manufacturer in Medical Equipment Innovation." *R&D Management* 15 (1985): 283–292.

Shrout, P. E., and J. Fleiss. "Intraclass Correlations: Uses in Assessing Rater Reliability." *Psychological Bulletin* 86, no. 2 (1979): 420–428.

Silveira, A. "Na Vila Zumbi, um exemplo de melhoria." Gazeta do povo, Last modified October 11, 2009. Accessed May 1, 2013. http://www.gazetadopovo.com.br/vidaecidadania/conteudo. phtml?id=932746

Silvertant, S. *Ideenwettbewerbe als Methode zur Ideengenerierung und Identifikation potenzieller Lead User im Kontext schnelllebiger Konsumgüter: Eine empirische Analyse von KMU der Lebensmittel- und Getränkeindustrie.* Hamburg: Dr. Kovac, 2011.

Simanis, E., and S.L. Hart. "The Base of the Pyramid Protocol: Toward Next Generation Bop Strategy." 2nd ed., Working Paper, Cornell University, 2008. Accessed May 1, 2013. http://www.stuartlhart.com/sites/stuartlhart.com/files/BoPProtocol2ndEdition2008_0.pdf

Simanis, E., and S. L. Hart. "Innovation From the Inside Out." *MIT Sloan Management Review* 50, no. 4 (Winter 2011): 9–19.

Simanis, E., S. Hart, and D. Duke. "The Base of the Pyramid Protocol: Beyond 'Basic Needs' Business Strategies." *Innovations* 3, no. 1 (2008): 57–85.

Simanis, E., and M. Milstein. "Back to Business Fundamentals: Making 'Bottom of the Pyramid' Relevant to Core Business." *Field Actions Science Reports*, Special Issue 4 (2012): 82–88.

Simon, H.A. "Bounded Rationality and Organizational Learning." *Organization Science* 2, no. 1 (February 1991): 125–134.

Slater, S. F., and J. C. Narver. "Does Competitive Environment Moderate the Market Orientation-Performance Relationship?" *Journal of Marketing* 58, H. 1 (1994): 46–55.

Smith, A. *The Wealth of Nations: An Inquiry into the Nature and Causes of the Wealth of Nations*. London: Stratton & Cadell, 1776.

Soll, J. H. *Ideengenerierung mit Konsumenten im Internet*. Wiesbaden: Deutscher Universitäts-Verlag, GWV Fachverlage GmbH, 2006.

Sridharan, S., and M. Viswanathan. "Marketing in Subsistence Marketplaces: Consumption and Entrepreneurship in a South Indian Context." *Journal of Consumer Marketing* 25 (2008): 455–62.

Sternberg, R.J., and T. I. Lubart. *Defying the Crowd: Cultivating Creativity in a Culture of Conformity*. New York: Free Press, 1985.

Styhre, A. "Rethinking Knowledge: A Bergsonian Critique of the Notion of Tacit Knowledge." *British Journal of Management* 15 (2004): 177–188.

Subotnik, R.F., and K. D. Arnold, eds. *Beyond Terman: Contemporary Longitudinal Studies of Giftedness and Talent*, Norwood, NJ: Ablex, 1994.

Subrahmanyan, S., and J. T. Gomez-Arias. "Integrated Approach to Understanding Consumer Behavior at Bottom of Pyramid." *Journal of Consumer Marketing* 25, no. 7 (2008): 402–412.

Surowiecki, J. "The Wisdom of Crowds: Why the Many Are Smarter Than the Few and How Collective Wisdom Shapes Business, Economies, Societies and Nations." New York: Doubleday, 2004.

Takeuchi, H., and I. Nonaka. "The New New Product Development Game." *Harvard Business Review,* January-February 1986.

The Economist. "The Power to Disrupt." Last modified April 15th, 2010a. Accessed May 1, 2013. http://www.economist.com/node/15879393

The Economist. "The World Turned Upside Down." Last modified April 15th, 2010b. Accessed May 1, 2013. http://www.economist.com/node/15879369

Thomke, S., and E. von Hippel. "Customers as Innovators: A New Way to Create Value." *Harvard Business Review* 80, no. 4 (2002):74–81.

Tidd, J., J. Bessant, and K. Pavitt. *Managing Innovation: Integrating Technological, Market and Organizational Change.* 3rd ed. West Sussex: John Wiley & Sons Ltd., 2005.

Tietz, R., J. Füller, and C. Herstatt. "Signaling – an Innovative Approach to Identify Lead Users in Online Communities." In *Customer Interaction and Customer Integration*, edited by T. Blecker, G. Friedrich, L. Hvam, and K. Edwards, 453–468. Berlin: Gito-Verlag, 2006.

Tiwari, R., and C. Herstatt. "India - A Lead Market for Frugal Innovations? Extending the Lead Market Theory to Emerging Economies." Working Paper No. 67, Hamburg University of Technology, 2012a. Accessed May 1, 2013. http://www.tuhh.de/tim/downloads/arbeitspapiere/ Working_Paper_67.pdf

Tiwari, R., and C. Herstatt. "Frugal Innovations for the 'Unserved' Customer: An Assessment of India's Attractiveness as a Lead Market for Cost-effective Products." Working Paper No. 69, Hamburg University of Technology, 2012b. Accessed May 1, 2013. http://www.tuhh.de/tim/ downloads/arbeitspapiere/Working_Paper_69

Tiwari, R., and C. Herstatt. "Open Global Innovation Networks as Enablers of Frugal Innovation: Propositions Based on Evidence from India ." Working Paper No. 72, Hamburg University of Technology, 2012c. Accessed May 1, 2013. http://www.tuhh.de/tim/downloads/arbeitspapiere/ Working_Paper_72.pdf

Torrance, E. P. *Torrance Tests of Creative Thinking*. Lexington, MA: Personnel Press, 1974.

Trommsdorff, V. *Konsumentenverhalten*. 2nd ed. Stuttgart: Kohlhammer, 1993.

Tromsdorff, V. "Involvement." In: *Handwörterbuch des Marketing*, 2nd ed., edited by B. I. Tietz, R. Köhler, and J. Zentes, 1067–1078. Stuttgart: Schäffer-Poeschel, 1995.

UN. *World Population Prospect: The 2012 Revision*. New York: United Nations, 2013. Accessed May 1, 2013. http://esa.un.org/wpp/Documentation/pdf/WPP2012_HIGHLIGHTS.pdf

UNFPA. "Linking Population, Poverty and Development." Accessed May 1, 2013. http://www.unfpa.org/pds/trends.html

UNDP. *Creating Value for All: Strategies for Doing Business With the Poor*. New York: United Nations Development Programme, 2008.

UNDP. *The MDGs - Everyone's Business: How Inclusive Business Models Contribute to Development and Who Supports Them.* New York: United Nations Development Programme, 2010.

UNDP. *Realizing Africa's Wealth: Building Inclusive Businesses for Shared Prosperity*. New York: United Nations Development Programme, 2013.

Urban, G. L., and E. von Hippel. "Lead User Analysis for the Development of New Industrial Products." *Management Science* 34, no. 5 (1988): 569–582.

Utterback, J. M., T. J. Allen, J. H. Hollomon, and M. A. Sirbu. "The Process of Innovation in Five Industries in Europe and Japan." *IEEE Transactions on Engineering Management EM* 23, no. 1 (1976): 3–9.

Verworn, B., and C. Herstatt. "Strukturierung und Gestaltung der frühen Phasen des Innovationsprozesses." In *Management der frühen Innovationsphasen*, 2nd ed., edited by C. Herstatt, and B. Verworn, 111–134. Wiesbaden: Gabler, 2007.

Verworn, B., C. Herstatt, and A. Nagahira. "The Fuzzy Front End of Japanese New Product Development Projects: Impact on Success and Differences Between Incremental and Radical Projects." *R&D Management* 38, no. 1 (2008): 1–19.

Verworn, B., H. Cornelius, and A. Nagahira. "The Impact of the Fuzzy Front End on New Product Development Success in Japanese NPD Projects." Working Paper No. 39, Hamburg Technical University, May 2006. Accessed May 1, 2013. www.tuhh.de/tim/downloads/arbeitspapiere/ Working_Paper_39.pdf.

Viswanathan, M., and J. A. Rosa. *Product and Market Development for Subsistence Marketplaces: Consumption and Entrepreneurship Beyond Literacy and Resource Barriers. Advances in International Management Series.* Edited by. J. Cheng and M. Hitt. Oxford, UK: Elsevier, 2007.

Viswanathan, M., and S. Sridharan. "Product Development for the BoP: Insights on Concept and Prototype Development from University-Based Student Projects in India." *Journal of Product Innovation Management* 29, no. 1 (2012): 52–69.

Viswanathan, M., A. Yassine, and J. Clarke. "Sustainable Product and Market Development for Subsistence Marketplaces: Creating Educational Initiatives in Radically Different Contexts." *Journal of Product Innovation Management* 28 (2011): 558–569.

Von Hippel, E. "The Dominant Role of Users in the Scientific Instrument Innovation Process." *Research Policy* 5, no. 3 (1976): 212–239.

Von Hippel, E. "Successful Industrial Products from Customer Ideas: Presentation of a New Customer-Active Paradigm with Evidence and Implications." *Journal of Marketing*. 42, no. 1 (1978): 39–49.

Von Hippel, E. "Get New Products from Customers." *Harvard Business Review* 60, no. 2 (1982): 117–122.

Von Hippel, E. "Lead Users: A Source of Novel Product Concepts." *Management Science* 32, no. 7 (1986): 791–805.

Von Hippel, E. *The Sources of Innovation*. New York: Oxford University Press, 1988.

Von Hippel, E. "Sticky Information and the Locus of Problem Solving." *Management Science* 40, no. 4 (1994): 429–439.

Von Hippel, E. "Perspective. User Toolkits for Innovation." *Journal of Product Innovation Management* 18, no. 4 (2001): 247–257.

Von Hippel, E. *Democratizing Innovation.* Cambridge, Massachusetts: The MIT Press, 2005.

Von Hippel, E., N. Franke, and R. Prügl. "Pyramiding: Efficient Search for Rare Subjects." *Research Policy* 38 (2009): 1397–1406.

Von Hippel, E., and R. Katz. "Shifting Innovation to Users Via Toolkits." *Management Science* 48, no. 7 (2002): 821–833.

Von Hippel, E., S. Thomke, and M. Sonnack. "Creating Breakthroughs at 3M." *Harvard Business Review,* (September – October 1999): 47–57.

Waibel, P. *How Base-of-the-Pyramid Ventures Can Learn from Development Approaches. London:* Greenleaf Publishing, 2012.

Walcher, D. "Der Ideenwettbewerb als Methode der aktiven Kundenintegration: Eine empirische Untersuchung zu Eignung und Kundenverhalten mit Implikationen für den Innovationsprozess." PhD diss., Universität München, 2007.

Webb, J.-W., G.-M. Kistruck, R. D. Ireland, and D. J. Jr. Ketchen. "The Entrepreneurship Process in Base of the Pyramid Markets: The Case of Multinational Enterprise/ Nongovernment Organization Alliances." *Entrepreneurship Theory and Practice* 34: (2009): 555–81.

Weick, K. "What Theory is Not, Theorizing is." *Administrative Science Quarterly* 40 (1995): 385-90.

Weidner, K. L., J. A. Rosa, and M. Viswanathan. "Marketing to Subsistence Consumers: Lessons from Practice." *Journal of Business Research* 63 (2010): 559–569.

Weiser, J., M. Kahane, S. Rochling, and J. Landis. *Untapped: Creating Value in Underserved Markets*. San Francisco: Berrett-Koehler, 2006.

Wenger, J., and J. Haller. "How to Design Prizes – Incentives in Innovation Contests." Conference Paper, Conference: Service Science – Neue Perspektiven für die

Informatik. Lecture Notes in Informatics (LNI) - Proceedings, Series of the Gesellschaft für Informatik, Leipzig, 2006.

Whitney, P. "Reframing Design for the Base of the Pyramid." In *Next Generation Business Strategies for the Base of the Pyramid: New Approaches for Building Mutual Value*, edited by T. London, and S. L. Hart, Chap. 6. Upper Saddle River, New Jersey: Pearson Education Inc., 2010.

Wirtz, M., and F. Casper. *Beurteilerübereinstimmung und Beurteilerreliabilität. Methoden zur Bestimmung und Verbesserung der Zuverlässigkeit von Einschätzungen mittels Kategoriensystemen und Ratingskalen*. Göttingen: Hogrefe, 2002.

Worldbank. "Poverty." Last modified April 2013. Accessed May 1, 2013. http://web.worldbank.org/WBSITE/EXTERNAL/TOPICS/EXTPOVERTY/EXTPA/0,,contentMDK:20040961~menuPK:435040~pagePK:148956~piPK:216618~theSitePK:430367~isCURL:Y,00.html

Yin, R.K. *Case Study Research. Design and Methods.* 3rd ed. Los Angeles: Sage Publications, 2003.

Zahra, S. A., and G. George. "Absorptive Capacity: A Review, Reconceptualization, and Extension." *Academy of Management R*eview 17, no. 2 (2002): 185–203.

Zeleny, M. "Human Systems Management: Integrating Knowledge, Management and Systems." *World Scientific* (2005): 15–16.

WEBSITES

Ashoka Changemakers website. Accessed May 1, 2013. http://www.changemakers.com

Cohapar. "Déficit habitacional no Paraná." Accessed May 1, 2013. http://www.cohapar.pr.gov.br/modules/conteudo/conteudo.php?conteudo=7

Copel. "Tarifa Social de Energia Electrica." Last modified February 7th, 2013. Accessed May 1, 2013. http://www.copel.com/hpcopel/root/nivel2.jsp?endereco=%2Fhpcopel%2Froot%2Fpagcopel2.nsf%2Fdocs%2FC6A246BB78F860A6032573F7006959C9

Datafolha 2009. Accessed May 1, 2013. http://datafolha.folha.uol.com.br/mercado/top_index.php

EBSCO website. Accessed May 1, 2013. http://www.ebscohost.com/academic/business-source-premier

ECB. "The growing importance of emerging economies." Accessed May 1, 2013. http://www.ecb.int/ecb/tasks/international/emerging/html/index.en.html

Empowering people. Award, Siemen's website. Accessed May 1, 2013. http://www.empowering-people-award.siemens-stiftung.org

Grameen Shakti website. Accessed May 1, 2013. http://www.gshakti.org/

IBGE. "IBGE Dá Início à Pesquisa Nacional de Saúde (PNS)." Accessed May 1, 2013. http://www.ibge.gov.br

IBGE. "IBGE Inaugurates National Health Survey (PNS)." Accessed May 1, 2013. http://www.ibge.gov.br/english/

India Knowledge@Wharton. "Reverse Innovation': GE Makes India a Lab for Global Markets."
Last modified May 20th, 2010. Accessed May 1, 2013.
http://knowledge.wharton.upenn.edu/india/article.cfm?articleid=4476

Merriam-Webster Dictionary. Accessed May 1, 2013. http://www.merriam-webster.com/ dictionary/characteristic

Minha Casa Minha Vida. Accessed May 1, 2013. http://www.minhacasaminhavida.com.br/

OpenIDEO. Accessed May 1, 2013. http://www.openideo.com

Project 10 to the Hundred. Accessed May 1, 2013. http://www.project10tothe100.com

SafariCom website. Accessed May 1, 2013. http://www.safaricom.co.ke/

SEED Initiative. Accessed May 1, 2013. http://www.seedinit.org

SRISTI website. Accessed May 1, 2013. http://www.sristi.org/hbnew/aboutus.php# and http://www.sristi.org/cms/

The GlobalGiveback Initiative Challenge, InnoCentive website. Accessed May 1, 2013. https://www.innocentive.com/ar/landing/global-giveback.gsp

The String Cleaner website. Accessed May 1, 2013. http://www.thestringcleaner.com

Tigre website. Accessed May 1, 2013. http://www.tigre.com.br

MIX
Papier aus verantwortungsvollen Quellen
Paper from responsible sources
FSC® C105338

If you have any concerns about our products,
you can contact us on
ProductSafety@springernature.com

In case Publisher is established outside the EU,
the EU authorized representative is:
Springer Nature Customer Service Center GmbH
Europaplatz 3, 69115 Heidelberg, Germany

Printed by Libri Plureos GmbH
in Hamburg, Germany